GRAIN AND FIRE

GRAIN AND FIRE

A History of Baking in the American South

REBECCA SHARPLESS

THE UNIVERSITY OF NORTH CAROLINA PRESS   CHAPEL HILL

This book was published with the assistance of Texas Christian University.

Designed by Lindsay Starr
Set in Quadraat Pro
by codeMantra

Manufactured in the United States of America

The University of North Carolina Press has been a member
of the Green Press Initiative since 2003.

Cover illustration courtesy Chicken Bridge Bakery,
www.chickenbridgebakery.com

LIBRARY OF CONGRESS CATALOGING-IN-PUBLICATION DATA
Names: Sharpless, Rebecca, author.
Title: Grain and fire : a history of baking in
the American South / Rebecca Sharpless.
Description: Chapel Hill : The University of North
Carolina Press, 2022. | Includes bibliographical
references and index.
Identifiers: LCCN 2021052597 |
ISBN 9781469668369 (cloth ; alk. paper) |
ISBN 9781469668376 (ebook)
Subjects: LCSH: Baking—Southern States—History. |
Cooking, American—Southern style. |
Food habits—Social aspects—Southern States—History. |
Cultural fusion—Southern States—History. |
Southern States—Social life and customs—History.
Classification: LCC TX763 .S424 2022 |
DDC 641.7/10975—dc23/eng/20211130
LC record available at https://lccn.loc.gov/2021052597

For Amaya, Alex, Hannah, Sarah, Trey, Elizabeth, and Kayley,
our beloved future
Amanda, Nathan, Jennifer, Joshua, Jan, and Richard,
our precious center
Les,
the best brother ever

Contents

Illustrations

INTRODUCTION

....

The Meeting of Grain and Fire

iscuits, the little quick breads made of wheat flour, tender and white on the inside and crusty-brown on the outside. Cornbread, white or yellow cornmeal, with or without sugar, fashioned into a cake, muffins, or sticks. Sweets, perhaps an elaborate layer cake—coconut comes to mind—or a pie: lemon, chocolate, pecan.

Southern baked goods are many things. And they mean a whole lot to southerners.

Baked goods fill southern spaces with both deep sentiments and wonderful aromas as they cook. Sweet baked goods often form the centerpiece of celebrations like birthdays and weddings. Southern holiday tables feature not just one dessert but many. People remember these joyful times, and they remember deeply the sweet things associated with those times. They also connect baked goods with the people who produced them, very often a grandmother. Those feelings are real, and they matter to people.

But reality must set in. Advocates of baking in the South have nurtured sentimentality to bolster the reputation of the region, arguing that southern baking is different and better than the baking in other parts of America. This is not a new notion. After the Civil War had barely ended, writers began publishing flowery praise of southern cooking, including baking. Once-wealthy white southerners seldom acknowledged the Black people who cooked the food, or the Native Americans who showed their ancestors how not to starve.

They never mentioned the enslaved people who died growing sugar in the Caribbean. Even now, when writers postulate a specialness about southern food, they often whitewash the cruelty that made it possible.

FOR BLACK SOUTHERNERS, the feelings for food may be more ambivalent than those of white people, but the positive side is important. For some African Americans, food links to the trauma of insufficiency. For others, the love of ancestors shines through. I recently watched a cooking video in which the cook repeated the phrase "Just like my grandmother" as she demonstrated how to make hot-water cornbread. She acknowledged her deep culinary and emotional debt to her grandmother.

Since the end of slavery, southern food has varied more by class than by race, and as Black southerners climbed from poverty to the middle class to comfort, they and their white neighbors ate more alike than differently. Food has become more a factor of unity than division, and baking holds a high position in the pantheon of southern food. Ward, a middle-aged white male, told interviewers that at a family funeral, in addition to fried chicken and multiple vegetables, "we are also going to have seven kinds of cake and seven kinds of pie as well as biscuits and corn muffins."[1] That kind of plenty speaks loudly to the cherished ethos of southern hospitality and baking.

I aim to hold sentimental notions, Black and white, up to the light of day. By looking at the realities of baking, I intend to show how southerners have related to each other through time and how they used baking to demonstrate their relationships, for good and for ill. By way of grain and fire, this history of southern baking kindles the broader history of the South and its people. Baking is one way to view the history of a place and its people: Who laid the fire, provided the grain, did the baking, did the eating? What did they use for materials and tools? How did they use baked goods to shape and show their connections to one another? How did these practices change over the centuries? And what did they mean to people? These questions go far beyond the simplistic romanticism often associated with southern baking.

Baking has shaped the South, and the South has shaped baking. Like everything else about the South, baking is far more complicated than a luscious cake might imply. *Grain and Fire* explores how distinctive baking practices have demonstrated the complexities of the region and its people for more than 500 years. Centering the collision and amalgamation of three global baking traditions—Native American, European, and African—over the course of five centuries not only reveals the story of key and beloved foods but also shows how the people of the South came to live together.

In the American South, three foodways came together, and they included baking. Southerners, like humans everywhere, used baked goods to distinguish among themselves and figure out the social order. Higher-status people have long had access to the more desirable nuts, seeds, or grains. An example of this is the chestnut, which, in the seventeenth century, the Powhatan reserved for their leaders. What we will see throughout this book is that powerful southerners employed baked goods to discriminate among themselves and others: who ate chestnuts and who ate acorns; who ate corn and who ate wheat; who had access to sugar, who had to settle for molasses, and who had no sweetening at all; and much more. This book traces those distinctions and why they matter for southern society, and for the United States more broadly.

STUDYING BAKING in one specific region raises the question: Is there really such a thing as southern baking? The primary distinction of the South, of course, is the historic confrontation of Indigenous peoples, Europeans, and Africans, more than in any other place in North America. The union of these three cultures, one brought by force, shaped a distinctive set of foods. Native Americans set the baseline, having made comfortable homes for themselves in the Southeast long before Europeans arrived. Then, for 400 years, Black hands prepared the dishes that wealthy southerners waxed rhapsodic about. The role of African-descended people in southern cooking cannot be overemphasized. At first under horrendous conditions of slavery, and later under continuing and often violent oppression, Black people made their innovative best with what they had, augmenting their diets and creating distinct foodways.

Further, southern food is the most recognizable regional cuisine in the United States, and it does have genuine distinctions. The baked goods of the South have differed from those of other regions particularly in the continued use of cornmeal and the preference for individual portions like biscuits, rolls, and muffins.

The tortured history of the South makes baking complicated, part of a "complex regional cuisine of both privilege and deprivation." The South has had some of the nation's richest people and many of its poorest. Racism, sexism, stark poverty, and class struggle have abounded. And the differences in what people ate provide strong examples of these struggles.[2]

WHY BAKING AS a particular lens with which to view the South? Aside from all the sentiment surrounding hot biscuits and so on, the process and history of baking has had a powerful impact on human life, providing both essential nutrition and pleasure. The material aspects of baking—the ingredients, the tools, the labor involved in creating the goods—demonstrate a lot about how humans have fed their families and themselves and how they have treated each other, over time, in one particular place.

At its most basic, baking is a form of indirect cooking: the food changes chemically in the warm air that surrounds it rather than directly in the flame. Like all other types of cooking, baking starts to break down structures in the food, making it easier to digest. Baking is slower, gentler, and considerably more complicated than boiling or roasting. And while many foods can be baked, we often think of the word as designating foods made from grain.

For most of human history, baking has meant bread—sustenance—rather than sweets. For thousands of years, people have made nuts, grains, and roots into powder, mixed that powder with liquid, and baked it. Baked goods are strikingly portable, unlike a boiled dish such as porridge, and they are more digestible than the raw grains and nuts that go into them. The more the grains are processed before cooking, the finer the texture of the finished product, and all kinds of ingredients can be added for taste and texture: fats, liquids, sweeteners, leavens, spices, nuts, and fruit.

A pone made only of corn and water, butter-laden puff pastry, and a four-layer coconut cake are all forms of baked grain. The people who baked such items and ate them have differed considerably, however, over the centuries. From the ovens and hearths of Native American women, enslaved women, housewives, and professional bakers have come a wide array of items. These bakers have fed everyone from their families to the people who enslaved them to customers who paid money for their breads and cakes. And for the people who ate them, baked goods have ranged from simple subsistence to markers of opulent celebrations, with sweet tastes making even sweeter memories. The array of foods and associated experiences have meant many different things to people over the centuries.

Baking requires fire, one of the essential components of life on Earth; compared by many cultures to earth, wind, and water; and the topic of numerous ancient myths. Fire is a complicated chemical reaction of fuel and oxygen that creates light and heat. I recently fumbled with the fire in my fireplace—a sturdy brick box with an excellent chimney—trying to light pieces of oak hewn by someone else and delivered to my house, using a Bic lighter and fine fatwood kindling. I reflected on how our ancestors *knew* fire: how to start it, how to keep it going, how to conserve it. Managing fire was a matter of life, not aesthetics, for them. Today fire is delivered to our houses through electrical wires and gas mains, and we forget about how important it is, but we still absolutely depend on it.

Archaeologists are not sure when humans began to cook—maybe as recently as 30,000 years ago—and the first cooked foods were probably meat. Baking developed even later than that.

Before people discovered how to farm, they gathered seeds, nuts (including acorns), and grains and learned to bake them. After they began farming, perhaps 12,000 years ago, humans started growing grain, the type depending on their location. Baking technology, particularly ovens, evolved unevenly. Where people remained mobile, they needed quick, portable fires. Ovens benefited only those societies that were rooted in place. Archaeologists are still figuring out the nuances of the earliest bread baking, examining Neolithic-period (roughly 10,000 BCE) ovens from western Asia for traces of grain, for example.[3]

People around the globe learned to bake seeds, nuts, roots, and grain into bread. Indigenous peoples inhabited the South for perhaps 15,000 years before Europeans arrived around 1500 CE. They baked their bread on earthen hearths or in stone ovens. When corn agriculture arrived from Mexico, thriving in the warm South, Native Americans recentered much of their food on the cultivation and cuisine of the coarse yellow grain.

Europeans—French, Spanish, and English—began invading the South between 1564 and 1607. They came from bread-eating societies, where grain provided up to 70 percent of their daily calories.[4] The grains included wheat but also barley, buckwheat, rye, millet, and other heavy varieties. In lean times, Europeans ate acorns, too. Wheat was the most favored because it could rise the highest, using various forms of yeast, and because the highly refined flour made from it was white. The Roman Catholic Church reinforced Europeans' affinity for wheat, dictating in its councils that the Eucharistic host, which became the body of Christ during the sacrament of Holy Communion, could be made only from wheat flour.

The first enslaved Africans arrived in Virginia in 1619. In West Africa, people baked their local grains—millet, rice, and sorghum—in open fires.[5] The Portuguese brought corn, wheat, and oven technology to Africa before they began transporting enslaved people to North America, and some enslaved people might have known about these foods and practices in their African homelands.

As these three cultures came together, sometimes gradually, sometimes in sudden violent clashes, people in the South learned about food from one another. Indians adapted European ways with careful consideration. Europeans learned to eat corn, taking on Native American ways. In the words of poet Stephen Vincent Benét, "They ate the white corn kernels, parched in the sun, / And they knew it not, but they'd not be English again."[6] At the same time, the most powerful southerners imposed their ideas of proper baking on others, particularly the Africans whom they enslaved. Baked goods remained symbols of rank and wealth, and enslavers tightly controlled enslaved people's access to high-status ingredients. But Black people found ways, even under the most dreadful circumstances, to contest those limitations and to enrich their diets beyond cornbread and fat pork.

After the Civil War, transportation, communications, and technology brought the South into the mainstream of American cooking culture. At that point, the words of southern chef and historian Bill Neal became true: "What makes a dish southern is its complete acceptance by the southern community and its general recognition as a southern food."[7] Southerners began to eat more like people everywhere else in the United States. But the food remained southern because it was in the South, it was cooked and eaten by southern people, and southerners claimed it as their own. As we will see, it provided a battleground for ideas about continuity and change, particularly in terms of race and class.

WHO AM I, the person writing this book? In the spirit of reconciliation, I acknowledge that my southern roots reach back to Jamestown and include European enslavers (most notably the Peirce family and John Rolfe), fighters against Native Americans, and a lot of small farmers. I'm also a baby boomer, one of that privileged generation of fawned-over kids. My daddy fixed pancakes on Sunday, a throwback to his time as a messman in the Marine Corps during World War II. My mother liked making cakes and cookies, but she always used canned biscuits, thought that brown-and-serve rolls were plenty good enough for the fanciest meal, and bought our birthday cakes at the bakery. I never knew either of my grandmothers, so I don't have those associations that many people do. I describe myself as a competent home baker. I enjoy baking, but my products are not notable.

Maybe because of my grandmother-less state, I'm not particularly sentimental about food, and I tend to be unsympathetic to those who are. People in the South—even some who ought to know better—have used food to buttress strongly held notions of a romantic past. I don't think there is anything unique about southern hospitality, and I don't believe that southerners have more of a childlike affinity for sweets than any other people. All cookbooks, not just southern ones, have large sections devoted to baked goods because so much of baking is chemistry. The proportions must be exact for the product to turn out right. You can ad-lib a stew, but doing so with a layer cake will only spell disaster. And so I evaluate with a steely eye the baking heritage of one American region.

By design, this is not a cookbook. The bibliography has numerous cookbooks in it, however, and many of those published before World War II are available full-text on the internet. My personal contemporary favorites are

The author on her second birthday, 1960, beginning her lifelong love of buttercream icing. Photo by Jimmie Willis.

by Nancie McDermott—*Southern Cakes* and *Southern Pies*—but there are lots of good ones out there.

With regard to terminology, I have used the tribal names for Native Americans and Africans when I knew them. I have used the more general terms in the absence of specific group names. When it is not in a direct quotation, I also have rendered seventeenth-century English into that of the twenty-first century.

LET'S SEE what happened when southerners put grain with fire.

Chapter 1

ACORN BREAD

....

Grinding Only Looks Easy

*T*he first baked goods in the South might seem humble, but getting, processing, and cooking them were far from simple. For maybe 10,000 years before the domestication of corn, southern Native Americans ate bread made from nuts and roots that women gathered while men hunted.[1] From the Gulf Coast to the Chesapeake Bay, oaks, chestnuts, hickories, and black walnut trees rained down their fruits in the fall. Native women ventured to the woods to collect nuts and acorns, loading their heavy booty into baskets they had woven and lugging it back to their homes.

Every year, the pressure to gather enough nuts until the next fall must have been intense. Most nut trees bear every two or three years, and even then the yields can be inconsistent.[2] Later, working to control the harvest, southeastern Native American women likely grew trees intentionally. Planting a nut-bearing tree required patience, for a young tree could take up to a decade to fruit.[3] Across the South, each fall, women bent and stretched to collect the precious harvest, laboring diligently as the daylight shortened and the air grew cool.

Gathering was the easy part, for making nuts and acorns edible was difficult. Black walnuts (*Juglans nigra*) have outer husks and thick shells. After soaking the nuts in water, the women broke the husks and shells with rocks, leaving deep stains of tannic acid on their hands. The meats usually fractured during the cracking and came out in fragments, but they were tender and tasty, rich in iron and potassium.[4] Similarly, hickory nuts (*Carya sp.*) yielded their meats only reluctantly. The pieces could be boiled and strained, then baked into bread.[5]

The most delectable nuts for bread, often saved for only elite men, came from trees we know as chestnuts (*Castanea*). They grew profusely in the southern forests and yielded a meat that early English visitor Ralph Hamor described as "luscious and hearty."[6] Chestnuts were relatively easy to process.[7] Their spiky burrs opened by themselves, and the shiny brown skin peeled easily most of the time. Women boiled the chestnuts before shaping them into bread. Across the South, Native Americans served chestnut "dough bread" to visitors.[8] In October 1540, messengers from the Native American town of Mabila (in present-day central Alabama) brought Spanish invader Hernando de Soto "much bread made from chestnuts, which are abundant and excellent in that region."[9] In Virginia sixty years later, the Powhatan served chestnut bread to "their chief men, or at their greatest feasts."[10]

Many kinds of oaks (*Quercus*) graced the southern forests, some of their acorns as small as a fingertip and others as big as a golf ball. More than any other tree in the South, the oak provided ingredients for bread to the Natives long before corn arrived.[11] Besides being abundant, acorns also kept well. If they were parched quickly after gathering to prevent them from germinating, they could easily hold over until the next year.[12]

The taste of an acorn varies widely according to the variety of tree. The main types are white oaks (*Lepidobalanus*) and red oaks (*Lobatae*). In the Deep South, the live oak (*Quercus virginiana*), a white oak, dominated the landscape. White oaks produce acorns every year and red oaks every two. Acorns from white oaks have a much milder flavor than those from red oaks, which are loaded with tannic acid.[13] Some Native Americans preferred the piquancy of the red oak over the blandness of the white.[14]

Most people wanted to get rid of the bitterness. The most common method of leaching the tannic acid was to bury the acorns in earthen pits. Father Alonso Gregorio de Escobedo described the process in eastern Florida about 1600: "They gather large amounts of the acorn which is small and bitter and peel the hull from the meat. They grind it well and during the time they bury it in the ground the earth is warm from the heat of the sun." While some Native Americans kept their acorns in the ground only briefly, others left them for eight days or longer.[15]

After the acid was tempered, next came the tedious labor of grinding or pounding. As historian Rachel Laudan comments, grinding looks easy, and it is—for the first ten minutes. The sustained labor of grinding nuts—and later, grain—took hours of a woman's day, putting her on her knees and straining

Chickahominy mortar and pestle. National Museum of the American Indian, Smithsonian Institution, catalog number 10/6576. Photo by NMAI Photo Services.

the muscles and bones of her arms, shoulders, back, and elbows. Small wonder that so many Native women's skeletons appeared arthritic at early ages.[16] Southern Native women used the same tools for centuries: a base, called a mortar in English and a *metate* in Spanish, and an instrument to grind or pound with—a pestle or *mano*. The base could be a movable piece of rock or the bedrock itself. In some places across the South, Native women hollowed out mortars in the bedrock to accommodate their handmade rock grinders.[17] They made those grinding stones of local materials—granite, sandstone, quartz—whatever was available that was harder than a nut, sized to fit a woman's hand.[18]

Seeds of all kinds also provided grist for bread. Native American women encouraged seed-bearing plants to grow in disturbed areas, and they then farmed those plants—deliberately saving seeds, planting them, and cultivating them. Best known to us, sunflowers have been in use for thousands of years, yielding large nutlike seeds that could be ground into "a very palatable bread."[19] Archaeological evidence shows that the seeds consumed by southern Native Americans included goosefoot (*Chenopodium*), amaranth, sumpweed (*Iva*), ragweed (*Ambrosia*), and knotweed (*Polygonum*).[20] European observers compared native seeds to those that they knew, identifying them as similar to rye, guinea corn, or millet. The seed that looked like rye, Englishman William Strachey noted, made "dainty bread, buttered with deer's suet."[21] Seeds could be stored easily and took up little space, but they had to be kept from germinating, put away dry and in the dark. They would be ground or pounded into flour before baking, meaning more time on her knees for the would-be baker.

Like their peers in the tropics, who often fed their families on cassava, southeastern Native American women also made bread from roots. Most bothered with them only when other foods were in short supply, but some southern Native Americans used roots regularly.[22]

Roots offered several advantages: rich in calories and nutrients, they often grew abundantly, particularly in marshy areas. They could be harvested year-round. But they were also a hassle. Full of water and heavy, roots were hard to transport. And, no small matter, many were poisonous.[23] Early European arrivals noted the root-based cuisines with their benefits and dangers. Spanish priest Alonso Leturiondo warned that the root called "ache" had to be processed correctly, or "the dough came out very black and if the pungency was not removed, 'the mouth is set on fire.'"[24] Similarly, the "tockawhoughe," or tuckahoe (probably *Peltandra virginica*, or arrow alum), that grew in Virginia had to be detoxified to be edible. Natives cooked the tuckahoe root in a pit to dissolve the poisonous calcium oxalate, as John Smith described: they "cover a great many of the[m] with oak leaves & fern, and then cover all with earth in the manner of a coalpit; over it, on each side, they continue a great fire 24 hours before they dare eat it."[25]

After detoxification came the tedious process of grating the root, perhaps with a sharpened stone or the jawbone of an animal such as a deer.[26] Then the root was dried and pounded into flour, probably with a stone pestle. Only then could a woman take the flour, most likely mix it with water, and make it into cakes to be baked. After such intensive labor, the baked product must have been precious.

Water also could not be taken for granted. Water is essential for human life, but it can also be deadly. Humans cannot drink salt water, fresh water can contain lethal pathogens, and standing water provides breeding ground for insects, especially mosquitoes. So finding pure, fresh water remained a constant concern for every adult. Once people found water, they had to bring it to the home. Each gallon of water weighs eight pounds. Every time we casually mention "water," we should think about the effort that went into finding it, making sure it was okay, and toting it (in a vessel one had made or found) to the place it would be used.

Once the acorns and roots had the acids and poisons removed and the nuts and seeds and roots were ground, they could be baked into cakes. The historical and archaeological records are sadly quiet about how these cakes were made and cooked. Most cooks used an open fire, although throughout the Southeast, archaeologists have found the remains of earth ovens, three to six feet in diameter, ranging in depth from two to four feet, dating back to perhaps 200 CE and used for hundreds of years. Remnants of numerous seeds and nuts in them indicate that the users baked bread.[27]

Fire, of course, was and remains a crucial feature of human life. Once started, a fire could be moved from place to place. Among the Native Americans of the Southeast, making and keeping fires was women's work, and knowing how to do it was vital. The first step was gathering material for the fire, an endless task sometimes delegated to children. Optimally, the cook—almost invariably female—had a supply of various types and sizes of wood. She began with a nest of tiny bits of tinder and kindling and created sparks, perhaps with a piece of rock or another hard surface. Once the kindling ignited, she added small bits of dry wood. In the Southeast, pine twigs, sticky with resin, flamed quickly. After this small fire got going, she added hardwood such as oak or hickory to create deep, even heat and a stout layer of ash.[28] The woman would also know how to bank her fire—to keep the embers glowing at a slow rate—overnight so that she wouldn't have to restart the fire the next day. She would likely rake the embers together in a place sheltered from the wind and then cover them with ash. If she were skilled—and lucky—the next morning the embers would erupt into a fresh flame. Working with fire was inherently dangerous, and the life-sustaining blaze, which could also be deadly, had to be treated with utmost respect.

The breads of the southeastern Native Americans cooked beautifully in the ashes below the flames, as long use hardened earth into a surface as dependable as any fired ceramic. In the summer, the baking often took place outside. In the winter, each family group's house had an earthen hearth or oven in the center, with a hole in the roof to let out the smoke. Hearths and ovens at ground level meant that each woman stooped and bent as she baked her family's meal. The seeds, nuts, and roots, mixed with water and baked with care, fed her loved ones.

WHILE SOUTHEASTERN Native American women gathered and grew their families' sustenance, a new plant was making its way northeast from Mexico. *Zea mays*, known in English as corn or maize, was the product of agriculture: human intervention in its growth. For centuries before Europeans appeared, Native American women sowed corn every spring. They cultivated it using tools made of wood, stone, or bone, then harvested, dried, and pounded it into meal. In sum, they participated in the cycle of events that sustained most

Zea mays
(maize, corn)

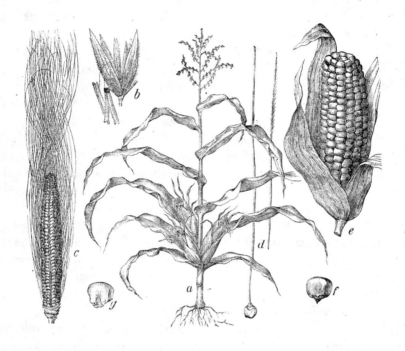

Corn botanical illustration showing stalk, kernel, and ear. iStock.

human life in Native America for a thousand years: growing and processing the most favored baked food of generations of southerners.

Corn arrived fairly late in the story of humans. Botanical geneticists generally agree that corn descended from a wild grain called teosinte and that it developed as the result of plant breeding by humans in the highlands of southwestern Mexico perhaps around 7000 BCE.[29] From its Mexican origins, corn spread throughout the Americas, stopping only where the climate became too cold, dry, or wet.[30] Corn, amazingly adaptable, grows in almost any moderate climate (tolerating a growing season as short as 120 days), and neither drought nor frost will completely kill it. In milder climates, staggered planting allows for two harvests. Because it has no tap root, it can thrive in shallow soils. Every corn plant is extremely productive. A stalk emerges from a single seed and produces two or three seedpods, known as ears, each with hundreds of kernels of grain. It stores easily for long periods of time. Ripe corn can stay in the shuck, or outer husk, indefinitely and once dry will remain edible for years.[31] And, unlike industrially produced corn, these early grains provided good, though incomplete, nutrition—vitamins A, C, and E and carbohydrates.[32] The Native Americans also discovered that soaking corn in water mixed with lye, made from ashes, made it more nutritious. (Today we call the process nixtamalization, and we know that it releases niacin, vitamin B_3, from the corn. We most often see lye-treated corn as hominy and as grits. The Native Americans figured it out without chemistry labs.) With all of these attributes, it is no wonder that corn became the centerpiece of the southeastern American diet.

The marvelous grain arrived in north-central Florida by 750 CE, eastern Tennessee by perhaps 800 CE, and as far north as the Chesapeake by 900 CE. When Europeans arrived at the end of the sixteenth century, Native American women were growing corn almost everywhere in the South.[33] While the men still hunted and gathered, southeastern Native Americans drew increasing amounts of their nutrition from the plants that women purposefully cultivated and stored for future use.[34]

As corn increased in significance to southeastern Native Americans, it took on strong cultural meanings. Sacred stories demonstrate the importance of corn to southern Native Americans. Perhaps the best-known tale is that of the Cherokee, in which Selu, the Corn Mother, produced corn from her blood.[35] The Cherokee used the story of Selu to explain their division of labor, in which women bore responsibility for almost all agricultural tasks.[36] Other Natives across the South also acknowledged the significance of corn with numerous rites asking their gods for fertility and celebrating harvest. In Mississippi, each Natchez bride presented a stalk of corn to her new husband as part of their pledges to one another.[37] During their fertility rites, the Creek offered the gods thick cakes made of corn. Spanish observer Pietro Martire d'Anghiera noted in 1530, "The natives are convinced that their prayers for harvests will be heard, especially if the cakes are mixed with tears."[38]

People worked diligently to adapt Mexican corn to their best advantage. From region to region, it varied dramatically: tall, short, many-colored, early- or late-ripening, with eight, ten, or twelve rows of kernels, and everything in between. Many varieties flourished with specific soils and rainfall, so that corn grown on the Atlantic coast differed from that in eastern Texas, for example. Planting several types worked to the Native Americans' benefit: the labor required for harvest could be spread out over time, and if one kind failed to thrive, another might produce plentifully. In the South, corn fell generally into two categories: flint and dent. Flint corns are harder, ripen earlier, and keep better than dent. Dent corns are softer and ripen later, and they were historically preferred for cornmeal.[39]

The corn of the fifteenth century was not the sweet, tender delicacy that we enjoy during the summer. The only time that Native Americans ate corn fresh off the cob was when it was still green. Women sliced the soft, milky corn off the cob and pounded it. They then wrapped the juicy grains in leaves from the stalk and boiled the bundles.[40] The appearance of green corn in early summer touched off annual celebrations. In Louisiana, the Great Corn Feast featured "shouts of joy," a "general feast," games, and dancing through the night.[41] For the Cherokee, the Green Corn Festival marked a time of renewal and reconciliation, with the ritual cleaning of their towns' public spaces. Women also scrubbed their houses, washed their cooking utensils, and disposed of ashes and leftover food. The Cherokee fasted, then feasted and danced.[42]

After the green corn celebrations, Native Americans settled down to wait for the grain to ripen. As the kernels darkened and the tassels dried, they harvested the ripe ears by hand, simply pulling them from the stalk. For the most part, Native Americans refrained from processing their corn until they were ready to use it. Once it is ground, corn turns rancid quickly, so Natives either left it in on the cob to dry or parched it immediately after grinding.[43] Across the South, Native Americans built structures dedicated to keeping corn dry and free from would-be thieves like rats and raccoons. The Choctaw, for example, stored grain in particular edifices raised eight feet from the ground.[44] Others kept their corn in pits in the ground, lined with bark and layered with dry grass, bark, and dirt.[45] At some point, they would remove the husks and strip the corn from the cob, a process later known as shelling. Whatever their means, Native Americans carefully provided for their families' continued sustenance.

The onerous task of grinding corn, like nuts, was women's work, and it consumed many hours each day. Sometimes women lightened their labor by doing it in the company of others, creating a rhythm as each worked at her separate mortar. Englishman John Lawson commented, "The Savage Men never beat their Corn to make Bread; but that is the Womens Work, especially the Girls, of whom you shall see four beating with long great Pestils in a narrow wooden Mortar; and every one keeps her stroke so exactly, that 'tis worthy of Admiration."[46]

By the sixteenth century CE, southern Native American women used mortars made from tree trunks and carved wooden pestles as a favorite grinding

Native American village of Secotan, North Carolina, showing multiple plant-
ings of corn. Engraving by Theodor de Bry based on a 1585 drawing by John
White. Published in Hariot, *Briefe and True Report*, [97].

method. First, they cut down a sturdy tree, maybe eighteen inches in diameter, to about waist height. Next, they lit a fire in the middle of the stump to begin hollowing out the tree trunk. Once the fire burned enough of the inner part of the tree, the women began planing it with "stone instruments, patiently continuing the slow process" until the stump had a well of the correct depth.[47] Although some southeastern Native Americans continued to use stone for pestles, others preferred wood, especially hickory. They shaved the edges of an appropriately sized log, creating a handle that allowed the worker to grasp the instrument and exert maximum force on the corn in the mortar.[48]

Native American women also fashioned a wide variety of other tools to help with their work. Among the most important were the baskets that they wove. Made from split reeds or lightweight wooden splints, baskets served crucial functions in preparing grain. The fanner basket was woven "in the shape of [a] shovel about thirty inches long, with one end open and flat; the other end, with the edges rolled up about four inches forms a pocket-like receptacle." The woman held the fanner in her hand and shook it to separate the husks from the broken pieces of grain. After she disposed of the husks, she placed the grain in a woven sifter, from which the smallest pieces fell into a large flat basket. Once the husks were gone, the woman could place the grain back into the mortar to be pounded even more finely.[49]

Any good cook improvises dishes, and southeastern Native American women were no exception. To her corn or nut dough a cook could add bear fat or deer suet to make a more tender cake.[50] Bakers commonly enhanced their dishes with the fruits that grew wild across the South—grapes, plums, strawberries, mulberries, blueberries, blackberries—using seasonal bounty for variety and taste.[51] Indeed, in the absence of honeybees and sugarcane, ripe fruits often provided the only sweetness in Native diets. Two other kinds of sweetener came from trees: the honey locust and the maples that grew in the uplands. The honey locust (*Gleditsia triacanthos*) bears a pod with a sweet pulp that can be used to flavor doughs.[52] English naturalist John Lawson noted the use of the sugar maple (*Acer saccharum*) in the North Carolina mountains where the Native Americans followed a procedure like their neighbors to the north: "The *Indians* tap it, and make Gourds to receive the Liquor. . . . When the *Indians* have gotten enough, they carry it home, and boil it to a just Consistence of Sugar, which grains of itself, and serves for the same Uses, as other Sugar does."[53] Maple sugar can be stored indefinitely and traded, so people beyond the mountains likely enjoyed it too.

And sometimes the additions were by necessity, not choice. In the periodic droughts that overtook the Southeast, Native American women stretched their ground corn by roasting corncobs and pulverizing them to a powder, called *pungnough* in Virginia, then adding the powder to the meal. The result, John Smith observed, "never tasted well in bread, nor broth."[54] But need sometimes overshadowed flavor.

As she prepared the dough from her painstakingly made cornmeal, a Native American woman surely thought about the baking process. She had to consider her wood carefully, because the type that she chose would flavor the bread, for better or worse. Her fire had to be at the right level, with a healthy supply of ash and ember, or her oven heated to the right temperature, so she had to plan ahead to build the fire hot and then let it die down. She carefully combined the precious meal with water; added any fat, fruit, or sweetener; then patted the mixture into cakes and carried them to the fire. Like her foremothers, with their roots and nuts, she might simply tuck the bare cakes into the ashes of the fire on an earthen hearth, hardened by repeated exposure to high heat.[55] The alkali in the ash leavened the cakes, adding air to the thick dough.[56] Or she might take broad leaves, such as maple or sycamore, larger than her hands, and wrap each cake in one before placing it in the ashes. She had to choose her leaf wisely, however, for it would also impart flavor to the bread.[57] Or she might put the dough on a smooth stone before placing it under the ashes. Such a stone—or later, pottery—griddle provided even temperatures for baking. Southeastern Native Americans often used stones found nearby—for example, soapstone slabs from the Savannah River, "thick as a board, some as big as a sheet of paper."[58] The baking surely occasioned an anxious eye from the baker. After all the time invested in those little cakes, the last thing she wanted was for them to burn.

When the cakes were done, the cook carefully brushed off the ashes or scorched bits of leaf, and sometimes she rinsed them in water to ensure that each bit of ash came off. Whatever else was on the menu—meat, squash, beans—it was time for her family to eat.

THE NATIVE AMERICAN WOMEN had been tending the field of corn northeast of the bay since early spring. By July 1539, it was tall and lush and green, with ears of grain swelling and just beginning to ripen. Surely, they must have thought, they would have a good year ahead, with an ample store of the life-giving corn laid in. Their hopes were dashed, however, when a group of light-skinned men, astride long-legged beasts that the Native Americans had never seen, went into the fields and stripped the tender corn from the stalks, taking all that they could. These horse-riding men were part of an expedition of 600 Spaniards under the command of Hernando de Soto, who had arrived on the west coast of Florida from Cuba six weeks earlier. In addition to killing various Native Americans along the way, the Spaniards helped themselves to food and other resources. They were conquistadors, after all, and everything—including corn—was meant for them. Or so they thought.[59] The stolen corn was just the beginning of changes for the Native Americans of the Southeast.

Europeans who began moving into the Americas in the sixteenth century came from bread-eating cultures. Most Spaniards received almost three-quarters of their daily nutrition in the form of grain, either boiled or baked. And they also came from cultures that determined social status partly through the foods a person consumed. Peasants ate bread made of rye, millet, barley, spelt, or oats, and in hard times they, like the Native Americans, baked acorns or chestnuts. The wealthy elite, on the other hand, consumed wheat, the finer and whiter the better. They didn't understand the chemical composition of wheat flour, which has a protein called gluten that provides a structure for leavening gas during baking, but they surely noticed that it rose higher and incorporated more air than any other flour. Upper-class Spaniards also enjoyed baked goods sweetened with sugar and spiced with cloves, ginger, nutmeg, and cinnamon.[60]

Certain foods, educated Spaniards argued, were essential for good health.[61] The Roman Catholic Church, too, made the case for the superiority of wheat over all other grains, requiring that the holy bread for a proper mass be produced from wheat flour.[62] Thus, when Christopher Columbus made his second voyage to Hispaniola in 1493, he brought wheat seeds and sugarcane cuttings—provisions for replicating an elite European diet—to try in the territory newly claimed for Spain. While the wheat failed to take hold in the tropics, the sugarcane thrived, changing the American landscape drastically.[63] As the Spaniards took over central Mexico, they found that wheat grew readily in the highlands, and a mere four decades after Columbus, they were growing enough wheat to export it to other Spanish colonies.[64]

In the southeastern part of North America, however, newly arrived Europeans had to make do with what they found there. The members of the de Soto expedition came to Florida planning to provision themselves off the land.[65] They knew corn as good food. They might have had it in Spain, brought by expeditions returning from America, or they could have encountered it in Cuba before their arrival in Florida. In any event, they delighted in the stolen abundance that the Native Americans' grain provided them. The de Soto expedition members also quickly found use for American nuts. A month after their arrival, they came to the Native American town of Colupaha, where in addition to corn they found "a great quantity of dried chinkapins that had prickly burs on the nut pods."[66] They may have recognized the chinquapins as types of the chestnuts that poor Spaniards ate. As they gobbled up the grain and nuts that the southeastern Native Americans had carefully stored for themselves and their families, de Soto and his fellow travelers were adapting to American foods.

Two decades after de Soto, about 200 French Huguenots—women, men, and children—sought a haven on the Atlantic coast just north of present-day Jacksonville. Creating a colony known as Fort Caroline in 1564, they brought with them European cooking technology as well as hopes for religious liberty. The French Protestant colonists built a village within a triangular palisade, and outside the wall they created a beehive-shaped oven, most likely of local clay, "some distance from the fort because the houses were covered with palmetto leaves and when fire starts in them it is hard to put out," as founder René Goulaine de Laudonnière observed.[67] A 1591 etching by Theodor de Bry, based on a watercolor by Jacques le Moyne de Morgues, who accompanied the Huguenots, shows the oven clearly, several feet wide and several feet high, under its own thatched-roof cover, safe from the elements. The colonists of Fort Caroline were likely the first to bring European-style oven technology to present-day America.

The oven at Fort Caroline, like many European ovens, was built for the community, and it may have operated in the European manner: a designated baker (most likely a man) made dough himself and baked and sold it, or a woman could make her own dough and bring it to the oven to be baked.[68] Oven baking was and is quite different from cooking with an open fire. The user first builds a fire inside the chamber to warm the floor, walls, and inside air. Once the oven reaches the proper temperature, the baker removes the fire. This process of moving fire around is treacherous, and oven baking is not for the faint of heart. The oven floor conducts heat directly into the loaves of bread, the domed roof radiates heat from above, and hot air surrounds the top of the baking loaf.[69]

The residents of Fort Caroline may have had a European-style oven, but the materials they baked were often strictly American. Awaiting resupply from France, the group ran perilously low on food in the winter and spring of 1565, and they survived only because the Natives traded with them for maize and acorns.[70] In the late summer of 1565, the French people got some decent European grain when the English fleet commanded by John Hawkins appeared. The French traded arms for food, including flour, "wheat bread," "meal," and "biscuits," which were versions of hardtack, the thick, hard, salty, dried wheat-flour bread that had sustained sailors and soldiers since the early Egyptians. Taking pity on the French "since [they] had not lately had anything to eat but grain and water," Hawkins also made a gift of a "barrel of white biscuits."[71] John Sparkes, a member of Hawkins's entourage, evaluated the food near Fort Caroline positively: "roots passing good. . . . These be things wherewith a man may live, having corn or maiz wherewith to make bread: for maiz maketh

Oven at Fort Caroline. Detail of Theodor de Bry engraving based on watercolor by Jacques le Moyne de Morgues. Published in le Moyne de Morgues and de Bry, *Brevis Narratio*, 10.

good savory bread, and cakes as fine as flower."[72] Adaptations by the Huguenots became moot, however, a month later, when the Spanish laid waste to the fort, killing the men, taking the women and children as prisoners, and permanently eliminating the French presence on the southern Atlantic coast.

The Spanish soldiers who destroyed Fort Caroline then established a stronghold thirty miles south, near present-day St. Augustine. They liked what they saw there: explorer Juan Pardo noted that the land was "good for bread and wine, and all kinds of livestock." Surely the new land could be made to grow the crops that the Spaniards cherished at home.[73]

With American settlement in mind, two ships left Spain on October 7, 1568, with 225 emigrants: families, most with children; widows; and single men—laborers and small farmers. To maintain the travelers on the voyage across the Atlantic, the ships carried flour and several varieties of hard biscuit, which they called "biscocho." A year later, their new town of Santa Elena, on present-day Parris Island, South Carolina, had a population of 327 people, and they soon enslaved Native Americans, some of whom probably helped with baking.[74] For seven years, the residents of Santa Elena tried to figure out life on the island. When they abandoned their project in 1576, after repeated attacks from the inhabitants of the Native towns of Orista and Escamacu, the Santa Elena residents relocated 200 miles south to St. Augustine, a town growing next to the fort that the Spanish had established there after destroying Fort Caroline.

As the Spanish tried to grow the colony around St. Augustine, biscuits and wheat flour arrived from Spain, along with sugar, honey, lard, and kindling.[75] Flour and biscuits also came from "New Spain," made from wheat grown in the Mexican highlands.[76] Wheat flour was in ample supply for the elites. When the Spanish governor died in 1576, his estate included a large store of flour as well as fine tableware and other luxury goods.[77] In the 1590s, each soldier's rations included 1.5 pounds of flour a day.[78] Yet a report from 1578 demonstrates the difficulties of trans-Atlantic supply: the galleon *Santiago Menor* delivered "77 *pipes* [each about 120 gallons] of flour, in bad condition; 14 *pipes* of flour, broken. 240 *arrobas* [each about 3 gallons] of flour was salvaged from the lot and put into 8 *pipes* of 30 *arrobas* capacity."[79] Less than 20 percent of the flour arrived in usable shape.

At first the Spaniards in North America had little to sweeten their fare, with sugar appearing only rarely. Although sugar production was already in full swing in the Caribbean, the sweetener that came from Havana to North America was honey, not sugar.[80] The honey may actually have come all the way from Spain, as the Spanish were slow to set up beekeeping in the Caribbean.[81] As the population of St. Augustine grew, however, the residents planted sugarcane along with other European fruits and vegetables, and sugar became more common.[82]

From Havana and Mexico, Spanish Floridians also brought baking ingredients native to the Americas, particularly corn. The imported corn, planted alongside the native variety, gradually changed the genetic composition of southern grains.[83] Also from Cuba came the root that the Spaniards called *cazabi*, or cassava (*Manihot esculenta*). Occasionally, finished baked goods showed up in addition to the dreadful biscuit. At least one shipment from Cádiz included four barrels of "rosquetes de azucar," sugary ring-shaped fried breads dear to the Spanish heart. And in 1570, the frigate *San Pablo* brought finished cassava bread from Havana.[84]

While the Spanish government wanted all its colonies to supply them-selves either by growing their food or trading with the Natives, that expec-tation proved unrealistic. The newcomers arrived determined to grow their own wheat, bringing millstones and grindstones from Spain to Santa Elena.[85] But the climate held no promise for such ventures. One of the colonists soon complained that the land was suitable only for maize, "as a little wheat and barley has been planted there by hoeing and after having headed badly, there is nothing to it but the husk. . . . We have suffered and do suffer great hard-ships."[86] By 1572, the farmers had settled on corn and hogs as their primary endeavors, depending on resupply from Spain for everything else.[87]

Even after the Spaniards abandoned hope for wheat, grinding corn remained an ongoing problem. The Spanish government knew that grinding would be essential, importing metates and manos, made of volcanic basalt, from Mexico as early as 1565.[88] An early traveler noted two problems that would per-sist into the twentieth century: the time required for grinding and the perish-able nature of the corn once ground. The residents were "busy half of each day grinding the maize to eat that day. It cannot be kept ground or cooked for another day, [yet] to grind it each day by hand is hard, continuous labor." Even the soldiers had to provide their own meal from their ration: "As they come in, tired from work and have to grind and cook the food (because they do not have anyone to do it for them), they have a bad time of it."[89] After 1578, the situation improved, as government buildings in St. Augustine included a "horse-powered mill for grinding corn."[90] The mill was so important that it could not be trusted to private hands.

By the mid-1570s, St. Augustine was a mix of families, both civilian and mil-itary, unmarried soldiers, and enslaved Native Americans. Women, whether Spanish or Native American, made corn cakes, probably several times a day.[91] Roman Catholic missionaries, who arrived with the soldiers, surely baked bread for the Eucharist from the wheat ration, as church law dictated. Sol-diers became proficient at baking. When Father Andrés de San Miguel ship-wrecked, along with his comrades, north of St. Augustine in 1595 and was awaiting transport back to Cuba, the soldiers baked his allotted ration for him each day. The priest reported that "they knew how to do [it] well, and they did it with much care." When the time came for Father Andrés to return to Havana, the soldiers baked his flour into biscuits for the voyage south.[92]

While many residents of St. Augustine likely had to make do with baking in the ashes of an open fire, at least some of them had access to an oven by 1576. Built with clay from the nearby marsh, it was probably a beehive style similar to the one that the French created at Fort Caroline.[93] After English forces burned St. Augustine in 1586, the Spanish residents rebuilt with care.

The governor, responsible for improving the St. Augustine food supply, stressed the importance of growing food locally, and he boasted to Spanish authorities that he increased production of corn sixfold. He also built a plaza where residents could barter their produce, and he set up a standard system of weights and measures. He constructed a second horse mill, observing that it was "a welcome relief for this city, for the inhabitants suffer much in grinding the corn by hand and in mills of logs."[94] Yet for many people in St. Augustine, supplying food for their families remained a daily challenge.[95]

Some Spaniards adjusted to American foods only with difficulty. Sailors from the shipwrecked *Nuestra Señora de la Misericordia* complained in 1595 that the Florida Native Americans who rescued them brought a few corn cakes but mostly "other cakes of holm-oak acorn, yellow and red, that are sour and bitter, and this was most of what they brought, and we could not eat them." Despite their hunger, the Spaniards' palates were defeated by the tannin-loaded nuts.[96]

Sometimes adjustment came not at all. The determined Catholics of the de Soto expedition carried with them wheat flour from Spain to make Communion bread. At the battle of Mabila in present-day Alabama, October 18, 1540, Native American forces under Chief Tuskaloosa caused the Spaniards to lose their precious store of wheat flour and wine. In the aftermath, the Spaniards debated among themselves whether they could consecrate bread made of corn for the Eucharist. They sadly concluded that the Roman Catholic Church "in her holy councils and sacred canons orders and teaches us, that the bread shall be of wheat and the wine from the grape." So they simply went without Communion until they straggled into Mexico City in 1543.[97]

At least some Spaniards developed a taste for corn, however. Married soldiers in St. Augustine commonly sold their flour rations to a local store and fed their families on cheaper Native American corn, pocketing the difference.[98]

While the Europeans adapted to American foods, particularly corn, by necessity, the southeastern Native Americans apparently ate European foods only sparingly. From the beginning, Europeans gave the Natives wheat flour as gifts designed to impress, and in the 1590s, flour was a substantial part of the provisions for the missions that were popping up.[99] But Native Americans were slow to develop a taste for wheat. They did quickly come to love peaches, which grew and spread easily and brought sweetness to their foods early in the summer.[100] Some cultural transference was happening.

AS THE SPANISH were energetically going about their business in Florida, the English reached the Outer Banks of North Carolina in 1585. The English knew what they wanted to have as food in the new land, bringing barley, oats, and peas in their initial foray onto Roanoke Island. But the wheat failed to make the trip across the Atlantic, getting soaked with salt water and turning "musty." English scientist Thomas Hariot mournfully observed that the "Suger canes" that they brought to Roanoke were "not so well preserved as was requisite," so they could not try them out either.[101]

The Roanoke experiment failed, but the snug world that the Spanish envisioned in Florida was about to change. As the seventeenth century began, Native Americans and Europeans from Spain and England contended for the right to live, bake, and eat in the South.

Chapter 2

ROSQUETES DE AZUCAR

....

America, Europe, Africa

he Angolan woman's feet touched solid ground for the first time in weeks. Months before, she had been snatched from her home on the west coast of Africa and taken across a big sea on a ship, then on a second long voyage to this place. She was alone in the world, surrounded by pale-skinned men speaking a strange language. We can imagine the trip across the rough terrain between Point Comfort, jutting into the Atlantic, and the tiny village the pale men called Jamestown. Soon the woman lived in the household of Joane and William Peirce and was assigned the name Angela. The Peirces were planning a fine house on several acres in the Newtowne section of Jamestown. Joane Peirce would need more help in the household, and Angela could be useful, even if she weren't English.[1]

In this way, in 1619, began the story of the African, European, and Native American encounter in colonial Virginia. Archaeologists working at Historic Jamestowne have excavated the Peirce home and may have found the kitchen where Angela labored. Captain William Peirce played a key role in the conflicts between Virginia Native Americans and the Europeans, stealing and destroying the corn crops of the Powhatan during the ongoing war. Angela may have cooked corn for the Peirces that belonged to Natives who had planned to use it for their own families, only to see it taken by the English.[2] So went the rhythm of stolen lands, grains, and people in colonial Virginia.

FOR MUCH of the seventeenth century, Native Americans and Europeans vied for control of eastern North America. Between 1600 and 1700, the Spanish clung to their toeholds on both the Atlantic and the Gulf. Native people, weakened by new diseases, threats to their land, enslavement, and warfare, responded by creating confederations to secure their livelihoods. By the time the French arrived on the Gulf of Mexico coast in 1699, the English, in large measure due to the Africans whom they enslaved, had thriving colonies in Virginia and Carolina. All the South's peoples would learn to live, bake, and die as their cultures mingled and collided.

For the Spaniards in Florida, the turn of the calendar from 1599 to 1600 meant little, as their ways of life went on as before. During the first part of the seventeenth century, the *situado*, or supply, from the Spanish government continued. Food came to St. Augustine from Veracruz by way of Cuba, stored in the royal warehouse at the fort and distributed by the governor. After 1635, the shipments from Mexico began to fall into arrears, and local governors had to scramble to get food for the colony. They paid premium prices to private merchants for provisions including maize, flour, cassava, and olive oil.[3] In 1651, a Spanish official assessed the situation: "We now depend on that brought in by ship, endangered by shipwreck and robbery by our enemies, which we lose a great deal."[4] By 1683, Floridians hungered enough that the governor allowed them to trade with a Dutch merchant for goods including flour and grindstones.[5]

Recognizing the precarious state of imported foods, the Spaniards in Florida tried to cultivate their own, and they began establishing missions throughout the region. Besides saving souls by turning Native Americans into Catholics, the missions were supposed to grow food for the Spanish residents. Throughout the seventeenth century, Spaniards created more than eighty of these small and often short-lived ventures to convert heathens and raise victuals.

With the introduction of iron tools such as axes and hoes, the Native Americans in the Apalachee, Guale, and Timucua areas of Florida increased their production of corn.[6] The Spaniards in St. Augustine came to depend on the agricultural skills of the Natives, who harvested, shucked, and ground the corn before sending it to the fledgling city.[7] Native women brought maize to market, as well as other goods, from pottery to tobacco.[8] The European market provided them an opportunity as well as a threat.

But the Spanish craved wheat. Plus, they had their ecclesiastical reasons for wanting wheat to bake Communion bread. Thus, at Mission Santa Catalina de Guale, the Spanish ate not only the native maize and acorns as bread but also wheat imported from Europe.[9] When their supplies from home dwindled, the Spaniards wanted to grow the ingredients for their Eucharist as well as for their daily consumption.[10] They soon added wheat cultivation to the native corn, turning Mission Santa Catalina into the so-called bread basket of the area.[11] (How they got wheat to grow in Florida, after their previous failures, is unknown, but apparently they did.) The Spanish also established farms, or haciendas, to produce both wheat and corn for the military and the missionaries.[12] By 1700, nine ranches in Apalachee raised wheat or livestock.[13] Against the odds, the Spanish persevered.

Some Spaniards ground their wheat by hand, but in St. Augustine, two mills, likely powered by animal treadmills, produced enough flour to necessitate the construction of "a large house of palm" to store it.[14] In 1651, Spanish officials built a larger mill and hired a miller who, they said, would bring in new millstones.[15]

The St. Augustine mills were almost surely the traditional kind with two parallel millstones. This type of mill had been in use for almost 2,000 years and would remain so, in extraordinary instances, well into the twenty-first century. A pair of parallel circular stones, usually fashioned from quartz, sandstone, or limestone, with grooves cut into them, formed the nucleus of these mills. The fixed bottom "bedstone" remained stationary, while the top "runner" stone turned on a spindle attached to the bedstone. The two stones ground the grain between them, and the runner stone could be adjusted to make the grind coarser or finer. This kind of milling required skill, because if the stones created friction, that could cause a spark, and the dust that comes off grain when it is milled is extremely flammable. A careless miller could burn down an entire village. The power to turn the runner stone could come from wind, flowing water, or treads powered by horses, mules, or oxen. Smaller mills, known as hand mills, worked similarly but on a lesser scale, with people providing the power.

And who did the baking in St. Augustine? The numbers of women varied over time. Spanish women came in the early years, but eventually their numbers declined, resulting in a ratio of perhaps one Spanish woman to every three of her countrymen. The men then turned to Native American women as wives.[16] In 1600, about twenty-five enslaved African women lived in St. Augustine. We know little about them, except for a few of their Spanish names: Gratia, Ana, Francisca, and María. These women, and others like them, almost surely did domestic work in addition to laboring in the fields.[17] Gradually Spanish laws restricted slavery, and Floridians began luring enslaved people from the English colonies in the north to irritate their global enemies. Many people escaping English enslavement came to St. Augustine. African women worked as paid domestics in private homes, including that of the governor.

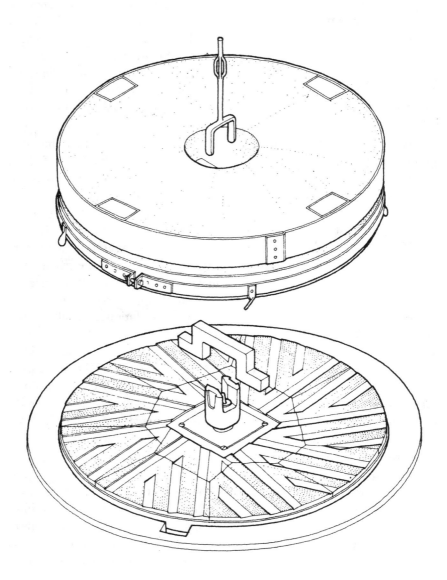

An exploded view of a bedstone (on the bottom) and a runner stone (on the top). J. Reynolds, *Windmills and Watermills*, 46.

On November 7, 1693, King Charles II issued a royal cedula, or decree, "giving liberty to all the men as well as the women."[18]

Africans rapidly became part of the St. Augustine baking culture. In 1695, Chrispin de Tapia, "a free *pardo*"—a person of Native American, European, and African lineage—was a *tienda de pulpería*, or keeper of a grocery store or bar. Two Apalachee Native Americans, Andrés de Escovedo and Ajalap Cosme, bought from him two reales' worth of *rosquetes*, the fried sweet spiral cake that earlier Spaniards had brought by the barrel from the old country. Isavel de los Rios, "a free morena [dark-skinned woman]," also sold *rosquetes* to Escovedo and Cosme. The transactions made it into the official record because the Native Americans paid with pieces of pewter and were convicted of forgery. But the episode raises questions about the nature of entrepreneurship by African Americans in St. Augustine. The record notes that Rios also "sold rosquetes for the house of the sergeant major don Nicolás Ponse de León and for the house of the corporal Ysidro Rodrígues." Was she making them? If so, where did she get capital to buy flour and sugar and the fat (probably lard) to fry the cookies in? Did she supply them to Tapia for sale in his store? Or were Rios and Tapia merely reselling Spanish-made *rosquetes*? The record remains quiet on these questions. What is clear is that the Africans engaged in the commerce of baked goods and the two young Native American men craved the sweets enough to commit a crime to get them.[19]

Overall, however, the Natives still limited their adoption of European foods.[20] When English colonists shipwrecked off the east coast of Florida in 1696, the Jobe took from them first their corn and clothing, leaving the rum, sugar, and molasses for later.[21]

The historical records on Spanish Florida are uneven. But we know that Native Americans, Spaniards, and Africans came together there and that they baked corn and wheat, the grains of the New and Old Worlds.

SOME 650 MILES north of St. Augustine, the English—Spain's chief rival for international dominion—redoubled their efforts to colonize North America. After the debacle at Roanoke Island, the English waited twenty years before seriously attempting to return to the Atlantic coast. The first new colonists, a group of forty men, arrived near the mouth of the James River in May 1607 and built a fort.

The area was already thickly populated with Native Americans from the Powhatan confederacy, well organized and prosperous. The Powhatan raised corn in community garden plots near water sources, tended by the women of each group. Four varieties of corn ripened at different times, keeping a constant supply of fresh ears throughout the harvest season.[22] The first Englishmen in Virginia made careful notes about the Natives, including their baking habits. John Smith observed grain preparation: "Their old wheat [corn] they first steep a night in hot water, in the morning pounding it in a mortar. They use a small basket for their Temmes [hulls], then pound again the great [grit?], and so separating by dashing their hand in the basket, receive the flower in a platter made of wood scraped to that form with burning and shells."[23] Smith's fellow invader George Percy noted that in "Potatans Towne," the women "do all their drudgery" making bread: "After they pound their wheat [corn] into flour, with hot water they make it into paste, and work it into round balls and Cakes, then they put it into a pot of seething water: when it is sod thoroughly, they lay it on a smooth stone, there they harden it as well as in an Oven."[24] Smith commented on the process of baking bread in an open fire: "Tempering this flower with water, they make it . . . in cakes, covering them with ashes till they be baked, and then washing them in fair water, they dry presently with their own heat."[25] Corn cakes and ash cakes abounded among the Powhatan.

The English, however, did not fare well in Virginia. They failed at raising food, and supplies from England arrived infrequently. New colonizers landed in 1608 and 1609, bringing food but also more mouths to feed. Colonist Richard Potts described the supply in unflattering terms: wheat and barley that "having fried some twenty-six weeks in the ship's hold, contained as many worms as grains."[26]

Soon the English had to beg or steal food from the Powhatan to survive. Percy observed, "It pleased God, after a while, to send those people which were our mortal enemies to relieve us with victuals, as Bread, Corn, Fish, and Flesh in great plenty, which was the setting up of our feeble men, otherwise we had all perished."[27] The English found themselves accepting even roots and acorns.[28] In England, only the poor ate "the scourge" of acorns, and even then they did so only "in times of dearth."[29] The Jamestown gentry were obliged to ingest baked goods they likely had not encountered in their privileged lives back home.

The Powhatan soon tired of their bossy visitors, and their encounters with the English deteriorated into mutual distrust and violence. The English brought the infamous starving time of 1609–10 largely on themselves by storing their corn badly and losing much of it while also experiencing severe drought. John Smith recalled, "In searching our casked corn, we found it half rotten: and the rest so consumed with the many thousand rats, increase first from the ships, that we knew not how to keep that little we had. This did drive us all to our wits end; for there was nothing in the country but what nature afforded."[30] The Europeans pressured the Natives to share their supplies, which the Powhatan, also drought-stricken, could ill afford to do. Relationships soon turned deadly. Percy told of an English delegation who went to the Native Americans in 1609 for grain: "Within [a] few days after Lieutenant Sicklemore and diverse others were found also slain with their mouths stopped full of bread, being done as it seems in contempt and scorn that others might expect the like when they should come to seek for bread and relief among them."[31] The Natives laid siege to the fort, and by the spring of 1610 the English population of Jamestown was reduced by three-quarters, to about sixty people.

Lord De La Warr's ship bringing relief in May 1610 found a colony in chaos. The new deputy governor quickly enacted the "Laws Divine, Moral, and Martial," a lengthy series of rules for the colonists, which included strict regulations on the ingredients for bread. Colonists who traded "Butter, Cheese, Bisket, meal . . . [and] Spice" at "unreasonable rates, and prices unconscionable" might be prosecuted "upon pain of death." Speculating in food became a capital crime.[32]

Bakers, for millennia the objects of suspicion for selling underweight, poor quality, or adulterated products, also came under a severe set of new rules. These men were ordered not to "steal nor embezzle, lose, or defraud any man of his due and proper weight and measure." There would be no "dishonest and deceitful trick to make the bread weight heavier, or make it coarser upon purpose to keep back any part or measure of the flower or meal committed unto him." A first-time offender would lose "his ears," while a second offense brought a year's imprisonment and the third offense a term of three years. Corporal punishment was a harsh penalty for cheating bakers.[33] Extreme times called for extreme measures.

It is unclear exactly who these bakers were. In 1619, however, two bakers, one miller, one brewer, three cooks, and a butcher were included among the eighty-nine men who arrived in Jamestown on the *Bona Nova*.[34] Surely more bakers came with the 3,000 or so English people who arrived before 1622.

After the starving time, the English attempted to stabilize their colony, and their numbers grew. In 1621, fifty-seven English women arrived to become wives for male colonists. The two oldest women in the company were Alice Burges, age twenty-eight, who could "brew, bake, and make malt etc.," and Ann Tanner, who at twenty-six could "brew, and bake, make butter and cheese, and do housewifery." Sara Crosse, the daughter of an English baker, might have learned her father's skills. Burges's and Tanner's ability both to brew and bake indicates competence and comfort with handling grain in a variety of ways.[35] Home baking was starting in earnest.

During the early years of English settlement, the Native Americans adapted English ways as they saw fit. For example, before 1614, Chief Powhatan asked for "a grinding stone, not so big but four or five men may carry it, which would be big enough for his use."[36] The Native Americans would use the stone for their traditional task of grinding corn. It would simply let them do their usual work faster. Despite the Native Americans' concerted efforts, however, their lot declined. As early as 1610, the English routinely destroyed Native American cornfields and burned their houses.[37] By 1615, the Native Americans, not the English, were begging for grain. Governor Thomas Dale loaned 400 or 500 bushels to "some petty Kings," who would "sell the very Skins from their Shoulders for Corn." In return, Dale "took a Mortgage of their whole Countries," which, according to colonist John Rolfe, were nearly the sizes of English shires.[38] Forced by hunger, the Native Americans leveraged their land and lost.

When the English neglected to plant enough corn because they were focusing on tobacco, they relied on murder to get grain from the Native Americans. In 1614, the English coerced the Chickahominy into signing a "treaty" obliging each "fighting man" to bring two bushels of corn in tribute—sort of like protection money—to the English. In 1616, Governor George Yeardley "sent to the Chickahominies for the Tribute Corn." When the Chickahominy gave him "a slight and affrontive answer," Yeardley gathered a force of a hundred men and went to demand the tribute. After an exchange of words, Yeardley ordered his men to fire, and they killed twelve Chickahominy and took "many Prisoners." The Native Americans ransomed their hostages with a hundred bushels of corn, which they then loaded onto the boats of the English. The Chickahominy had reason for vengeful laughter, however, for the English "crowd[ed] onto" the first boat to "bring the first News to James-Town," which "was unhappily overset, all her Corn lost, and eleven Men drowned."[39] Corn mingled with Native American and English blood.

Despite the obvious unwillingness of the Natives to supply the English, in 1620 Jamestown leader Sir Edwin Sandys confidently declared that the colony "began generally to prosper so well as they did not desire any more provision of Meal to be sent unto them" from England but would prefer "a few trifling Commodities As Beads and such like toys" to trade with the Native Americans.[40] The English also continued to steal corn from the Native Americans throughout the 1620s. In one raid in 1622, Yeardley captured from the Pamunkey more than a thousand bushels of corn worth up to a thousand pounds sterling.[41] Such continued tensions over land and food contributed greatly to the attack by the Powhatan in 1622, in which they killed three-quarters of the English population of Virginia. After a truce in 1632, the Native Americans retreated, and the Virginia coast gradually became the dominion of the English and the site of enslavement for Africans.

After the 1622 attacks, the English intensified their colonization efforts, and their hamlets spread up and down the James River. The number of European women also increased. Many came as indentured servants, with more than 500 women landing in 1624 alone. As we have seen, the first Africans arrived in 1619. When Jamestown officials counted their population in 1624,

Captain William Tucker and his wife, Mary Tucker, had seventeen servants in their Jamestown home, including Africans Anthoney and Isabell.[42]

As the numbers of English people grew in Virginia, they began to distinguish among themselves and other people by race and social class, and grains became an important part of that discrimination. In the beginning of the Virginia colony, the diet of indentured servants (who were almost all white and British) and that of enslaved people (all Native American or African) was the same. English indentured servants were poor men and women who contracted to come to Virginia and work for a certain number of years in return for their ship fare. At the conclusion of their contract, they were to receive various supplies that might include land. Enslaved people were considered property and served for life.

Servants and enslaved people, irrespective of their origins, suffered in early Virginia. Indentured servant Richard Frethorne wrote to his parents in 1623 bitterly complaining about, among many things, food supplies: "A penny loaf must serve for 4 men which is most pitiful." One of his fellow servants stole his cloak and likely sold it for "butter and beef." If the supply did not improve, Frethorne predicted, they would have to "eat bark[s] of trees, or mould[s] of the Ground."[43] He was dead by the next year.

Masters of indentured servants and enslaved people were responsible for giving their workers decent provisions.[44] As times got better in England and the flow of servants from Europe to America slowed, the fare of enslaved people became ever more meager. By the end of the century, some enslavers fed their captives not even bread but merely corn mush, made from the dregs left from hand-milling their grain. Bread and meat came as treats only at Christmas.[45]

Some Africans came to Virginia already familiar with corn as a staple food. The Portuguese arrived on the coast of West Africa in the 1480s, and in less than twenty years, the native Africans saw their traditional grains of millet, rice, and sorghum giving way to corn and even some wheat.[46]

By the early sixteenth century, Portuguese traders were stocking slave ships with corn to feed their cargoes on their journeys to America, and the Dutch and English rapidly followed suit.[47] African women learned to bake the imported grains, both under duress and as a source of profit. They prepared ship's biscuits, the dry breads that would sustain their fellow Africans in the voyage across the Atlantic, from maize.[48] On the coast of Guinea, entrepreneurial women were selling the cornbread known as kangues or kenkey to the Portuguese by 1700. The cook dried maize grains and then soaked them in water for a day. After draining and mashing the grains, she allowed them to ferment for several days. She next combined the mash with water and salt and boiled it. After the mash was cooked, she wrapped it in leaves—perhaps from a banana tree—or in a maize husk and baked the bundle under the cinders or on heated rocks, just as Native American women did in America.[49] Some enslaved West Africans might have taken a shred of comfort in their American diet of corn, for it was what they had known at home.

European colonists in Virginia also wanted the grains of home, and they came quite determined to make their new land into a little Britannia. Wheat, an anonymous writer said in 1649, would be a civilizing force in America. He made no effort to conceal his hatred of the "Savages" who had opposed the English. Now that they had been driven far away and "their Towns and houses ruinated," their "clear grounds" had been "possessed by the English to sow Wheat in."[50] The land the Natives had used for corn would now be used for wheat, that most English of grains.

The reality, however, was that growing corn made more sense than grow-ing wheat. Planted in small hills rather than straight rows, it required no plowing and no animal power, a real plus in a land heavily covered first with trees and then with stumps. A person raising corn could plant in the spring, transplant the young plants to hills, weed with a hoe, and expect a good har-vest.[51] In lower Virginia, two crops a year were not unusual.[52] Wheat, on the other hand, demanded clear fields for growing. It was difficult to harvest and process, and it required complicated milling.[53]

Few Virginians ate wheat prior to 1700—sometimes very few. And when they did, people noticed. In 1702, Swiss visitor Francis Louis Michel lodged in Gloucester, Virginia. He found cornbread baked on the fire almost inedible and cornbread baked in the oven "better." He observed bluntly, "Bread is also made of wheat, but not for the slaves or servants."[54] The social distinctions of baked goods stood obvious, probably for those who ate corn as well as for those who imposed the limitations.

Corn dominated for everyone, however. The Jamestown muster (census) of 1624 showed that almost all English households had corn and "meal," measured in hogsheads, barrels, and bushels.[55] When the English arrived in Maryland in 1632, the governors moved quickly to ensure the food supply, requiring that farmers plant two acres of corn for each person employed in raising tobacco.[56] In Carolina, traveler Thomas Ashe observed in 1682, the chief "Provision" was Native American corn, which yielded two harvests a year. Wheat cultivation in the colony remained experimental, though small crops "grew exceedingly well."[57] Corn continued to outstrip wheat in every southern English colony.[58]

Whether the grain was corn, wheat, or even rice (as we will discuss in a later chapter), most English colonists had to pound or grind it just as the Native Americans, French, and Spanish continued to do. Much of that labor was done by housewives, indentured servants, or enslaved people, for hours each day.[59] Like the Spanish soldiers before them and generations of enslaved and poor people after them, the enslaved people and indentured servants of early America had to face grinding after their day's work. Dutch colonist Jasper Danckaerts expressed horror: "The servants and negroes after they have worn themselves down the whole day, and come home to rest, have yet to grind and pound the grain, which is generally maize, for their masters and all their families as well as themselves, and all the negroes, to eat."[60] Grinding was such a despised task that Maryland servants negotiating their contracts for the ends of their indentures sometimes insisted that they be exempted from "beating at the mortar & grinding at the mill."[61]

Former governor George Yeardley built the first wind-powered mill in Virginia in 1621.[62] By 1649, Virginians had four windmills and five watermills to "grind their corn," as well as "many horse-mills of several kinds" and "hand-mills for several uses."[63] Large mills, whether for wheat, corn, or both, required capital investments that far exceeded ordinary people's means, and only the wealthy or hopeful entrepreneurs erected them. When Edward Chisman built a mill in York County, Virginia, in 1675, he itemized his expenses, which included the importation of millstones from England. The total cost amounted to 21,405 pounds of tobacco, the equivalent of £170. Chisman expected the mill to pay for itself in about five years.[64] Such large expenditures put the culinary fate of entire communities in the hands of the few.

The English set up the system of paying tolls for milling that remained in place for more than two centuries. A farmer paid the miller a fraction of the cornmeal or flour in return for his services. Unhappy customers often accused millers of charging rates that were too high or lying about weights. "To rectify the great abuse of [by] millers," the Virginia legislature ordered in 1645 that millers could not take more than one-sixth of the ground grain as their toll, and they set penalties for violating that rule and for using inaccurate scales.[65] As much as colonists benefited from having mills and were willing to travel long distances to use them, they found the powerful millers untrustworthy.

As Virginia colonists prospered, wealthy landowners built mills on their plantations. The mill that Lewis Burwell II erected in Gloucester County before 1680 provides an excellent example of the labor and capital needed for a water-powered mill. First, a builder needed land with a strong supply of running water, in Burwell's case Carter Creek. Second, they needed a good place to build a mill dam to slow the water as well as a millrace, the canal that funneled water to the waterwheel that turned the millstones. Skilled enslaved people and white craftsmen excavated the millrace and built the dam and the mill building. These millstones came by ship into Carter Creek. With a well-trained miller at work, Burwell sold flour in the county seat and also exported it to England.[66]

ONCE MILLED, of course, cornmeal and flour had to be cooked to be edible. We don't have a lot of details about the cornbread that European colonists ate in seventeenth-century America. Most cornbread was probably baked on the hearths of the fireplaces in simple homes. In the early years of the British colonies, a lot of indoor cooking, including baking, was done in large open fireplaces vented with chimneys. The earliest chimneys in Virginia and Maryland were built of wood daubed with clay, just as they had been in various parts of Britain. Most of the houses had dirt floors, and the hearths were made of clay that hardened through repeated heating, just as they did in Native American homes.[67]

We know far more about what the most elite Virginians may have eaten because of the records of Frances Culpeper Berkeley Ludwell. Born in Kent, England, in 1634, Frances Culpeper arrived in Virginia with her parents around 1650 and married three times to wealthy, prominent men.[68] For seventeen years she was the wife of Virginia governor Sir William Berkeley and presided over his mansion, Green Spring. Her "household book" of handwritten recipes, bound in brown leather, made its way through the generations and is now at the Historical Society of Pennsylvania. Household books like these were common in rich European families during the medieval period, and women carried them to the colonies and passed them down to their American daughters. Lady Berkeley died around 1695, so her recipes likely reflect cookery only in the wealthiest houses of Virginia in the mid-seventeenth century.[69] Almost everyone else would have lacked access to the wheat flour, sugar, spices, and dairy products that Lady Berkeley recorded, as well as the expert cooks required to pull off the baking.

It is highly doubtful that Lady Berkeley ever did any actual cooking. Indentured British servants formed the core of workers at Green Spring, and some of them were women and probably worked in the house. Sir William also enslaved people, but that is basically all that we know. We can only speculate that Lady Berkeley may have supervised enslaved people in her kitchen.[70] Some enslaved cooks may have come to Virginia already versed in European cookery. In Ghana, enslaved cooks first learned to cook European-style from Portuguese women known as *degradadas* who had been banished from their homeland to Africa for various crimes.[71] Enslaved women probably then taught each other as well as learning from their enslavers and figuring things out for themselves.

The recipes in the Berkeley manuscript cover all aspects of cooking, from capon roasted with oysters to raspberry marmalade. Not surprisingly, of course, numerous recipes are for baked goods, less forgiving of carelessness than a roast beef and thus more needful of a precise formula. While many of the recipes for baking are for bread, the majority are for sweets—forerunners of the pies, cookies, and pound cakes of today. These were the foods of the wealthy, who had access to the best ingredients. There is no corn in the cookbook. The recipes are thoroughly English, with no nods to their transport to America.

The easiest recipes were for griddle cakes, which we would call pancakes, baked on the hearth. They were "fried" in butter, perhaps crisper and closer to crêpes than their modern-day counterparts. Lady Berkeley's pancake recipes included flour, eggs, and cream; ale for leavening; and nutmeg, rose water, "sack," salt, and cinnamon for flavor.[72] Wafers were thin cakes baked over the fire in specially made irons, often with a honeycomb pattern. "Excellent Wafers the French Way" contained cream, flour, egg yolks, yeast, melted butter, salt, nutmeg, cinnamon, mace, grated "naple bisket" (a cookie we'll discuss later), and ambergris dissolved in rose water.[73]

Despite the simplicity of preparation, the ingredients indicate that these quick breads were only for the affluent. The English who colonized Virginia expected milk, cream, butter, and cheese to be regular parts of their diet, as they had been in England,[74] but dairy products were precious in the colonies. Though by 1622 colonists were boasting of their fat cattle, most of the larger cow herds were intended for meat, not milk, and they belonged to individual families, not to large dairies.[75] Butter was valuable enough in early Virginia that when Jamestown merchant Thomas Warnet died in 1629, he left to a friend a firkin (about eleven gallons) of butter.[76] By the 1660s, Rebecca Cole of Maryland had access to the production of twelve cows, and she, like other colonial women, owned a churn—almost surely made of wood or pottery with a wooden dasher—and two "great butter pots." The women in her household, with the help of indentured servants, made enough butter to sell the surplus.[77] Butter production was seasonal, tied to the calving of the cows, and it entailed a great deal of work.

One of the biggest factors in baked goods is leavening: introducing air, and thus tenderness and loft, into the product. Other than ash from their fires, Native American baked goods had little leavening and so were apt to be tough and chewy. Europeans, on the other hand, treasured light, soft baked goods made with yeast and starters. Yeast is a tiny fungus that, when activated, emits carbon dioxide into dough. Egyptians discovered the use of yeast more than 4,000 years ago. As strange as it sounds, this little fungus remains the heart of bread baking today.

All of Lady Berkeley's bread recipes call for ale yeast or barm, the froth that forms on top of fermenting ale and has been used as leavening "through the ages."[78] A product of the household brewing that was common in early America, barm compelled a baker's highest skill. It might be strong or weak, by chance, and it could be bitter or strongly tasting of hops.[79] Surely every cook making yeast bread held her breath until the first cut of the loaf proclaimed success.

The flavorings in Lady Berkeley's pancake recipes had medieval origins. Sack was a sweet white wine, similar to sherry, imported from Spain. Rose water, popular until the late nineteenth century, was simply rose petals steeped in water, and it could be manufactured at home or bought commercially. Two prized and expensive spices came from animals: musk (secreted from the glands of the male musk deer) and ambergris (secreted from the digestive system of sperm whales).[80] Cinnamon, imported from Asia, was the inner bark of trees in the genus *Cynnamomum*, dried and probably powdered.[81] Nutmeg and mace, which both derive from the *Myristica fragrans* tree, and cloves, flower buds of *Syzygium aromaticum*, originated in the Dutch colonies in the South Pacific.[82] All these spices were imported into Virginia as early as the 1620s, although only those with money or goods to barter could get them.[83] Spices remained precious enough in colonial Virginia that they were enumerated in estate inventories.[84]

With baking on their minds, the English built ovens from the time of their arrival. Sometime between 1608 and 1610, Jamestown settlers fashioned large ovens into the clay walls of the cellars of two structures. They built a second set, side by side, after 1610. The facades of the ovens were brick, and they probably had thick wooden doors. The brick fronts helped prolong the lives of the ovens, for hearths endured a lot: loading wood, moving fire, unloading ashes, sweeping, and the heat from the oven. The clay that formed the oven floors and walls fired over time, showing "extensive use."[85] Curved clay roofs gave the ovens an "igloo-shaped interior."[86]

The most affluent private homes had durable cooking surfaces. In Maryland, John Lewger built his house in 1638 with a huge center fireplace, fashioned from "brick and yellow loam mortar," where most cooking took place for at least two decades.[87] Robert Burle constructed his house in the 1650s in Maryland with a hearth laid with alternating green and yellow pavers.[88] English colonists also built ovens, both interior and exterior. Builders often installed small brick ovens to the side of interior fireplaces. When Marylander Charles Calvert leased his house to Henry Exson in 1678, he stipulated that Exson "Build a good new Oven and Build a Shade over it," indicating that the oven was outside.[89] According to seventeenth-century bread-baking instructions, an oven took an hour and a half to heat. The bread then baked for another hour and a half.[90] Careful cooks staged their baking to best use the heat in the oven, which cooled gradually after the initial fire was removed: in

Early ovens at Jamestown. Photo by Michael Lavin. Courtesy of Jamestown Rediscovery (Preservation Virginia).

one example, the "household bread" went first, when the oven was hottest, then gingerbread. Third would be "manchet," a fine white bread "baked with a gentle heat," and finally the cookies known as jumbals.[91] Everything would be cooked correctly, and no precious oven heat would be wasted.

By the middle of the seventeenth century, affluent colonists began to separate kitchens, along with servants' and enslaved peoples' living quarters, from the main house to avoid contact with the workers as well as odors, noise, and fire danger.[92] When cooking left the central house, it traveled in one of two directions: down into the basement or out into a separate building.

Lady Berkeley's house, Green Spring, was the finest European house in early Virginia: a fifteen-room brick structure built by her second husband in 1645, before their marriage. In the early days, the kitchen and pantries, with brick and tile paving, were at one end of the structure, separated from the family living quarters by a reception hall. Eventually Lord Berkeley moved the kitchen to the basement.[93] Cellar kitchens developed across the Chesapeake throughout the second half of the seventeenth century.[94]

Kitchens also began to move into separate outbuildings by 1650.[95] The distances from the kitchens to the houses in Isle of Wight County, Virginia, varied from 15 to 130 feet, with an average of 65 feet—many steps for the people who had to hustle the food onto the dining table before it got cold, through the rain, snow, or heat.[96] If the goal was to push servants' work to the periphery of the main house, a well-worn path surely helped.

As kitchens became more sophisticated, so did the gear for cooking in them. Most colonial families in the seventeenth century had only a few pieces of cookware, perhaps an iron pot or a small kettle.[97] Larger estates, however, had numerous utensils, some specifically geared for baking. Pie pans, biscuit pans, and "patty pans," designed for small cakes, all had precise purposes.[98] These pans would have been used for both leavened and "quick breads"— breads that didn't use yeast to rise. Two of the most basic ways of introducing air into quick baked goods are adding eggs—whose proteins bond as they bake and add structure to the product they are a part of—and repeatedly striking a dough. The recipes in Lady Berkeley's cookery manual use both methods.

Breads called "biskets" more resembled crackers or the tough products used on ships than the flaky creations of later periods. Lady Berkeley's recipes required "flowre," almost surely wheat. Her recipes for "bisket bread" had no leavening other than eggs and instead directed beating the dough at length, in one case for two hours and in another "till it will bubble," noting, "Ye longer you beat it ye better it will be." These particular biscuits were sweetened with sugar and seasoned with anise seeds, coriander, musk, and rose water.[99] Coriander, native to southern Europe, is a tiny seed whose flavor is "startlingly floral and lemony." From the eastern Mediterranean, anise seed, known to us as aniseed or simply anise, is the "aromatic and sweet-tasting" spice that we most commonly associate with licorice.[100] "Prince biscuits" were beaten for an hour and then baked in "frames," which were like wooden springform pans. They might be garnished with "caraway comfits," caraway seeds coated with sugar.[101] Caraway, with its pungent, distinctively flavored seeds, grew throughout Europe. We mostly know it from rye bread.

Lady Berkeley's recipes for "biskets" and "biskitello" resembled ship's biscuits in their keeping power. French biskets were made in long rolls, baked, sliced, and baked again, with the promise of staying edible two or three years.[102] "Biskitello" employed gum tragacanth, a dried sap, to stabilize its dough of sugar and spices—aniseed, musk, ambergris, and rose water. Made into loaves and then dried, it would keep good "all ye year."[103]

The recipes in Lady Berkeley's book contained sugar, reflecting changing English custom. Until the British colonized Barbados in 1627, sugar was rare even for the wealthy.[104] When Caribbean sugar became available, well-heeled English people imported ever-increasing amounts.[105] Sugar came in various stages of refinement, cooked and strained repeatedly to remove bitterness from the syrup. Muscovado was the darkest, with the highest molasses content. It had a warm, robust, slightly smoky taste and a high moisture content. Panela was brown sugar, slightly more refined than muscovado. White sugar was the most highly refined and sometimes powdered. It was dry, light, very sweet, and greatly prized.

English colonists in America knew and appreciated good loaf bread. Bread, graded accorded to its coarseness, formed an important part of the English diet as early as the thirteenth century. Wheat flourished in southern England, and expert milling made possible a fine white loaf.[106] The English would try their best to bring their style of baked goods to America.

Lady Berkeley's most basic yeast bread recipe, "To Make White Bread," consisted only of "fine flower," salt, lukewarm milk, and "good yeast," mixed well, left to rise by the fire, and baked for an hour and a half.[107] A second yeast bread, the "buttered loaf," called for more numerous ingredients: milk and rennet (an enzyme from the lining of a calf's stomach, which makes milk coagulate), eggs, ginger, and flour, leavened with ale yeast. The name came from the recommendation of serving the bread with butter and sugar.[108] Ginger was the cheapest and most common spice in England and in the colonies. It came from the root of the tropical plant *Zingiher officinale*, scraped and dried. Colonists used ginger often, probably because of its relative affordability.[109]

Bread can be formed in two basic ways: cast, or formed by hand, and baked on a flat surface; or baked in a pan with high sides that support the loaf as it rises. Cast bread has a tougher crust. Virginia colonists, like their cousins in England, preferred soft-crusted, pan-baked bread. Lady Berkeley did, however, also include a recipe for crisp-crusted French bread. The cook placed the dough, made from flour, salt, ale yeast, and warm milk, on a "peele" for baking in an "oven pretty hot."[110] Peels were flattened, shovel-like surfaces with handles for inserting and removing baked goods from an oven.[111] Berkeley's recipes also included a twice-baked, heavily spiced yeasted bread called "cinamon bisket": fine flour, cinnamon, coriander, aniseeds, eggs, ale yeast, and warm water baked in long rolls. The next day, the baker sliced the rolls and spread "searced" (sieved) sugar over the pieces, then baked the rolls again until dry.[112]

"Cakes," small and large, were plentiful in Lady Berkeley's recipes. These cakes, made with yeast, were more like bread than the fluffy creations we now apply the word to. "Carraway" cakes strongly resembled traditional English seed cakes, cherished throughout the empire. Lady Berkeley's version was kneaded with an entire pound of caraway comfits. The little cakes rose "before ye fire" for half an hour before baking. "Annyseed Cake" was composed simply of flour, butter, and aniseed comfits.[113] Lady Berkeley had four recipes for yeasted "Great Cake" leavened with ale barm. The seasonings varied—some combination of nutmeg, cinnamon, cloves, mace, rose water—and the recipes also sometimes called for currants and caraway seeds. Food historian

Karen Hess speculates that these cakes were cast rather than baked in pans and so would have come out as big rounds of crusty goodness.[114]

The most enduring cake in the South is the fruitcake. Centuries before it became the punch line of jokes, fruitcake graced English and then American tables. Fruitcakes are labor-intensive creations of dried fruits and nuts, chopped and then bound with a flour-based batter. They are often soaked with liquor and actually will remain edible for years if stored properly. Lady Berkeley's "Excellent Cake" had a batter of flour, sugar, eggs, cream, and butter, seasoned with nutmeg, cloves, mace, rose water, and lemon juice. The fruits included currants and candied orange, lemon, and citron peel, and the alcohols were ale and sack, with ambergris "if you please." The whole, "mingle[d] and knead[ed] up," was leavened with ale barm.[115] Currants, the berry of the genus *Ribes*, were used frequently in English cookery and remained in southern kitchens for centuries, usually in dried form.[116] While early colonists tried growing tropical fruits, most were probably imported from warmer locations.[117] Citron, *Citrus medica*, is a fruit with thick skin and only a little juice and pulp, strong in smell and taste. Today it has very little use in American cooking—except in fruitcakes! Candied fruit peel, still a fruitcake staple today, has been around since the medieval period, with sugar keeping the peel from rotting.

Another amazingly persistent sweet in English and southern kitchens is gingerbread, baked as cake and as cookies. Lady Berkeley's six recipes attest to the ongoing popularity of the spicy yet sweet treat first documented in England about 1430. Four of them, more like cookies than cakes, were "baked in molds" or "printed"—what we would call rolled and cut. They started with a base of grated bread crumbs and sugar or honey and then were flavored with ginger (of course) and some combination of licorice, anise, sandalwood, cloves, nutmeg, mace, and cinnamon. Sandalwood, used more today in perfume than in cookery, is made from the bark of the *Santalum* tree, which in powdered form gives a warm taste and red color to foods. Licorice (*Glycyrrhiza glabra*), native to southern Europe, is distinct from anise, although the tastes are similar.[118] Unlike the Spanish, the English colonists speedily brought bees from England for both wax and honey.[119] By midcentury, an anonymous promoter noted stores of bees in the woods and also "tame bees in hives about their houses," providing "plenty of honey and wax."[120] "Pepper Cakes That Will Keep good in Ye House for a Quarter or Halfe a Year" were made of treacle (a sweet sugar syrup similar to a light molasses), fine wheat flour, ginger, coriander seeds, caraway, aniseed, "suckets" (candied fruit peel), and orange peel, all worked into a paste and made into "pritty large cakes."[121] Fruitcake and gingerbread have remained with southerners throughout the centuries.

Pies and pastries formed an important part of elite English diets. Some foods were put into a "coffin," a closed, freestanding crust, thick and sturdy enough to hold its own weight and its contents—"stiffe and tough," according to English cookbook writer Gervase Markham in 1615. Others were baked on "plates," which we would likely call a pie pan. A tart had a thinner bottom crust and was baked open, or without a top crust. Markham advised that "fine wheat flower" made an excellent crust kneaded with "a good store of butter" and hot water.[122]

Fruit pies were popular in the colonies. When French immigrant Durand de Dauphiné visited Virginia in 1686, he noted that each farmer grew only a bushel of wheat, exclusively for making pies from the local apples.[123] Lady Berkeley's recipes for fruit pies or tarts used quinces (Cydonia oblonga, a relative of apples and pears), stewed with sugar, and apples coddled in "faire water" and garnished with sugar and cinnamon.[124] Apples seasoned "for puffs" were quartered and boiled with nutmeg, ginger, cloves, candied orange and lemon peel, citron peel, "a little red wine," and sugar.[125] Eighteenth-century American cooks could also easily have made pies from other fruits. English gentry in Virginia, Maryland, and Carolina swiftly planted apple, pear, fig, cherry, apricot, and peach trees. All those fruits thrived, and by midcentury "great orchards" provided their bounty for their wealthy owners.[126]

The other fruit-based sweet in Lady Berkeley's book was apple fritters, with sliced or chopped apples, dipped into a batter of eggs, flour, nutmeg, mace, and cloves. The more elaborate of the two recipes added ginger, cinnamon, saffron, eggs, rose water, and "new milk." Saffron, even more precious then than now, came from Middle Eastern crocus flowers. Both versions were dropped quickly into boiling fat—suet (rendered fat from around a cow's kidneys) or lard (rendered from the fat around a hog's kidneys, back, or belly)—and strewn with sugar and cinnamon after they were cooked.[127]

Custards formed the basis of two pies in Lady Berkeley's book. One was made of eggs "rosted" in the ashes of the fireplace and then minced, beef suet, nutmeg, currants, rose water, sack, salt, sugar, egg yolks, sugar, and orange or lemon peel, with no instructions for a crust. The second was baked in a "coffin," thick enough to stand on its own. The custard consisted of cream, mace, nutmeg, cinnamon, bay leaf (Laurus nobilis, native to the Mediterranean), eggs, sack, and blanched almonds. Almonds, one of the most popular tree nuts in the world, were widely used in colonial cooking. The cultivated almond, Prunus amygdalus, originally came from Asia and was imported into the colonies as early as 1620.[128] Yet another sweet pie was made of rose hips, the seed pods of roses left after the blooms have faded, stewed in white wine and flavored with sugar, cinnamon, ginger, and rose water.[129]

Much like fruitcake, mince pie, a medieval dish, has persisted into the present day. In the seventeenth century, it occupied a middle spot between sweet and savory pies. The meat part of the mincemeat was much more prominent than it is now. It contained many ingredients, all of which had to be prepared and chopped before baking: leg of veal (young cattle) or tongues from neats (older cattle), beef suet, raisins, currants, apples, and candied orange, lemon, and citron peel, flavored with sugar, cloves, mace, nutmeg, cinnamon, and rose water and doused with "muskadine" or sack.[130]

In the medieval fashion, meat and vegetable pies combined sweet and savory flavors. The meats that the Berkeley household consumed in pie included parts of beef, sheep, venison, chicken, pigeon, and pork, from the tongues to the hooves. "Humble pie" included the "humbles," or heart, kidneys, liver, and other organs of a deer, along with beef suet, cloves, mace, nutmeg, ginger, verjuice (sour fruit juice, often made from unripe grapes), and salt, baked in a crust and served with a sauce made of claret (red wine from Bordeaux), melted butter, and sugar.[131] Vegetables also filled pies: "hartichoaks," the root vegetables parsnips and skirrets (Sium sisarum), and "lettis cabbage." The veggies were cooked with butter and seasoned with sugar, cinnamon, and ginger, as well as rose water, "wine," and lemon juice. The artichoke and cabbage pies also contained bone marrow, which added savor and heartiness.[132]

Today we would call some of Lady Berkeley's recipes cookies, although she called them cakes. Sugar cakes started with flour, sugar, eggs, and butter, flavored with a combination of rose water, sack, or cinnamon. They might be rolled and cut with a glass—one recipe stipulates a beer glass—or shaped into "round cakes."[133] Jumbals, later known as jumbles, had a run of several hundred years, into the twentieth century. The seventeenth-century version consisted of flour, sugar, eggs, sweet cream, rose water, and butter, seasoned with aniseed or caraway, ambergris, and musk. They were rolled, made into "what forms you please"—usually a fancy pattern—and baked on pie plates.[134] Shrewsbury cakes, which persisted into the late nineteenth century, began with flour, butter, and sugar, seasoned with varying combinations of cinnamon, cloves, mace, rose water, nutmeg, or ginger. The cook rolled and cut the dough and then baked it on floured paper.[135] Finally, Lady Berkeley's "little cake" is a cookie similar to today's Fig Newton. The cook made a dough of wheat flour, sugar, eggs, butter, nutmeg, and saffron, then rolled it out and beat it "well with a rouling pin." The cook next topped half of the tenderized dough with a filling of currants, nutmeg, and rose water, then covered that filling with the other half of the dough.[136] And of course there was gingerbread in the form of cookies.

Through Lady Berkeley's book, we know a lot about the super-rich. We know much less about middling people, the poor, the enslaved. We know almost nothing about the people who couldn't bake at home. Presumably there were commercial bakers in Jamestown, but records speak little. Not until the British capital moved to Williamsburg in 1699 do the sources become clearer.

THE YEARS BETWEEN 1600 and 1700 saw unprecedented change in the southeastern part of North America. The Native residents tried to hold onto their lives and traditions amid disease and warfare while adapting to the new technologies and foods brought by strangers. Arrivals from Africa and Europe brought foods from home and learned to tolerate eating corn. The next eighty years would bring even more outsiders, speaking yet more languages, and eventually the creation of a new nation. Through it all, Native people, African people, and European people continued to bake, bringing together ingredients and technologies, both old and new, in ways that made sense to them and sometimes to each other.

Chapter 3

PLUMB CAKES

....

Wheat and Corn, Like It or Not

"*T*he men who are in Louisiana are accustoming themselves to eat [corn], but the women who are for the most part from Paris eat it reluctantly. This makes them grumble a great deal against the Bishop of Quebec who had made them understand that they would be in the Promised Land."[1] So began an enduring fable in southern culinary history, the so-called Petticoat Rebellion in early Louisiana.

The story starts truthfully enough. The first French women arrived in the colony in 1704: twenty-three young women, poor but respectable. All but one quickly married French men already there. Unhappy with their food, the women took to the streets of Mobile in April 1706 to protest. But then the tale gets murky. According to lore, the governor, Sieur Bienville, instructed his cook and relative, Madame Langlois, to share with the young women the cooking skills she had mastered from local Native Americans. The young women learned to cook corn for their husbands and to like it themselves. Bienville and Langlois, so the story goes, saved the colony and created Creole cuisine.

The Louisiana colony did survive, and Creole cuisine did develop. But Madame Langlois likely never existed.[2] The made-up story does, however, demonstrate the cultural adjustments necessary for Europeans and Africans coming to America. French women adapted to corn, and so did everyone else, over the course of the eighteenth century, like it or not.

THE FRENCH reached the Gulf Coast in 1699, establishing forts near present-day Biloxi, Mobile, and Natchez, with New Orleans developing in 1718. Several hundred miles to the northwest, French colonists also created the town of Natchitoches. Early French invaders enslaved Native Americans and began importing African enslaved people as early as 1710. Spanish Florida stretched as far west as Pensacola by 1698. The Spanish also moved north of the Rio Grande, establishing the hamlets of Nacogdoches, San Antonio, and Los Adaes. The English continued to spread down the Atlantic Seaboard, founding the colony of Georgia in 1732. Itchy English colonists moved west, too, pushing the line of settlement toward the Appalachians and pressing the Native Americans. Everywhere they went, the English took enslaved Africans. Almost 300,000 Africans arrived in the South between 1700 and 1800.[3] They learned to cook a hybrid cuisine with alien ingredients and new methods of preparation.

Whatever the culture, grain—particularly bread—served as the staple, more than meat, fish, or vegetables. Only the wealthy had sweets often, though poorer people savored them as occasional treats. Baked goods played a central role in the lives of southern people, demonstrating power and social status in new ways.

FORAGED FOODS—acorns, nuts, seeds, and roots—continued to nourish many people.[4] Enslaved Africans learned about the nuts in their new environment. In Virginia, for example, they came to rely on black walnuts and hickory nuts to augment their limited diets.[5] As in Virginia, the Natives in Texas and Louisiana cultivated sunflowers (*bah-hum* in Caddo), sumpweed (*Iva annua*), chenopod (*bah-ha-tse* in Caddo), amaranth, knotweed, maygrass (*Phalaris caroliniana*), little barley, and panic grass, all of which yielded seeds suitable for grinding into meal.[6] Mississippi Native Americans gathered from the riverbanks small grains that they called *ollogolle* and *chipicholle*, which French soldier Dumont de Montigny thought resembled millet.[7] Some Native Americans still ate roots as a matter of course. In North Carolina the Natives boiled and then baked the root of the "Tisinaw, or Bastard China Root" (*Smilax pseudochina*).[8] A similar root provided bread for runaway African enslaved people in the Louisiana maroon settlement of Ville Gaillarde.[9] And Florida officials were still requisitioning cassava from Mexico.[10] French soldiers were horrified by it, reporting that prisoners near Pensacola in 1719 received "nothing to eat other than rancid cassava bread."[11]

For all southerners of all backgrounds, however, corn remained the staple.[12] European observers noted the ways of Native Americans with grain. The

Cherokee so valued corn that it was part of their marriage rite: "[The groom] presented [the bride] with a leg of venison, and she gave him an ear of corn, denoting that he would keep her in meat, and she would keep him in bread."[13] Natives in North Carolina mixed their corn with beans and sometimes pumpkins, "pleasant to the taste," according to Moravian travelers.[14] Louisiana Native Americans called their corn-and-bean bread *cooedlou*.[15] Swedish scientist Peter Kalm described Native Americans making cornbread for special occasions, enhanced with dried blueberries, blackberries, or wild grapes or with wild strawberries in season. He observed that the fruit-studded corn dough could be boiled, fried, or baked, or it might be wrapped in "herbs" and cooked like ash cake. The result was delectable: "This kind of bread tastes good and is generally eaten warm."[16]

Most English colonists raised their own corn, sometimes swapping their surplus for goods such as cheese or butter. A growing group of merchants sold surplus corn to those unfortunate enough not to have their own source.[17] As Anglo-American families prepared to move west from the Atlantic colonies, they sent men ahead in the spring to plant corn. Some of the men stayed in the new location while others returned east to fetch the women and children, timing their arrival with the corn harvest. Even with careful planning, Europeans heading into new territories almost always ended up needing to acquire food from the Native Americans. When Swiss colonists arrived in New Bern, North Carolina, around 1711, they sold their clothes to the Tuscarora for corn, almost surely grown by women.[18] Groups including the Houma and Pascagoula proffered corn and bread to the new French arrivals on the Gulf Coast.[19] In fact, French colonists found trading with the Native Americans so convenient that officials complained that it led the French to disdain farming.[20] At Natchitoches (Louisiana) and neighboring Los Adaes, the Caddo supplied corn and bear grease to the French and Spanish.[21] If the Natives had to tolerate the new arrivals, at least they could make some profit off them. Unfortunately, their products did little to satiate the newcomers' greed for their land.

In St. Augustine, *situado* goods, including corn, continued to come irregularly from the Spanish government even as officials hoped in vain that the colony would become self-sufficient. In 1738, the government established Fort Mose for African Americans who had escaped slavery in the English colonies. The Spaniards expected Fort Mose residents to produce enough food to feed themselves, but they also occasionally provided supplies, including corn.[22]

Corn milling occupied many southerners' time and attention. For green corn, Anglos adapted the grater from the Native Americans, fashioned from "a half circular piece of tin, perforated with a punch from the concave side, and nailed by its edges to a block of wood." The method was slow, recalled Shenandoah Valley colonist Samuel Kercheval, but "necessity has no law."[23]

Southeastern Native Americans continued their long-standing practice of pounding grain with wooden mortars and pestles. A Moravian missionary attested to the labor involved: "They can scarce prepare as much in a forenoon as they consume the rest of the Day."[24] Europeans modified the Native American method of pounding corn in a hollowed-out tree trunk with a device called a sweep mill or hominy block. A sweep, or pole of "springy elastic wood," maybe thirty feet long, eased the work. One end of the sweep was anchored securely on the ground, and forked supports elevated the center about fifteen feet in the air. Then a piece of sapling, with the end carved into a pestle, was attached to the suspended end of the sweep. A handle on the pestle allowed two people to raise and lower it, exerting double effort. Samuel Kercheval recalled making an "excellent sweep" from a "sugar tree sapling" and said that it was "kept going almost constantly from morning till night by our neighbors for several weeks."[25]

Hand mills supplied small quantities of cornmeal. According to traveler Johann Schoepf, "a negro briskly turn[ing] it about could grind several bushels of corn in a day"—a testament to the labor of Black people in providing foodstuffs, likely for others as well as for themselves.[26] Slave quarters often had hand mills, with which weary laborers ground their evening supply of meal after long days in the fields.[27] (Remember, cornmeal spoiled easily and had to be prepared often.)

Baked, ground corn sustained American colonists. For years, Samuel Kercheval said, "johnnycake and pone" were the only breads in his backcountry home.[28] The simplest cornbread consisted of cornmeal and water kneaded together to form a small cake that was generally baked as a "cast" bread, on a flat surface, and variously called pone, hoecake, or johnnycake. The only difference among them was the cooking surface. Pones were baked directly on the hearth.[29] Hoecakes cooked on a flat piece of metal—usually a plate, not the garden implement, despite the name. In 1739, even in sophisticated Charleston, Justinius Stoll sold "new Iron Plates to bake Johnny Cakes or gridel bread on."[30] By the 1770s, Native Americans in Louisiana were acquiring iron plates from the French for baking their corn cakes, perhaps liking the portability and relatively easy cleaning of a plate rather than a hearth.[31] A johnnycake was made of thick dough set on a flat piece of wood, which could lend a distinctive taste to the bread, then propped in front of the fire rather than in or over the ashes.[32] To Los Adaes, the Spanish brought the ways of

Mexican Native Americans. They baked corn into the unleavened round bread known as a tortilla (Spanish for "little cake"), probably on a flat metal or pottery disc known as a comal.[33]

Before the importation of domesticated animals, both Native Americans and European colonists used the fat of wild animals in their baking.[34] The most abundant sources were black bears, which developed layers of highly nutritious fat to prepare for hibernation. In Louisiana, the Caddo had a lively trade in bear oil with the French and Spanish, and bear oil also came downriver from Arkansas and Illinois.[35] The French accommodated their palates to it readily enough: Dumont de Montigny, who had not known about bears before coming to America, commented, "This oil is nearly as white as lard, never congeals, and is just as good as olive oil or even better. . . . It can be eaten spread on bread, like butter."[36] The English in the backcountry likely also availed themselves of this handy source of tenderness in their cornbread.

People on the move also adapted to new sweeteners. As they went west, Europeans learned to make maple sugar, while enslaved people in Virginia adopted the Native American practice of sweetening food with pulp from the honey locust tree.[37] Everyone—Spanish, English, Native Americans, and Africans—liked honey from the bees that the Europeans brought with them. Colonists kept domesticated bees, and adventurers could find honey from bees gone feral.[38]

Wealthy white southerners, obligated with provisioning their indentured servants and enslaved people, considered corn to be the most appropriate, and often only, source of food for their charges. Enslaved people often had cornbread three times a day, sometimes with fat pork or salt herring on the side.[39] Not only was corn cheaper and easier to grow than wheat, but Europeans thought that it provided more energy for working people.[40]

How well did Europeans adapt to cornbread? Snobby travelers despised it, describing it as "harsh," "coarse," and "unpleasant," an acquired taste at best.[41] But poor people ate it readily, even on special occasions. Traveler Janet Schaw observed a humble funeral feast near Wilmington, North Carolina, with lots of rum and "vast quantities of pork, beef, and corn-bread."[42] People's tastes evolve, of course, and to the dismay of some English colonists, their countrymen began to develop a liking for corn. Robert Beverley reported in the 1720s that some "gentlemen" in Virginia preferred "pone" made of "Indian meal" over wheat bread.[43]

Yet class distinctions remained. It was most proper for upper-class Europeans to eat wheat bread.[44] And so Europeans worked mightily to grow wheat. Though their villages were at sea level, with a constant flow of warm, moist air, the French tried diligently and persistently to grow wheat. Governor Bienville ordered wheat planted every year between 1704 and 1710.[45] Near Natchez, the

Triticum aestivum
(common wheat)

Wheat botanical illustration, showing heads and kernels. iStock.

colonists sowed the grain every month for a year, trying to discover through trial and error when it would thrive and learning that the answer was never.[46]

Climate made all the difference. German-speaking Moravians on the edge of the Appalachian Mountains in North Carolina harvested their first wheat in the fall of 1754. By 1759, they were growing enough to relieve the hunger of their non-German neighbors: "Counting all the kinds of grain we have had something over 1400 bushels, so that we have been able to help many poor people in their great need, for the only grain crop of most of the settlers here,—corn,—was a failure last year, and there has been a wide-spread lack of bread."[47]

Virginia and Maryland, particularly the Shenandoah Valley, provided the greatest amount of wheat for the English colonies. By the 1720s, Virginians grew sufficient wheat to export the surplus to New England and the West Indies, and by midcentury, planters across Virginia and Maryland had begun to shift their tobacco crops into wheat.[48]

Even in the eighteenth century, wheat farming was capital-intensive.[49] Harvest, usually in early summer, presented particular challenges. Workers, almost all male and sometimes enslaved, cut, or reaped, the grain with sickles, scythes, or cradles. Ancient tools (more than 12,000 years old), sickles and scythes had curved blades attached to handles of varying length. The harvester grabbed a handful of grain stalks, swung the blade by the handle, and cut the stalks, which then fell every which way. The grain cradle, which was invented in the 1760s, was a substantial improvement. A cradle was a straight scythe with long perpendicular arms to catch the grain as it was cut, laying it in neat rows and making it easier to pick up. A deft worker using a cradle could harvest up to two acres a day by himself, more than twice the quantity possible with a scythe.[50] Skilled enslaved people hired themselves out—that is, worked for people other than their enslavers for cash wages—and sometimes exploited the frenzy around harvest to run away. When Peter Deadfoot took off from Loudoun County, Virginia, in 1768, his enslaver described him as ingenious, able to turn his hand to anything, and "one of the best scythemen, either with or without a cradle, in America."[51] Whether Deadfoot's skill brought him freedom, we are left to guess, but clearly, enslaved people formed important parts of harvesting crews.

The final step before milling was threshing, or separating the grain from the stem and husks. Most wheat farmers used a flail (two sticks joined by a short chain) to beat the grain by hand.[52] Less advanced farmers employed simple poles, and more technologically savvy growers deployed horses and oxen to trample on the stalks and release the grain. Because reaping and threshing were so labor-intensive, southern farmers hired or shared workers, and crews roamed the countryside, going from farm to farm.[53]

Southerners celebrated successful harvests, continuing a tradition of thousands of years, and they feted the wheat harvest as no other. John Brickell noted in 1737 that the only harvest festivals in North Carolina were upon the reaping of "the European Wheat." Revelers—presumably all white—traveled as far as thirty miles to join the parties, which included feasts and music.[54] In Maryland in 1774, Nicholas Cresswell described a "reaping frolic": "The people very merry, Dancing without either Shoes or Stockings and the Girls without stays."[55] The Moravians marked the end of threshing with their cherished "Liebesmahl," or Lovefeast, a shared meal of yeasted buns and coffee.[56]

As the European American population spread across the South, mills popped up at any handy location, usually near flowing water. Sometimes they ground corn, sometimes wheat, and occasionally both, requiring different types of stones for the two grains.[57] Most mills had only a single set of grinding stones, but larger ones had multiple "runs," or pairs, of stones. Americans so valued fine stones that they imported them from Germany and France.[58] These stones were remarkable works of both utility and beauty. After quarrying, they were hammered into blanks. Highly skilled millwrights used chisels to cut grooves into the grinding surface.[59]

Local milling grew rapidly in wheat-growing areas. Frederick County, Virginia, had 17 mills in 1748, and by 1800 the number had grown to more than 400.[60] Wealthy southerners like Augustine Washington and his son George Washington erected mills on their properties.[61] Conversely, the utopian founders of Savannah erected a public corn mill in 1733, though it saw little use before falling down. This mill, right in the middle of town, was probably powered by an animal treadmill. Although animal-powered mills could be sited anywhere, colonists preferred water power, which did not need to be fed or rested.[62] Water-powered mills had to be sited carefully, with enough water to dam into a pond and a suitable place for the millrace, a sluice that carried water from the stream to the waterwheel that powered the stones.

Mills played numerous roles in community building across the South. In 1714, the Virginia legislature required that mill dams be ten feet wide so that they could serve as bridges.[63] Though the mills themselves were almost entirely masculine spaces, places near them served as sites of hospitality both for customers and travelers. Jacob Funk's mill on the Great Wagon Road in Virginia, for example, became a regular stopping place for tired sojourners. In North Carolina in 1756, Moravians Johann Friedrich and Maria Schumacher Schaub "moved to the mill," where she could "care for those who come to have grain ground." As customers might have long journeys to and from the mill, the entrepreneurial Moravians concluded that they would do well to provide food and perhaps lodging for them.[64] Colonists frequently chose homesites near newly established mills, creating communities like Waterford, Virginia, which grew up in the 1740s around the mill operated by Amos and Mary Janney.[65]

Despite their difficulty in growing wheat, the French also built mills in their southern territories. The first mill in the lower French colony opened in Natchez in 1720, where the commissioner had brought several millstones with him from France as well as a "very smart" miller. The Native Americans

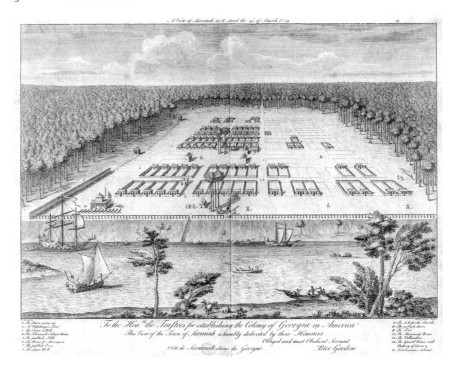

"A View of Savanah as it stood the 29th of March 1734," by Peter Gordon. The public mill is structure 5, centrally located in the village. (A detail of the image is opposite.) Hargrett Library, University of Georgia.

welcomed the convenience of the mill, coming "in droves" to get their corn processed.[66] New Orleans had a highly problematic mill, subject to fluctuations in the Mississippi River, tended by "blacks" who lived in a nearby cabin.[67]

In addition to the hard labor of digging the millraces and constructing the buildings, enslaved men did the skilled work of millers and millwrights: they built mills, maintained them and the all-important millstones, and ground the grain. In 1767, Philip Ludwell III, owner of the large Powhatan Mill in tidewater Virginia, left to his daughter Hannah Philippa Ludwell both the mill "& the Miller."[68] In 1770, Nick, a millwright who worked with "Mr. Nathanial Gordon . . . in many parts of the country," ran away from the Norfolk area.[69] The itinerant nature of Nick's work meant that he spent a good deal of time traveling around and probably learned where to go in his bid for freedom. His skill would presumably allow him to make a living as an independent worker.

Where wheat wouldn't grow, Europeans remained determined to have it, even if it meant paying high prices for imported flour. After half a century, the

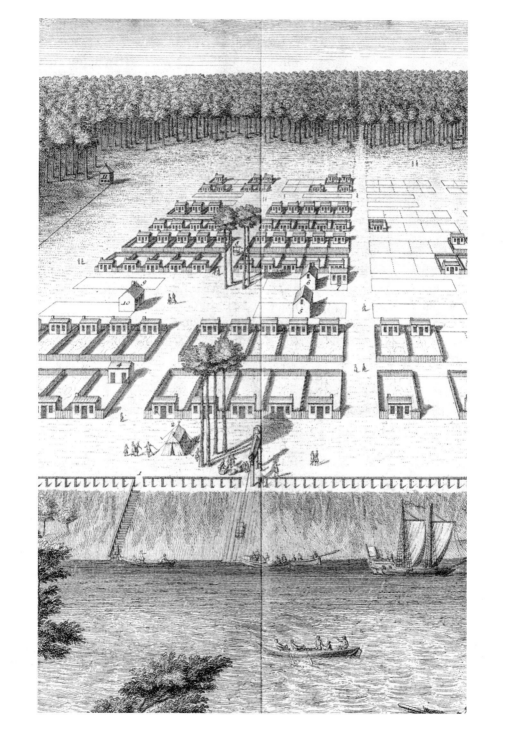

Spanish finally quit trying to grow wheat in Florida and instead brought flour from Mexico and Spain. In northwest Louisiana, the people of Los Adaes grew wheat with limited success.[70] More typically, they received their flour from the Spanish government. Getting it overland was never easy, however. Los Adaes was the eastern terminus of El Camino Royal, the road from Mexico City, 1,200 miles away, rough and split by often-impassable streams. In 1723, one load of flour from the Rio Grande was delayed seven months, and most of it spoiled due to floods.[71]

The French on the Gulf Coast brought flour across the Atlantic with them.[72] The time of travel often worked against the quality of the flour. In 1699, French leaders complained of "six barrels of flour like dust and turned sour, which had to be jettisoned."[73] In 1751, a poorly loaded shipment from France brought flour soaked with coal oil, "totally destroyed."[74] French officials finally concluded that it was best to import flour from their colonies in the Illinois country.[75] The journey between Louisiana and Illinois was rarely easy, however, and supplies arrived irregularly. With the uncertainties of the Illinois trade, Louisianans never completely lost their reliance on European flour.[76]

The French also had ongoing problems with hoarding flour and fraud. In one notable instance, in 1757, the commander of Cats Isle, off the coast of present-day Gulfport, Mississippi, sold for his own profit the government-issued flour intended for his soldiers. He forced the soldiers instead "to make their bread of the flour saved from the wreck of a Spanish ship, which was lost on the coast." The soldiers' complaints to the governor had no effect, so they formed a firing squad, killed the commander, and threw his body into the sea. He would cheat his men of good bread no more.[77]

In coastal English settlements, merchants imported flour from New York, Philadelphia, or their own interior—"Carolina" flour or that brought from Richmond.[78] To get such flour, customers had to have cash or goods to barter, thus limiting it to more affluent people only.

Whether they grew or bought their grain, colonists stored it carefully until they needed it. Most southern women did their own cooking, but we know most about the cooking of the wealthy, who kept records of their foods. Even as we consider these elaborate foods, we should keep sight of the ordinary Native American and European women who cooked for their families multiple times a day and of the enslaved women who often fed their own families in addition to performing their other duties for their enslavers.

And as we think about the foods of the wealthy, we must think of the hands that prepared them—whether as indentured servants or as enslaved people. Some of these cooks attained great skill in their work, creating elaborate masterpieces. We know the names of only a few of those cooks and bakers, and even less of their lives, but we can catch a few glimpses.

A handful of the cooks were white indentured servants. As late as 1754, Richard Mynatt, a white English indentured servant, cooked in the household of Thomas and Elizabeth Lee at Stratford Hall, Virginia. After Mynatt won his freedom in 1754, however, Caesar, an enslaved African American man in his early twenties, may have succeeded him in the kitchen on the Potomac.[79]

More often, the cooks in the kitchens of wealthy southerners, like Caesar, were enslaved: usually—but not always—female, sometimes Native American but more typically African. John Lawson was mightily impressed by a Native American woman whom he saw at a "House of great Resort" in the Carolina up-country in 1709: "This She-Cook . . . made us as White-Bread as any English could have done, and was full as neat, and expeditious, in her Affairs."[80] In Louisiana, Dumont de Montigny recorded Native American women who for only small pay "served as your wife and your slave all at once. She looked after the cooking, made the flour and the bread, both fluffed up the bed and helped to flatten it. Others hire themselves out for one or two days like field enslaved people to pound the corn and make flour from it, and this for very little, perhaps a handful of salt, a yard of ribbon, or an assortment of green, blue, red, white, or black beads such as on a rosary."[81] In Natchitoches, most Native American enslaved people were women, used for domestic work and as "concubines."[82] These Native women learned to prepare the foods of their vanquishers.

While Native American slavery in the American colonies declined in the eighteenth century, African slavery grew rapidly, with cooks and bakers among their numbers. Early in the eighteenth century, virtually all enslaved women worked in the fields. By the time of the American Revolution, a minority— maybe about 5 percent—worked exclusively in their enslavers' houses. On large estates, particularly in Virginia, greater numbers of women performed domestic work. In 1769, at Westover, the Virginia plantation of William Byrd III, enslaved women working in the house included two cooks and two "poultrywomen and bakers."[83] In Louisiana, too, African American women did domestic work for families great and ordinary. Dumont de Montigny recalled that in 1737, he, his wife, and two children lived in New Orleans with "only a single negro woman at home to make our rice bread."[84] In Natchitoches, a woman named Françoise cooked for the family of Pierre Derbanne, whose cruelty to his enslaved people was notorious.[85]

Enslaved women who appeared for sale in newspaper ads often bore descriptions like the one in 1749 Charleston: "a good and neat house-wench, that can cook . . . and bake bisket and bread."[86] Others are listed in plantation records only by their name and occupation: "Frank the cook wench" lived and worked along with eighty-five other enslaved people at Ralph Wormeley's Virginia estate. Doll became the cook at Mount Vernon when she accompanied her enslaver, Martha Dandridge Custis, to the home of Custis's new husband, George Washington. Daphne cooked for the Ludwell family on Jamestown Island.[87] The cook named Rachel became part of an estate after her enslaver died, and she ran away after John Aylett bought her.[88] Sukey Hamilton cooked for Virginia governor Francis Fauquier and was sold twice in a span of months after his death in 1768. In Norfolk, Pleasant was the cook for James Parker, whose family also benefited from the services of eight other domestic workers.[89]

These women, and thousands like them, spent long days in the kitchens of their enslavers, cooking dishes that they would never be able to share with their loved ones. They handled live fire, toted gallon after gallon of water, lifted heavy containers of flour, and fought mice and weevils. They stirred and rolled and measured and guessed at what their enslavers would like. They judged when doughs were ready to bake and when they were properly cooked. They were on their feet from before dawn till at least late afternoon. They bore the summer heat and the winter cold. To my knowledge, we have no voices of colonial enslaved cooks. To reconstruct their work, we must read between the lines written by others.

While most southern housewives baked in the fireplaces of their simple houses, detached kitchens continued to increase among the wealthy colonists.[90] Kitchens affected the lives of the people who worked in them. Often, their workspace was also their living space. On one horrific night in 1741, eleven enslaved people died when fire swept through the kitchen where they were sleeping at Roswell Plantation in Virginia.[91] The distance between their workspace and their enslavers' homes continued to present problems for the enslaved. As always, the people who delivered hot food to their enslavers' tables had to figure out the optimal path for getting from the outbuilding to the dining room. Even in urban settings, the kitchen might be fifty feet from the main house.[92] For the cook, the separation may have created some autonomous space away from the prying eyes of supervisors. But it may also have enhanced the enslavers' efforts at psychological warfare, restricting enslaved people into only their workspaces.[93]

Wealthy English colonists still constructed ovens next to their kitchen fireplaces. The kitchen of the Heyward-Washington House in Charleston, built in the 1740s, has an excellent example of one of these ovens. The brick fireplace opening is five and a half feet across, four and a half feet high, and twenty-eight inches deep. The oven, also brick, is immediately to the right, its arched facade jutting forward from the chimney face. Its bottom is thirty inches off the floor. The oven is forty-one inches deep and twenty-one inches wide on the inside, with an arched door that is sixteen inches wide and twelve

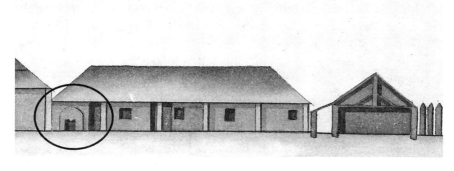

Plano del Presidio de Nra Señora del Pilar de los Adaes Capital de la Provincia de los Tejas by Joseph de Urrutia, 1768. British Library / Granger.

inches high at its highest point. A cook could heat the oven or move bread in and out without stooping or bending.[94]

The ovens in fancy Spanish buildings could be in the main building or detached. In St. Augustine, the governor's kitchen had an *hornillo*, or small oven.[95] The separate main kitchen for the estate of Diego de Espinosa was fashioned of coquina, a fire-resistant sedimentary rock made from ancient seashells, with a coquina oven built into the wall.[96] The governor's house in Los Adaes had an oven on the porch, sheltered from the elements.[97]

Colonists of all descriptions erected outdoor ovens. When French soldiers came to a location where they intended to stay for a while, building ovens was high on their list of priorities. Dumont de Montigny observed in 1733, "Our soldiers built, on the right side of the camp, several ovens in which bread was baked for the sustenance of the army, which was rather tired of eating only biscuits made from a mixture of half rice flour and half wheat flour from France."[98] Ads for properties in Virginia, Georgia, and South Carolina touted exterior ovens as desirable features.[99] And in remote Natchitoches, women cooked their breads of rice and corn in adobe (sun-dried brick) ovens behind their houses.[100]

As in Europe, people without their own ovens could sometimes bake their raw dough at community bakehouses. A few of the bakehouses were civic enterprises. In Savannah, there weren't enough bricks for each house to have an oven, so the town founders built a short-lived communal "glorious large Oven" adjacent to the public mill.[101] For the English who moved into Fort Frederica, Georgia, in 1736, the community oven provided a welcome reminder of normalcy: "An oven was built, and an indented servant, a baker by trade, was detailed to bake bread for the colony. . . . This fresh bread, in the language of one who partook of it, was a great comfort to the people."[102]

Most bakehouses, however, were private property. In rural areas, plantation owners often built them adjacent to their mills and charged for their use.[103] In cities, some commercial bakers made their ovens available to paying customers. For example, William Patterson, a pastry baker newly arrived in Charleston, announced that he would "keep his oven hot every day between 10 and 11 in the forenoon, to bake for dinner whatever may be sent to him for purpose, at the reasonable price of one shilling and three pence per dish."[104] These ovens operated both for profit and as a sort of public service, allowing people without ovens to have their own fresh baked goods.

While ordinary southerners had few kitchen implements, affluent colonists boasted a variety of baking gear. Their households often had dozens of "patty pans" as well as specialized pans for cakes, Naples biscuits, pies, and tarts.[105] An immediate hit in eighteenth-century southern kitchens was the Dutch oven, a cast-iron pot with legs and a tightly fitting rimmed lid. Cast iron absorbs and holds heat to provide steady, even cooking. By closing the pot tightly and surrounding it with coals, a cook could imitate the indirect heat of an oven, where hot air rather than flame cooks the item. The legs kept the pot from touching live fire and permitted heated air to circulate under it. The rimmed lid allowed the cook to pile live coals on the top without worrying about them sliding off. After seeing them made in the Netherlands (hence the origin of the name), in 1708 Abraham Darby patented the process of casting iron pots in sand and began cranking out cookware from his foundry in Shropshire, England. Colonial merchants sold them in coastal cities and the backcountry alike.[106] Creative cooks used Dutch ovens for all sorts of baking. The only downside was that cast iron rusts in a heartbeat, and the pots had to be tended carefully, sometimes scrubbed with salt or sand to get rid of the oxidation.

And what, besides cornbread, came out of these pots and ovens? As we have seen, wealthy southerners had much greater access to wheat bread than did their poorer neighbors. Throughout many of the colonies, wheat bread remained a luxury. William Logan, traveling through North Carolina in 1745, commented on getting wheat bread in New Bern, "which is a great Rarity here."[107] In central Tennessee, the colonists enjoyed "English bread" only on Sunday mornings.[108] Enslaved people could get wheat flour occasionally, sometimes through barter, sometimes through theft, and infrequently as gifts from enslavers.[109]

Almost all the wheat breads in southern elite homes were English-style. We learn this from the household books of four affluent white women: an

"Anonymous Housekeeper" from 1700 Virginia; Jane Bolling Randolph of Virginia, whose cookery book dates to 1743; and Eliza Lucas Pinckney and her daughter, Harriott Pinckney Horry, of South Carolina.[110] Historian Katherine Harbury has traced many of the Virginia recipes directly to English cookbooks of the period. How much custom followed the recipes, we cannot know, of course, but these recipes give detailed descriptions of baked foods that are missing from other sources. Like the book of Lady Berkeley, the books have no recipes for corn.

Southern women also owned printed English cookbooks. The first cookbook produced in the colonies was *The Compleat Housewife* by Eliza Smith, an English volume reprinted in Williamsburg in 1742. A truly southern cookbook would wait another eighty years for publication.

Most eighteenth-century recipes were merely listings of ingredients. The few with instructions give telling hints of the amount of work involved in baking. Jane Randolph's recipe for "Cakes very Fine" instructed the baker to knead all the ingredients together and let the mixture sit for an hour or two, then make into cakes and bake in an oven "not too hot not shutting up it's Mouth." Once baked, the cakes were iced with a mixture of egg whites, fine sugar, and rose water and strewn "thick" with caraway comfits, baked again, iced again, several times. Such cakes would stay good for a month.[111] A recipe from 1700 explained how to measure seasonings: "as much Salt As will ly upon a Sixpence," a British coin slightly larger than a dime.[112] "A Butter Cake" required the cook to use her body as a tool. She was to mix her ingredients "together in a kettle over ye fier stirring it with your hand till tis very smooth[;] let it be as hot as you can bear." Presumably stirring by hand made sure that the batter was perfectly smooth. This risky treat was then baked in a "hoop" (a round, bottomless mold made of metal or wood) with "a paper flowered at ye bottom"—rather like a springform pan.[113] Generally operating without instructions, southern bakers either had to be taught by another cook or had to learn by trial and error, which could be costly in time, ingredients, and anxiety.

One of the hallmarks of southern baking has long been rolls: individual portions of bread, served hot from the oven. Rolls suit the southern climate, taking less time to bake, and thus creating less heat in the kitchen and using less fuel, than loaf bread. A large loaf, designed to last longer, molds quickly in warm humidity. Visitor Hugh Jones commented disapprovingly in 1724 that planters "bake daily, Breads or Cakes . . . tho' it be pleasanter than what has been baked a Day or two."[114] (What Jones meant, of course, was that *enslaved people* baked for planters every day—a hot, complicated routine.) Jane Randolph recommended "French Bread, or Royls, for Oisters," made with flour, eggs, butter, sack, and warm milk, baked in little patty-pans.[115] Harriott

Horry's recipe for "Bops" contained flour, butter "rub'd in the flour till you cant feel the Butter," and milk made into a "very thick Batter then put it into a marble Mortar and beat it till 'tis quite light"—again, striking the dough to introduce air.[116]

Getting European-style ingredients remained a challenge, particularly those that came from live animals.[117] Milk cows required the most attention of all domestic animals. Louisiana administrator Pierre Le Moyne d'Iberville reported in 1699 that the cows he brought from France survived the Atlantic crossing, but those he purchased in Saint-Domingue all died.[118] The Germans who settled in North Carolina and Louisiana proved expert at cow husbandry, and they sold "exceedingly good" butter to nearby city residents with cash to spend.[119] Colonists also continued to import butter from Europe. The English who arrived in Georgia in 1735 were guaranteed nine pounds of butter a year by the founders, while in Louisiana, a 1747 bill of importation included butter as well as brandied fruit and "goose thighs."[120] Milk, butter, and cream remained mostly for rich people.

Southerners used hog lard both as an ingredient and as an oil for frying. Hogs originally came from Europe—Spain, England, and France alike—but they thrived in the South as though they had always been there, living mostly in the woods and eating fallen nuts and acorns.[121] Pork has played a crucial part in southern cooking ever since. Virtually every part of the animal is edible, and smoked or salted pork keeps well. Hog butchering typically took place in the autumn, and the fat would be rendered—cooked until the impurities separated and could be strained out—into lard shortly thereafter. Fortunate families stored enough lard to last till the next year, while others learned to do without during lean times. Many free rural families had hogs, but urban white families and enslaved people had to get their lard from other sources. European colonists, particularly in town, also bought lard imported from Europe.[122]

Chickens were the easiest to raise of all domestic animals. They required little in the way of food or shelter, and they provided both meat and eggs. Most white families and some enslaved people had at least a few chickens. But for those unfortunates who did not, enterprising farmers brought eggs to town for sale.[123]

Breads leavened with yeast took various forms. Jane Randolph had numerous recipes for small, relatively simple cakes—again, individual portions—made with yeast that would have been served freshly baked. Her muffins, which resembled what we call English muffins, consisted simply of flour, yeast, and water, baked in a mold. Her "French Rouls" were made from flour, yeast, butter, and "new milk from the cow."[124]

Wigs were barely sweet buns, seasoned with caraway seed or sack, enjoyed particularly during Lent.[125] Rusks were crisp yeasted rolls, often twice-baked. Leavened with ale barm or yeast, they were composed of flour, eggs, sugar, butter, and sometimes milk or caraway seeds.[126] (Similarly, the Moravians in North Carolina made twice-baked zwieback from their fine flour.)[127] Caraway, either plain or as comfits, still went into seed cakes. Comfits could be "rough" or "smooth," designating how the layers of sugar were coated around the caraway.[128] Jane Randolph's recipe for seed cake used an entire pound of comfits, plus flour, butter, eggs, and cream or milk, leavened with ale barm.[129] Other seed cakes included combinations of wine, almonds, candied citron, lemon peel, orange peel, or musk.[130]

Ale barm remained common as a leavening. Some bakers caught wild yeast, which exists everywhere, simply by setting a container of flour and water outside.[131] Commercially made yeast came on the market in Philadelphia and New York in the 1760s, but it is hard to tell when it became available in the South. In 1770, Harriott Horry gave directions for making yeast from boiled, mashed Irish potatoes, hops, and brown sugar.[132]

Larger "cakes"—more like loaves of bread, not our layer cakes—were meant to be cut into individual servings. Almost all the recipes for these were variations on a theme: flour, butter, currants, sugar, and ale yeast. Beyond that, the sky was the limit: variations with eggs, cream ("made blood warm"), or sack, seasoned with selections of rose water, nutmeg, cloves, cinnamon, mace, or candied orange, lemon, and citron peel. While a few raisins came from dried American grapes, most dried currants were imported from England.[133] In ports such as Annapolis, Charleston, and Savannah, moneyed consumers could buy a wide array of seasonings.[134] In the backcountry, the choices remained simpler, with allspice, ginger, nutmeg, and cinnamon the most widespread.[135]

Sweets became more common and yet highly problematic in the colonial period because they used sugar. Europeans in North America originally failed at growing sugarcane, so colonial merchants imported molasses and sugar from the Caribbean.[136] Sugar plantations were places of brutality and disease, where enslaved people worked until they died, and colonial consumers enjoyed sweet tastes at a high human cost. Sugar, as always, came in various grades, from muscovado to white sugars of several levels of refinement and texture.[137]

The wealthiest southerners, of course, enjoyed the most sugar. Ordinary, poor, and even enslaved people bought it as they had cash or items to barter. In New London, Virginia, an enslaved man named London bought sugar with the money he earned by picking the seeds out of raw cotton, and we wonder if he knew the pain his fellow enslaved people endured to produce it.[138] Back-country merchants also received goods in trade for sugar. In 1750, Jane Carr of Hanover County, Virginia, traded two pairs of sheets that she had sewn.[139]

Some extravagant colonial recipes used large quantities of eggs, beaten for long times, as leaven. The "Anonymous Housekeeper" of 1700 included a recipe for a huge pound cake, with four pounds each of sugar, flour, and butter. The ingredients also included forty eggs, two nutmegs, "Cinnomon," cloves, and caraway seeds. The eggs were beaten "one houer" and then the sugar added and the mixture beaten for another hour. The rest of the ingredients were added and "beaten up with one's hand." The batter was poured into a "Tin pudding pan," but "It must be kept beating with ones hand till it goes into the Oven Else it will fall."[140] One can only imagine the trepidation with which a cook made this cake. If it didn't turn out, more than twelve pounds of expensive ingredients and hours of physical labor would be for naught.

Plum cakes and fruitcakes continued as popular treats throughout the colonial period, with recipes handed down through the generations. Jane Randolph had four recipes for "plumb cake," all with flour, sugar, butter, cream or milk, and as many as two dozen eggs. They might be leavened with yeast and loaded with various fruits, nuts, and flavorings, including orange flower water made by steeping orange-tree blossoms in water. One was baked in a "Coffin of Paper" (likely a boxlike form made of thick paper rather than pastry, as in the past), another in a "frame" (possibly a wooden square), and a third in a hoop.[141]

In Bethabara, the first home of the Moravians in North Carolina, Christian worship services centered around the Lovefeast, in which church members shared coffee and a loaf of bread. The bread was traditionally made from wheat flour, leavened with yeast, and seasoned with sugar and sometimes cinnamon and mace.[142] In 1753, however, the newcomers demonstrated their adaptability to different circumstances by baking their Lovefeast bread from cornmeal.[143]

The well-organized, prosperous Moravians had joyous Christmas celebrations that they quickly shared with their poorer neighbors. In 1760, the Bethabara residents invited "the English children from the mill . . . so poorly clad that it would have moved a stone to pity. We told them why we rejoiced like children and gave to each a piece of cake."[144] They don't say what kind of cake, but traditional Moravian ginger cakes are paper-thin and crisp, with molasses, brown sugar, cloves, cinnamon, and ginger.[145] Tricky to prepare because of the expected thinness and snap, the cakes required forethought and care on the part of the Moravian bakers. In 1770, the Lovefeast at the South Fork community included telling the Nativity story, followed by "honey-cakes and verses." Again, "the children were full of wonder and joy, it being the first time they had attended such a service."[146]

Among the English, the terms "biskets" and "cakes" seem interchangeable, referring to small creations variously dropped, rolled and cut, or baked in "molds." Jane Randolph's "Bisket Drops" featured sugar, eggs, sack, "Seeds in pouder," flour, and sugar.[147] "Naples Biskets," which were dry, oblong cakes, had medieval roots. They consisted of flour ("well dryed in an Oven"), sugar, and eggs, flavored with caraway, coriander, and rose water. Harriott Horry seasoned hers with rose water, "a few peach kernels," or orange peel. Why peach kernels? Cooks made a flavoring called noyau by steeping the kernels of fruits such as peaches, plums, or apricots in alcohol. Noyau mimicked the flavor of bitter almond, a type of almond that contains a toxin called amygdalin, without having its poisonous side effects.[148] Naples biscuits could be baked in buttered molds, or, as Harriott Horry said, "the principal thing to be observed is to bake it extremely thin" on paper or tin sheets.[149]

A few "biscuits" began to resemble those small breads that we cherish. The closest is Horry's recipe of hot milk, butter, and flour, kneaded for an hour, then rolled, cut with a cup, and baked in a "pretty hot oven."[150] The lengthy kneading, which introduced air into the dough, was the only leavening. Jane Randolph's "Tavern Biskets" consisted of flour, butter, and eggs leavened with yeast, then rolled and cut with the lid of a large canister.[151]

Shrewsbury cakes and jumbals still had many fans, and gingerbread retained its exalted status.[152] The word "cakes" also described something closer to our cookies, with numerous options. The cook mixed the ingredients, beginning with flour and sugar, into a stiff paste and then shaped them into rounds or "what form you please." They could range in size from "the Bigness of a Hand" to "about the size of half a crown" (a British coin, about an inch and a quarter across). They might have currants, nutmeg, rose water, cloves, mace, or sack, and they might be iced "over with Sugar" or garnished with caraway seeds. They were baked on tin plates, probably resembling our cookie sheets.[153]

For pies and pastries, the heavy cases of the past had disappeared by 1700. The "Anonymous Housekeeper" of that year gave only ingredients and no directions for the three pastry recipes in her household book: "Past[e] for a high Pye" (flour worked up with melted butter and "boyling liquar"); "Past[e] Royall for Patty Pans" (a sweet, rich dough of flour, butter, sugar, and eggs); and "Past[e] for a Custard" (simply flour and boiling water).[154] Jane Randolph included directions for her recipe for puff pastry, very similar to modern methods, although hardly adequate to teach an inexperienced hand. Fine flour, eggs, and a little cold water made a stiff paste. Then, Randolph said, "role it abroad & Lay little pieces of butter upon it very thick & sprinkle Little flower & fold your paste role it out again." Repeat this process eight or nine times, Randolph said, "always putting butter between ye Folds."[155]

Almost all the recipes labeled "pie" in these eighteenth-century household books are for meat pies, not desserts. The closest things to sweet pies were mince, which changed little over the centuries. One relatively light, fruity version had a foundation of suet, currants, and apples (specifically, "right golden runnets," a highly favored English apple of the period) seasoned with spices and citrus fruits.[156]

English colonists brought apples with them, and by the eighteenth century, apple cultivation in the upper South had become highly sophisticated.[157] In 1709, John Lawson listed ten varieties of American-grown apples, from Leather Coat to Redstreak to Lady-Finger, each with its own advantages and drawbacks.[158] Native Americans in the up-country learned to grow and adapt apples for their own use.[159] In the lower South, prosperous people bought apples imported from cooler regions. Pears, "plentiful and good," and quinces, less common, joined their botanical cousins in southern orchards.[160]

To find what we would call pie recipes, we have to look instead for puddings and "Florentines," which was a term for something baked in pastry. Made with puff pastry bottoms and "lids," Florentines somewhat resemble our fruit pies. They could be made of oranges, apples, currants, or combinations of the three.[161]

Puddings were custard-like fillings made with eggs, butter, cream or milk, and sugar, often baked in a puff pastry. One almond pudding consisted of Jordan almonds (almonds with hard shells of sugar) and pistachio nuts (imported from the Middle East) ground together, grated biscuits, "sweet spice," sack, and orange-flower water.[162] Jane Randolph made orange pudding with preserved orange peel, sack, rose water, and nutmeg, while her lemon pudding was made with only lemons for flavoring.[163] Her apple pudding combined apple pulp with eggs, grated Naples biscuits, and orange or lemon rind boiled and then beaten in a mortar, all of which was placed in a buttered dish "with a past[e] at top & Bottom & Bake[d] not to mch."[164]

By the eighteenth century, European fruits had been growing in parts of North America for more than 200 years. The colonists continued to import plants, trying to replicate the gardens of England and Spain. Stone fruits— with a big center seed—generally adapted nicely to the southern climate. Colonists quickly added plum trees to their orchards, and apricots, though less common, also made the trans-Atlantic journey.[165] European cherries, too, flourished in the southern up-country.[166] According to John Brickell, the Native Americans in North Carolina were smitten with the English cherries: "this Fruit is in great Request amongst the Indians, which they sometimes dry and preserve for the Winter."[167] Europeans planted many cultivars of peaches in lush orchards.[168] James Glen noted that "Fourteen or Fifteen Sorts" of peaches grew in South Carolina.[169] Europeans brought figs with them, and the fruit quickly established as trees wherever it went. Like peaches, by the eighteenth century they had gone wild and could be enjoyed by the multitudes.[170] English colonists prized oranges and lemons, trying with mixed success to grow them outside in South Carolina and in greenhouses farther north.[171] Wealthy southerners occasionally bought imported oranges.[172] In Florida, oranges grew wild but weren't used much.[173] The French colonies did better, as oranges, lemons, figs, and pineapple all found homes on the balmy Gulf Coast.[174]

Stale bread and other forms of sturdy baked goods became the basis of new dishes, as we saw with the puddings above. Desserts called charlottes, which were combinations of baked goods, fruit, and custard, served either warm or cold, appeared in the colonial period. No one is quite sure where charlottes, like many dishes, started or why they were called that, but that never stopped southerners from loving them. Harriott Horry's book contained a recipe, not in Horry's handwriting, for "Charlotte à la façon [method] de Mr. Short," possibly given to Horry by William Short, a diplomat to France. This version started with buttered slices of stale bread sprinkled with brown sugar, then apple slices, followed by more brown sugar, "grated bread," and cinnamon or nutmeg. The cook repeated identical layers until the pan was full. The recipe warned that the dish "requires a great deal of baking and the oven must not be too hot."[175] Many charlottes would emerge from southern American kitchens in the next 200 years.

Rice culture likely came to the South with enslaved people in the 1690s when a Portuguese ship brought a "considerable quantity" of rice as food for the enslaved cargo. Africans, particularly those from the Windward Coast (west of present-day Ghana) knew how to grow rice, liked eating it, and presumably began growing it in small garden patches in America. South Carolina enslavers, in search of a cash crop, realized that they had both a viable commodity and the skilled workforce required to grow it.[176] Thus, they began cultivating rice in swamps along the Atlantic Coast. In the next twenty years, white South Carolinians imported so many enslaved people to grow rice that Africans outnumbered Europeans in the colony. The working conditions were brutal, and even enslaved people accustomed to humid environments succumbed to malaria, yellow fever, and cholera.[177] Rice also came to Louisiana from Africa with enslaved people.[178] By 1731, Louisianans grew enough rice to export surplus to the Caribbean.[179]

Planters used both natural low spots and dams to capture water for growing rice. Enslaved people cleared swampland and excavated earth for dams that opened and closed with sluice gates. In early spring, women sowed rice on dry ground and men covered it with a light layer of soil. Next, they flooded the field, the rice sprouted, and cycles of draining, weeding, and flooding went on until about September. Both men and women harvested rice with sickles known as rice hooks. They then bound it in sheaves to cure and prepare for threshing and milling.[180]

In both South Carolina and Louisiana, small mills for hulling and grinding rice soon developed.[181] Each grain of rice has two covers: the outer hull, which comes off easily, and an inner bran layer that is difficult to remove. Africans brought with them the basic method of hand milling, very similar to that used by the Native Americans for corn. A log served as the mortar and a wooden pestle was suited "to the Strength of the Person who is to pound it." Workers winnowed and strained the rice several times before packing it in barrels.[182]

As rice cultivation accelerated in the Low Country and in Louisiana, people usually boiled the small, hard grains, but eventually they became the basis for bread.[183] I have been able to find very little on how raw rice was turned into flour, but food historian Karen Hess speculates that it had been done for millennia. Grains broken during milling, more difficult to sell than whole grains, may have been used for flour.[184] Traveler Johann Schoepf noted that Carolinians ate "small, thin cakes . . . baked, either of rice alone or mixed with maize, and served warm."[185] He observed that for Carolina "negroes," rice served as "almost the only food."[186]

Some people thought rice bread was acceptable. James Freeman of South Carolina wrote in 1712, "Rice bread, whilst new, eats as pleasant, and is as white to compare with the finest wheaten bread."[187] Many people, however, found it inedible. William Logan complained in his journey south of the Santee River in 1745, "We Could get no Bread . . . but Rice Bread & that Exceedingly sour."[188] During the Revolutionary War, soldier William Feltman grumbled that rice was "a very poor substitute for bread, and it is a mystery to see how to make it into bread." Craving cornmeal, he marveled that "the Carolinians say they are fonder of rice bread than they are of the best wheat."[189] Karen Hess regards the mixture of wheat and rice flours to be "the most original culinary development of the European minority" in the Carolinas.[190] Apparently white Carolinians' palates adapted, and Black Carolinians had no choice.

When Louisianans faced shortages of wheat flour, they stretched their supplies by mixing it with cheaper rice flour.[191] Combining the two was "problematic," according to a New Orleans baker. Rice flour is soft, with low protein, and has no gluten to give it structure. The wheat must do double duty to raise itself and the rice.[192] In the 1790s, during a period of scarcity, the New Orleans government worked with two bakers to discover the best proportions of rice and wheat to achieve edible results.[193]

Among the home bakers, only Harriott Horry included recipes for rice bread, which is not surprising since both her parents and husband made fortunes raising rice. Her formulas contained cooked rice, wheat flour, yeast, milk, and salt. Notably, the gluten in the wheat flour provided the structure that would allow the dough to rise into "excellent white Bread."[194] The cooked rice was likely easier to raise than crunchy rice flour.[195] Other cookbook writers of the antebellum period limited themselves to the grains they found easier to make palatable.

ALTHOUGH MOST southerners prepared their foods at home, an increasing number bought cooked victuals. The sellers ranged from proprietors of eating and drinking establishments, to individuals peddling all kinds of foods, to stores with delicacies processed in Europe and then shipped across the Atlantic.

Inns and taverns provided for travelers and locals alike, and they served large quantities of bread to their patrons.[196] John Owens of Savannah offered "Good entertainment for men and horses. . . . Also good bread, cakes, &c. sold."[197] Enterprising individuals hawked baked goods throughout the South, rural and urban. Native women sold to European troops. In Keowee, a Georgia Cherokee village, in 1756, women carried to the English troops "a great Number of Cakes of Bread of their own make . . . every Woman bringing something of this Kind in a Basket." Soon after the establishment of Fort Loudoun in eastern Tennessee, Native American women had a thriving trade vending corn and other "Eatables."[198] In the French colonies, they sold fresh cornmeal as well as bread.[199]

Enslaved Africans, especially women, began selling food in cities by 1725. For these workers, the process of selling baked goods involved a constant search for ingredients, whether grown, salvaged, bought, or stolen. Even the most enterprising enslaved persons had difficulty getting their hands on wheat flour or sugar. Then they had to find the time and the means to make up and bake their goods and sell them. Though such women dearly earned their income, some sellers did extremely well. In New Orleans in the 1760s, Mandingo women Comba and Louison sold cakes along the streets and made enough money to throw a feast for friends.[200]

Enslaved peddlers sometimes used their imperfect independence to run away. In 1760, an Angolan woman named Flora, with limited command of English, sold cakes "within ten miles of Charles-Town . . . pretending to have permission from me [her enslaver]." She took her leave in December and was still missing six months later.[201] Hannah Bullock was "well known in Charlestown . . . selling Cakes and other things in the Market." With smallpox scars, a missing front tooth, and a pigeon-toed walk, she had been gone at least three months when her enslaver offered a reward for her return in 1766.[202] Both her trade and her appearance made Hannah distinctive, yet she remained at large. Perhaps Flora's and Hannah's successful flights testified to the pluck and creativity demonstrated by their baking enterprises.

For city governments, peddlers created problems, both by their mere existence and with the fragments of autonomy that their sales brought to them. To maintain control, Low Country cities began licensing enslaved peddlers by the 1730s.[203] In New Orleans, officials tried to require enslaved peddlers to carry written permits from their enslavers, but the trade was too helpful to too many people for the government to make much headway.[204] The city of Norfolk wrestled with regulation for decades. In 1773, it banned "Indians, mulattoes or negroes Bound or free from selling any kind of dressed meat, Bread, or bakes," and then it repealed the law in 1783.[205] Despite white people's protests, enslaved women maintained lively trades in cake, confections, and bread in all the cities of the colonial South.[206]

White women from the countryside also sold baked goods in cities. Mary Holt Harnett had a thriving business near Wilmington, North Carolina, in the 1770s, making "minced pies, cheese-cakes, tarts and little biskets, which she sends down to town once or twice a day." English traveler Janet Schaw noted that Harnett refused to "run tick," or give credit, to anyone, acting rigorously as a businesswoman. Harnett likely had at least one enslaved person to help with her enterprise, whether in making the goods or delivering them to Wilmington.[207] Her business perhaps gave her some autonomy as a white woman.

The number of commercial bakeries in southern cities grew throughout the colonial period. All the large cities had multiple bakeries, and by the 1770s, even a small place like Camden, South Carolina, in the backcountry, had a bakery, a brewery, and a distillery.[208]

As late as midcentury, white indentured servants played a role in the commercial baking industry. An ad for the indenture of George Michael Woller in South Carolina stated that he "claims to be a Butcher and Baker."[209] A 1766 Charleston ad noted for sale "the Indentures of eight Dutch SERVANTS, among which are a shoe-Maker Butcher and Baker."[210]

Enslaved Africans, particularly men, proved crucial to the development of commercial baking in the South. While they did the manual labor of carrying water and delivering orders, they also understood and executed the intricate and delicate steps of baking.[211] In Louisiana in the 1730s, the French government paid bakers to provide bread for the troops "while a negro at the Balise [the French fort near the mouth of the Mississippi River] was doing the same work quite as well for his clothes and a soldier's rations."[212] A Charleston writer complained in 1772 that it was "well Known, that the Management of . . . Baking, is generally left to Negroes at Night as well as in the Day."[213] To the enslaved people of Charleston fell the responsibilities of rising from their beds in the tiny hours of the night to heat the ovens and raise and bake the dough so that the white consumers of the city could have fresh bread by first light. The *Georgia Gazette* in 1766 offered for sale an "exceeding good cook, house painter, barber, baker, and in every respect a useful negroe man," while at the same time in Williamsburg, an enslaved man named Will was advertised as "a lusty well made Fellow, bow legged, and round shoulder'd, about 30 Years old, he is a Baker by Trade."[214] Sometimes bakers came as part of a package deal: a 1771 lease near Norfolk included windmills, a bakehouse, a granary, and "some Negroes, among whom are Millers, Bakers, and a Wench."[215]

As the South filled with immigrants from England and Germany, the number of bakers rose accordingly.[216] While many immigrant bakers were German, the majority were English: John Herbert, a "Pastry-Cook from London"; Joseph Calvert, "Baker from London"; John Barrell, "Baker, from Bristol," for example.[217] These men produced impressive arrays of goods. An elaborate bill of fare came from the Charleston ovens of John Meek, "lately arrived from England," in 1767. Meek offered a variety of tarts ("Citron, cinamon, chocolate, almond, bisket & bread"); breads ("Lemon, cinamon, almond, coffee, aniseed, chocolate, Vienna, French, Spanish, and Swedish"); "Savoy, Spanish, King's, citron, rock, and all sorts of light BISKETS"; "sweet and cinamon macaroons"; and "French and Free-Mason cakes," plus comfits, almonds, ratafias (almond-flavored cookies), and more.[218] While most immigrant bakers were men, Englishwomen Margaret Nelson and Elinor Bolton ("late house-keeper to Lord Charles Greville Montagu"), who opened shops in Charleston in 1768 and 1769, also sold fine wares such as apple "cheese-cakes" and orange tarts.[219]

In the Louisiana colony, most housekeepers bought their bread rather than trying to make it at home, and the commercial baking industry thrived from the early days of French settlement. The first bakers arrived in the 1720s, with their numbers increasing steadily throughout the colonial period.[220] Despite the challenge of producing bread in hot, humid conditions and the recurring shortages of wheat flour, Louisiana bakers produced French-style bread, cast rather than baked in a pan, with a crisp crust and tender interior. As the premier historian of New Orleans baking Roger Baudier observes, "They were French and from France and brought with them their formulas and methods." Loaves were dense and round, available in sizes ranging from one to five pounds.[221] Fine baking came to New Orleans by 1721, when a "pastry cook" named l'Abbe introduced "Paris type pastries." Even when the Spanish gained control of Louisiana in 1769, New Orleans bakers retained their French ways.[222]

The baked item most sold in the colonies was ship's bread, the unleavened flat cakes that had been used for hundreds of years on ocean voyages. The trans-Atlantic trade in ship's bread thrived, with bakers on both sides of the sea. English business writer Malachy Postlethwayt gave detailed directions for its production in 1774. It could be made only from wheat flour of first quality, odorless and "like velvet to the touch" when sifted. After being baked into eight-ounce cakes, the ship's bread was stored in a prewarmed, tightly sealed chamber for at least two months and preferably for six before loading onto ships.[223] Bakers in all southern Atlantic ports made ship's bread, ready to supply outbound voyages.[224] The Spanish also used biscuits as rations on land— not for themselves but for the formerly enslaved people at Fort Mose, African Americans whom they enticed to Florida to irritate the English. Despite their free status, Black people in Florida did not receive wheat flour or have access to soft wheat bread.[225]

Bread was so important that cities and states continued another ancient tradition, passing ordinances to protect consumers. Fraudulent baking in New Orleans began less than a decade after the city's establishment. The French government decreed that each baker furnish buyers bread "of full weight." When a royal inspector paid surprise visits to the city's bakeries, he found François Lemesle to be cheating. Lemesle's punishment was to have all his four-pound loaves dumped in the Mississippi, a problematic solution because he held the contract to supply the bread for the Royal Hospital.[226]

In 1749, the South Carolina government scolded "covetous and evil-disposed persons, taking advantage . . . [who] have, for their own gain and lucre, deceived and oppressed his Majesty's subjects, and more especially the poorer sort of people." The colony, accordingly, passed the Act for Regulating the Assize of Bread. The 1749 South Carolina law, like most others, did three things: tied the price of bread to the price of flour, required bakers to mark or imprint the bread they sold so that it could be traced, and set penalties for cheating. The law authorized justices of the peace to make surprise inspection visits. Any bread found wanting would be seized and given to the poor of the parish.[227] Periodic updates on the price of flour subsequently ran in the newspapers.[228]

BY 1780, the South's time as a colony was drawing to an end. The Seven Years' War eliminated French authority from America in 1763, and the United States separated from England in 1776. Only Spain remained alongside the new nation.

The ways of multitudes of people—Native American, African, French, German, eastern European, Spanish, and English; enslaved and free—were coming together to make a unique southern cuisine, a hybrid of all these types. Cities grew, and more people became involved in trade. The people of the new United States would continue to learn from one another the ways of baking in a diverse society.

Chapter 4

HOECAKE

....

Who Ate What, and Who Decided That

rowing up in Maryland, the great thinker and writer Frederick Douglass heard a fellow enslaved person sing:

We raise de wheat,
Dey gib us de corn;
We bake de bread,
Dey giv us de crust;
We sif de meal,
Dey gib us de huss.[1]

Transcribing the passage into his book *The Life and Times of Frederick Douglass*, Douglass described it as "a sharp hit . . . to the meanness of slaveholders." From the time they arrived in America until emancipation, enslaved people saw the disparities between their diet and that of their enslavers. They ate corn; their enslavers ate wheat flour. They expended their time and sweat baking bread but received none of the good parts. They sifted the ground corn but got only the leavings. The recitation of wrongs in the song went on, but baked goods headed the list of the many ways that enslavers lorded their power over the enslaved people who created their wealth. Who ate what, and who decided that, exemplified the inequalities of the new American nation.

As slavery cleaved the young country, its people were on the move. White Americans and the people they enslaved went west, breaking and fencing lands that had long been home to Native Americans. Pressed to surrender their lands, the Natives paid dearly for their attempts to remain in the region. In 1813, U.S. soldiers razed the fields and storehouses of the Creek in eastern Alabama, leaving the Natives scrounging for leftover corn.[2] By the late 1820s, some Creek were subsisting on roots and tree bark.[3] In 1836, the U.S. government forced them into Oklahoma and opened the last of their lands to white interlopers.

The Cherokee tried to stave off American aggression by demonstrating their "civilized" nature. One way they showed their assimilation was by printing Anglo-style recipes in their newspaper, the Cherokee Phoenix. "Receipts for the Ladies," published in 1831, included jumbles, ginger cake, and more.[4] Their attempts to show themselves as suitable Georgians failed, of course, and the United States dispatched most of the Cherokee to Oklahoma. Some Native American families remained in the East, but by and large, by 1840, southern people were mostly considered Black, white, or a combination of the two. The territories of Louisiana and Arkansas became part of the United States in 1803, and Texas joined in 1845. The boundaries of the South crashed against the Apache and Comanche to the west and the young nation of Mexico to the south.

CORN REMAINED the staple food for most southerners, whoever they were. Rural people mostly grew their own while urban dwellers bought their supplies with cash or bartered for them.[5] Most adult enslaved people received about a peck of corn or cornmeal a week, about five cups a day, as their ration.[6] Many enslaved people, after long days in the fields, waited their turn to grind their corn before it could be cooked for supper. When he was enslaved, Charles Ball witnessed such a scene in South Carolina before 1835: "After it was quite dark, the slaves came in from the cotton-field, and taking little notice of us, went into the kitchen, and each taking thence a pint of corn, proceeded to a little mill, which was nailed to a post in the yard, and there commenced the operation of grinding meal for their suppers, which were afterwards to be prepared by baking the meal into cakes at the fire." The grinding proceeded with consideration for the youngest and oldest: mothers of small children and the elderly went first. Ball particularly noted the irony of the cooks having to grind their cornmeal: "The two women who had waited at the [enslavers'] table, after the supper of the white people was disposed of, also came with their corn to the mill on the post, and ground their allowance like the others. They had not been permitted to taste even the fragments of the meal that they had cooked for their masters and mistresses."[7] Ball captured nuances of these provisions: enslaved people took care of each other, and being a house servant did not ensure a person better food. And no matter how late one got to bed, freedman Solomon Northrup observed, an enslaved person dared not be late to the fields the next morning.[8]

Larger corn mills retained their old features: two balanced stones, powered by water or a treadmill. In a particularly cruel turn of affairs, in the 1820s the State of South Carolina erected a treadmill in the back of the prison powered by "negro slaves" in Charleston. Traveler Karl Bernhard described the activity that produced cornmeal:

> [Each wheel] employs twelve prisoners, who work a mill for grinding corn, and thereby contribute to the support of the prison. Six tread at once upon every wheel, while six rest upon a bench placed behind the wheel. Every half minute the left hand man steps off the tread-wheel, while the five others move to the left to fill up the vacant place; at the same time the right hand man sitting on the bench, steps on the wheel, and begins his movement, while the rest, sitting on the bench, uniformly recede. Thus, even three minutes sitting, allows the unhappy being no repose. The signal for changing is given by a small bell attached to the wheel. The prisoners are compelled to labour eight hours a day in this manner. Order is preserved by a person, who, armed with a cow-hide, stands by the wheel. Both sexes tread promiscuously upon the wheel.

The "negroes," observed Bernhard, "entertain a strong fear of the treadmills, and regard flogging as the lighter evil."[9] The means of sustenance became a method of torture at the hands of the white people in charge.

Industrialization made cornmeal available to faraway markets. To stabilize the corn, inventors experimented with drying methods, such as heating it in a kiln.[10] Many consumers disliked the dried cornmeal, as the process changed the taste, but it became common anyway. The long-standing debate over yellow and white cornmeal may have its roots in the bitter, scorched flavor of kiln-dried yellow corn. White cornmeal was supposed to be sweeter and tastier than yellow, and of course whiteness had symbolic overtones of purity and race. Wealthy white North Carolinian Catherine Edmondston declared adamantly, "White is the only corn fit for bread."[11] Merchants frequently advertised white corn and cornmeal with superlatives—"best," "clean," "prime," "beautiful," "superior"—giving them license to charge 10 to 15 percent more for white than for yellow.[12]

AS THE WHITE American population streamed west across the Appalachians, so did wheat cultivation.[13] Southern farmers favored soft red winter wheat, which had less gluten and less water than northern varieties. It was easier to grind than hard wheat, and the flour had a dazzlingly white appearance.[14]

Wheat cultivation changed little after the American Revolution, but mechanization altered harvesting methods. Harvest still required a frenzy of activity, however, with enslaved people forming an integral part of the workforce.[15] Because they needed maximum flexibility, enslavers swapped labor and also allowed enslaved people to hire themselves out to other farmers. Enslaved people still used their harvesting skills to escape their bonds. Arch, "a fast reaper," would no doubt "procure a sickle and attempt to pass as a freeman," according to his enslaver. "Negro Ned," another escapee, "understands felling, mowing, cradling."[16] But white laborers also did a goodly portion of the work, in return for cash wages, barter, or repayment of debts.[17]

The threshing machine, invented in the 1780s, greatly sped up harvest. A thresher had a rotating set of blades that snapped the wheat heads from the straw, then beat the heads to remove the kernels, reducing the amount of labor required by 75 percent.[18] The machines, with their whirling sharp edges, could be quite dangerous, and stories abounded of crushed and mutilated limbs.[19] One Virginia slaveowner used a thresher as an instrument of torture. Freedman Horace Muse recalled, "One woman, ole Toots Smith, make ole marser Riles mad one day. She answer him back. He took her an' tied her to de thrashin' drum o' de wheat thrasher. Den he let de fan beat her 'till she fell, an' tol' her ole man ef he want her, to come an' git her. He took her to his cabin an' de po' thing died de nex' mornin'. He tol' de res' o' us, 'Dat's what you git effen you sass me.'"[20] The enslaver terrorized the enslaved with technology.

With the increased wheat crops and the expanding human population, the number of corn and wheat mills also surged in the decades before the Civil War.[21] Even a small mill had enormous cultural and environmental impacts. Millers were among the wealthiest people in rural communities.[22] As people moved west, the mills they established became anchors for new communities. To cite just one example, the little town of Temperance Hall, Tennessee, grew up around the mill that the people enslaved by Samuel Caplinger built in 1820.[23] Native Americans adapted milling technology. In 1825, Alabama Cherokee owned thirty-one grist mills, which they were forced to abandon a decade later.[24] Millraces and ponds slowed the flow of water in creeks and small rivers, impeding the movement of fish and breeding mosquitoes, increasing the risk for malaria.[25] Mill ponds had other social significance as well: in the late 1820s, enslaved mystic and later rebellion leader Nat Turner baptized himself and a companion in Pearson's Mill Pond in Southampton County, Virginia.[26]

Skilled enslaved people frequently ran the mills of their enslavers. In an unnamed Virginia community, "Uncle Radford," an "old" enslaved man,

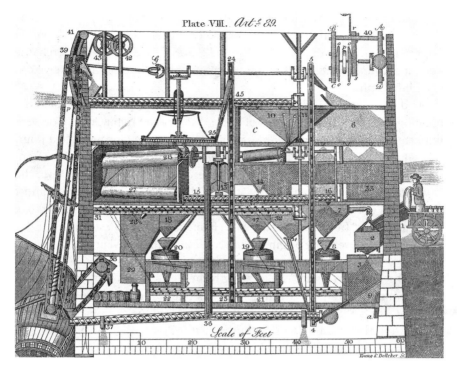

Plate VIII. *Art.ᵈ 89.*

Oliver Evans's automated mill. Published in O. Evans, *Young Mill-wright*, n.p.

ground wheat and corn for the "entire neighborhood." In Caroline County, Virginia, "Uncle Junius" operated the mill for his enslavers. Each day he went to their house to sum up the work: "Muster Brown, two bushel—Corn. Muster Black, five bushel—Wheat. Muster Green, one sack—Flour. Miss Molly White, three bushel—Corn."[27] Men like Radford and Junius bore enormous responsibilities but likely had little authority over their work.

Mechanized wheat milling began in the 1780s when Delaware native Oliver Evans devised series of elevators and conveyors to move grain through the process.[28] New steam engines further sped up milling. The steam engine in Isaac McKim's 1818 mill in Baltimore could drive eight pairs of millstones and produce 200 barrels of flour a day. While small millers found steam engines beyond their financial abilities, the machines allowed entrepreneurs to set up mills in places with limited water supplies.[29] Baltimore and Richmond became centers of capital-intense industrialized milling.[30] In 1860, the Gallego and Haxall mills in Richmond were among the largest wheat-milling complexes in the United States.[31] About 70 percent of their workers were enslaved men.[32]

Most of the lower South continued to buy wheat from other regions, particularly the Old Northwest.[33] The Spanish colonies of Louisiana and Florida imported flour from the northern United States.[34] While Florida merchants bought sugar and rum in Havana, their grain and flour came from New York and Philadelphia.[35]

As the railroad spread across the South, easier transportation created the ongoing debate about the origins of flour: Was it better to buy locally, or were imported products preferable?[36] Some merchants touted locally milled flour. J. G. Glass of Chattanooga, for example, in 1844 offered "superior" flour from Washington County, Tennessee.[37] Other merchants perceived flour from the North to be of higher quality. In 1807, consumers in Nashville paid almost three times the price of local for "imported flour."[38] Savannahians could buy "Genesee Flour" from New York, which claimed to be the finest in the world.[39] Disagreements over flour origins would continue into the twenty-first century.

FOR MANY SOUTHERNERS, cooking technology stayed the same. Left to their own devices, some African Americans built cabins with fireplaces that spoke of African traditions, placing their hearths in the centers of their cabins, venting them through a hole in the roof.[40] Enslaved women sometimes did their summer cooking outside over open fires.[41]

Chimneys called "mudcats," made of sticks and mud, still ventilated the homes of Native Americans, white settlers, and enslaved people.[42] Sylvia Cannon of South Carolina recalled the cabin provided by her enslaver: "De ground been us floor and us fireplace been down on de ground. Take sticks en make chimney cause dere won' no bricks en won' no saw mills to make lumber when I come along."[43] Such chimneys washed away in heavy rain, and they frequently caught fire. More prosperous southerners constructed fireplaces and chimneys of brick or cut stone.[44] In the antebellum period, some enslavers began erecting better lodgings for their enslaved people—whether for health reasons, for public perceptions, or in hopes of making their workforce more docile—and that included better-quality fireplaces.[45] On Butler Island, Georgia, for example, the fireplaces in the slave quarters were made of brick, either made on-site or bought in Charleston and Savannah.[46]

Outdoor ovens persisted in many places. The Koasati (Coushatta), displaced from Alabama, built large earthen ovens adjacent to their houses in northeast Louisiana.[47] Texas freedwoman Hagar Lewis clearly recalled her white enslavers' ovens, dedicated for specific purposes: "My mother was the cook. . . . There was a big light bread oven in the yard of the big house and in front of the quarters under a big tree. That one baked the pies."[48]

Banished from Canada by the British, the Acadians (later called Cajuns) began settling west of New Orleans in the 1780s. Many of them built outdoor ovens near the backs of their houses. Lacking brick and stone, the Acadians constructed ovens of a material known as *bousillage*. First they assembled a wooden platform, several feet off the ground, supported by heavy wooden posts. Then they built an earthen base on the platform and placed half a barrel, split lengthwise, on top of the base to create an arched form. The next step was making ropes of Spanish moss and immersing them in a mixture of clay and water. They then laid the ropes over the form to a thickness of six inches, leaving a hole in the rear for smoke to exit. After the clay dried for several days, they burned the wooden form, curing the clay from the inside. The builders then added a wooden door to the front and maybe a shed-type covering to protect the oven from the rain.[49]

Florida and Texas remained part of Spain until 1819 and 1821, respectively, and the houses there still reflected Spanish traditions. In St. Augustine, the detached kitchen of the Ximenez-Fatio house, built in 1798, featured a large fireplace with a domed, or beehive, coquina oven to the side.[50] In the Texas outpost of Nacogdoches, most chimneys were the mudcat type, and residents baked on the fireplace hearths. The Spanish government enacted strict laws for the highly flammable construction, with fines and jail time for careless users.[51]

On southeastern plantations, kitchens were usually in separate outbuildings: either a single room with a fireplace and chimney at one end, or two rooms with a fireplace and chimney in the middle, with one side used as housing for enslaved people.[52] At Rosegill plantation, in Virginia, for example, by 1801 the brick kitchen was a one-story building measuring twenty by forty feet, connected to the house by a covered walkway eighty-six feet long and nine feet wide.[53] In the urban South, antebellum kitchens could be either in cellars or detached. As always, the southern custom of serving freshly baked breads challenged the enslaved cooks to get their products to the table in peak condition. Thomas Bullitt observed that, though their kitchen was seventy-five feet from the house, the pancakes, waffles, and beaten biscuits arrived at the table hot, "even in the coldest winter weather."[54] This feat may have seemed magical to the enslavers but hardly so to those doing the running.

Most antebellum kitchens retained large fireplaces and hearths, with openings of five to eight feet in width, and baking still took place in the ashes.[55] The best kitchens kept the traditional brick baking oven next to the fireplace. At Cannon's Point, on St. Simons Island, Georgia, the baking oven was about three feet deep and two feet wide, big enough to bake several items at a time.[56]

The invention of the cookstove in the 1790s began to move baking from the fireplace, although the change took well over a century to complete.[57] Early cast-iron cookstoves combined ovens and cooking surfaces. They were rectangular boxes on four legs, with ovens beneath the cooking surface. The oven

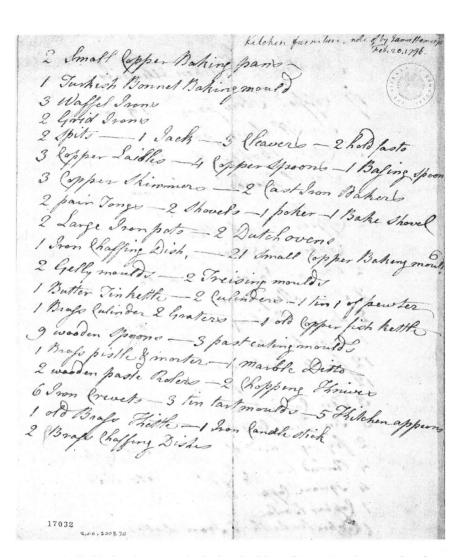

Monticello kitchen inventory in the handwriting of James Hemings, enslaved chef. Library of Congress, Manuscript Division.

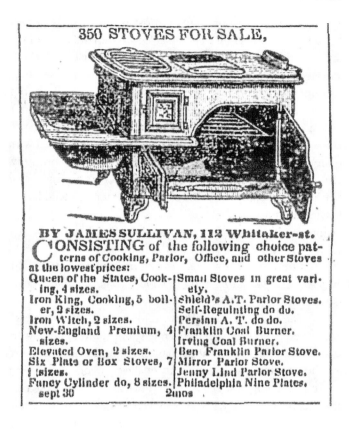

Ad for stoves, *Savannah Daily Republican*, November 17, 1851.

opened from the front or side of the rectangle, and the cook regulated the temperature by opening or closing dampers. Stoves saved a lot of fuel, and ovens in them could heat for baking in only ten or fifteen minutes. But ovens in stoves also posed considerable problems. The baker had to stoop to access the oven and open the dampers. The heat in a cast-iron oven was more uneven and patchier than the steady warmth of an old-style brick oven, producing bread that was noticeably inferior.[58]

Despite the drawbacks, southerners embraced the cookstove, and the new appliances became available as far west as Little Rock by 1819.[59] Early stoves came from the northeastern United States, often with cheery, patriotic names like "The Republic."[60] The "western market," with limited access to coal, required wood-burning stoves.[61] Southern companies also ventured into stove manufacturing, using iron from Tennessee and Georgia, guaranteed "to be equal to any made at the North in workmanship and durability."[62]

Whether with a fireplace or a stove, most ordinary white women in the South cooked for their own families. Enslaved women did most of the cooking for wealthy families, learning their skills well. The poshest households had multiple enslaved cooks, some designated as pastry cooks.[63] Some elite southerners apprenticed their enslaved cooks to pastry chefs, willing to pay freedwomen for sharing their knowledge. In Charleston, Sally Seymour and her daughter Eliza Lee taught enslaved cooks, who then brought high prices when they were sold.[64] A young enslaved woman named Amy trained with Camilla Dunstan, another well-regarded free pastry cook in Charleston. Amy's enslavers paid Dunstan for Amy's room and board as well as her instruction.[65] The enslavers either could enjoy the skills of these women or could have the profit of the sale with the added value.

Some white southerners acknowledged the labor done by enslaved cooks. Georgian Emily Burke observed, "Of all the house-servants, I thought the task of the cook was the most laborious." The morning's first chore, Burke commented, was gathering kindling and firewood: "To get as much fuel as she will want to use in preparing the breakfast she is often obliged to go into the woods several times." The cook then set about grinding the corn for breakfast meal. The cycle repeated itself three times each day, until, after cooking supper and washing dishes, the cook began the preparations for the next day's breakfast.[66]

Besides the physical work, being an enslaved cook included emotional labor—the toll of being under constant critical scrutiny and facing often unreasonable expectations. Wealthy southerners worried incessantly about enslaved people stealing sugar and flour. They often kept supplies under lock and key, allowing just enough for a given project so that any theft would be obvious.[67] Harriet Jacobs recalled the cruel stinginess of her enslaver, Mrs. Flint: She "weighed out by the pound and ounce, three times a day. I can assure you she gave [the enslaved people] no chance to eat wheatbread from her flour barrel. She knew how many biscuits a quart of flour would make, and exactly what size they ought to be."[68] Enslaved people took advantage of lapses in security to get some of the good stuff for themselves. David Lee recalled swiping sugar: "Missus, she had a big barrel ob lumpy sugah in de pantry. De doo' was ginnerly liked, but sometimes when hit was hopen, ah'd go in and take a han' fu'."[69] Enslaved people also stole finished baked goods, such as biscuits, but those were harder to get away with.[70]

Enslaved cooks suffered harsh penalties for performing less than perfectly. Elizabeth Sparks bitterly remembered punishments meted out by her enslaver's mother, "a mean ol' thin'": "She'd give the cook jes' so much meal to make bread fum an' effen she burnt it, she'd be scared to death 'cause they'd whup her. I remember plenty of times the cook ask say, 'Marsa please 'scuse dis bread, hit's a little too brown.' Yessir! Beat the devil out 'er if she burn dat bread."[71] Liza Brown recalled even worse treatment of her mother, the cook for an "ol' 'oman [who] was de devil" and a "hell pigeon": "When mother was in pregnant stage, if she happened to burn de bread or biscuits, Missus would order her to the granary, make her take off all her clothes . . . sometimes 'twon' but one piece. After she had stripped her stark naked she would beat mother with a strap. You know it had so many prongs to hit you wid."[72] These white women had no empathy for their enslaved cooks.

Some slave-owning women baked or knew enough about it to supervise and instruct their cooks. Alabama minister's wife Lucilla McCorkle observed in 1850, "The mistress should herself know how to perform these [duties of enslaved people] and if she occasionally *chooses* to do it *her self cheerfully* it will have an excellent effect."[73] Published cookbooks became plentiful in the new nation. The first came from England. Many southern matrons owned copies of Hannah Glasse's *Art of Cookery*, an English cookbook originally published in 1747 and first printed in the United States in 1805.[74] In Norfolk, Virginia, Elizabeth Myers and the women who worked in her household dog-eared their copy of *The Experienced English Housekeeper*, written by Elizabeth Raffald in 1789.[75] When American cookbook publishing exploded in the early nineteenth century, with northern experts such as Catharine Beecher spreading their wisdom, southern women acquired those volumes, too. Southerners published their first cookbooks in the antebellum period. The first was *The Virginia Housewife*, by Richmond boardinghouse keeper Mary Randolph in 1824. Next was *The Carolina Receipt Book*, published in 1832 by "A Lady of Charleston," whom historians Jane Aldrich and Donna Gabaccia identified as New England immigrant Caroline Howard Gilman.[76] Mother of nine and the wife of a physician, Lettice Bryan wrote *The Kentucky Housewife* in 1839. Sarah Rutledge, the unmarried daughter of a wealthy rice planter, published *The Carolina Housewife* in 1847. These southern cookbooks all tied themselves to specific locations, perhaps indicative of differences in climate and growing nationalism. Elite women consulted all these books as well as many published in the North.

WE KNOW A LOT about the foods of enslaved people in the nineteenth century because of oral history interviews led by the Federal Writers' Project in the 1930s. For the most part, the daily diet of enslaved people consisted of cornmeal and fat pork, distributed by their enslavers, sometimes in short supply. Many enslaved people augmented their foods as best they could with garden plots, foraging, hunting, bartering, or stealing. If they had any chance to earn cash, they often spent it on food.[77] Enslavers, whatever their motivations, occasionally gave victuals as treats, including lard, sugar, molasses, and wheat flour, and sometimes gingerbread and plum pudding at Christmas.[78] Solomon Northrup observed, "Only the slave who has lived all the years on his scanty allowance of meal and bacon, can appreciate such suppers."[79] But on ordinary days, most enslaved people dealt with relentless rounds of corn and hog.

Enslaved people called cornbread "Johnny Constant," for it was always on their menu. Some suspected that it would accompany them to the afterworld, singing,

> W'en I come to die, you mus'n' bury me deep,
> But put Sogrum molasses close by my feet.
> Put a pone o' co'n bread way down in my han'.
> Gwineter sop on de way to the Promus' Lan'.[80]

Large plantations often had central kitchens from which enslaved people received cooked meals, theoretically a gesture toward efficiency.[81] Beverly Jones from Virginia remembered his mother cooking for the fieldworkers. "My mother was they cook, used to have to get up at sunrise to fix the food for the great house. First thing she did was to feed the [enslaved people]. That didn' take no time. Jes' give them home-made meat an' hoe-cake, an' sometimes fish. . . . She used to cook hoecakes in a big iron pan, two or three at a time."[82]

Virtually all enslaved people who cooked for themselves used open fire. Austin Pen Parnell from Arkansas vividly described the skill with which his grandmother baked ash cakes. First, "she'd take a poker before she put the bread in and rake the ashes off the hearth down to the solid stone or earth bottom, and the ashes would be banked in two hills to one side and the other." She then made a batter of cornmeal and water. "She could put it together and take it in her hand and pat it out flat and lay it on the hearth. It would be just as round! That was the art of it!" The cakes, Parnell recalled, were "about an inch thick and about nine inches across." His grandmother put three cakes down at one time and let them bake until they were almost firm, then covered them with ashes: "The cakes had to be dry before they were covered up, because if the ashes ever stuck to them while they were wet, there would be ashes back on the top of the cakes." The cakes baked about ten or twelve minutes, "then she'd rake down the hearth gently, backward and forward, with the poker till she got down to them and then she'd put the poker under them and lift them out." He concluded, "We'd get that hoecake out of the ashes and wash it off until it looked like it was as clean as bread cooked in a skillet. . . . The bread would have a good firm crust on it. But it didn't get too hard for us to eat and enjoy."[83] Enslaved people also continued the practice of wrapping their cakes in leaves, including collards and corn shucks, before baking them on the hearth.[84]

Horace Pippin, *The Hoecake*, 1946. New Jersey State Museum.

As their ancestors had done, enslaved people made hoecakes of meal, water, and fat if they had it and baked them on flat pieces of metal on open hearths.[85] So close was the association of enslaved people with corn cakes that Harriet Jones of Texas recalled a racist rhyme in which the body of the enslaved person literally became the utensil for baking the hoecake, either putting it on an enslaved person's heel and "hold[ing] it to the sun" or wrapping it around the person's stomach and "hold[ing] it there all day."[86]

A special treat, at hog-killing time in the fall, was cracklings, the pieces of crisp pork left after rendering lard, added to the cornbread to give taste and texture. Aleck Woodward of South Carolina recalled, "Us didn't get white flour bread, but de cracklin' bread was called on our place 'de sweet savor of life.'"[87] Crackling cornbread was probably available only to a select group of enslaved people, for few of them had hogs of their own.

Enslaved people with relatively humane enslavers received molasses regularly. Meaner enslavers allowed molasses, rich in iron, only for nursing mothers, skilled laborers, and the oldest enslaved people. The stingiest enslavers gave molasses only at Christmas, or not at all. Enslaved people who could earn wages or produce goods for barter supplied themselves with the sweet syrup.[88] They topped their cooked bread with molasses rather than baked it into the dough. Alex Montgomery from Mississippi recalled, "We had thick black lasses an' sometime we got a piece uf bread an' dug a hole inside uf it an' den filled dat hole wid lasses, an' dat wus jes' like cake to us. All de cake we eber had to eat wuds made wid meal and lasses."[89]

Just as cornbread was "Johnny Constant," enslaved people called bread made from wheat flour "Billy Seldom."[90] Some enslaved people never tasted wheat bread, and others experienced it only on special occasions.[91] Monroe Brackins, from Texas, remembered, "Once in a while, on a Sunday morning, we'd get biscuit flour to eat. It was a treat to us. . . . We lived on cornbread, mostly."[92] The flour that enslaved people received was often of poor quality. One Virginia enslaver sent wheat for his enslaved people to the mill, only to have the miller reject it because it had weevils.[93] Many enslavers issued their enslaved people "middlings," "shorts," or "seconds"—coarsely ground flour with large portions of bran still in it. Lizzie Williams, from Mississippi, remembered, "Sometimes we'd have biscuits made out o' what was called de 2nds. De white folks allus got de 1st's."[94]

White southerners consumed wheat flour as their locations and budgets allowed. As always, the easiest, most common types of wheat breads were pancakes, waffles, and wafers. Still often served for breakfast, they might also appear on the midday or evening table as the entrée or dessert. One fashionable variation was called "quire of paper" because the cakes were extremely thin—like a sheet of paper—and one needed a stack of them to make a serving. (A quire is about twenty-five pieces of paper.)[95] The family of Robert E. Lee served them for dessert at their Arlington plantation, perhaps from flour made of wheat grown and milled by people enslaved by the Lees.[96]

In the seventy-five years after the American Revolution, the availability of sugar in the South skyrocketed and prices plummeted. Fast ships brought sugar from Brazil, Cuba, St. Croix, and "Portorico."[97] Domestic sugar production also jumped. Ribbon cane, originally from Jamaica, arrived in Louisiana in 1825, and fifty years later, Louisiana sugar made up almost a quarter of the world's supply.[98] With increasing availability and falling prices, sugar consumption in the United States grew from ten pounds per capita in 1820 to almost thirty-three pounds per person by 1860.[99]

Southerners enthusiastically acquired sugar by barter and purchase. Alexandria, Virginia, merchant John Murray offered three kinds of sugar in return for "cash, tobacco, flour, or ginseng," the wild root prized as a folk medicine.[100] Inhabitants of early Nashville took animal pelts and corn to New Orleans and returned with sugar as well as coffee, tea, rice, and molasses.[101] Enslaved southerners worked extra hours for money to buy sugar and molasses as well as flour.[102]

Solomon Northrup, a freedman who was kidnapped into slavery and hired out on a sugar plantation in Avoyelles Parish, Louisiana, described sugar cultivation in the 1840s. Gangs planted cane in January and then hoed the fields three times. In October, enslaved people cut the ripened cane with thin-bladed knives, "fifteen inches long, three inches wide in the middle, and tapering toward the point and handle." Young enslaved people gathered the cane into a wagon and took it to the sugarhouse on the plantation.

At the sugarhouses, enslaved people operated the mills and the boiling kettles.[103] Some mills turned with animal power, but Northrup's employer ran an "immense" mill with the latest technology—and enslaved people. Enslaved children unloaded cane onto "an endless carrier." A steam engine powered "two great iron rollers, between two and three feet in diameter and six or eight feet in length . . . [that] roll in towards each other." The rollers crushed the cane and extracted the juice, which was then filtered. The juice heated to boiling in kettles perhaps six feet in diameter and then flowed through iron pans and into wooden boxes with fine-wire bottoms, called coolers. When the boiling juice hit the coolers, the sugar granulated—turned into grains—and the leftover liquid, molasses, ran through the wire into a cistern.[104] Cheap in dollars but dear in cost, slave-made sugar spread into Americans' kitchens.

Quick wheat breads without yeast were easily made and served hot and fresh. Some "Bunns" and batter breads were made from wheat flour, eggs, and milk, then baked in "moulds" in a "quick," or hot, oven.[105] Other cakes, some with fanciful names like "bops" and "Zephyrinas," had the same ingredients, sometimes baked in pans or on "plates" or rolled flat before baking.[106]

Particularly in the Low Country, cooks created quick breads from rice. Though rice by itself still made poor bread, Charleston merchants increasingly offered rice flour in the early nineteenth century.[107] More commonly, cooks combined boiled rice with wheat flour, dressing it up with varied combinations of eggs, salt, butter, or milk. They baked it in a variety of forms: loaf bread, griddle cakes, crumpets, muffins, waffles, wafers.[108]

Enslaved Low Country people usually ate their rice boiled rather than baked, and their bread was usually made from corn. On Sapelo Island, however, they kept African traditions with a rice cake called *saraka*. The daughters of Bilali Muhammad, a captured Guinean man, continued making *saraka* from soaked rice and honey or sugar for Muslim fast days. Shad Hall recalled his grandmother Hester Smith creating cake of rice or cornmeal and honey on the first of every month. She gave every family member a cake, "den we all stands roun table, and she says, 'Ameen, Ameen,' an we all eats cake."[109]

Almost all white rural southerners had chickens, and sometimes enslaved people kept hens and sold or bartered eggs.[110] Housekeepers might trade eggs and other goods with their neighbors. Still, eggs could be hard to come by, particularly when the hens slowed or stopped laying during the fall and winter. Anna King wrote to her daughter in 1851, "I did want so much to send you cake but there was not an egg to be had for love or money."[111]

The South had only a quarter of the cows in the United States, and those were held in small numbers rather than at large dairies.[112] Even the wealthy sometimes had trouble getting dairy products. Sarah Watkins of Mississippi complained that her husband wanted dessert every day: "That is too often to suit my convenience. This time of the year the eggs are needed for setting. The cows are decreasing in milk and it takes eggs, butter and milk to make most deserts [sic]."[113] Even rich people had to bow before the seasons.

The southern climate made making and keeping butter difficult. Traveler Emily Burke commented that one never saw "good butter" in the "warm seasons"; rather, it came to the table in a "fluid state."[114] Those who could afford it bought butter from the North.[115] The most prized butter had the appellation of "Goshen," from the Hudson Valley of New York. By the 1840s, merchants sold "Goshen butter" all the way to Texas.[116]

Sweet quick breads were old friends—Naples biscuits, for example, and gingerbread in many forms.[117] Rusks were still baked to last. Eliza Middleton Fisher wrote of their usefulness on her journey from Charleston to Philadelphia in 1841: "Had it not been for Mrs. F's kind present of Rusks I should have almost starved on the road. I ate 4 for 2 days—the bread was not eatable at the inns, & all the party partook of the rusks."[118]

Southerners still used the English word "biscuit" for some labor-intensive, un-yeasted antebellum sweets. Beaten almonds—whether sweet, bitter, or mimicked with peach kernels, like noyau—and flour formed the basis of popular sweet breads. Almonds were by far the most common nut imported into the South, and a few wealthy southerners cultivated almond trees.[119] Delicate sponge biscuits had twelve egg yolks beaten for half an hour, powdered sugar, egg whites, flour, and lemon rind, baked in "tin moulds."[120]

In the nineteenth century, "biscuit" also gradually came to mean the small cakes with brown exteriors and soft interiors that hold such a strong place in southern sentiments. They were a special treat to the enslaved southerners. Benny Dillard, from Georgia, observed, "Us had biscuit once a week, dat was Sunday breakfast, and dem biscuits was cakebread to us."[121] Having one's fill of biscuits and molasses delighted enslaved people at hog-killing time, according to Henry Barnes of Alabama.[122]

Beaten biscuits, the thin, crunchy cakes tenderized with many whacks of a heavy weight such as an ax handle, were common in the antebellum period, at least in part because enslaved people could be compelled to do the repetitive, tedious labor. Cookbook author Mary Randolph stipulated that the biscuits should be beaten for half an hour with a pestle, rolled "past thin," and baked carefully, as they burned quickly.[123] While white southerners waxed rapturous over them, to the enslaved, beaten biscuits had quite a different connotation. Freedman Louis Hughes, from Mississippi, recalled the attack on Delia, an enslaved woman, by her enslaver after guests left: "By this time she was in the kitchen, confronting Delia. Her face was flushed as she screamed out: 'What kind of biscuits were those you baked this week?' 'I think they were all right, Mis Sarh.' 'Hush!' screamed out the madam, stamping her foot to make it more emphatic. 'You did not half cook them,' said she; 'they were not beat enough.'" Hughes continued, "They did not use baking powder, as we do now, but the biscuits were beaten until light enough. Twenty minutes was the time allotted for this work; but when company came there was so much to be done—so many more dishes to prepare, that Delia would, perhaps, not have so much time for each meal. But there was no allowance made."[124] Delia and Miss Sarah had opposing interpretations of the greatness of beaten biscuit.

The simplest biscuit doughs were wheat flour, butter or lard, and salt. Others might have eggs, sugar, milk, butter, or cream. Henry Barnes recalled, "Dey made up biscuits in de big wood trays. Dem trays was made outten tupelo gum an' dey was light as a fedder."[125] The dough could be dropped from a spoon or patted out and cut into round cakes with a drinking glass or a biscuit cutter.[126]

Many nineteenth-century biscuit makers took quickly to chemical leavening, which introduced air into baked goods through the reaction of acid and alkali. Caroline Howard Gilman recommended pearl ash (potassium carbonate), made from ashes soaked in water, for a "Fine Light Biscuit," saving "all that tedious process of beating."[127] Soda (sodium bicarbonate) and saleratus (potassium bicarbonate) became more prevalent.[128] All these alkaline chemicals needed acids to activate them. Lettice Bryan understood the chemistry, emphasizing the need for sour milk in her biscuit recipes: "Otherwise, it will not rise so well."[129] The greatest innovation before the Civil War was Eben Horsford's patented combination of monocalcium phosphate, made from beef and mutton bones, and baking soda.[130] Confoundingly, Horsford called the combination "yeast powder," though it had no yeast in it. His invention, the forerunner of baking powder, guaranteed that baking would never be the same.

Because of the large number of pigs in the South, almost all free southerners had some access to lard.[131] In town, residents bought lard from local grocers.[132] The priciest was leaf lard, the fat from around the pig's kidneys and loins, mild in flavor and thus ideally suited for baking. Although there were plenty of local pigs, a Little Rock merchant touted his leaf lard "just received direct from Cincinnati," which was quickly gaining its reputation as "Porkopolis."[133] For enslaved people, however, lard could be scarce, reserved by enslavers as an indulgence. After enslaved people cooked their pork, they sometimes baked bread in the remaining grease, tenderizing and flavoring the dough.[134]

Loaf bread made from wheat flour and leavened with yeast, often called "light bread," had high value in the antebellum South.[135] Bread was suitable as a gift or for elegant refreshment. Sarah Haynsworth Gayle received "with infinite pleasure . . . an enormous loaf, a fine one of wheat-bread," from a Mrs. Peck, and she noted that the wife of Dr. John Hunter served "light-bread, butter and jelly" to callers.[136]

Southern women, whether enslaved or free, knew that good loaf bread did not appear by magic but rather through careful action and some luck. Tryphena Fox wrote about the shortcomings of Mary, an enslaved woman, who "cooks almost everything in good order, excepting light-bread. I have let her try twice & she has brought me in, both times heavy, sour bread, not fit to be eaten in any way."[137] Letitia Burwell recalled that in her Virginia community, her elite peers enjoyed "hot loaf" in the morning and evening, with cornbread at midday. Each plantation, Burwell contended, "was famed for its loaf bread," distinct from all others.[138] Fresh bread in the morning meant that an enslaved woman had gotten up in the wee hours to make sure the bread was ready when her enslavers wanted it.

While urban cooks could buy yeast from commercial bakeries, many antebellum households continued to manufacture their own.[139] "Common yeast" was made from hops, usually imported from the North, boiled in water, and strained. The maker then added enough flour to create a thin batter, yeast from a previous batch or purchased from a local brewer, enough "corn meal as will make it the consistency of biscuit dough," and sometimes brown sugar. Experts recommended fashioning the yeast into little cakes that could be dried and stored.[140] Potatoes—boiled, mashed, and mixed with hops—also provided good rising material.[141] Women shared gifts of yeast and recipes for its manufacture. A Mrs. Hawkins gave Sarah Watkins some "Magic Yeast" and the formula to mix more. It made, Watkins said, "right good bread."[142]

Many southern cooks continued to shape their yeasted doughs into individual rolls, buns, or cakes rather than large loaves.[143] These small breads usually consisted of wheat flour, milk, butter or "good lard," yeast, salt, and sometimes eggs.[144] Inventive cooks might add currants or raisins or change the starches with potatoes, rye flour, or rice.[145] Raisins were by far the most common dried fruit in the South. Nearly every general store in the South stocked them, and, as in the past, families could make their own from grapes.[146] A new favorite was "Sally Lunn buns," a rich bread supposedly named for a woman in Bath, England, which appeared in England in the 1780s and became a big hit throughout the United States early in the nineteenth century. Caroline Gilman made hers from milk, yeast, and flour, after which she added butter, let it rise, and baked it on tins.[147]

By 1800, pies and pastry crusts had evolved into highly prized concoctions of wheat flour, fat, and little else, with the elusive goals of tenderness and flakiness. The value of an enslaved cook could rise with her pastry-making ability. Rosalie Stier Calvert of Maryland observed in 1796, "Fanny is an excellent cook. She can make all sorts of cakes, pastries, sausages, bread, etc."[148] Some plantation mistresses claimed to make pastry—with the help of enslaved women. South Carolinian Keziah Hopkins bragged, "Sylvia and myself . . . succeeded in making beautiful paste for the pudding."[149]

Cookbook author Lettice Bryan cataloged the variety of pastes and their purposes. Plain paste, a simple mixture of flour, butter, salt, and water, was useful for pies, dumplings, and breakfast cakes. Standing paste, a tougher mixture of butter, salt, and sweet milk, beaten with a rolling pin, was for fruit pies and rolls. Pastry for meat pies could be created with lard, suet, or beef drippings. Sweet paste, made with flour, powdered white sugar, eggs, and wine, was "for shells and tarts of the finest quality." Puff paste remained the crowning glory of pastry.[150]

Still-popular mince pies retained their bases of beef—tongue, roast, or suet.[151] Lettice Bryan offered six versions, all baked in a double crust (a crust on both the bottom and top). She pulled out all the stops for "the Finest Mince . . . too costly to be used for common purposes." To beef tongue and suet, she added raisins, "the best pippin apples," currants, sugar, preserved citron, sweet and bitter almonds, orange and lemon juice and peel, nutmeg, mace, cinnamon, Madeira (Spanish wine), and French brandy, all to be baked "in the finest puff paste."[152]

Apples grew abundantly in the up-country, and elite southerners prided themselves on their orchards.[153] A major breakthrough in apple cultivation occurred in 1792, when Quaker minister Ann Jessup grafted cuttings from England onto North Carolina trees. Enthusiasts planted Jessup trees all over North Carolina and then to the west.[154] Southerners in areas too warm to raise apples imported them, sometimes by the barrel.[155] Pears grew easily across the South.[156] Formerly enslaved Levi Pollard recalled that pears were considered special "for de house" of his enslavers—but he also took the opportunity to enjoy them. "Co'se I stole 'em," he admitted, adding, "Dey sure was good."[157]

Tarts were small, individual pies, often filled with preserved fruit or jelly and baked in patty-pans.[158] The celebrated—though enslaved—St. Simons cook Sans Foix served "marmalade tartlets" to an elite gathering in 1821.[159] Lettice Bryan created tarts from all sorts of fresh fruits, particularly berries— homegrown, gathered from the wild, or store-bought—stewing them and putting them in crusts of plain or puff pastry.[160] Enslaved people picked wild berries and sold or bartered them for other foods. At least one enslaved woman staked her freedom on them. In 1814, Betty, declared a runaway, was last seen by her enslaver on her way to Savannah "with a basket, some huckle-berrys and a quart measure."[161]

Peaches for tarts could be "mash[ed] to a smooth marmalade" and added to sweet cream and powdered sugar, or they could be stewed and baked in a double crust in a patty-pan.[162] Peaches grew abundantly in the wild, and Native Americans and enslaved African Americans made good use of them.[163] They were also the subject of horticultural experiments, with at least thirty-eight varieties in cultivation on Thomas Jefferson's estates.[164] Cherry tarts were made from pitted cherries, baked in a double crust.[165] Cherries flourished in cooler parts of the South and received intense interest from elite planters. They were shipped to warmer parts of the South in boxes.[166]

Cooks also baked small individual pies to eat out of one's hands. "Puffs" were fashioned of puff or sweet pastry. The cook rolled the paste into circles, added stewed apples or strawberry or raspberry jam, and then folded the pas-try into a "half moon" before baking. Fried pies could be made of "any kind of nice fruit," especially dried. The pastry was sturdy and fried in "a pan of boil-ing butter" before being sent to the table warm.[167]

The treasured dish that today we call cobbler was more often called a pot pie, and southerners considered it "homely" fare.[168] Louis Hughes viv-idly remembered peach cobblers made in Dutch ovens for enslaved people's (ironic) Independence Day celebrations: "The crust or pastry of the cobbler was prepared in large earthen bowls, then rolled out like any pie crust, only it was almost twice as thick. A layer of this crust was laid in the oven, then a half peck of peaches poured in, followed by a layer of sugar; then a covering of pastry was laid over all and smoothed around with a knife. The oven was then put over a bed of coals, the cover put on and coals thrown on it, and the process of baking began."[169]

Southern cooks still called egg-based pie fillings puddings. Some were cooked custards of eggs, milk, sugar, and lemon, poured into prebaked shells.[170] Sometimes the filling baked along with the crust, as for Sarah Rut-ledge's "Citron Pudding." She made a layer of paste, then covered it with cit-ron. The top layer was a mixture of butter, sugar, eggs, nutmeg, rose water, and lemon juice.[171] These pies all rested on a single, or bottom-only, crust.

Tropical fruits might be homegrown in warm climates or greenhouses, but most people bought them in stores. Oranges and lemons were available as far west as Little Rock by 1839.[172] Exotic fruits like coconuts, pineapples, and citron appeared in southern stores by the 1820s.[173] "Pine Apple Pudding"— grated fresh pineapple, butter, sugar, eggs, and grated bread—could be baked either with or without a crust.[174] Pineapples became more plentiful with the establishment of plantations to grow them and the invention of steamboats to bring the fruit from the tropics.[175] Coconut puddings were baked in puff paste. Caroline Gilman's recipe was particularly rich, with three coconuts "grated and dried," sugar, butter, fifteen egg yolks, and rose water.[176]

Cheesecakes—different from the cream-cheese confections that we enjoy—occupied a middle space between custards and pies and were often served at fancy occasions like balls and weddings.[177] The recipes had been around since the 1750s, but they were daunting for home cooks. The cook first prepared the soft cheese by boiling whole milk, then adding white wine, rennet, or eggs and stirring the mixture until a curd formed. The cook then drained the whey and added butter, sugar, and sometimes flour. The mixture could be flavored with nutmeg, cinnamon, lemon, brandy, wine, or rose water. The individual cakes could be baked in small pans or in puff pastry shells.[178]

Fried wheat dough had its place on southern tables. The most common kind, balls of dough cooked in boiling lard, were called fritters. The ever-practical Lettice Bryan offered her counsel: make the batter thick, "as if made thin, they will soak the lard in which they are fried, and be greasy and heavy, and of course not good."[179] Apples and peaches could also be made into fritters: seasoned with nutmeg, cinnamon, or brandy, dipped in a flour-based batter, and fried in butter or lard.[180]

Sweet fried breads, variously called crullers and doughnuts, or even by the Dutch name oly-koek, were also popular.[181] Before the Civil War, doughnuts were shaped like nuts—hence the name.[182] They were generally combinations of flour, eggs, sugar, and milk, sometimes with yeast and sometimes without.[183] Caroline Gilman seasoned hers with rose water and ginger, and she advised, "Hogs-lard is better than butter to fry them in," probably because lard could get hotter than butter before burning.[184] Lettice Bryan added raisins, lemon rind, wine, eggs, pearl ash, and sour milk. She rolled the dough several times and fashioned it into "little cones or oval shaped cakes" before frying it in butter.[185]

Many sweets were the flattened doughs, rolled and cut, that we today would call cookies, but people in the nineteenth century still called them cakes.[186] After centuries, gingerbread was still the most common type of cake/cookie. Cretia Stewart made gingerbread, rolled thin and cut in squares, every

Sunday for the children of her enslavers in Charleston. Susan Pringle, away at school in New York, received a shipment of Stewart's ginger cakes in 1845.[187] The basic ingredients varied little, though sometimes cooks added orange marmalade or peel, cinnamon, mace, cloves, allspice, or citron. They might cut the dough into strips or diamonds or circles.[188]

Jumbles were still rolled thin and twisted into fancy shapes.[189] Lettice Bryan, never content to leave things plain, added nutmeg, cinnamon, cloves, essence of lemon, and white wine to hers. She instructed the cook to cut the dough into strips, put them on buttered tin sheets, and then "twist them round, regularly concatenating them together so as to form small rings," finally brushing them with egg white and sprinkling with sugar before baking.[190]

Wafers, the thin cakes baked in special irons, could also be sugary indulgences. Like their plainer counterparts, sweet wafers started with flour, butter, and eggs. They might be flavored with nutmeg, citron, cinnamon, lemon, peach water (similar to noyau) or rose water, wine, or brandy. Once the wafers came out of the irons, cooks generally rolled and served them quickly.[191] They required a deft hand.

The sweets that we call cakes—large creations intended to be cut into pieces before serving—were offered by wealthy southerners on special occasions.[192] Jane Henry Thomas remembered an 1829 party in Nashville to celebrate an election victory. The fare included "all kinds of large and small cakes, confectionery, and fruits."[193] Weddings and birthdays merited cakes as well. Sarah A. Watkins wrote to her daughter in 1861 about the efforts of their enslaved male cook: "I had a cake made in honor of your birthday. I told Robin if he made it nice, I would write that you must bring him a present. He baked it very nice so you will have to bring him a pipe for it."[194]

If enslaved people got to enjoy cake, it was usually as a gift from their enslavers, and even then not of the best materials. Elizabeth Croghan of Kentucky recorded a "blunder" made by the cook enslaved by their family in 1810: "Aunt had a large cak made of brown sugar for the servoants and Coock Robin thru mistake toock one of Aunts best cakes and left her the one that was made of brown suger."[195] We might wonder how much of a "mistake" Cook Robin really made as his comrades enjoyed top-notch cake for a change.

Cakes remained labor-intensive. Lettice Bryan gave careful instructions for preparing ingredients that she specified should be only of the highest quality—a note repeated by many cookbook authors throughout the nineteenth century. Sugar was to be weighed, broken up, spread on a cloth, crushed to a fine powder with a rolling pin, and sieved. Butter was to be washed once or twice, making sure to remove all salt, then worked with a wooden paddle to eliminate all the water. Egg whites were to be beaten "in an earthen dish to a stiff froth, using a broad-bladed knife, small hickory rods or a bunch of wire, bent in hoops or broken." Fruits and seasonings should be prepared a day ahead, "as a good deal of time is required to prepare them in a proper manner." Raisins had to be seeded, cut in half, and then sprinkled with flour to prevent them from sticking together. Almonds were to be scalded in hot water until the skins slipped off, then dried and "pounded one or two at a time in a marble mortar, with a little orange flour [sic] or rose water, to prevent them oiling and to make them white and light, removing them as you pound them." Citron was to be cut in large slips, as it couldn't be tasted if cut too finely. Currants and coconuts had to be prepared the same day they were used—the currants picked over, washed, dried, and dredged with flour; coconuts peeled, washed, and grated fine. Seasonings were to be pounded fine, then strained. Bryan concluded, "If these directions, together with what I will hereafter give in each receipt, be carefully followed and dexterously performed, you may safely calculate on having the best of cake."[196] That is, of course, if one could then mix the cake and bake it successfully.

Fruitcakes became a way for enslaved cooks to make their reputations. Nellie Smith of Georgia recalled, "Why, Child, two of the best cake-makers I ever knew used them old ovens for bakin' the finest kinds of pound cakes and fruit cakes, and evvybody knows them cakes was the hardest kinds to bake we had in them days. Aunt Betsey Cole was a great cake-baker then. She belonged to the Hulls, what lived off down below here somewhere but, when there was to be a big weddin' or some 'specially important dinner in Athens, folks 'most always sent for Aunt Betsey to bake the cakes. Aunt Laura McCrary was a great cake-maker too."[197] The cooks' enslavers might have loaned them to their neighbors as favors, or they might have charged for the labor of their human property. One wonders if Betsey Cole or Laura McCrary received any reward other than praise. On the other hand, enslavers complained about unsuccessful fruitcakes. Anna King grumbled in 1856 that her daughter would have to get her fruitcake "iced over as Clementine made quite a botch of it."[198]

Elite southerners served fruitcakes at their weddings. Guests took slices of cake home with them, and the family of the bride sent pieces to distant friends and relatives. Eliza Middleton Fisher wrote to her mother in 1840 that her wedding cake, shipped from her hometown of Charleston, had finally arrived at her new Philadelphia home after almost a year. She commented, "After 10 months delay, it is of course not quite as fresh as ever but is still in sufficiently good preservation to be sent round, and accordingly it is cut up for that purpose."[199] Fisher's new friends would have tokens almost surely made by one of the many hundreds of people enslaved by her father.

Enslavers, perhaps pleased that enslaved people wanted to form stable unions, sometimes made big deals over their human possessions' weddings, providing cakes or other goodies.[200] Maggie Bond of Arkansas remembered that her enslaver baked her wedding cake, and two other white women "made two baskets full of maple biscuits for my wedding. They was the best cake. Made in big layers and cut and iced. Two laundry baskets full to the brim."[201] The enslaved peoples' wedding cakes were not the extravaganzas that white people enjoyed, but baking marked a happy occasion anyway.

Sponge cakes, light with eggs and no fat, dairy, or leavening, developed during the eighteenth century and attained great favor in the antebellum period. They were difficult to make and served mostly on special occasions.[202] The basic recipes separated numerous eggs—usually between twelve and twenty, sometimes as many as thirty-six—into yolks and whites, with the whites whipped by hand and combined into the batter separately. In those days before rotary eggbeaters, a cook would be fortunate to have a sturdy whisk or wooden "rods" for the job. Sponge cakes were most often flavored with lemon rind and juice, sometimes iced and sometimes not.[203]

And sometimes cake was all about the icing. Sarah Rutledge's recipe for boiled icing was challenging: a pound and a half of sugar boiled in water "until it ropes" (thread stage, 234 degrees Fahrenheit), seven egg whites beaten "to a stiff froth," and then the whole beaten for an hour.[204] Lettice Bryan recommended colored icing. Pink came from cochineal, a dye produced from an insect of the same name, while purple, pink, and yellow colorings were concocted from the juice of preserved fruits.[205]

Iced cakes sprouted all kinds of ornaments. Jane Henry remembered a dance in Nashville about 1812: "At supper they had iced cakes with sprigs of cedar stuck in them. Tied to the cedar were white roses made of tissue-paper. I made the roses."[206] Lettice Bryan used "devices and borders in white sugar, which you may obtain at the confectioner's," and leaves and flowers, both artificial and real.[207] But it would be hard to top Catherine Ann Devereux Edmonston, who went to great pains to ice a "marvellous cake" for her parents' fiftieth wedding anniversary. (Apparently someone else, likely an enslaved person, baked the cake, and Edmondston decorated it.) She brought ornaments from New York and added her parents' monograms and the initials of their children, comfits, "sugar plums" (presumably some sort of hard-sugar candy), and "festoons." She concluded that she was "more proud" of her creation than any French chef.[208]

Charlottes became ever more desirable.[209] The cook began with a base of sliced sponge cake or bread, placed on the bottom and sides of a dish, perhaps soaked with sweet wine or almond-flavored ratafia liqueur. The filling could be a varied combination of apples, brown sugar, butter, or lemon peel, layered with bread or cake, and baked.[210] Another version featured raspberry jam or jelly, mixed with beaten egg whites.[211] The charlotte russe, invented by the French chef Marie-Antoine Carême in the early nineteenth century, appeared often in the most stylish homes. Consisting of flavored whipped cream poured over sponge cake and then chilled (which required ice or another cooling method), a charlotte russe proved that those who provided it were among the fashionable people of the world.[212]

AS TOWNS DEVELOPED, so did the outlets for southerners to buy baked goods. For travelers, eating at an inn or a hotel was the closest thing to being at home. Charlestonian Eliza Middleton Fisher wrote to her mother from Richmond of "Pancakes and Pound cake with tumblers of milk! . . . We were glad to find ourselves once more on the verge of civilization if not at its very center."[213] Although travel writers loved to complain about food, some hotels provided excellent baked goods. Frederick Law Olmsted compared the inn-keeping ability of a Mrs. Barclay near Raleigh to Robert Burns's talent as a poet. A supper of many dishes included two "preparations" of maize and wheat cakes.[214] Even plain fare could be fine, as English visitor John Smyth found, as breakfast at Stewart's "ordinary," or inn, probably in southern Virginia, consisted of "toasted Indian hoe-cake and very excellent cyder."[215]

Locals, too, enjoyed eating at hotels. When William Bullitt craved the cherry pie that his health-conscious wife, Mildred, forbade him, he got it at the original Galt House in Louisville.[216] In Tallahassee, the Planters' Hotel in 1830 hosted a sugar-soaked version of "ladies' night." At a cotillion party, the "Gentlemen of the City and vicinity" had to buy their own food and drink, but "WINE, CAKE, TEA &c." were "furnished for the LADIES."[217]

Peddlers selling cake and gingerbread popped up at public events like musters (assemblies of local troops), elections, and even religious meetings. The peddlers were often free people of color such as Lige Whitely, who vended ginger cakes at the courthouse in Smithville, Tennessee, "on days of occasion."[218]

In urban areas, enslaved people, mostly women, regularly made and sold baked goods in the streets and the marketplaces. In Gordonsville, Virginia, for example, African American women met each arriving train with bread and fruitcake, provisions for hungry passengers.[219]

Cities still struggled with the conflicts between the need for these women's goods and the problems that the vendors' success presented. By the late eighteenth century, enslaved women "virtually monopolized the vending of cakes and confectionery in Savannah's public market."[220] In the early nineteenth century, Charleston and Savannah required free Black and enslaved vendors to wear stamped copper tags verifying their right to move around the market and streets.[221]

Scotsman James Stuart, visiting the New Orleans market in 1833, commented, "Negroes, Mulattos, French, Spaniards, Germans, and Americans, are all crying their several articles in their peculiar languages. The women of colour seem very strong, carrying baskets of bread, and every thing on their head."[222] The most famous New Orleans street food was cala, a sweet rice fritter made from day-old cooked rice, milk, eggs, sugar, and sometimes cinnamon. Enslaved African Americans, mostly women, fried them in portable furnaces on the street and sold them while they were *tout chaud*—"very hot!" Sometimes women worked in pairs, with one frying and the other selling. At least a few cala vendors made enough money to purchase their freedom.[223]

The numbers of commercial bakeries rose as cities grew.[224] In 1803, Charleston had twenty-one bakers.[225] New Orleans in 1820 had almost sixty bakers, most of them French, with enslaved people selling their breads from wicker baskets.[226] By the 1850s, Richmond's bakers numbered eleven.[227] Bakers' ads across the South listed impressive arrays of goods: many types of breads, cakes, cookies, tarts, crackers, biscuits, and European specialties such as a French nut cookie called a *croquant*.[228]

Baking, as always, was a tough business. In Cahawba, Alabama, in 1819, new bakers Volz and Gray informed the public that they were now ready to furnish "Warm Bread . . . every morning at sun-rise." Warm bread was available at dawn only because someone had labored through the night.[229] Both enslaved and free Africans and African Americans worked as commercial bakers. In New Orleans, the lease of a large bakery included "eight certain negroes" as well as the building.[230] In Charleston, freedwoman Camilla Dunstan hired enslaved people to help in her pastry shop until she could afford to buy four female enslaved people.[231] But exclusion could prevail as well. In Montgomery, Alabama, in 1847, Irish immigrant Thomas Lindsay declared that racists need not worry: "*I attend to the business MYSELF.*"[232]

Free Blacks excelled as baking entrepreneurs. In early nineteenth-century Annapolis, Lucy Smith catered for wealthy families and sold goods both from her kitchen and on the street "from her basket."[233] In Savannah, pastry cooks were among the most successful free African Americans. Aspasia Cruvellier, who with her sister Justine Cruvellier established their business in the 1820s, eventually made enough money to buy a three-story brick house.[234] William Claghorn hired both Black and white workers, particularly immigrant German bakers who brought European-style baked goods to the city. He owned a stunning $4,000 worth of real estate in the late 1850s.[235]

In Charleston, numerous African American bakers and pastry cooks plied their trades.[236] Most prominent were free women Sally Seymour and her daughter, Eliza Lee. Seymour bore four children with the planter Thomas Martin. She trained under a professional pastry chef, and when Martin manumitted her in 1794, she opened her own shop. Seymour bought and trained enslaved people to help with production, and she taught her daughter both to read and to cook. When Seymour died in 1824, Eliza Lee took over the business. She and her husband, John Lee, a free tailor, ran numerous establishments in Charleston. At least seven other free black pastry chefs in Charleston also enslaved people.[237]

From the 1830s, Germans' immigration to southern cities accelerated because of political unrest in their homeland.[238] In Richmond, the German population doubled between 1850 and 1860, and at least eight of the immigrants were bakers.[239] Germans, with a long tradition of fine yeasted bread, brought their knowledge and skill with them. Among the most successful German bakers in the South was Johann Christian Heinrich Claussen, who came to Charleston in the 1850s. He began as a baker and quickly expanded his holdings, enslaving eleven people by 1859.[240] In Savannah, Anton Borchert became "celebrated" for his Passover bread even though he was Lutheran.[241]

Because bread remained important in the diet of urban southerners, the governments of most southern cities continued to regulate the weight, quality, and prices of flour and bread.[242] Spanish authorities set prices in New Orleans in the 1790s.[243] In Alabama, Mobile officials drew up the first "tariff for bakers" only three weeks after the city was incorporated in 1814, tying the price of bread to the price of flour.[244] Most southern cities confiscated underweight bread loaves and distributed them to the poor.[245] An increasingly complicated economy demanded solutions.

IN 1860, white southerners wanted to keep all the good stuff—all the way down to wheat bread and fancy cakes—for themselves. Enslaved people reached for better lives, including food that wasn't just hoecake from hand-ground meal. Although the South was never just one entity, most of its white population held attitudes toward slavery that people in the North found intolerable. By 1860, the rifts in American society were irreparable. As eleven southern states left the Union and formed a new country, food supplies, including baked goods, became a part of the war experience for many southerners.

Chapter 5

RAISON CAKE

....

The Eye Was Well Deceived, but to the
Taste It Was Rather Sour

*T*he Civil War lasted only four years, from 1861 to 1865, but it had pro-
found effects, both temporary and enduring, on how southerners ate.
As the South seceded from the United States, its people were already
divided into rich, poor, enslaved, and free, and then segmented further into
military and civilian. All southerners confronted challenges, though the
rich and free of course fared the best. Those nearest the lines of combat—
particularly in Virginia, Tennessee, Georgia, and Mississippi—faced the
greatest peril and, for the enslaved, the greatest opportunity for freedom.
Some privileged individuals came through with their food supplies relatively
untouched. Farm families in remote areas, accustomed to eating corn and
syrup rather than wheat flour and sugar, sometimes did all right. And at the
end, 4 million enslaved people had to find their ways into freedom, pretty
much unaided, often hungry. Baked goods numbered among the real problems that both Black and white southerners faced.

When the fighting began in April 1861, the Confederate government
focused on feeding its troops, and it commandeered the output of private
grain mills. By 1862, Gallego Flour Mills, the largest in Richmond, had "a
giant contract with the government to furnish flour," and smaller mills also
sold meal and flour to the Confederacy.[1] Likewise, numerous bakeries contracted with the government to provide bread for the soldiers. An observer
in Mobile in March 1862 commented, "The bakeries are destitute of all cakes,
pies, and other delicacies, their whole time being occupied in baking bread

Ruins of an oven at Fort Sumter after Union occupation. Library of Congress, LC-DIG-ppmsca-40725.

for the soldiers."[2] The Confederacy also operated its own bakeries at various outposts, trying to keep the soldiers nourished.[3]

Military bread supplies remained adequate in the early years of the war. The Seventeenth Virginia Infantry near Manassas had "hot rolls and bread, good butter" as part of a "sumptuous supper for a blockaded army."[4] Three ethnic German units from Richmond all had multiple bakers, along with two "oven builders," who continued practicing their trades for their comrades.[5] At Fort Sumter in 1863, the commandant told a visitor that the firing of mortar shells at Union troops spoiled their bread, "as it shakes the foundation so that the yeast cannot make the dough rise."[6]

Units with professional bakers counted themselves lucky, for untrained bakers turned out some dreadful messes. One hapless soldier baked biscuits with stolen tallow—beef fat—rather than lard. Complaints were numerous: biscuits were hard, or burned, or raw, or—maybe worst—"burned out side & raw in side," as a Virginia soldier griped. The problem of baking became so bad that Confederate generals Joseph E. Johnston and P. G. T. Beauregard blamed it for massive diarrhea outbreaks and ordered ovens built so that soldiers could have "decent bread a few times a week."[7]

The women working in Confederate hospitals paid careful attention to the quality and quantity of bread served to the ill and wounded. Phoebe Yates Pember, matron of the huge Chimborazo Hospital in Richmond, wrote, "After the flour or meal had been made into bread, it was almost ludicrous to see with what painful solicitude Miss G. and myself would count the rolls, or hold a council over the pans of corn-bread, measuring with a string how large we could afford to cut the squares, to be apportioned to a certain number."[8] Confederate nurse Kate Cumming, near numerous battlefields, often wrote about bread, which was sometimes all she and her coworkers had to serve their patients. In 1862, she found the bread to be "black and sour." A few months later, they fed the men "wheat-bread (very nicely made at the government bakery)." She fretted in times of shortages, using stale bread in batter cakes and making puddings without eggs.[9] Even the fragile wounded sometimes went hungry.

WHILE THE MILITARY depended on the government to supply it, civilians had to fend mostly for themselves, contingent on their location and financial means. Delicacies imported from the North, like butter, disappeared almost immediately.[10] Greedy merchants and individuals hoarded staples to drive up prices or to ensure supplies for their own families. In Alabama, David Marshall Scott, son of an extremely wealthy manufacturer, blithely remembered, "Everybody bought what was needed at the beginning of one year to last until the next. Flour, sugar, molasses, coffee, tea, wines and liquors, brandies, spices and condiments were all bought in wholesale quantities and stored away in the spacious storerooms attached to every residence."[11] Wealthy people gave gifts of baked goods and treated guests till near the war's end. The family of an Atlanta Presbyterian minister frequently enjoyed presents from church members: loaves of bread, pound cake, and fresh butter to go with them.[12] And in January 1864, well into the hardest days of the war, the First Lady of the Confederacy, Varina Davis, served chocolate jelly cake at a women's luncheon.[13] The rich seemed oblivious to others' woes.

For some southerners, however, particularly those closest to the front lines, deprivation arrived early and stayed long. Sugar shortages came first. Winchester, Virginia, which was occupied by the Union army five times in four years, ran out of sugar in July 1861, only four months into the conflict.[14] The blockade of southern coasts by the Union navy effectively stopped almost all imported goods. Union control of New Orleans beginning in 1862 further disrupted the flow of sugar throughout the Confederacy as the northern army burned nearby sugar mills and stopped commerce east and west across the Mississippi River.[15]

Sugar was never completely unavailable, however. In the first year of the war, merchants stocked sugar, presumably brought through the blockade or stored up before the ports closed.[16] In October 1862, Mississippian Sarah A. Watkins wrote to her daughter, "We have sugar, flour and coffee yet." As the war wore on, Watkins commented in January 1864, "Provisions and goods are very scarce and dear. . . . All our white sugar was used in cake, the icing was made of your sugar you left here that I had put away for you. Necessity compelled me to use it. I will replace it or pay you for it."[17] The family felt the need to carefully account for what sugar belonged to whom, but at least they still had some. And in March 1864, George M. Goodwin advertised four hogsheads of "fine brown sugar" (which would have been considered an oxymoron before the war) for sale in Columbia, South Carolina.[18]

Families in warm climates grew a little sugarcane to make into molasses, and the dark liquid remained for sale in limited quantities.[19] The most common substitute for sugar, however, was sorghum syrup. Sweet sorghum came to the South in the 1850s. It didn't crystallize like sugar, so people used— and loved—it in liquid form. Families erected mills with wooden cylinders to grind the sorghum cane, and they boiled the extracted juice to make syrup.[20] Watermelon rind, which had some natural sweetness, also stretched sugar supplies. With a small amount of sugar, it could be made into "molasses" or candied for use in baking, a frugal use of an otherwise cast-off food.[21]

Wheat flour, never common in the antebellum South, became even rarer shortly into the war. The lower South seldom received shipments because of the limited railways and the Confederate government's seizure of flour. In the upper South, labor shortages and the inability to repair or replace equipment created problems. Price gouging by farmers, millers, and merchants, as well as hoarding by random citizens, made wheat and flour unaffordable even in places where they were abundant.[22]

As the Union hardened its tactics against the Confederacy, grain mills became casualties of war. Northern soldiers tore up and burned mills and set fire to stores of grain, flour, and cornmeal.[23] The damage hurt both the Confederate government, which was deprived of military supplies, and individuals. William H. Rhea of Arkansas toted up his losses after the battle of Prairie Grove, December 7, 1862. He calculated that between goods taken and the Union army's uncompensated use of his mills, his losses topped $7,000.[24]

The most widespread destruction took place in the Shenandoah Valley of Virginia. Before the Civil War, the Shenandoah's fertile soil, farmed by large numbers of enslaved people, produced millions of bushels of wheat and corn each year.[25] U.S. general Philip Sheridan reported in 1864 destroying more than 2,000 barns filled with wheat, hay, and farming implements and more than seventy mills loaded with flour and wheat.[26] Both the northern and southern armies also took stores of food for their own use, including large amounts of corn and wheat flour.[27]

To make matters worse, the Confederate army sometimes destroyed mills as they retreated, for example torching the facilities at Crum's Mill on the Hatchie River near the border of Tennessee and Mississippi after the battle of Corinth.[28] Most spectacular was the ruin of the gigantic Gallego and Haxall mills in Richmond, burned by the Confederates as they abandoned their capital in April 1865.

People in areas away from the fighting tried to supply themselves with wheat as well as corn. The Jones family of Georgia, for example, grew "a small crop of wheat" in 1864 and had it milled into flour.[29] Some tough Alabama women not only raised wheat but processed it as well. One woman flailed wheat by whacking it against the side of a barrel, able to separate "as much as a bushel or two at one time." She then threshed the wheat by pouring it onto a sheet placed on the ground, letting the wind carry away the chaff. Another ingenious woman put the wheat into crude wooden troughs, and she and her "little children" beat the grain with "heavy sticks and little wooden mauls she had roughly shaped" to separate the grain and husks.[30] For white women, the act of going to the gender-segregated mill challenged the social order. In Georgia, Dolly Lunt Burge wrote of accompanying the family's coachman, Elbert, to the mill to keep "straggling soldiers" from taking her mules. Burge wrote, "Never did I think I would have to go to mill! Such are the changes that come to us!"[31] She did not comment on any concern over Elbert's personal safety or whether he received any of the flour that he risked himself for.

Flour shortages occurred unevenly among the elite. Virginia Clay-Clopton observed that by the summer of 1862, some residents of Richmond could no longer find fine flour but were "reduced" to eating the coarsely ground flour

Ruins of the Haxall Flour Mills, 1865. Library of Congress, LC-DIG-ppmsca-34928.

called "seconds." Then, in 1863, she remarked, "Molasses and 'seconds' . . . came to be regarded as luxuries by many."[32] Flour became a generous gift. Kate Stone recorded in September 1862 a Mrs. Hardison sending her family "a little homemade flour," from which the family made cake, "a most rare occurrence." Stone reflected on the Hardisons' generosity: "But for them we might forget the taste of wheaten bread."[33]

The families and survivors of Confederate soldiers suffered from hunger during the war because of the absence of men to raise the crops in rural areas and because of ongoing shortages and price gouging in urban areas. Some cities created charities and relief efforts to assist them. In New Orleans, relief work began early, after 300 women staged a public protest in August 1861. The resulting Free Market, supported by donations, fed 1,900 families in November 1861, barely six months into the war.[34] Other large cities followed suit, provisioning soldiers' families with flour, sugar or sorghum syrup, cornmeal, and small amounts of pork.[35] By December 1864, almost 20 percent of the white women and a third of the white children under the age of eight in Orange County, North Carolina, were on relief.[36]

Across the South, white women instigated public uprisings as they confronted crushingly high flour prices and shortages, calling out speculators and hoarders. As wives, daughters, and sisters of Confederate soldiers, they

GᴿAND REAPING.

SOUTHERN WOMEN FEELING THE EFFECTS OF REBELLION, AND CREATING BREAD RIOTS.

Depiction of the Richmond bread riot. *Frank Leslie's Illustrated Newspaper*, April 2, 1863.

expected the nation to help provide for them.[37] A group of forty to fifty hatchet-wielding women describing themselves as "Soldiers' Wives" targeted speculators in Salisbury, North Carolina, in March 1863. When merchant Michael Brown refused to sell them flour at a reasonable price, they attacked his storerooms. He gave them ten barrels of flour. The group eventually amassed twenty-three barrels of flour as well as salt, molasses, and cash.[38]

Richmond faced problems as refugees from the war zones flooded in and food supplies dwindled.[39] In early spring 1863, the situation reached a breaking point. A group of women decided to call on the Virginia governor to air their complaints. Armed with stones, clubs, knives, hatchets, and guns, the women were turned away by an unsympathetic aide. The angry crowd of perhaps a thousand women then surged into downtown Richmond and broke into several grocery stores, stealing flour, among other items.[40] Troops dispersed them, and eventually the city government set up special markets for poor residents.

The women in Mobile marched down Dauphine Street in September 1863, bearing banners emblazoned with the words "Bread or Blood" and "Bread and Peace." They began breaking into stores and stealing clothing and food, which was available but scandalously priced. The Seventeenth Alabama Regiment, sent to quell the disturbance, sympathized with the women and refused to intervene. The crowd dispersed after local officials promised to ensure adequate supplies of staples.[41] And so it continued—in 1863 in Bladen County, North Carolina; Petersburg, Virginia; and Atlanta and Columbus, Georgia; in 1864 in Raleigh, North Carolina; Savannah, Georgia; Randolph County, Alabama; and Barnwell, South Carolina; and as late as February 1865 in Macon, Georgia.[42] Hunger and need drove the women of the Confederacy into the streets.

As flour soared in price or disappeared, families turned back to cornmeal.[43] Parthenia Hague commented that cornmeal, "when sifted through a thin muslin cloth and mixed up with scalding water to make it more viscid and adhesive, was as easily moulded into pie crust with the aid of the rolling-pin as the pure flour."[44] Even wealthy southerners had to adjust their ideas of luxury. Kate Stone thought it odd to have no flour or "'boughten' delicacy" to serve company in 1862, but she admitted that they could eat well on corn, combined imaginatively with sugar, molasses, and lots of eggs.[45] Three years later, that abundance was a thing of the past as Kate Cumming, in Georgia, reveled in cornbread made with lard, soda, and "a *whole egg*."[46]

Creative southerners tried to ease flour shortages by making new dishes with corn. The editors of the *Houston (Georgia) Tri-Weekly Telegraph* in September 1862 offered a prize to "the person furnishing them with the greatest number of ways that corn meal can be served." A young woman won the contest by submitting seventeen different recipes, many of them familiar delicacies with new twists, such as cornmeal ginger cake.[47] In Florida, Sarah Pamela Williams created a recipe for "Confederate cake" that included cornmeal, butter, eggs, and dried peaches.[48] Southern women renamed their corn-based recipes to honor southern icons: Jeff Davis muffins, Jackson batter cakes, Beauregard cakes, and Stonewall hoecakes.[49]

Slave-owning families sometimes sent enslaved people to forage for cornmeal. North Carolinian Fannie Ransom Williams recalled that her refugee family had no bread and could not buy cornmeal, "so our old mammy went out and got a little, I don't know how."[50] In Petersburg, Virginia, Sara Agnes Rice Pryor wrote, "My faithful John foraged right and left, and I had reason to doubt the wisdom of inquiring too closely as to the source of an occasional half-dozen eggs or small bag of corn."[51] We might speculate that enslavers compelled enslaved people to commit theft on their behalf. We don't know if "mammy" or John got any of the cornmeal.

Other substitutes for wheat flour also emerged: white potatoes, sorghum, and even acorns.[52] A few southern cooks used flour made from arrowroot, a tropical plant whose dried root was typically used for thickening.[53] Some southerners tried their best to work with rice flour. In October 1862, Charleston merchant J. C. H. Claussen advertised "fresh ground rice flour, a substitute for Wheat Flour, at reduced prices," adding helpfully, "A receipt for its use will be given gratis," as though Low Country cooks did not already know how to make bread from rice flour.[54] A Vicksburg woman reported disappointing results from rice: "I had nothing left but a sack of rice-flour, and no manner of cooking I had heard or invented contrived to make it eatable. A column of recipes for making delicious preparations of it had been going the rounds of Confederate papers. I tried them all; they resulted only in brick-bats, or sticky paste."[55]

The most reviled flour came from dried cowpeas, which we call black-eyed peas, considered indigestible and "peculiar and disagreeable" in taste and used only in the direst circumstances.[56] A southern soldier recalled that as it cooked, the pea bread became very hard on the outside and increasingly soft on the inside, and it usually had raw meal left in the center.[57]

As the war continued, sweets became increasingly rare, reserved for special occasions. In 1863, Mary Dawson Ravenel, the wife of botanist Henry William Ravenel, made a cake for his birthday. He apologized in his diary for the extravagance, commenting that she "insists upon keeping up the usual custom of cake and wine, even at the cost of some little self-denial afterwards."[58] When a Colonel Hood visited the Jones household in Georgia in January 1865, they had "a little raised ginger cake" on hand, and they insisted that he share it and then take the leftovers with him.[59]

Wartime often speeds romance, and as weddings continued throughout the Civil War, so did cakes, whether made of wheat flour or something else. Fruitcake remained a part of many Confederate weddings. The sweetness of dried fruit covered a shortage of sugar, and even persimmons could be pressed into service.[60] North Carolinian Catherine Edmondston carefully analyzed the cake from Kate Miller's wedding: "The *Raison* cake was really a clever substitute for the genuine article, being made of dried cherries and whortleberries. The eye was well deceived, but to the taste it was rather sour tho' not more so than cake made from old raisins often is. '*Confederate Raisins*' are dried Peaches clipped to bits with scissors."[61]

Some families kept stores of local and imported dried fruit throughout the war.[62] Tropical nuts remained available in the early part of the conflict, as merchants advertised "almonds, filberts, pecans, Brazil nuts, English walnuts" in January 1862.[63] When shortages hit, native hickory nuts, black walnuts, and pecans filled the void.[64] In 1863, Georgian Gertrude Thomas referred to peanuts as "Confederate almonds."[65]

Georgia Griffing Wilcox recalled her sister Eliza's wedding to Robert Elliott in Mississippi around 1862. The sisters were determined to have cakes of the latest fashion, with white icing, even though the layers were made of "dusted corn meal." They used an elaborate process to create a sugar substitute, grating sweet potatoes and steeping them in water. The sediment from the steeping was "pure white," and they dried it, made it into powder, "mixed it with the beaten whites of eggs, and thus made a splendid frosting for our cakes." The bride's cake, as trends dictated, was stacked "two feet and a half high, frosted to a dazzling whiteness and trimmed with wreaths of pure white japonicas." The groom's cake was "alternated layers of the richest pound cake and the most delicate strawberry jelly. This cake was heavily frosted, and was ornamented with great clusters of lovely roses, buds, and green leaves."[66] The cakes may have lacked flour and sugar, but they sure looked good.

One of the fanciest wedding receptions in wartime Richmond celebrated the September 1863 marriage of LaSalle "Sallie" Corbell and General George Pickett, fresh from defeat at Gettysburg. Years later, Sallie Pickett remembered—perhaps with some embellishment—having "thousands of delicious beaten biscuit" and cakes with distinguished pedigrees: "Not having sugar, we had few sweets, but Mrs. Robert E. Lee had made for us with her own fair hands, a beautiful fruit-cake, the General's aunt-in-law . . . sent us as a bridal gift a black-cake that had been made and packed away for her own golden wedding."[67] As Pickett recalled, prominent women generously provided for her wedding. As in the past, guests still received pieces of cake to take home.[68]

People who weren't rich and famous enjoyed wedding galas, too. In 1864, Tennessean Jorantha Semmes attended a celebration that included jelly cake and strawberry pie.[69] And, as in the past, enslavers used weddings to control the lives of their soon-to-be formerly enslaved people. When the enslaved woman Elvira married in 1864, her enslaver gave her "some substantials and a syrup cake and pone," indicating her approval of Elvira's life choice.[70]

In the early months of conflict, leavenings remained easy to find in urban areas.[71] By late 1862, Charleston merchants were manufacturing yeast cake and yeast powder to sell.[72] Further afield, families returned to making homemade leaven. Parthenia Hague recalled cooks burning corncobs to make ashes, covering them with water, and using the resulting alkaline solution as leavening.[73] As in the past, people gathered fig and peach leaves to get wild yeast, and some families used "old-fashioned milk yeast," made from milk, flour, and boiling water.[74] The *Confederate Receipt Book*, a collection of recipes for wartime published in Richmond in 1863, gave instructions for making homemade yeast from flour, brown sugar, and salt.[75]

Even close to battle, sometimes people were able to buy ingredients for baking. Shortly before the siege of Vicksburg, a local woman recalled her husband procuring a "hogshead of sugar, a barrel of sirup, four pounds of wheat-flour, and a small sack of corn-meal, a little vinegar, and actually some spice!"[76] In 1864, prices in Augusta, Georgia, skyrocketed as refugees from Atlanta streamed in. Yet wheat, sugar, and eggs remained available, though at absurd prices.[77] In Alabama, Parthenia Hague recorded shortly before the end of the war that "Aunt Phillis" brought hot biscuits "just from the oven,—for no one thought of finishing breakfast without a relay of hot biscuits toward the middle or end of the meal."[78] It is unclear how these ingredients remained plentiful, but sometimes it was from hoarding. In Richmond in 1864, a visitor was stunned when his host "simply took me to his bed-room, and raising the coverlet, showed several barrels of flour, sacks of coffee, sugar, and other groceries snugly stowed away. This, he said, I would find to be the case in nearly every household in the city."[79]

Shortages of baking materials arose gradually and varied by location. In the autumn of 1863, Charleston merchants Laury and Alexander offered a single keg of butter for sale, for cash only.[80] The *Confederate Receipt Book* assured its readers that "bad butter" could be cured by melting the rancid butter in hot water, skimming it off "as clean as possible" and "work[ing] it over again in a churn," adding salt and sugar, and pressing it well to remove the water.[81] Salt itself was often in short supply, with uses (including basic nutrition) that extended far beyond baking.

Supplies of fresh fruit gradually diminished. By September 1864, in Richmond, apples were going for fifty cents apiece, a price, one resident complained, that would "make pippins blush for themselves."[82] The blockade kept Caribbean fruit from coming into southern ports, and prices grew high, while in Florida, oranges, lemons, pomegranates, limes, and citrons rotted for lack of transportation.[83]

Some spices continued to slip through the blockade so that a few fortunate Charlestonians could buy cloves and cinnamon in November 1863.[84] As supplies grew dear, southerners worked to create passable copies of their cherished recipes. Richmond resident Clara Minor Lynn devised a "ginger snap" recipe with no ginger or sugar, making the spicy cookies from flour, sorghum syrup, and black pepper.[85] By and large, most southerners just went without seasonings in the latter part of the war.[86]

DURING THE CIVIL WAR, as always, baked goods could show affection, loyalty, social status, or control. They could even be part of the paranoia about slave insubordination. White southerners were always willing to believe the worst of enslaved people, and their accusations grew more fanciful during wartime. Officials leveled false charges of poisoning a cake against Amanda, an enslaved woman in Richmond, in 1864. Amanda often made "little dainties" for her enslaver's children to carry to school. One day, four of the children became nauseated after eating a shortcake that Amanda had sent with them. A local doctor charged that they had been poisoned. Although the children's mother and another doctor testified on behalf of Amanda, she remained in jail for at least a month.[87] She might have been using bad ingredients because of wartime, but her labors for the children were wrongly punished.

White southern women baked to show their support for the Confederacy. In August 1861, the women of Savannah raffled off a "colossal pyramid . . . victory cake" for twenty-five cents a chance.[88] In Chattanooga in 1863, a mere seven months before their city became a battle site, the locals auctioned off 600 pounds of sponge cake—a huge outlay of eggs as well as sugar and flour.[89] In January 1865, a month before much of the town burned, the "gentle patriots" of Columbia, South Carolina, held a bazaar where each of the Confederate states was depicted with a remarkable display of sweets. The Texas booth had "cream and chocolate cakes," and Louisiana's included treats like French rolls and charlotte russe.[90] Artistic women ornamented cakes with Confederate symbols: Mary Jones of Georgia topped a cake with a "cockade" of blue ribbon, representing the Confederate states, then added live oak and magnolia leaves, rice sprigs, and cotton bolls. In New Orleans, one fundraiser fashioned a Confederate flag of icing on the top of her cake.[91]

At least one highly placed southern woman tried to use cake for espionage. To help Confederate spy Rose O'Neal Greenhow escape Union custody, Adele Cutts Douglas, widow of U.S. senator Stephen A. Douglas and Greenhow's niece, made a cake and hid between the layers cash for bribing Greenhow's guards and a plan for her escape. Northern soldiers found the goods before Greenhow could get them. When Greenhow and her daughter Little Rose went to jail in early 1862, women brought cakes and pies to them and other imprisoned Confederates.[92]

Confederates supported southern troops by baking for them, individually or in groups, family members and strangers alike. Because the war took place almost entirely in the South, troops were often within easy reach of sympathetic bakers. In the summer of 1861, "Baby" Watkins baked a silver cake, made with egg whites and no yolks, to send to a "dinner given for soldiers at Tobin's Spring." Ironically, she enlisted enslaved people Martha and Robin to help in her endeavor.[93] As late as June 1864, organizers of a barbecue for soldiers in Galveston desired "large contributions of cakes . . . enough of them so that all can feast on cake alone if they wish to."[94]

Families sent boxes to their loved ones in military service. Catherine Edmondston loaded a parcel for her brother-in-law with loaves of bread and "some Wedding Cake for him to dream on"—referring to the old tradition of putting a piece of wedding cake under one's pillow to conjure dreams of one's future spouse.[95] W. L. Barry of the Ninth Mississippi Infantry complained to his family that "the bread you sent was a little moulded all over."[96] People dreamed and whined, war or no war.

Hospitality extended to times of disaster and deprivation. Lida Lord Reed remembered the retreat of southern troops from battles in Mississippi in the late spring of 1862: "From early dawn the cook [Chloe] was busy boiling coffee and baking biscuit, which Minnie, our zealous mulatto maid, handed in buckets and big trays to the scores of dusty, ragged, and foot-sore men who pressed up to the front door."[97] Again, enslavers forced enslaved people into extending kindness to southern troops, and they still had wheat flour and coffee. Savannah residents cooked "great kettles" of soup and pans of cornbread for freed prisoners of war in the fall of 1864.[98]

Baking for wounded and ill soldiers became a way for individual women to help as war took its toll. After the first battle of Bull Run, women loaded a wagon "with comforts" for the hospital, including "nice bread, biscuit, sponge cake."[99] Supplies for "sick soldiers" near Charleston in 1862 included "cake bread" and "ginger nuts" as well as butter, eggs, meal, and grist.[100] Susan Bradford Eppes wrote in 1864, "Three times a week Mother fixes up a basket to send in to the Tallahassee hospital . . . always two large loaves of delicious home-made bread. This last is a luxury as flour is hard to get."[101] The family would sacrifice for the Confederate cause.

Ironically, the southern cities that fell to the Union fared much better in terms of food than those that remained within the Confederacy. Shortly after the Union army occupied New Orleans in April 1862, officials allowed city residents to send flour, corn, cornmeal, meat, and rice to the country "for family and plantation purposes." The city had stored enough food to provision the countryside.[102] With the opening of the Mississippi River, food once again flowed into the Crescent City: butter, fresh flour, lard, leavening, and spices.[103] Natchez, occupied in the summer of 1863, likewise rebounded with "a new customer base in the form of occupation troops." By the end of 1863, old businesses were thriving and new ones springing up, "providing every kind of good and service."[104] Stores were selling all manner of goods by the middle of 1864, from flour to cooking extracts to condensed milk. Chattanooga, where the United States built facilities to rebuild the railroads, was flourishing by the summer of 1864. Restaurants served travelers night and day. Sutlers (private businesspeople who traded with the soldiers) and traders in the city offered strawberries, olive oil, figs, cinnamon, and other delicacies.[105]

Despite sugar and flour shortages, African American women somehow got the supplies to make baked goods for sale throughout the war. In Richmond, "the cake, pie and apple women" hawked their wares in the Virginia State Capitol during legislative sessions.[106] A traveler to New Orleans in 1864 marveled at the "cake wagons."[107] Their public ventures exposed the vendors to danger; a group of Union soldiers robbed "a number of poor cake women" on the Mississippi levee in 1865, while "one of the negro-hating element" in Beaufort, South Carolina, took "a colored woman's pies" and then slapped her.[108]

Soldiers proved ready buyers for goods baked by African Americans.[109] A Confederate soldier near Petersburg complained about the "cake and pie venders" who took soldiers' wages.[110] Union soldiers, too, enjoyed baked treats: apple pie for the sailors on Sapelo Island, biscuits for Thanksgiving in Milledgeville, corn cakes for the pickets at Hampton Roads.[111] We don't know if the bakers sold these delicacies or gave them in gratitude to their liberators.

In the latter half of the war, white women, likely out of desperation for cash, also began selling or trading baked goods to northern soldiers for profit. In 1863, Cornelia McDonald and others in tormented Winchester, Virginia, exchanged fresh bread for sugar, meat, and coffee.[112] In Natchez, "impoverished gentlewomen" sold cakes, pies, and cornbread "at the army camps near the town."[113] Mary Mallard reported from Savannah in early 1865, "We hear that many of the most respectable ladies are compelled to make cakes and cornbread and sell to the Yankees to enable them to live."[114] We can only speculate on how the women got their hands on flour and sugar and how they felt about peddling their baked goods, but it seems likely there was some humiliation involved.

Confederate soldiers even sold baked goods to each other. A North Carolinian soldier near Fredericksburg, Virginia, in 1863 commented that "immense quantities of apples, ginger cakes, goubers [sic], &c, are disposed of here at the most extravagant prices." He relayed the story of "two men carrying a barrel of ginger cakes from the Railroad to their Brigade several miles off" who unsuccessfully tried to cross a creek with the barrel and lost the entire load.[115]

The fortunes of commercial bakers went up and down during the war, depending on the availability and cost of ingredients, the demands of the military, and the ability of customers to pay for their purchases. Seven months before the battle of Chattanooga, M. B. Parham was selling cake and "best sugar."[116] As late as November 1863, a Richmond writer bragged that the city's bakeries could supply the army and the military prisons and still have enough left to sell to "citizens, sutlers and soldiers." The bread, he wrote, "is always fresh and sweet . . . served on the tables of private families, boarding houses, and the hotels of Richmond."[117] In Charleston and Columbia, South Carolina, bakeries continued to produce cakes and bread and to hire workers into 1864.[118]

Yet shortages caught up with commercial bakers as they did households. In South Carolina in 1863, Emma Holmes observed, "The ten cent loaves made here are so small, about *four inches* square & *two* thick."[119] Richmond bakers temporarily stopped baking bread in April 1864 when flour prices reached $300 a barrel.[120] Although the Oriental Saloon in Richmond continued to serve sumptuous meals, the baked goods were pricey: $1.00 per person for bread and butter, $1.33 for cake, and $1.50 for hot rolls.[121]

Commercial bakers thrived in areas of Union occupation. In New Orleans, Jacob Ott sold cakes and pies at his confectionery.[122] George Mallery's baking in Natchez was "highly appreciated."[123] And the invaders also turned entrepreneurial. On the Natchez square, a Wisconsin soldier oversaw the construction of a large brick oven. While he "calculate[d]" to bake primarily for his fellow Wisconsinites, he also planned to sell to "the rest of mankind occasionally, intending to keep the usual supply of baker's goods, as cakes, pies, bread, &c."[124]

And so it remained until the end of the war. While some southerners faced great shortages, others enjoyed unlimited access to baked goods. When nurse Kate Cumming arrived at the Cook House in Columbus, Georgia, in March 1865, she was shocked at the plenty: "cold turkey, sausages, roast pork, biscuits, hot rolls, cornbread; and I could scarcely believe my senses when I saw cake." For breakfast the next morning she had "pure coffee" with milk, sugar, and buttered toast.[125] FitzGerald Ross similarly found "universal profusion" in hotels and boardinghouses across the South, amazed at "hot rolls and cakes, several kinds of bread."[126] In January 1865, an optimistic baker opened his new establishment in Selma, Alabama, announcing that he "will always have on hand a good assortment of Bread, Cakes, &c, &c."[127] Success might not be assured, but optimism reigned even as the Confederacy faced its death knell. We wonder how this business fared after Selma fell to the Union three months later.

AS ENSLAVED PEOPLE contemplated their choices of staying or going when Union troops drew near, food became part of their calculation. The Union army haphazardly made supplies available. Individual soldiers gave food to African Americans. Sarah Wooden Johnson, near Petersburg, Virginia, remembered, "Does you know dem soldiers jes would take dem ole hard biscuits and throw 'em at we chillun? I picked up a coat tail full . . . carried dem biscuits home and dropped dem in de pot of pot liquer dat was settin' down dar on de fir[e] place."[128] Louise Jones recalled, "When Yankees come to a store dey would break it open, an' give you all you could tote. Dey broke into smoke houses an' dey would throw de bigges' hams, whole meat sides, an de lak. Flour, meal, corn an' everything was yours."[129] Enslaved people couldn't depend on such supplies, but they clearly appreciated the food when it became available and may have particularly enjoyed the redistribution of enslavers' stashes.

Enslaved people who left the homes of their former enslavers and followed Union troops were often gathered into so-called contraband camps, where their rations consisted mostly of hard bread, molasses, fat pork, and water. Others received cornmeal, flour, sugar, rice, and soda to bake their own bread with.[130] In Port Royal, South Carolina, African Americans got corn on the cob that then had to be shelled (removed from the cob) and hand milled before they could bake it.[131] In some places, they also received rations of wood for cooking.[132] In January 1864, the U.S. War Department set subsistence rations for adults at "one pound of cornmeal five times a week; one pound of flour or soft bread or twelve ounces of hard bread twice a week . . . eight pounds of sugar," plus meat, with children under the age of fourteen receiving half rations.[133]

Many would-be freedpeople fared poorly, however, as the Union provided for them only scantily, far worse than they did poor white southerners.[134] In Nashville, the federal government paid meagerly the laborers whom they forced to work and fed them bread that its commissary had rejected. Primarily because of slim provisions, more than 25 percent of these impressed laborers died between 1862 and 1863.[135] In the fall of 1864, freedpeople accused government officials of trying to starve women and children to death.[136]

Feeding freedpeople had never been the U.S. government's plan. The *Chicago Tribune* commented in 1864 that "contraband" had originally been supplied with rations "at an immense expense to the government" but that helpful northerners were now trying to make them self-sufficient. The government expected formerly enslaved people to earn their bread. At a camp in Decatur, Alabama, "useful old men, strong, muscular women, accustomed to work in the field, and children" grew corn and wheat and operated a gristmill, probably abandoned by its owner.[137] Northern white women working in the camps tried to instill domestic ideals, asking their peers to contribute housewares and teaching freedwomen how to raise yeast bread.[138] And when forty

African American couples living in "Sabletown" near Norfolk married, missionaries provided them with huge slices of rich, iced wedding cake and "lemonade without stint," presumably to reinforce their respectable decisions.[139]

White southerners also came to rely on the Union army as a source of food, including flour and cornmeal.[140] "Gently nurtured" Virginians disdained the "musty corn-meal and strong cod-fish" that the Yankees offered.[141] More to their liking, perhaps, were the "carloads of bacon, flour, cornmeal, lard, and other items such as sugar and coffee" distributed by Sheridan's commissary to the people of Winchester in late 1864.[142]

But women grew tired of making do. During the Union occupation of Petersburg, Sara Agnes Pryor met her friend Louisa Bland Weisiger "trudging along with her basket." Pryor asked Weisiger if she were going to receive her rations of meat, sugar, and canned vegetables from the northern government. Weisiger replied, "No indeed! I'm going, with the only five dollars I have in the world, to the sutler's! I shall buy, as far as it goes, currants, citron, raisins, sugar, butter, eggs, brandy, spice—" Pryor responded, "Mercy! Are you to open a grocery?" and Weisiger rejoined, "Not a bit of it"—solemnly—"I'm going to make a *fruit cake!*"[143]

AFTER FOUR YEARS OF WAR, an uneasy peace came in April 1865. The infrastructure of the southern milling industry lay in shambles. More than a quarter of a million southern men were dead. And 4 million freedpeople had to figure out their way in the world, for little help existed for them. The South rejoined the Union grudgingly, to share the fortunes of the nation once more. In the decades ahead, the baking habits of southerners would come to resemble those in other parts of the nation, even as some of them remained distinctive.

Chapter 6

WHITE MOUNTAIN CAKE

....

Poverty and Opulence

By 1868—just three years after the end of the Civil War—Alabama had resumed its annual State Agricultural Fair, with baking contests among the multitude of activities for white people. Bakers could win prizes in five time-tested categories: loaf light bread, a prize of $1; pound cake, $5; fruit cake, $5; sponge cake, $5; and jelly cake, $5.[1] In Georgia twenty years later, the opportunities had almost doubled for bakers wanting to flaunt their talents. Along with the same five cakes and breads, new competitions included light rolls, soda biscuits, coconut cake, silver cake, orange cake, chocolate cake, and spiced cake.[2] With cheap flour and sugar, flavoring extracts, baking chocolate, and, above all, chemical leavening, southern baking had entered a new era.

For 4 million formerly enslaved people, however, abundance remained elusive. With only erratic help from their former enslavers and the U.S. government, many went hungry, and most had little variety in their diets. African Americans were no longer property but citizens, though subject to continuing and often violent attempts by white people to undermine that status. Black Americans were determined to get paid for their work, but white supremacists quickly moved to keep the ways of slavery as intact as possible. Limiting access to food was one way they sought to maintain dominance. This pattern of limiting food continued unabated well beyond the nineteenth century.

While some African Americans acquired farmland, most did not, and an economic system called the crop lien rapidly developed. Under this system, a landowner and a landless farmer signed an agreement for a year. The landless farmer was to raise corn and the staple crop—usually tobacco or cotton. In return, he and his family got a place to live, seed, and the use of farm equipment and draft animals, usually mules. At harvest, the landowner would theoretically receive either a third or half of the corn and the cotton or tobacco as payment. The hitch in the system was that anything that sharecroppers bought on credit while awaiting harvest, including food, went against their bottom line, and rural stores charged outlandish prices with ridiculous interest. Some landowners owned commissaries that sharecroppers had to trade at, while others arranged for credit with local merchants. At Henry Long's store in Waverly, Mississippi, tenants paid almost twice what landowners did for cornmeal.³ All too often, sharecropper families ended the year in debt, with nothing to show for their work. Landlords also decided if sharecroppers could keep chickens or hogs or raise a garden.⁴ With the limitations of poverty and oppression, the diets of many rural African Americans weren't much different from what they had been before the Civil War: corn, pork, and syrup.

IN THE DECADES after the Civil War, many rural people, Black and white, still cooked their meals on the open hearths of small fireplaces. Freedpeople near Brunswick, Georgia, built chimneys of salvaged bricks and mortared them with marsh mud, doing the best they could with meager resources.⁵ The poorest houses, in fact, still had mudcat chimneys.⁶

Stoves became increasingly common throughout the South, however, particularly in towns.⁷ Sizes and models abounded, with names like "Queen of the South" and "Southern Bell."⁸ Ovens still lacked thermometers, so cooks had to figure out ways to determine baking temperatures. The unnamed author of *Housekeeping in Alabama* advised her readers to use their own bodies: "Test the oven with your hand. If you can keep your hand in it thirty-five seconds, or while you count to thirty-five, it is a quick oven; for forty-five seconds, it is a moderate, and for sixty seconds, a slow oven. Sixty seconds is a good oven to begin a fruit cake."⁹

Many of the women risking their bodies were African American. After the Civil War, the number of African American women working as cooks in private homes expanded dramatically, and more white southern women had the service of domestic workers than ever before. Most enslaved African American women had worked in the fields rather than in houses. After emancipation, for many African American women, going to town and getting a "cook job" seemed like a better option than field labor. As cooks became more

Old African American Couple Eating at the Table by Fireplace, Rural Virginia, 1899. Photo by Frances Benjamin Johnston. Frances Benjamin Johnston Collection, Prints and Photographs Division, Library of Congress, LC-USZ62–61017.

available, an increasing number of white women hired them. But the transition to domestic work came hard for many, with demanding employers and circumstances. On the other side of the equation, some affluent white women had to do their own cooking, at least in the short run, when their formerly enslaved cooks departed, and they learned to do basic tasks that enslaved people had always done for them.[10]

Experts stood ready to help would-be cooks. The number of published cookbooks shot up in the second half of the nineteenth century, with white southerners like Mary Virginia Terhune, who wrote under the name Marion Harland, giving instructions with strong, authoritative voices. At least two African American women also produced cookbooks before 1900. Freedwoman Malinda Russell, originally from Tennessee, self-published her *Domestic Cook Book* from her new home in Paw Paw, Michigan, in 1866. Abby Fisher, born in South Carolina, moved to San Francisco and wrote *What Mrs. Fisher Knows about Old Southern Cooking* in 1881. Russell's recipes were terse, mostly lists of ingredients, but Fisher sometimes explained techniques. African American women's voices became audible in a new way.

Southern women also read cookbooks written by white northern women such as the prolific Maria Parloa and Sarah Tyson Rorer. Groups of white southern women, like their peers elsewhere, began assembling and publishing cookbooks—for example, the *Gulf City Cook Book Compiled by the Ladies of the St. Francis Street Methodist Episcopal Church, South, Mobile, Alabama*—usually as fundraisers for worthy causes. Community cookbooks provide invaluable information on local foods, sometimes reflecting what people actually ate and sometimes what the contributors wanted people to think they ate. Cookbooks by white women also articulated racial attitudes of the time and place through reflections on Black cooks—sometimes praise, sometimes scorn, almost always patronizing.

WHETHER COOKED in a stove oven or on a hearth, corn continued to sustain most rural southerners. William Edwards, born in 1869, lived with his aunt, a freedwoman, in Alabama. He recalled hard times: "We very seldom had enough to eat." The two of them raised about twenty bushels of corn a year on their five-acre plot. Edwards remembered, "Saturdays were mill days and I had to take the corn on my shoulder and go to the mill, which was four or five miles away. It always took me from four to five hours to make this trip, as I had to stop by the way several times to rest."[11] People also continued to use hand mills to grind small amounts of corn for their families, although the cost of one was beyond the reach of the Edwards family.[12]

Southerners also bought cornmeal, the quality varying with their buying power. Poor African Americans ate unsifted cornmeal, containing large amounts of bran, making their cornbread rough and unappealing.[13] More affluent southerners could afford to be picky about their cornmeal. White cookbook author Mary Stuart Harrison Smith insisted that the right cornmeal (which was also white) completely did away with the need for sugar: "Good meal is essential to its perfection. It should be made of white corn, and ground in a mill worked by water-power. Any addition of sugar is thought to spoil it, the native sweetness of the corn being all-sufficient."[14] The Macon merchant W. A. Huff could have read Smith's mind, advertising in 1866 "Prime White Meal, Water Ground."[15] Yellow, industrially ground meal had no place on fine tables, according to the connoisseurs.

Cornmeal continued to be the first thing that many women, Black and white, learned to cook. Privileged white women, no longer enslavers, had to start somewhere. Fannie Caison wrote in 1866, "I am learning to do every thing . . . down to baking a hoe cake. I think I *excell* in cooking: but poor little

Floy often wishes 'we could get a good cooker.'"[16] Susan Bradford Eppes, from northern Florida, complained that she was "the poorest hand at making a fire." But she reported that she "baked some corn bread for breakfast; batter bread, it was, with eggs and milk. We had plenty of butter to eat with it." Then the family had batter bread again for the midday meal.[17] Apparently that was the extent of Eppes's repertoire.

Dairy products represented luxury. As always, cows were expensive to feed and tough to care for. In small southern towns, residents sometimes kept cows at their homes. But someone had to care for the animal. Susan Eppes whined in early 1866, "Mrs. James . . . (fortunate woman) can milk her own cow. I fear I could never learn to do that. You see I am so terribly afraid of Bossy. She looks like a dreadful monster to me."[18]

Southern women who could get cream continued to churn butter at home. Although some had new barrel churns that turned with a crank, most probably used the ancient dasher churn, which employed an up-and-down motion.[19] C. C. White, an African American East Texan, remembered his mother's efforts to make butter after their landlord "let us have a cow to milk":

Mama got hold of a old crock jar and made herself a churn. She got me to help her whittle out a wooden lid and put a hole in the middle of it so the dash handle could go up and down. Then we made the dash. We took two little flat boards and whittled them down nice and smooth and fitted them together like a cross, and nailed them on the end of a old broom handle, and got them wet and rubbed them real good with salt so the butter wouldn't stick to them. We made the best butter in that old churn.[20]

Many urban consumers and a few sharecroppers bought butter.[21] While the dairy industry in the South remained small, dairy farms served the larger cities.[22] The Vineville Dairy outside of Macon, Georgia, in 1897 touted its Jersey cows that produced "the purest milk. The sweetest butter."[23] Southern merchants also imported butter from the North.[24]

Southern housewives worried about keeping butter fresh and sweet.[25] Refrigeration was an obvious answer. Wealthy southerners had long had icehouses, but family-sized iceboxes appeared only after the Civil War. The clumsy technology spread slowly throughout the upper and middle classes.[26] In 1867, the "Louisiana Fair Premium Zero Refrigerator" was built of "well-seasoned pine," filled with charcoal for insulation, and lined with zinc for rustproofing and cleanability and had galvanized wire shelves and "good locks with accessoried keys" to keep out would-be thieves.[27] By 1900, cheaper models were made of "hardwood" and lined with "galvanized iron."[28] Leaky, humid, and smelly, few iceboxes were genuinely effective, and many southerners simply could not afford them, even if they could occasionally buy ice. Refrigeration would have to remain a dream for the future.

Artificial products became another solution to the butter problem. Invented by a French chemist in 1869, the first oleomargarine was made from beef tallow and milk. In the United States, the early industry used lard and "oleo oil," pressed from beef tallow. The well-organized dairy industry went into a rage, and in the 1880s, anti-margarine legislation took effect in numerous states.[29] State governments required food vendors and bakers to post conspicuous signs telling consumers that they used "oleomargarine" or "imitation butter."[30] But the cow was out of the barn, as it were, and artificial butter gained an increasing market share, as we will see later.

For poor southerners, milk and butter were only dreams. In 1898, researchers in the new field of sociology found that African Americans in Virginia still made their cornbread as their ancestors had done: "simply of meal wet up, without salt or leavening material, and baked, as a rule, in the ashes."[31] C. C. White remembered his mother making the best with what she had:

> Mama had fried us a corn cake before she left to walk to Shelbyville to cook and sweep and iron for her white folks. I'd set there by the fireplace and watched her scrape off the top ashes and pull out some live coals and set the big old Dutch oven on them and pour in a little grease. . . . She was pouring the corn cake in the Dutch oven. It sizzled, and kind of bubbled around the edges. And it smelled *oh so good*. Mama put the lid on and shoveled some hot coals and ashes on top. . . . Then Mama lifted the lid, and the corn cake was done, all nice and crinkly brown on top. It *did* give out. Mama divided it between Frank and Liza and me, and it sure was good, but it didn't last half long enough.

White's childhood notion of heaven was where "everybody's mama didn't have nothing to do but stay home all day and cook corn cakes and fatback and turnip greens."[32] A "field holler"—a song sung by African American laborers as they worked—in Tennessee in the late nineteenth century showed the continuing importance of hoecake: "I wants a piece of hoecake I wants a piece o' bread / Well Ise so tired an' hungry dat Ise almos' dead."[33]

Most southerners called fried cornbread "fritters." African American cookbook author Abby Fisher explained her technique. The cook took "young and tender corn" still on the cob and cut half of the kernels away whole and cut the others about halfway, releasing sweet liquid. With the corn she made a batter of eggs, powdered crackers, and wheat flour. She next heated lard or butter "hot enough to brown the fritters in two minutes" and dripped the batter into the fat from the end of a spoon.[34] White cookbook writer Marietta Gibson's fritters, also made with fresh corn, were rich with cream and fried in butter, and Gibson recommended them for dessert with wine sauce.[35] Several women cautioned bakers about the amount of lard required for frying the fritters, but, as Virginia housewife "Mrs. S. T." noted in a rare nod to frugality, "it is not extravagant, as it may be used again. Strain what remains and put it by for use."[36]

Recipes for cornbreads changed mainly in the way they were leavened, which we will discuss in detail shortly.[37] But even time-tried recipes sometimes needed instructions for baking in stoves. One unnamed recipe donor updated the directions for "Awendaw" cornbread, a buttery, eggy cornbread named after its coastal South Carolina place of origin: "Bake with a good deal of heat at the bottom of the oven, and not too much at the top, so as to allow it to rise."[38] Fashionable cooks made corn sticks in "Krusty Korn Kobs Baking Molds," cast-iron pans with impressions in the shape of an ear of corn from the Ohio-based Wagner Manufacturing Company.[39]

The proportion of wheat in southerners' diets grew substantially, even as they depended on corn. In the Shenandoah Valley and on the prairies of North Texas, wheat cultivation thrived.[40] Many small farmers continued to raise small wheat patches for their families. Urban southerners bought flour made from wheat grown in the rapidly developing fields of the Midwest, brought in on ever-expanding rail lines.[41]

For a time, small community mills continued much as they had before the Civil War. In DeKalb County, Tennessee, for example, Allan Wright built a mill in 1866 on the site of one that had been burned during the conflict.[42] Urban mills processed large amounts of meal and flour. In Richmond, the Haxall Flour Mills, destroyed in the Confederate retreat from the city, reopened in 1874 with forty sets of wheat stones and six sets of corn stones.[43] Some new mills upgraded to steam power. Nashville's Elevator Mills, established in 1874, employed a 160-horsepower Corliss engine, providing ample power for multiple runs of stones.[44]

But the era of stone grinding was ending, as a so-called new process took over. Invented in Switzerland in the 1830s, the roller mill, which used horizontal rollers made of steel or porcelain, dramatically changed milling around the world.[45] The roller mill made the Midwest the center of the U.S. wheat industry, as it could handle the hard winter wheat grown on the Great Plains better than stone mills could. Southern mills of all sizes retrofitted their facilities with rollers.[46] Madison Mills, for example, had ground wheat on Virginia's Rapidan River since 1795. When the mill's owners installed rollers, mill capacity grew to seventy-five barrels per day by 1895.[47] Building a roller mill took even larger investments than a mill with grinding stones did, and investors formed stock companies to finance their ventures. The new mill at Liberty, Tennessee, for example, was capitalized in 1887 at $6,000.[48] The cost of a roller mill limited mill building to the wealthy even more than in the past.

With the industrialization of wheat-growing and the changes in milling, the flour output of the United States rose by more than 50 percent between 1860 and 1880.[49] Southern flours, made from softer wheat with less gluten and protein than northern hard wheats, began claiming the loyalty of home bakers. Two brands beloved into the twenty-first century, White Lily, from Knoxville, and Martha White, from Nashville, debuted in 1883 and 1899, respectively.[50] Smaller local mills made numerous grades of flour, differing by purity and fineness, and each with its own trade name.[51] According to nationally revered cooking writer Maria Parloa, once a cook found a brand she liked, she should stick with it: "The best flour is the cheapest, as there is no waste in using it."[52]

White housewife Tryphena Fox, from Mississippi, mourned the effects of bad flour in 1866, when she "made a mistake, & the chicken pie was made of my old dark flour & *was* so tough & black that it required a good appetite & poor eyes to manage it—Of course the biscuits were the same."[53] Virginia cooking teacher Harriet Curtis Cringan gave careful instructions on how to evaluate flour: "Good flour, when pressed with the hand, remains in shape and retains the impress of the lines of the skin. It has a yellowish-white tinge when mixed with water, and when well kneaded is tough and elastic."[54] Cookbook writer Marion Cabell Tyree summed up the situation: if the cook tried a barrel of flour twice and it became wet and sticky both times, "you had better then return it to your grocer."[55]

Landowning African American families often raised wheat, but even sharecropping families began to eat more wheat flour. Sometimes they received wheat flour as part of their "furnish" from the landowners.[56] William Pickens remembered that his family ate corn between fall and spring, then switched to flour during the growing season. They had to buy flour on credit, so it was a calculated risk.[57] White supremacists recognized what the change to wheat bread meant: African Americans were choosing what they could eat, and the bullies were losing an element of control. A writer in the *Richmond Dispatch* complained in 1898, "Now the darkies eschew [cornbread] where wheat bread is to be obtained."[58] Such equality appalled white observers.

Griddle breads—pancakes and flannel cakes, waffles, and wafers—continued to be among the simplest and fastest ways of baking wheat flour. Pancakes took a noteworthy turn in 1889 when two white businessmen bought a bankrupt flour mill in St. Joseph, Missouri. With no background in cooking, they worked by trial and error and eventually hit on a mixture of wheat flour, corn flour, "lime phosphate," and salt that, when mixed with milk, made good pancakes. Their luck ran out, though, because they couldn't market it successfully. The next year, they sold their company and recipe to R. T. Davis Milling Company. Davis added powdered milk, so that the home cook had only to add water, and he included rice and corn sugar to improve the flavor and texture. Most notoriously, Davis created the persona of Aunt Jemima to market the mix, creating one of the longest-running racial stereotypes in American advertising.[59] Thus, Aunt Jemima pioneered two parts of American culture: baking mixes and racist marketing.

A stovetop waffle iron, patented in 1869, made cooking waffles easier and presumably less dangerous.[60] Abby Fisher noted, however, that the process still took care: "Always have your irons perfectly hot and well greased."[61] If not, the result would either be soggy or stuck—a mess in either case.

As flour grew cheaper, countless women rose each morning and made pans of biscuits, measuring the ingredients by hand, sight, and memory. Poor women cooked them in Dutch ovens on open hearths.[62] More affluent women baked them in pans in stove ovens.

Biscuits represented prosperity. B. W. Orrick, son of a poor white farmer, remembered that when his family lived in Arkansas, "it was cornbread three times a day." Once they moved to Texas, however, "we could eat biscuits for breakfast."[63] A break from cornbread was a step up the culinary and social ladder.

The quality of a woman's biscuits became a stand-in for her character. Cookbook writer Mary Stuart Harrison Smith sneered in 1885, "Nothing can be more inelegant than a large, thick biscuit."[64] Grace Buckingham Campbell, wife of a teacher, recalled her relief at the favorable judgment by her new neighbors in Joppa, Alabama, of her biscuits, made with sweet milk and baking powder.[65]

Most southern biscuits were simple combinations of flour, lard, and milk, sometimes salt, occasionally egg. Some used soda and cream of tartar for leavening.[66] Although rural landowners continued to own and butcher hogs, sharecroppers and city people usually bought lard from grocers. Increasingly, that lard came from large midwestern companies such as Armour (from Chicago) and Kingan (from Indianapolis). These companies touted the purity of their product to contrast it with adulterated goods appearing on the market.[67]

Biscuits offer a good place to explore the changes in leavening in the nineteenth century. The search for effective chemical leavens continued for a long time, with lots of flops. Baking ammonia (ammonium bicarbonate, also called "volatile salts" or "bakers' hartshorn," originally derived from the hooves and horns of male red deer) was a near miss.[68] The ill-named "yeast powder," a mixture of baking soda and monocalcium phosphate, continued to find users after the Civil War.[69] Still, it had its doubters. New Orleans writer Lafcadio Hearn observed that most biscuits made with yeast powder had a "screwed or drawn-up look."[70]

Baking soda (sodium bicarbonate) continued to grow in popularity as a leaven. The most widely used national brand was Arm & Hammer, begun in Massachusetts in 1846.[71] Recipes for baked goods of all kinds, from sponge cakes to pancakes, mixed soda with an acid to provide loft.[72] Biscuits, helpfully called soda biscuits, were one of the most widespread uses for soda, made with flour, milk, salt, sometimes egg, and sometimes lard.[73] The most popular acid to blend with soda was cream of tartar, or tartaric acid. The mixture was common in cakes and biscuits through the 1880s.[74] Amid the corruption of the Gilded Age, one had to trust one's supplier, as cream of tartar could be adulterated with plaster of paris, flour, or marble dust.[75]

Baking powder changed everything. In 1869, chemist Eben Horsford, of yeast powder fame, added cornstarch to a combination of phosphate (phosphoric acid) and baking soda, buffering the two ingredients to prevent them from exploding. The cornstarch also absorbed moisture, keeping the new product fresher longer. The newly stable compound could be packaged in small amounts and sold in grocery stores rather than drugstores. By 1896, Americans were buying almost 120 million pounds of baking powder a year.[76] Farmworkers and railroad hands, Black and white, spent their precious earnings to get the magic leaven.[77]

Baking powder companies competed fiercely. Some local manufacturers got into the game: the Southern Manufacturing Company in Richmond produced Good Luck Baking Powder, for example, while the Best Tea and Coffee Company in Atlanta gave its own name to its product.[78] Nationally, camps quickly divided over those powders that used alum (potassium aluminum sulfate), such as Horsford's, and those that used cream of tartar as the acid base, such as Royal. Royal was by far the more popular in the South.[79] At the Jones and Willaford store in Macon, Georgia, the brand was so commonly used that account books simply noted "Royal," with no further explanation.[80] But Mary Stuart Harrison Smith, author of the 1885 *Virginia Cookery-Book*, shrugged, "Most house-keepers keep a supply of both Horsford's powder and the Royal Baking Powder, to be used as occasion requires, and good recipes for their use accompany each package."[81] (Smith also pointed out how companies supplied recipes to market their products. Horsford first produced a cookbook in 1879.)

A direct outgrowth of the invention of baking powder was self-rising flour, sometimes called "self-raising": flour sold with the leavening already in it. An English baker, Henry Jones, in 1849 patented his formula of baking soda, tartaric acid, salt, and sugar mixed into flour.[82] Self-rising flour spread quickly throughout the South after the Civil War.[83] Makers of self-rising flour heavily marketed their product. Hecker's Flour offered a cooking exhibition, a new selling technique, at Savannah's Masonic Temple in November 1875. The company explained, "With this article in the larder there is no danger of having biscuits overcharged with saleratus."[84] The experts would keep the home cook from making mistakes.

Technology resurrected beaten biscuits, still made without leaven. Mary Stuart Harrison Smith whined, "Nowadays beaten biscuits are a rarity, found here and there, but soda and modern institutions have caused them to be sadly out of vogue. . . . Most servants object nowadays to the trouble of preparing this bread."[85] But in 1877, Evelyn L. Edwards of Vineland, New Jersey, received a patent for a dough-kneading machine, also known as a biscuit brake, which used a hand crank to turn two toothed rollers. The cook passed the dough repeatedly through the teeth until it became light and blistered, just as it would if it were beaten.[86]

In addition to biscuits, other quick breads graced southern tables, whether as loaves, muffins, or old favorites like Shrewsbury cakes and Naples biscuits.[87] After hundreds of years, people still found new ways to make gingerbread. In 1895, cooking instructor Harriet Curtis Cringan came up with "My Own Hard Gingercakes," consisting of flour, brown sugar, butter and lard, molasses, ground ginger, salt, allspice, cloves, and soda, rolled thin and cut.[88] Virtually all cookbooks published during this period had gingerbread recipes, so one wonders how original Cringan's formula could be, but she proudly asserted her inventiveness.

Crackers, a flat, more delicate version of ship's biscuit, became common in the late nineteenth century. Most were made commercially, but housewives also baked them at home. Mary Elizabeth Wilson of Nashville touted her crackers as "premium," which probably meant that they had been awarded a prize: flour, lard, cold water, and salt, rolled very thin, cut in three-inch squares on greased white paper, and baked three to four minutes in a quick oven. Like wafers, these crackers could burn in a flash, so the cook had to attend them carefully.[89] Other cooks augmented plain crackers with butter or lard and leavened them with soda and sour milk.[90]

Crullers and doughnuts became ever more popular. The doughs were well seasoned with nutmeg, cinnamon, and lemon, sometimes leavened with soda and sometimes with yeast. They were rolled and could be cut into various shapes, such as diamonds or triangles or the more familiar rings.[91] (We'll talk about beignets, the French doughnut revered in New Orleans, in a bit.) Another popular fried bread was a simple mixture of egg yolks and flour, rolled, cut, and fried in lard, then sometimes sprinkled with sugar. These bits of dough had several names attached to them—"non de scrips," "deceptions," "trifles," "vanities"—all highlighting the simplicity of the dish.[92] North Carolina Moravians enlivened their fried bits with sugar, cinnamon, and "spirits," calling them "strumbendles" or "tanglebritches."[93]

INCREASINGLY SOUTHERN WOMEN followed national cooking trends, including food reforms. Sylvester Graham began advocating in the 1830s for the use of whole-grain flours to combat the dreaded nineteenth-century malady known as dyspepsia—what we would call indigestion.[94] His breads combined graham flour—coarse whole-wheat flour—with cornmeal and brown sugar or molasses, usually leavened with soda, made into loaves, rolls, or muffins, baked or steamed.[95] By the 1870s, recipes for graham bread or "brown bread" had trickled into the South. An owner of a *Handy Housekeeping* cookbook handwrote into her copy the recipe for "graham wafers" from Philadelphia cookbook author Sarah Tyson Rorer.[96] First Lady Frances Folsom Cleveland sent to the women of St. Paul's Episcopal Church in Waco, Texas, in 1888 a recipe for "Boston Brown Bread" composed of graham flour, sour milk, cornmeal, molasses, soda, and salt.[97] (Cookbook compilers often asked celebrities for recipes for their collections, and Cleveland responded to numerous requests with the same brown bread recipe.) While it's hard to gauge how widely accepted graham and brown breads were throughout the South, at least some housekeepers made them regular parts of their repertoire.[98] Mrs. O. E. Edwards, a home cook from Anniston, Alabama, passed along a handy tip with her "Excellent Brown Bread" recipe: "If you have no brown-bread pan, Royal baking powder boxes do very well."[99]

Although its origins are unclear, the misnamed salt-rising bread gained acclaim in the mid- to late nineteenth-century South. Mary Stuart Harrison Smith called it a "favorite bread" in the Shenandoah Valley and noted that "some dyspeptics think it much more digestible than bread made up with other kinds of yeast."[100] Salt-rising bread began with a notably smelly starter, composed of milk and cornmeal mush or of salt, flour, and boiling water, which rose overnight. The next morning, the cook added water or milk, salt, sugar, and flour, and let it rise again. At that point she mixed in lard and baked the loaf.[101] Salt-rising bread was notoriously finicky, and Elizabeth Whitner Glover, a caterer from Warm Sulphur Springs, Virginia, proudly declared her recipe "Salt-rising Bread That Never Fails."[102]

After the Civil War, white cookbook writers stressed that white women, regardless of their class, should learn to bake bread. Marion Cabell Tyree haughtily observed, "Surely the loving hands of the poor man's wife and daughter will take as much pains to make his bread nice and light as hirelings will do for the wealthy." She assured her white readers that, if enslaved people could, they certainly could make good bread: "If persons without brains can accomplish this, why cannot you?" Knowing how to bake would enable a housewife to "give more exact directions to the cook" and be able to produce bread when "circumstances should throw her out of a cook for a short time."[103] On the other hand, the unnamed author of *Housekeeping in Alabama* learned both from a cookbook and her own cook, Elsie, who taught her how to properly raise and judge the timing of the dough.[104] Black freedwomen had plenty to teach their employers who were willing to learn.

Though southerners continued to make homemade yeast, they used it less and less. The Fleischmann brothers of Cincinnati began producing standardized compressed yeast—a soft, concentrated cake—and sales skyrocketed after they exhibited it in Philadelphia at the World's Fair in 1876. In the South, urban bakers had access to industrially made yeast by 1879. A few years later, the editors of a cookbook in Charlottesville commented, "To those who do not care to take the trouble to make yeast, we cheerfully recommend Fleischmann's yeast."[105] Reliable and convenient, compressed yeast became the preferred product and Fleischmann's became the household name.[106]

But bread baking remained a difficult, time-consuming task. One hopeful housekeeper handwrote two full pages of instructions to make "one loaf of bread" into one of her cookbooks.[107] Marion Cabell Tyree advised, "Knead without intermission for half an hour, *by the clock*. Otherwise five minutes appear to be a half hour when bread is being kneaded or beaten."[108] Not surprisingly, many African American housewives, with more limited resources than their white counterparts, declined to take the time to prepare yeasted bread.[109]

Success was possible. In 1867, Tryphena Fox praised her own bread-making skills and, in turn, those of Milly, a newly emancipated cook: "I have taught Milly to make *very fine rolls, light bread* & batter-cakes & pastry so she set a nice table all the time they [previous company] were here—I wish you could have a loaf of my bread. It is like baker's only better—Cant I brag?"[110]

Southerners still loved rolls and small breads for individual servings. Again, southern women happily adopted northern recipes. In 1898, the women of Central Presbyterian Church in Atlanta published a recipe for Parker House rolls, a Boston invention of light, buttery, slightly sweet rolls folded before baking. The unnamed author observed, "If rightly managed

cannot be beaten."[111] Sally Lunn buns became extremely popular, with cookbooks often featuring multiple recipes with slight variations.[112] Rusks also
remained common, although the practice of baking them twice diminished.
Lafcadio Hearn specified that "Miss Lester's Tea Rusk," flavored with mace
and nutmeg, should be served hot.[113]

Although pies changed little during the nineteenth century, standards for
their preparation became more exacting. Cookbook writer Mrs. M. E. Porter commented that "the manufacture of light, sweet and moderately brittle
paste or crust is the grand desideratum," condemning the "tough, rancid or
heavy compounds so frequently served up under the tempting appellations of
pies and pudding." She then gave eighteen hints for obtaining good pastry,
from rolling it out on a marble slab to eating it warm.[114]

The increasing availability of ice eased pastry making for urban housewives, who could chill the fat and use ice water in the dough.[115] Before the
1860s, southerners had access only to ice that had been brought from cold climates and stored. During the Civil War, a French ice-making machine, using
ammonia and water as a refrigerant, was smuggled from Mexico to San Antonio, and by 1867 three plants operated there. In 1868, the Louisiana Ice Works
opened in New Orleans, and before long, ice manufacturers dotted southern
cities.[116] Ice was a luxury and a revelation for those who could afford it.

Still, much depended on the skill of the pastry maker. Abby Fisher counseled, "Roll out to the thickness of an egg-shell for the top of the fruit and that
for the bottom of fruit must be as thin as paper. In rolling pastry, roll to and
from you; you don't want more than ten minutes to make the pastry."[117] Lafcadio Hearn warned about baking pastry in a coal oven: "When baking with
coal, if the fire is not brisk enough do not put on more coal, but add a stick or
two of hard wood; or if nearly done, put in a stick of pine wood."[118]

The poorest southerners still made pies from wild fruit, and pie plates
were among the few household items purchased by workers in Ascension Parish, Louisiana, during the 1870s.[119] Freedwoman Millie Evans, who lived in
southern Arkansas, gave her formula for persimmon pie: "Make a crust like
you would any other pie crust and take your persimmons and wash them. Let
them be good and ripe. Get the seed out of them. Don't cook them. Mash
them and put cinnamon and spice in and butter. Sugar to taste. Then roll your
dough and put in custard pan, and then add the filling, then put a top crust
on it, sprinkle a little sugar on top and bake."[120] Home canning accelerated
with the development of glass jars with metal lids, and women who had time,
sugar, and a stove could "put up" wild fruits like blackberries and peaches for
future pies.[121]

If the number of recipes in cookbooks is any indication, mincemeat pies
continued their centuries-long run. Mrs. M. E. Porter published eight recipes,

using various types of meat: beef tongue, "tender beef," suet, calf's feet, or pigs' tongues and hearts.[122] Beef tongue appears to have been the most common meat used by her peers. The traditional ingredients—fruits, nuts, and liquors—all persisted.[123] In a nod to rising sentiment in the nation, Porter included a "temperance" version of mincemeat, in which "good cider" substituted for wine and brandy.[124]

For the busy housewife, commercially made mincemeat offered relief. In 1883, Marion Harland in her *Dinner Year Book* touted the product of Philadelphia's Atmore and Son: if a housewife did not have all her Christmas supplies in store, she wrote, "let me advise you to get a box of 'Atmore's Celebrated Mince-Meat,' and fill your pastry-crusts. . . . It comes in neat, wooden cans, and is really *good*. If you like, you can add more sugar and brandy."[125] The company George McMechen and Son, from Wheeling, West Virginia, sold its "'Old Virginia Brand' Mince Meat . . . Prepared from Famous Old Virginia Homemade Recipes."[126] Perhaps appealing to southern sensibilities increased sales.

Apple pies remained favorites. Commercially grown apples came to the South from "the North" and "the West," probably brought by rail. A Charleston merchant in 1869 advertised "Prime NORTHERN APPLES: Red Baldwins, Spitz, Twenty Ounce."[127] Apples were cheap and common enough that they were stocked in the general store at Waverly plantation in Mississippi in 1887 and 1888.[128] While southerners continued to dry apples at home, they could also buy the fruit in "evaporated" form and reconstitute them for baking.[129]

Most apple pies remained simple affairs, with only sweetened, spiced fruit and perhaps nuts or raisins baked in a double crust.[130] Baked or boiled dumplings also centered on apples.[131] Mock apple pies, invented in the 1850s, became increasingly common: a base of soda crackers, wetted and then mashed, combined with lemon juice and lemon rind, sugar, and sometimes butter, baked in a double crust.[132]

Although citrus growers in California and Florida were beginning to make inroads into the U.S. market by the late nineteenth century, most lemons continued to come from Sicily.[133] Lemon pies were the usual familiar combination of lemon juice and rind, sugar, and egg, and sometimes the newly discovered ingredient cornstarch for a thickener, baked in a single crust and topped with meringue.[134] Orange pie never caught on the way that lemon pie did, despite the increasing availability of domestic as well as imported oranges. Florida experienced a boom in oranges between the 1860s and the 1890s, with groves expanding northward up the peninsula.[135] Most cooks who made orange pies followed formulas almost identical to those for lemon meringue.[136]

Sweet potato pie had two versions: one made with sliced sweet potatoes and the other in the more common mashed form. Malinda Russell baked the first kind in Michigan, and Abby Fisher took her recipe for the second type with her to California.[137] Southerners mostly regarded pumpkin pies as exotic imports from the North. Marion Harland recalled that in 1866, her father provided four pumpkins to be made into pie for Christmas, and her family's cooks had to figure them out.[138]

One of the great mysteries of southern baking is chess pie. No one knows exactly where or when it was invented or why it is called that. In 1853, Frederick Law Olmsted pouted because the Commercial Hotel in Vicksburg promised "chess cake," but it, like everything else on the menu except "grimy bacon and greasy cabbage," was unavailable.[139] An 1870 recipe for chess *cake*, published in New York by Sarah A. Elliott (about whom I have not been able to discover more than her name), sounds like pie: sixteen egg yolks, a pound of butter, and a pound of sugar, beaten, flavored with lemon extract, and baked in "shapes lined with puff paste."[140] But an early print recipe for chess *pie* came from Grimes County, Texas, in 1866, when Mrs. Samuel P. May (about whom I have not been able to discover more than her *husband's* name) sent a recipe to the New York–based periodical *American Agriculturalist*: eggs, sugar, cream, butter, flour, nutmeg, baked in a single crust. She added, "This is the best pie we ever ate."[141] Neither recipe has cornmeal in it. This evidence points to a midcentury origin, possibly in the North, with no illumination on why the pie is called *chess*. The mystery continues.

Malinda Russell and Abby Fisher both gave recipes for peach cobbler. Russell's was in her usual terse language—stewed peaches, sugar, and butter, covered with paste—while Fisher's was more fulsome: "Peel the peaches (freestones) and make a pastry, the same way as for pie, and roll out the dough as thin as for pie crust. Put one layer at the bottom of the dish, and cut the peaches into pieces the size of a plum and fill the dish with them, sprinkling them freely with fine sugar [and "powdered cinnamon," she adds later]. Cover them over with another layer of pastry, cut with a knife two or three air-holes on the top and put to bake. Let it bake brown."[142] White cookbook writers, however, shunned cobblers, perhaps considering them common.

In March 1865, Gertrude Thomas decided to make cookies, which she still called cakes, as her first foray into baking: "I went into the kitchen and made up the first cakes I ever accomplished." It took the help of enslaved cook Tamah to pull off the feat: "With Tamah's advice I at length succeeded." Thomas reflected on the effort: "The children stood around admiring 'Ma's performance' as I cut out men, thimble cakes &c—but my back ached when I was through, and I have seen things I liked to do better."[143] Making rolled cookies was harder than Thomas thought.

Many people continued to refer to cookies as cakes, but the newer term, derived from the Dutch word *koekje*, became increasingly common in the

United States after the Civil War. Cookies generally remained some combination of flour, butter, and milk or cream, leavened with cream of tartar and soda, and flavored with the usual seasonings: ginger, nutmeg, cinnamon. The old-fashioned ones might have caraway seeds or rose water, which was rapidly being replaced by flavoring extracts.[144]

Cookies and other baked sweets benefited from cheap sugar, even as sugar workers and the nation's nutrition suffered. After the Civil War, the availability of sugar rose sixfold between 1865 and 1900, and by 1915, the average American consumed eighty-six pounds a year. (Remember, in 1820, estimated consumption was ten pounds a year.)[145] The reasons for this increased accessibility were several. First, the United States mechanized sugarcane cultivation and greatly expanded acreage and production, particularly in Texas and Louisiana. Texas notoriously used convict labor to grow and refine sugar, with the state government building a "large, modern, well equipped sugarhouse with a five-roller mill" staffed by prisoners in Fort Bend County.[146] Second, sugar mills became industrialized, and as they grew in size, they increased production.[147] Third, the amount of sugar imported into the United States from Hawaii, the Philippines, and the Caribbean expanded dramatically as America enlarged its imperial presence in the tropics.[148]

While southern consumers gobbled up sugar, it remained a luxury for the poor. Some sharecroppers bought tiny amounts at the stores near them, but many confined their purchases to cane syrup and, particularly, sorghum syrup.[149] And sugar, like other foods, had problems with adulteration. It could be mixed with "plaster of Paris or other foreign elements" or the "white earth called 'Terra Alba,' which causes the sugar to harden like stone, and prevents the cake and frosting from being, as it should be, light and good." So even as sugar became widespread, its distribution remained uneven.[150]

Flavoring extracts, rare in the South in the 1850s, spread quickly after the Civil War. At first, local druggists made extracts from natural flavorings, such as vanilla beans or lemon peel, soaked in alcohol and water.[151] Increasingly, grocery stores began offering extracts from manufacturers such as the Joseph Burnett Company from Boston.[152] C. F. Sauer of Richmond was the largest manufacturer in the South.[153] Sauer, a pharmacist, first sold extracts to housewives who brought their own bottles to his drugstore. In 1887, he began packaging extracts in glass bottles and selling them in grocery stores.[154] Sauer advertised widely, and writers such as Harriet Curtis Cringan specified Sauer's in their recipes.[155] Vanilla and lemon extracts were such favorites that even hard-pressed sharecroppers bought them.[156]

As the enslaved woman Tamah undoubtedly knew, making rolled cookies was not easily accomplished, especially in a warm climate. But rolled cookies were quite popular in the late nineteenth century. Mass-produced, inexpensive cutters, fashioned of tin, became widely available.[157]

The simple cookie known as a tea cake became adored in the late nineteenth century, although it is unclear how a "cake" became a cookie. "Tea cakes" had been around forever, but they were soft and puffy, baked in pans. The change was underway by 1877, when "Mrs. F. C. W." of Virginia advised her peers to "roll out half an inch thick" and bake the tea cakes.[158] The basic cookie recipe began with flour, sugar (usually white, occasionally brown), butter or lard, and eggs, leavened with cream of tartar, soda, or hartshorn. Milk could add richness. The cookies could be flavored with mace, cinnamon, nutmeg, lemon, or orange peel, with almonds or raisins sometimes mixed in.[159] Cooks added their own twists to the recipe. Harriet Curtis Cringan proudly made "My Own Tea Cakes" with both butter and lard, brown sugar, and lemon and orange peel.[160] Lafcadio Hearn advised rolling and cutting "with fancy cutters."[161]

The love for jumbles and wafers continued. For sweet wafers, made of butter, sugar, grated orange, eggs, cinnamon, and flour, Abby Fisher counseled, "Roll out on a board and put them out about the size of a biscuit and roll again till thin as paper, and bake in a quick oven. Watch close while baking. You can roll them round on a fork handle while they are warm, if you like." Fisher had the skill to make the delicate cookies and to keep them from burning.[162]

Lots of new cookies came into fashion.[163] A marguerite was a fancy, pretty cookie made of sugar, butter, eggs, and flour, seasoned with cinnamon, mace, nutmeg, and rose water, and then rolled, cut, and baked. Each cookie was then spread with marmalade, jam, or jelly. A meringue flavored with sugar and lemon went on top, and the whole confection was browned in the oven.[164] Similar cookies, lacking the meringue but sporting fancy names like "Fanchonettes" (possibly named for a Charles Dickens character) and "Genoese Cakes" (a midcentury European concoction), were cut after baking—a forerunner of bar cookies, perhaps—then iced and "ornament[ed] with dots or stripes of any kind of bright jelly or preserves."[165] And some small cakes were cut after baking and then frosted simply with confectioners' sugar, water, and sometimes rum or egg white.[166]

The creation of cakes as we know them—rounds about the size of a dinner plate—flourished after the Civil War. Middle-class families could afford to buy tin pans especially for making cakes, and cakes tolerated baking in stove ovens. There were as many types of cakes as there were combinations of ingredients, cheaper and more widely available than ever before. And, perhaps above all, there was baking powder to make them tall and tender.

Serving cake became a sign of middle-class acceptability and gentility. At a supper in Farmville, Georgia, an African American grocer's wife offered cake

and ice cream as the dessert course following a meal of chicken, ham, potatoes, corn, and bread and butter. The family indicated, through their menu,
that they belonged to polite society.[167]

At the other end of the political spectrum, white southern recipe writers
kept the Confederate cause alive by naming cakes after iconic white southern men, most frequently George Washington and Robert E. Lee. Typically,
the Washington cake had currants or raisins—occasionally both—and sometimes citron, seasoned with cinnamon, brandy, nutmeg, and "wine."[168] (Raisins replaced currants almost completely after 1860.) The Robert E. Lee cake
always featured citrus in both the cake and the icing. A representative example came from cookbook writer Mrs. M. B. Moncure in 1870. The cake layers, "baked in jelly tins," were sponge made with lemon peel and juice. The
filling included egg whites, sugar, orange peel and juice, and more lemon
juice.[169] Confederate generals Stonewall Jackson and John Brown Gordon also
had cakes named for them, as did Confederate president Jefferson Davis and
Georgia governor William J. Northen.[170]

Cake baking was a challenge irrespective of one's politics. Mrs. M. E. Porter encouraged tenacity: The "most careful, painstaking housewife may meet
with discouraging results in her first attempt even though she may think she is
following most exactly the details of the recipe; total failure at the first, resulting in heavy, soggy or doughy cake, should not discourage her, but should
rather spur her to renewed efforts, with full determination to succeed. 'If you
don't succeed at first, try, try again.'"[171] Porter did not explain how to rectify
the problems. She merely promoted persistence.

The conversion from fireplace to stove took some reckoning. Mary Stuart
Harrison Smith advised, "It will be obvious to all that the above directions are
for cooking by an open fire, but any person of common-sense can accommodate them to our modern stoves or ranges."[172] Easier said than done. Without thermostats, heat regulation remained tricky. A cool oven could cause the
cake to fall; an overly hot one could make it "harden or crisp" on the top. Mrs.
M. E. Porter cautioned bakers, "This is a point that can be learned only from
experience." A good cook had to practice.[173]

As much as cake baking changed in the second half of the nineteenth century, much stayed the same. Fruitcakes of all kinds, also called plum cakes or
black cakes, were as big a deal as ever, suitable for celebrations or gift giving.[174]
Some brides still chose fruitcakes as wedding cakes.[175] Creative cooks added
their own twists to the traditional recipes. Lafcadio Hearn bragged on his
"Nougat Fruit Cake," which included almonds and coconut as well as conven-
tional ingredients: "This is much admired. It is an experiment of my own, and
has been very much in request."[176] Adherents to the temperance movement
objected to liquor-saturated cakes, and the unnamed author of *Housekeeping in*

Alabama addressed the fears of her non-tippling sisters: "The alcohol is converted into vapor using spirits in any way, and molasses will be found an excellent substitute."[177] So-called white fruitcakes also abounded. They often used egg whites rather than whole eggs and white sugar in the place of molasses or brown sugar, and they usually omitted the alcohol that drenched their darker counterparts.[178]

Urban housewives, likely tired of elaborate fruitcake production, began to avail themselves of shortcuts. Lafcadio Hearn advised his readers not to struggle with the huge cakes and long baking times: "It is safer to have it baked by a confectioner, if it is convenient to do so."[179] And in Atlanta in 1898, a merchant offered "cash bargains in . . . fruit cake. Don't throw away your money but come to Headquarters and save money on Christmas specialties."[180] A harried housewife could simply buy her cake and be done with it.

While cakes using dozens of eggs for leavening became rarer, they were still around.[181] Technology made beating easier than before. Eggbeaters, first patented in the United States in 1856, were metal whisks attached to gears attached to a handle, which took much of the labor out of beating eggs.[182] In 1877, Marion Cabell Tyree recommended using a "Dover egg beater" for her bride's cake with twenty eggs.[183] "Dover" was a generic name for a rotary eggbeater popularized by the Dover Stamping Company of Boston.

Sifting also became easier with technology. Rotary sifters with wire mesh were invented before 1820, and they gradually improved. In Louisville in 1897, "Mrs. Claudine Wheeler Harding, Inventor," created the "Claudine Flour Sifter" with "three successive sieves" designed to keep the cook from having to sift numerous times. She advertised in local cookbooks and sold her invention at a nearby dry goods store.[184] Sifters mattered enough that sharecroppers on the Waverly plantation in Mississippi spent dear money on them in 1887.[185]

Eggs largely remained a home production both in the country and in town. Urban matrons bought eggs from local groceries, and sharecroppers obtained them from the plantation stores.[186] The old challenges continued. Marion Cabell Tyree instructed her readers to break each egg into a saucer before adding it to a batter. That way, the cook would learn if the egg were spoiled or had been fertilized and thus avoid ruining a bowlful of other ingredients.[187]

While sponge cakes still relied on eggs for leavening, some late nineteenth-century sponge recipes also included chemical leavens. Mrs. M. E. Porter cautioned bakers that sponge cake was "one of the very nicest of cakes (when well made), and one of the most difficult to make just right."[188] Abby Fisher counseled bakers, "Have your pans in readiness, grease with butter, and place white paper at bottom of pan. . . . A sponge cake should not stand a second after made before it is baked. Bake in a medium oven, keeping heat at bottom."[189]

Lemon—juice, peel, or extract—was by far the most common flavoring, but cooks used everything from ginger to brandy. Almonds and coconuts were favored additions.[190]

Marble cakes—made with light- and dark-colored batters, swirled together—were extremely fashionable in the late nineteenth century. Unlike present-day cakes, however, the dark parts were not chocolate. Rather, they were made with molasses, brown sugar, egg yolks, and "plenty of all kind of spices to suit the taste."[191]

Rolled cakes filled with jelly or marmalade became so popular that a new pan was created just for them. "Jelly cake pans," shallow and rectangular, created thin cakes that could easily be rolled around fillings. The cakes were typically simple white cakes, sometimes flavored with lemon, and some of the jellies specified were plum, currant, and apple. Abby Fisher started her jelly cakes by making orange marmalade for the filling a day before baking the cake. She iced the finished roll with a mixture of egg whites and powdered sugar and then sprinkled "fine grated cocoanut" over it.[192]

Southern cooks eagerly embraced the "Scripture Cake" fad that emerged about 1895. The recipe gave a verse from the Hebrew Bible rather than the actual name of the ingredient so that the baker had to look up each scripture to discover what the ingredient was. The young women of the Methodist church in Clayton, Georgia, in 1896 made and sold scripture cake by the slice, along with the recipe: 4.5 cups of 1 Kings 4:22 (for flour), a pinch of Leviticus 2:13 (for salt), and so on. The mixing instructions said, "Follow Solomon's prescription for making a good boy, Proverbs 23:14, and you will have a good cake."[193] That verse, in the King James Version of the Hebrew Bible, was "Thou shalt beat him with the rod, and shalt deliver his soul from hell." Presumably, that meant to thoroughly beat together all the ingredients. The cakes were usually baked as a loaf.

If you ask people what an iconic southern dessert is, they might say cobbler or coconut pie, maybe banana pudding. But most likely they will say cake, meaning lots of layers and lots of icing. And they will be surprised to learn that those luscious, gaudy creations did not exist before the Civil War. They are the offspring of baking powder and inexpensive sugar. Baked in multiple layers and mortared together with icings and fillings ever more extravagant, layer cakes created spectacular presentations for upscale occasions.

The simplest layer cakes were white cakes, made with butter, sugar, flour, and many egg whites. They were leavened with cream of tartar and soda or baking powder and flavored with lemon or rose water. They might also contain milk, almonds, almond extract, or vanilla extract.[194] Frosted versions, called white mountain cakes, became the choice for "bride's cakes," although fruitcake sometimes retained the name "wedding cake."[195] White mountain cakes were baked in multiple shallow pans to create layers. The layers then were stacked with icing between each layer and sometimes on top, on the sides, or both. The icing often consisted of egg whites, sugar, and perhaps orange or lemon juice and peel.[196]

Most of those amazing creations called "coconut cakes" were simply white layer cakes with white icing and coconut between the layers and on the top.[197] With steamship and railway transport, coconuts were available even in the smallest towns. Urban housewives could purchase "freshly-grated cocoa-nut at a reasonable price" from "any confectioner," said Charlottesville resident Mary Stuart Harrison Smith.[198] Most cooks, however, still grated their own.

Silver cakes, sometimes called lady cakes, resembled white cakes. They usually consisted of egg whites, white sugar, flour, and butter, leavened with yeast powder or cream of tartar and soda. Cornstarch could be substituted for part of the flour to make the texture even finer. Silver cakes might be flavored with almond extract, vanilla extract, rose water, or peach flavoring. Almonds and coconut were popular additions.[199] White women in Atlanta in 1898 gave their silver cake a political twist, naming it a "Bryan cake" after the politician William Jennings Bryan, who famously opposed basing U.S. currency on the value of gold.[200] The counterpart of the silver cake was the gold cake, made with identical ingredients but egg yolks only.[201]

The invention and spread of baking chocolate brought another momentous change in late nineteenth-century America. In the 1890s the Baker Chocolate Company of Dorchester, Massachusetts, began marketing its unsweetened chocolate for baking rather than for drinking. (Keep in mind that Baker's Chocolate is a brand name, named for the Baker family, and does not refer specifically to chocolate made for baking. Likewise, German chocolate was named for Samuel German, the man who developed it, not for the country.)[202] Though other brands tried to compete, Baker's vigorous advertising ensured that it dominated the field.[203]

In the first decades after the Civil War, "chocolate cake" meant a light-colored layer cake with chocolate icing between the layers or on top.[204] By the 1890s, the cake we now recognize as chocolate cake had come into being, with the cake as well as the icing containing baking chocolate. It was not common, however.[205] That would wait for the new century.

With the development of layer cakes came fillings—soft, sugary confections to put between the layers. Some resembled custard.[206] Others consisted simply of cream and egg whites, flavored with lemon juice, or of eggs, sugar, and butter. Chocolate filling quickly became a favorite. Chunky fillings might have nuts or chopped apples.[207] And sometimes the filling stole the show. In the 1890s, Emma Rylander Lane of Clayton, Alabama, self-published a cook-book, *Some Good Things to Eat*. She included the recipe for "Prize Cake," which later became known as the "Lane cake" in her honor. The cake itself was sim-ple and delicate, baked in four layers. The flavor-packed filling consisted of egg yolks, sugar, butter, raisins, whiskey or brandy, and vanilla.[208] From Ala-bama, the Lane cake spread across the United States, as we will see later.

People in the nineteenth century often called the outside coating for cakes by its older name, icing, rather than by the newer term, frosting.[209] The most common, and trickiest, remained boiled icings. Usually left white, they could also be flavored with vanilla, orange juice, rose water, lemon, or even choco-late.[210] After all the work involved, that icing was best served on the day that it was made.[211] An easier formula for white icing contained sugar and egg whites, beaten together.[212] A simple caramel icing consisted of brown sugar, butter, and milk, cooked simultaneously.[213]

Some cooks put sauces over cakes rather than iced them. Some were pour-able, while others, called "hard" sauces, were more like spreads. Most sauces had bases of butter and sugar, flavored with wine or whiskey, lemon juice, or nutmeg.[214] Cookbook writer Annabella Hill cautioned bakers, "All butter sauces should be made of good, fresh butter. Nothing good can be made of rancid butter; the taste cannot be disguised."[215] Others were made of wine and sugar boiled together with egg yolks and lemon peel and juice, orange peel, or nutmeg added.[216]

Charlotte russes, built on sponge cake (sometimes in the form of lady-fingers), continued their great acclaim.[217] Wider availability of gelatin made delicate confections more stable. Unflavored dried gelatin, extracted from the bones of cows' feet, first came to the United States from England in the 1840s. American Charles Knox developed granulated gelatin in 1894, making it easier for housewives to incorporate in their cooking. By 1900, Savannah merchants were advertising five brands, including Knox.[218]

Various desserts used sponge cake soaked in wine as the base for flavored whipped cream or custard.[219] Although the British might call such a dessert a trifle, southern Americans used other names. Cookbook writer Mrs. E. J. Verstille's construction went by the name of "tipsy cake." The cook first baked six sponge cakes and steeped them in brandy. Next, she cut almonds "into spikes" and studded the cakes with them. The spiky cakes were then "piled" in a pyramid on a dish. The cook poured a custard around them and then "la[id] preserves in heaps" upon the cakes.[220]

IN THE LATTER PART of the nineteenth century, home cooks had at their disposal growing assortments of materials, recipes, and paraphernalia for all types of baking, much of it recognizable a century and a half later. Commercial baking also made inroads, however, as the number of people selling baked goods continued to grow in the postbellum years.

Freedpeople quickly entered the baking market. In 1865, Sidney Andrews observed a strong entrepreneurial spirit among them: "Half a dollar will start a whole family in trade, and a negro woman in Columbia, to whom that amount had been given, was next day selling corn-cake and peaches on a corner near the post-office, where I found her on every succeeding day of my stay."[221] African American men peddled ginger cakes during religious revivals and elections and to train passengers passing through.[222] Time, ingredients, and courage all played parts in freedpeople setting themselves up in the baking business.

Storefronts selling baked goods also increased. Following a national trend in the 1870s, concerned women created establishments called women's exchanges to give needy white women venues to make money. Most dealers sold textiles, but some also ventured into food sales. In Richmond, for example, women "whose circumstances make it necessary for them to dispose of their handiwork" supplied "Cakes, Breads, and orders filled daily for Desserts."[223] The Christian Woman's Exchange in New Orleans offered "meals at all hours . . . home-made bread, cake, pastries . . . entirely for the benefit of reduced gentlewomen." They also took orders for mince pies, fruitcakes, and plum puddings for the holidays.[224] Women's exchanges apparently met their charitable goals well enough, for they continued into the twentieth century.

In the decades following the Civil War, commercial baking businesses expanded dramatically. Even small towns boasted local bakeries. The Newnan Bakery in Georgia advertised its wares in 1885, everything from loaf bread to sponge meringues. The Columbus Bakery made sure that its goods were of the latest style, including rye bread, graham bread, "maccaroons," and ladyfingers. Bakers encouraged customers to shop locally: in 1899, the *Jackson Economist* from Winder, Georgia, admonished its readers, "Don't send off to Atlanta for what you can get at home."[225]

Southerners with cash gladly availed themselves of bakers' wares. Gertrude Thomas, a white housewife in Augusta, Georgia, "sent Uncle Jim down to the French Store for an iced pound cake" for the new year of 1866. Similarly, Marion Harland's father ordered a "Christmas fruit cake . . . of noble proportions and brave with ornate icing" from the revered confectioner Pizzini in Richmond for the holidays.[226] Even impoverished sharecroppers occasionally bought "baker's bread."[227]

Most bakers were white, with a significant number being German immigrants. For example, August Weidmann opened a bakery in 1896 in Corsicana,

Texas, awash with new oil money. He specialized in fruitcake, using a recipe that he brought with him from Europe. Weidmann's Collin Street Bakery developed into a mail-order business with a global following that continues in 2021.[228]

African Americans also launched new enterprises. Just after the end of the Civil War, skilled freedpeople in New Orleans founded a "People's Bakery," though it was undercapitalized and did not last.[229] In Washington, D.C., Mrs. J. Johnson offered "Wedding Cakes . . . made to order at the shortest notice."[230] In 1899, an Atlanta University survey found ten African American "bakers with shops"—entrepreneurs—in various places across the South. The largest was in Norfolk, Virginia, a baker who had been in business ten years and had a capital investment of $2,000.[231]

In 1877, Staunton, Virginia, baker John Hounihan clearly laid out the difficulties and profits of the work: "Cakes are not a necessary thing of life, and bakers must work to attract the eye and suit the taste." But there was money to be made. He observed that a Stonewall Jackson cake, with layers of pound cake, lady cake, and sponge cake, filled with jelly, iced with "pink water icing," and decorated with flowers and roses, could bring between three and five dollars. (Water icing may have been simply confectioners' sugar and water.) Slices of Robert E. Lee cake would "sell swell at five cents a piece."[232] He aimed his advice at his white comrades, as an African American baker would be unlikely to make or sell goods named for Confederate soldiers, but the profit motive was clear.

Larger cities brimmed with bakers. Charleston bakeshops employed almost 300 men.[233] Wholesale bakers, sometimes outside the region, sold goods to grocers for resale. Matzos, the unleavened bread for the Jewish Passover, probably came from Philadelphia and New York.[234] When Wiley H. Bates, an African American entrepreneur, opened his grocery store in Annapolis in 1884, his stock included ten pounds of gingersnaps, almost surely baked somewhere else and purchased by Bates for resale.[235]

New Orleans continued to shine in the commercial baking business. By 1871, New Orleans had 149 bakeries for 191,000 residents.[236] Among the many notable bakery owners was Margaret Gaffney Haughery, who emigrated from Ireland as a child. Although she was not literate, she was smart and shrewd. When her husband and only child died in 1836, Haughery began investing her money and loaning it to others. In 1859, she repossessed a large steam bakery and began running it herself. The business, simply known as "Margaret's Bakery," thrived, making numerous kinds of bread, biscuits, and crackers. Haughery gained local fame not only for the high quality of her baked products but also for her many acts of charity, especially for the children in

Statue of Margaret Haughery, Camp and Prytania Streets, New Orleans. The Charles L. Franck Studio Collection at The Historic New Orleans Collection, acc. no. 1979.325.5843.

the city's Catholic orphanages. After Haughery died in 1882, leaving most of her estate to multiple orphanages, admirers erected a statue of her that still stands in the Garden District.[237]

The Café du Monde opened in the French Quarter in 1862, serving coffee and doughnuts, made from pastry dough and fried, topped with powdered sugar, and served hot. Joseph Juresch opened a competitor, the Morning Call, in 1870, a few blocks downriver in the French Market.[238] As New Orleans grew, it attracted immigrants from across the globe. Abduhlaha Al Azize established the "first Arab bakery" in 1874, and French citizen Justin Langlés began baking Italian specialties in 1879.[239] Numerous Jewish bakers also set up shop in the Crescent City. In 1895, B. Moses named his business the "Southern Matzos Bakery."[240] The city's baking culture reflected its diversity.

Baking continued to be a strenuous occupation. Many bakers lived on the premises of the business because of the overnight schedule required to have hot bread ready by dawn. The workers united to improve their working hours and living situations. Like their peers elsewhere in the United States, the bakers in New Orleans organized into benevolent societies and then unions. In 1892, members of the Union of Journeymen Bakers and Confectioners won their demands for "an amelioration of their hard conditions": a twelve-hour workday Sunday through Thursday, a fifteen-hour day on Friday, and Saturday as the workers' one day off. The agreement also forbade any boss baker from "requiring his journeymen to board and lodge on his, the employer's premises."[241] How long the hours must have been before this "amelioration."

Invented in the 1840s, the process of steam baking sped across the United States after the Civil War. Introducing steam into the oven gave a finished loaf of bread a beautiful golden crust. A baker could bring in something as basic as a "moistened wisp of straw" to produce vapor.[242] Newer ovens had steam pipes built right into them. In 1871, the G&C Steam Bakery in Galveston swept the awards at the Texas State Fair for the best crackers, bread, rye bread, soda biscuits, and butter crackers. Clearly steam was the way of the future.[243]

Another significant change to industrial baking was the introduction of Viennese-style bread at the 1876 Philadelphia Centennial Exposition. The key difference between Viennese and regular bread was the use of milk rather than water, providing a more even crumb and a softer crust.[244] The new bread caught on widely in places like Waynesboro, Georgia, where Austrian immigrant Morris Blatt opened the New Vienna Bakery in 1893.[245] New bread pans produced a standard square shape. "Box bread," baked in tin boxes, had a thin, soft crust as well as a soft interior. Later given the name "Pullman bread," these loaves resembled those that we see stacked in grocery stores today.[246] National and international trends shaped southern baking.

THE PERIOD BETWEEN the Civil War and 1900 saw major changes in the South. White supremacists used racial violence to enforce the ever-hardening segregation of African Americans, but a significant number of African Americans made financial progress nonetheless, enjoying middle-class lifestyles and foods. Many white southerners remained poor even as the fortunes of wealthy white families soared. Industrialization and transportation increased the availability of baked goods for many southerners, while growing ethnic diversity and a national economy brought new tastes to the region. These changes would accelerate through the booms and busts of the early twentieth century, when baking would still represent prosperity and poverty in the South.

Chapter 7

JELLY ROLL

....

The Modernizing South

hen blues idol Bessie Smith sang in 1927, "I need a little sugar in my bowl, I need a little jelly in my roll," she invoked the tradition of comparing food with sex, given fresh attention through modern media. In the blues, angel food cake, cookies, and shortening bread all stood in for another kind of desire, but the jelly roll, a plain cake with sweet filling, was the favorite metaphor.[1] Music—whether live, on the radio, or recorded—and baked goods all told the same story. Desire and baking were central to understanding the modernizing South.

As the South increasingly assimilated into the greater United States between 1900 and 1940, baking played an integral role in the changes that reshaped southern culture. Developments in transportation (railroads and highways) as well as communication (through radios and telephones) meant that southerners became less isolated from the rest of the nation. At the same time, racism and poverty continued to characterize the South more than other parts of the country. Some southern baking practices remained distinct, while others took on more national trends. When a southern baker made a recipe created in Minneapolis, for example, that recipe became, in many senses, southern as well as midwestern.

World War I provides a good example of Americanization. During the war, in which the United States was directly involved for only nineteen months, the U.S. Food Administration urged voluntary conservation of wheat and meat to provide food for the troops and for starving allies in Europe. Patriotic Americans got on board in a variety of ways. At the Walker County Fair in Georgia in 1918, the only prizes given for baking were for brown bread, cornbread sticks, and "best economical war bread."[2] In Tampa, "American" bakers limited their production to three kinds of loaf bread and temporarily discontinued rolls and buns. The "Latin" bakers restricted themselves to an "Italian" and a "Spanish"—probably Cuban—loaf. German bakers suffered accusations of being disloyal to the United States.[3] For most southerners, eating corn during the war was not a big deal, though some recalled wheat shortages. Howard Matthies, whose German Texas family expected great bread, commented, "Well, during World War I, we had to eat rye bread and barley bread," and Myrtle Calvert Dodd observed, "Of course, during the war, they got out of flour and had to have cornbread for breakfast, and none of us liked that."[4] But Armistice Day came after a year and a half, and wheaten biscuits and hot rolls were again the breads of choice for southern Americans.

The consumer boom in the first part of the twentieth century brought changes to the kitchen. Although some southerners continued to cook on open hearths, most made the transition to stoves fired with wood.[5] Families saved their pennies to buy them, and the used stove market thrived. When East Texan Mary Cimarolli's family moved to a dilapidated house with only a fireplace in 1937, her father quickly paid four dollars for a used stove.[6] Mildred Council, the esteemed African American restaurateur born in North Carolina in 1930, remembered the challenge of making a wood fire. As a small girl she got chips and bark from the woodpile to start her fire and then "blew and blew on it until I was dizzy."[7]

Although stoves improved over time, they still had problems. Arkansan Genevieve Sadler recalled that the wind sometimes sent rank-smelling smoke back down her chimney.[8] When a family got the first woodstove in a neighborhood, the neighbors often came to see it. Georgian Nora Garland so loved the small stove that her family acquired about 1906 that she wrote a poem about it. The middle stanza read,

All the neighbors wondered
When we got the thing to go
They said it would burst and kill us all
Some twenty year[s] ago.[9]

The next generation of stoves burned kerosene. Texan Inez Folley recalled the change: "I had to get used to cooking on an oil stove; it's much different . . . than cooking with a wood stove." Her sister complained about the taste of kerosene in her biscuits, but Folley was willing to tolerate the taste in return for not having to cut stovewood.[10] Carey Snyder commented that his mother's baking suffered as she switched from wood to gas. She used the same American Beauty flour and Rumford baking powder in her biscuits, but the biscuits "never were right anymore."[11]

Inventors came up with new kinds of pans to use with these stoves. New smelting processes made aluminum widely available after 1900, bringing lightweight, rustproof bakeware to the household. In 1915, the Corning Company introduced Pyrex, the first glass bakeware, made of the same borosilicate as laboratory vessels.[12] Bakers had ever-increasing choices for their kitchens, easier to handle and clean.

Even when they had stoves, some southern women continued to bake in the fireplace, using the hearth or Dutch ovens.[13] North Carolinian Cherokee Mary Shell recalled, "Mother had a cook stove and then she had a fireplace right by the cook stove. . . . Had an oven [Dutch oven], you know, to bake the bread. That's the best eatin' you can eat, bread cooked on the fireplace oven."[14]

Outdoor ovens also persisted. Italian immigrants brought to the South their rich bread-baking traditions, including the outdoor brick oven.[15] Tony Monteleone remembered his grandparents' oven in Tangipahoa Parish, Louisiana, in the 1930s:

> Their bread-baking oven, which was built of mud bricks, was located outside. My grandfather would fill the bottom of the oven with wood, light it, and wait for it to burn down, which took about two hours. While waiting for the oven to heat, my grandmother would place the dough in the baking pans made from olive-oil cans which had been cut in half. Money was not spent on luxury items such as baking pans. Once the oven was heated, the pans of dough would be placed inside on a board attached to a long stick and then removed once the bread was baked. Ten to twelve loaves of bread would be baked at the same time.[16]

Refrigeration spread more slowly than stoves. Rural southerners continued to use cisterns and wells for cooling. Myrtle Dodd remembered, "We had a bucket that went down in the well to keep [milk] cool. . . . Sometimes it'd be a little blinky [slightly sour] and we didn't like that."[17] Crock jars wrapped with wet cloths served as a basic form of evaporative cooling. Store-bought "water coolers" consisted of metal posts holding shelves. The posts stood in a pan of water, and the water spread throughout a cloth wrapped around the shelves, keeping the foods inside cool.[18] Iceboxes were more common in urban areas than in rural settings; food reformer Dorothy Dickins commented, "Very few [rural people] purchased ice as it is expensive and troublesome to bring home. The majority consider it a luxury, especially as its season comes at a time when money is scarce."[19]

Electric refrigerators started appearing in southern homes in the 1920s.[20] The first electric refrigerators had all sorts of limitations, from the poisonous gases they used as coolants to the need for electricity for power.[21] Gradually, manufacturers addressed the hazards, and prices came down substantially. By 1940, Westinghouse offered "TWICE the Value at HALF the Cost" of its earlier models.[22] Even in cities, however, water, gas, and electric utility service spread unevenly, and many poor town dwellers still lacked these conveniences. For them and for rural families without electricity, the icebox remained the best choice for cooling.

The rural South did not share the prosperity of urban areas in the 1920s, and during the Great Depression, hunger increased for many southerners, especially African Americans. Black workers in the sawmill town of Bogalusa, Louisiana, sang of baking shortages to the tune of "Stormy Weather":

> Don't know why Mammy don't make no apple pie—
> Starvation—
> Since Pa lost his occupation—
> Keep hungry all the time. . . .
> Don't know why Mammy don't bake no banana and lemon pie.[23]

Slowly—way too slowly—the U.S. government began allocating commodities to poor families. (Commodity distribution was more about helping farmers sell their crops than about feeding hungry people.) Starting in 1932, the government distributed flour to hundreds of thousands of families—mostly white—across the South.[24] But the amounts were small. Between 1933 and 1935, the Federal Surplus Relief Commission distributed a measly half a pound of flour and half a pound of butter, on average, per recipient each month.[25]

Relief programs morphed throughout the Depression. In some places, southerners received the ingredients to bake at home—flour, cornmeal, lard, and molasses—and in others they got already baked white bread. Sometimes recipients were given varying amounts of canned milk, dried fruit, salt, baking soda, or butter and eggs.[26] Local boards decided who would receive relief, and many times they excluded African Americans.[27] Hunger was real, and it persisted.

THROUGH WAR, prosperity, and economic depression, many southerners continued to eat cornbread two or three times a day. Bread made of cornmeal was so central to the southern way of life that linguists in the 1930s recorded

332 terms for it.[28] When a cruel husband wanted to inflict maximum pain on his wife as he abandoned her and their children, he "pour[ed] the little coal oil that was left in their can into their cornmeal crock."[29] Cornbread was virtually all homemade, as bakeries couldn't supply it fresh and hot, and no one wanted it cold or stale. Although "Jiffy" cornbread mix was invented in Chelsea, Michigan, in 1930, it made its way south only slowly, and no cornbread mixes advertised in the region before World War II.[30]

The white and yellow cornmeal controversy continued. William Riley of Sylva, North Carolina, emphasized, "White corn is for folks, yellow for critters."[31] Farm families prized their white corn. Texan Pearl Wynn Guderian recalled, "Oh, my mother did not want the yellow meal. We always had to plant some white corn so we would have our corn meal for year-round use."[32] The accomplished cooks in famed chef Edna Lewis's African American family in Virginia specified it in many recipes.[33] Southerners loved having a choice about something as elemental as corn.

Native Americans continued to embellish their cornbread as their ancestors had, according to an observer in 1922. Cherokee, Creek, and Seminole all made bread with pumpkin and cornmeal, formed into pones or small loaves.[34] Bean bread consisted of kidney beans, cornmeal, and boiling water, made into patties. Dutch ovens were the vessel of choice for baking these breads.[35]

The Choctaw, Chickasaw, Creek, and Seminole all fermented cornmeal for bread. The Choctaw-Chickasaw version, *paluska hawushko*, was simple: soak cracked corn overnight, add it to cornmeal, and add boiling water to make a stiff batter. The baker let the batter stand until it fermented slightly and baked it in a Dutch oven.[36] The more complicated Creek-Seminole type, *tuk-like-tokse*, required three days to prepare. First the bakers soaked flint corn in warm water, pounded the corn to loosen the hulls, removed the hulls, and soaked the clean corn again. On the second day, they pounded the corn to a fine meal, sifted, and boiled it to a gruel, which fermented in an earthen jar overnight. The cooks then baked the fermented paste in a Dutch oven.[37] Creek and Seminole sometimes added European ingredients—flour, salt, soda, and yeast—to the sour cornmeal dough for loaf bread.[38]

Creek and Seminole also made long-lasting *chuto-ahake* (translated as "Resembling a Rock—Hard Bread"). The baker soaked shelled flint corn in a strong solution of ash lye and water and then pounded and husked the grains. She sifted it again to produce "a fine meal." She then mixed the meal with boiling water and more "strong ash-lye drippings" to make a stiff dough, shaped the dough into a ring, and baked it. The fresh-baked bread then sat in the sun until "perfectly dry . . . hard as wood." The baker strung the rings on heavy cord and hung them for storage.[39]

Southerners continued to enjoy fried cornbread. Hot-water cornbread was a favorite of African Americans. Cleora Butler recalled that her grandmother Bettie Sadler Manning made it from homegrown cornmeal, salt, sugar, and melted bacon drippings, plus of course boiling water, and she fried it in bacon fat as well. Sometimes she added cracklings for extra flavor and texture.[40] The boiling water began cooking the meal, rendering it softer and less gritty. The pones fried quickly, making the outside brown and crunchy while the insides remained tender. White Texan Hester Calvert fed her family of ten on cornbread patties, sometimes called "dog bread," during the lean times of late winter. Her daughter recalled, "She'd just put one big drop out of a spoon; be about like the palm of your hand. We had a big heavy skillet—she'd fill that full and then stack them and do it again."[41] The term "hushpuppies" came into common use in the 1920s, to mean cornbread fried alongside fish, in the same grease.[42] We'll discuss them more in the next chapter.

The newest form of cornbread in the South—and at the same time one of the oldest—was the tortilla, brought by Mexican immigrants as they came to Central and North Texas after 1900, escaping ongoing political violence. Women like Cleofas Hernandez made tortillas three times a day.[43] Adelaida Almanza left the cotton fields at midday to fix hot, fresh tortillas for her family's meal. The family purchased ground corn. She added lye to nixtamalize the corn (see chapter 1) and ground the resulting mixture, called masa harina, in her metate. She then shaped the dough into balls, rolled them into flat circles, and cooked them on a comal on top of the stove.[44] Some Mexican Americans preferred flour tortillas, which required wheat flour and lard or shortening, over corn. Susan Valerio Moreno remembered, "The only thing we didn't have was flour to make tortillas. We'd grind our corn. We could make our corn tortillas, but none of the kids liked the corn tortillas. We liked the flour."[45]

Yes, everyone loved wheat flour, whether it was because they liked the taste and texture or because it was the more prestigious grain. By World War II, almost all southerners had wheat flour at least some of the time. The poorest tenants in the Yazoo-Mississippi Delta ate biscuits one morning a week, with cornbread at all the other meals.[46] While landlords and store owners might veto expenditures by African Americans that they deemed extravagant or inappropriate, they gradually allowed flour.[47] Food reformers believed that wheat bread was more socially refined than cornbread. In eastern Kentucky, the founders of the Hindman Settlement School sought to replace mountain people's cornbread with more "civilized" wheat biscuits and bread.[48]

Some farmers still grew small wheat patches for their families' use. North Carolinian Harold Moss recalled, "They raised a field of wheat. . . . They just had enough of it to make their bread. That's all they ever grow, one field."[49]

Five-year-old Vera Hill with a flour sack picking cotton, Comanche County, Oklahoma, 1916. Photo by Lewis Hine, Library of Congress, LC-DIG-nclc-00616.

But most southerners bought their flour from stores, often in twenty-four- or forty-eight-pound bags.[50]

Those bags came in handy. By the 1920s, thrifty farmwives began reusing sacks from store-bought ingredients to make all sorts of items. A child's first cotton-picking sack might well be a ten-pound flour sack with a strap sewn onto it.[51] Some women sewed household goods such as pillow cases and dish towels.[52] But perhaps the most common use was for children's clothing, from underwear to dresses.[53] Women scrubbed the printed labels off the bags and then dyed them. In the late 1930s, manufacturers began printing their bags with colorful patterns. To soften the bags, Mary Cimarolli's mother washed them several times, dried them in the sun, and then ironed them.[54] Before long, women started choosing their brands of flour with the goal of getting enough matching bags to make garments.[55] An industrious woman could make something out of almost nothing. Tennessean Delilah Woodruff "raveled" string from the bags and crocheted bedspreads and doilies with it, and innumerable women made quilts from flour and sugar sacks.[56]

Self-rising flour continued to be an innovation for many southerners.[57] Ethel Marshall Faucette remembered, "Whenever they begin to put out this self rising flour, my momma bought that. But she didn't buy it regular, she used her old straight grade flour where it was ground at the mill." The self-rising flour, Faucette said, came from their company store (a stored owned by their employer, which likely charged outrageous prices).[58] An unnamed woman from the textile mill town of Marion, North Carolina, recalled, "I used to make my biscuits with plain flour and baking powder till my husband told me it was all right to use the self-rising kind. . . . I was just doing what I was supposed to."[59] She kept her expenses close to the bone and believed she had to have her husband's permission to indulge in self-rising flour.

Though American reformers got stirred up about food purity early in the twentieth century, flour was low on their list. It could be adulterated with numerous white powders—plaster of paris, borax, chalk, or alum, to name only a few—but that was minor compared with the problems in the animal products industries.[60] The biggest concern regarding flour, which is cream-colored when it is fresh, was the practice of bleaching it. Consumers unwittingly preferred white flour, and the industry obliged with numerous bleaching methods. The U.S. Department of Agriculture banned the most dangerous, nitrogen peroxide, in 1908. Other chemicals, such as nitrogen trichloride and chlorine gas, prevailed, however, and bleaching flour became common practice among large millers.[61]

As their industry centralized, corporate millers began to degerminate their corn and wheat—removing the oily, nutritious germ from the grain kernels. Although the process made cornmeal and flour less likely to turn rancid, it also removed critical nutrients.[62] Not surprisingly, the number of southerners diagnosed with pellagra, a disease caused by niacin deficiency, began to skyrocket. Pellagra was a horrific affliction, causing lesions of the skin and mucous membranes, diarrhea, dementia, and eventual death. As awareness increased, a stunning number of cases were diagnosed: by 1924, at least 90,000 southerners were detected with the disease. After much trial and error by researchers, nutritionists began experimenting with foods such as milk, yeast, and liver to combat pellagra. In the 1920s, many large commercial bakers began adding 6 percent nonfat milk solids to their breads to help combat the problem, and in the 1930s, bakers began voluntarily enriching bread with high-vitamin yeast or synthetic vitamins.[63] By 1939, margarine manufacturers, too, were adding vitamins A and D, mostly from fish liver oil, to their product.[64] Not until the 1940s, however, would pellagra be conquered.

Many of the forms in which people loved wheat flour were old friends from decades, even centuries, before. Take pancakes and waffles, for instance.

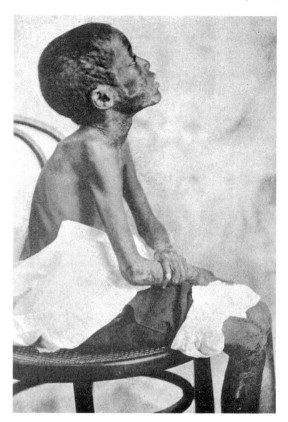

Child with pellagra, South Carolina, about
1909. Published in Marie, *Pellagra*, 182.

Aluminum stovetop griddles promised greaseless, perfect pancakes, while electric griddles and waffle irons provided constant, steady heat. Though advertisers might tout electric waffle irons as "essential," they remained expensive luxuries for many cooks.[65]

The period between 1900 and 1940, with cheap flour and reliable baking powder, might well be called the golden age of southern biscuits. Georgian John Patterson Vaughan exulted in the newfound prosperity that meant he could have biscuits instead of cornbread for breakfast, exclaiming, "Now I got yaller butter and biscuits ever mornin'."[66] Mexican immigrants learned to like biscuits in place of tortillas as their tastes adapted to their new situations.[67]

Many southern cooks, both white and Black, fixed biscuits for breakfast seven days a week and sometimes for dinner and supper as well, baking them hot and fresh. Alabaman Elma Lee Hall remembered, "I been making biscuits ever since I had to stand in a chair to reach the biscuit tray. . . . I always cooked biscuits three times a day. Paw and the others would've pitched a fit if they had to eat cold biscuits."[68] Seventy years after the fact, Texan Bernice Porter Bostick Weir could still recall her mother's biscuit ingredients: "She always used buttermilk to make her biscuits and that requires a pinch of soda and two pinches of baking powder and about a tablespoon full of lard. And then about a cup and a half of milk—that would make about fifteen or eighteen biscuits."[69]

The quality of a woman's biscuits still stood in for her worth as a house-keeper.[70] More than ever, biscuits also represented social class. Margaret McDow MacDougall remembered, "We had tiny little biscuits like this, and the mill children had great hunky biscuits. It was food for them; for us it was dainty little this, that, and the other."[71] And so it went, with small brown cakes carrying great social meaning.

Most biscuits were leavened with baking powder, though some recipes designated as "old-fashioned" used soda and cream of tartar or buttermilk.[72] Yeast biscuits, often called "Dixie biscuits," were a time-consuming alternative.[73] "Cathead biscuits" were shaped by hand rather than by rolling and cutting. They earned their name by being extra large—as big as a cat's head.[74]

A Kentucky wholesale baker named Lively Burgess Willoughby and his wife, Eliza Hall Smith Willoughby, pioneered premade biscuit dough in the 1920s. In 1931, Lively Willoughby patented the process for canned, refrigerated dough. He made biscuit dough with flour, baking powder, salt, sugar, shortening, buttermilk, and soda, and then he cut the dough, put it in a metal tube, glued the ends on, and refrigerated it. When he opened the tube a week later, the biscuit dough was still ready for baking. Willoughby refined the process and sold it to Ballard and Ballard Flour Mills of Louisville.[75] Thus was born the "whomp" biscuit, as humorist Jerry Clower dubbed it, from the sound the tube makes when you whack it against the countertop to open it.

Also in 1931, General Mills, the huge milling company in Minneapolis, introduced Bisquick, a biscuit mix. Like self-rising flour, Bisquick had leavening already mixed in. Like pancake mix, it contained dried milk. But what was new about Bisquick was that the fat was also included in the mix. According to General Mills lore, Cal Smith, a company executive, was traveling on the Southern Pacific railway and asked the dining car chef, an unnamed African American man, to prepare biscuits at an odd hour. Smith was astonished when the chef produced hot, delicious biscuits in short order. Upon inquiry, the chef explained that he kept all his ingredients—flour, baking powder, salt, and shortening—at the ready so that all he had to do was add liquid. Smith took the concept to Minneapolis, where the General Mills chemists determined sesame oil to be the correct fat. To use Bisquick, all a cook had to do was add water and then shape the dough. General Mills created a massive marketing campaign with movie stars and the fictional character Betty Crocker.[76] In early 1932, shoppers in Brenham, Texas, paid thirty-three cents for a forty-ounce package—which would make about three dozen biscuits—with the promise "Add water or milk, enjoy the finest Biscuits you ever baked—no failures."[77]

Even as poor southerners rejoiced in their wheat flour biscuits, some status-conscious eaters found a new preference: store-bought sliced bread. Booker T. Washington encouraged the use of "cold light bread" by the teachers and students at Tuskegee Institute, wanting his charges to know about supposedly more refined things in life.[78] Numerous people recalled their shame as children at bringing homemade biscuits in their school lunches. Black Texan Arthur Fred Joe remembered, "We'd take biscuits and syrup and stuff in a bucket. I'd always find the kids with light bread to change with. I wanted a light bread sandwich."[79] Mean kids made fun of their peers from the countryside. Anna May Peyrot Wharton, who went to all-white schools, recalled "smart-aleck girls": "They'd snigger and say, 'Look! Look! She's eating one of them old biscuits and we got light bread.' They'd do that every day, and I couldn't hardly take that."[80] Bread hierarchy mattered as much in southern elementary schools as it did elsewhere.

Mixes eased the preparation of old favorite gingerbread. In the mid-1930s, boxed gingerbread mixes spread across the South, including the Dromedary brand, made by the New York company Hills Brothers. Dromedary gave its mix a special southern twist by claiming to be based on the "200-year-old private recipe of the Washington family" obtained "by special permission of the Washington-Lewis Chapter, Daughters of the American Revolution." The Dromedary mix required only water, containing all other essential ingredients, but it still had a southern pedigree.[81]

Nut breads, leavened with baking powder and mixed with raisins, walnuts, or pecans, became increasingly popular.[82] Orange nut bread was sufficiently chic that Cleora Butler baked fifty loaves of it for a swanky Tulsa party in 1936, served with fresh local butter alongside spiced tea. She recalled that the recipe, which included "California oranges, pecans, and 'orange rind syrup,'" came from the metropolis of Oklahoma City.[83]

Pecans, the most common nut in the lower South, started showing up frequently in recipes in the twentieth century. Though horticulturalists such as an enslaved man named Antoine began working to improve pecans in the 1840s, the slow-growing trees took a long time to domesticate, and serious commercial production began only in the 1880s. By 1900, Georgia and Texas were the centers of the pecan-growing industry, and production in the South rose sixteenfold between 1900 and 1920. Pecan use in baking grew accordingly.[84]

In another use of nuts—actually legumes—George Washington Carver, an agricultural scientist at Tuskegee Institute, developed recipes using peanuts. He began his work trying to get farmers to grow peanuts to fix nitrogen in the soil, but peanuts also added nutrition (particularly protein and fat), texture, and taste to baked goods. Carver's baking recipes all started with wheat flour and added peanuts, but his attempts to improve the southern diet gained favorable attention.[85]

Although store-bought bread was becoming the norm, some women continued to bake yeast bread at home or for their employers. In the Ybor City area of Tampa, Florida, Italian immigrant women baked every Friday, tantalizing the neighborhood with the aroma.[86]

A few people continued to make yeast.[87] Cajun Eula Mae Doré recalled the technique of her mother, Semar Touchet: "She would take some peach leaves and she boiled them, like you would make a tea, and she would put cornmeal in it and a little piece of dough, and let it rise. Each time she would save a little piece of that homemade dough." With the yeast, Touchet made *pain leve*, or light bread, for her family's supper.[88]

Women prized their starters, which often began with flour, sugar, salt, yeast, milk, water, and sometimes potatoes.[89] Genevieve Sadler remembered, "This 'starter' yeast was given to me by Mrs. Turner. It was a yeast that was kept by adding sugar and flour and water each time the yeast was used for bread making. The neighboring women seemed to keep this yeast going year after year, those who neglected it borrowing from others and adding the sugar and flour and water until it bubbled in the fruit jar and was ready for use. Some one told me that the original 'starter' had been brought from Missouri."[90] Lou Folley called her starter "traveling yeast." Her daughter recalled, "You just kept on making batches out of the same—it would just travel. You wouldn't go down to the store and buy yeast cake to make the rolls."[91] Keeping the starter alive added to a woman's chores, but sharing meant that she could rely on others' help if she slipped up.

Individual yeast rolls, more special than biscuits, were sometimes reserved for the Sunday early-afternoon meal known as dinner. Eugenia Nixson, who ran a boardinghouse for white patrons in Silsbee, Texas, loftily observed, "On Sundays everybody from the churches came and ate. We made yeast rolls all the time. Never plain biscuits or anything like that."[92]

The new "icebox rolls" used modern technology to ease baking, as the dough rose in the icebox or refrigerator overnight. It could then be shaped and baked in the morning, with little preparation time needed before serving.[93] Happy breakfast eaters also enjoyed yeasted sweet rolls and cinnamon rolls. Although a quick version of Sally Lunn buns leavened with baking powder developed in the twentieth century, traditionalists continued to make theirs with yeast.[94]

In the late nineteenth century, German immigrants to Texas brought with them recipes for a sweet yeasted bread that they called coffee cake. Howard Matthies remembered, "Mother would make the coffee cakes out of that same dough that she made bread of . . . and let it rise. And then she put butter or cream on it and put sugar on it—and it was flat like that—and bake it."[95] Czech women from Moravia and Bohemia produced kolaches, flat buns with sweet toppings made from poppy seeds, peaches, or other fruits. *Buchta*, another Czech sweet bread, was a yeast dough with a fruit or poppy seed filling baked in a square pan.[96] New Texan families treasured these old-country transplants.

Reformers still blamed pie for dyspepsia, and people still loved it.[97] Atlanta food columnist Henrietta Dull commented, "Pies properly baked will refute the old argument that they are indigestible." Dull did her part to make sure that pie bakers were doing their work correctly, teaching her readers, for example, the difference between a pie pan (slanted sides) and a cake pan (straight sides).[98] Reformers were justifiably dismayed to learn that almost half of poor African American Mississippians ate fruit only when it was baked in pies.[99]

Vegetable shortening, used in the place of butter or lard, altered pastry making.[100] Researchers had sought a lard substitute for decades as prices went up and down and shortages sometimes occurred.[101] The cottonseed oil industry, looking to use seeds left after ginning, provided the real spur. Cottonseeds had to be bleached and deodorized before the oil could be used for cooking, but they soon emerged as a plausible substitute for lard. Memphis food chemist David Wesson in 1899 produced the first commercial shortening made from cottonseed under the trade name Snowdrift. Shortening consumption grew rapidly, and by in less than twenty years it equaled and then surpassed that of lard.[102] Shortening had numerous advantages over lard: it had a neutral, non-porky taste; it did not go rancid; it was uniform in quality; and it creamed, or incorporated air, more readily than lard. While shortening rendered pastry less flaky than lard, cooks were willing to sacrifice texture for convenience and neutral taste. The Cincinnati-based Procter and Gamble Company patented hydrogenation, a process that made cottonseed oil creamy and white, in 1911 and named its new product Crisco, a mashup of "crystallized cottonseed oil."[103] States and the federal government passed numerous statutes governing lard and vegetable shortening. Alabama, for instance, in 1909 decreed that edible cottonseed oil was to be "free from disagreeable tastes or odors."[104] Shortening arrived to stay.

The most popular new pie in the South was invented by a northerner in the 1930s. A woman from New York or Chicago likely came up with the combination of sugar, corn syrup, pecans, eggs, butter, salt, and vanilla that we know and adore as pecan pie. The Corn Products Refining Company of New York and Chicago introduced both light and dark Karo corn syrups in 1902. The pecan pie recipe, allegedly the creation of an unnamed company executive's wife, begin appearing on Karo bottles in the 1930s and instantly became a favorite.[105] Revered Black New Orleans caterer Lena Richard, who later pioneered cooking on television, featured the new pecan pie as the first recipe in the pastry section of her 1939 *New Orleans Cookbook*, showing how fast the recipe caught on with even the most discerning cooks.[106]

Vanilla, a key ingredient in pecan pie and so many other recipes, became readily available with the spread of vanilla orchid cultivation across the globe.[107] The biggest boon for rural southerners was the arrival of two northern companies: Watkins from Minnesota and Rawleigh from Illinois. Rawleigh encouraged its salesmen to ignore racial prejudice and sell to African Americans, and by 1912 both companies had branches in Memphis.[108] With their armies of peddlers traveling rural roads, accepting eggs, butter, and chickens as payment, Watkins and Rawleigh provided farm women with an unprecedented variety of spices and flavorings.[109]

As they did with many other products in the early industrial age, imposters faked or tainted extracts. Vanillin, the primary component in vanilla, could be concocted from pine bark, clove oil, or rice bran.[110] Frauds also made imitation vanilla from tonka beans, which contain coumarin, a chemical that can cause significant liver damage.[111] They adulterated almond extracts and produced lemon extracts with only small amounts of actual lemon.[112] State legislatures and the U.S. Department of Agriculture stepped in, setting purity standards for many extracts to protect sweet eaters.[113]

While southerners began putting pecan pies on their holiday tables, old friend mincemeat continued to show up too, even in sharecroppers' homes.[114] Most mincemeat pie recipes still had meat, particularly beef tongue, and suet as well as booze, despite Prohibition.[115] Or one could take the simple path of Mary Elizabeth Warren from Yazoo City, Mississippi, in 1922. Her "Delicious Mince Pie" recipe consisted of a "small box of mince meat," water, and sugar, baked in a double crust.[116] The State of Georgia made sure that its consumers got high-quality premade mincemeat, ordering that it be "not less than ten (10) per cent of cooked, comminuted [shredded] meat, with chopped suet, apple and other fruit," plus spices, sweeteners, and fruit juices or "spirituous liquors."[117] To the dismay of southern chauvinists, pumpkin pie also became a standard on southern holiday tables, sometimes in preference to sweet potato pie.[118]

When fruit was unavailable, thrifty southern cooks made vinegar pie, which substituted vinegar for produce. Commercially made vinegar had been around since the colonial period, but its use in pies followed the Civil War. Skeptics were put on notice: African American Alfreida Foster, remembering her Aunt Mattie Scott's vinegar pies, commented, "They were good, too."[119] Most people made theirs as a single-crust pie with a filling of butter, sugar, eggs, and vinegar.[120] Fancy versions could be topped with meringue or sweetened cream.[121]

Though rural southerners and some town dwellers continued to keep cows for their personal supplies of milk, cream, and butter, dairy production in the South became increasingly industrialized in the first decades of the twentieth century.[122] Southern dairies didn't attain the scale of their northern counterparts, but a growing number of farmers began commercial milk production after 1900. For example, Sicilian immigrants established dairies around Tampa, and by 1910 there were twenty-six Italian milk vendors in the city.[123] With leadership from Mississippi State University, the Magnolia State's farmers concentrated their efforts selling around Starkville, Memphis, and the port cities on the Gulf Coast.[124] The safety of the milk supply became a significant concern to health officials in the early twentieth century as reformers focused on bovine tuberculosis and sanitation.[125]

With the improvement in roads and the encouragement of home demonstration agents, an increasing number of rural women sold eggs and homemade butter to urban clients. Urban women, for their part, could know or assume that their butter was made locally and hence was fresh and good.[126] But grocers also continued to import dairy products from northern states.[127] Regulators and reformers raised warnings over "renovated butter," rancid butter that was reworked with various chemicals to hide its odor and state of decay.[128] Consumers had to be careful about their milk and butter.

Tropical fruits continued to become cheaper and more widespread. Hawaiian pineapples were now the product of an American company led by the Dole family.[129] In pies, they were most often grated into a custard, baked in a single crust, and topped with meringue or whipped cream.[130] Banana custard pies used the products of the vast United Fruit Company, an American corporation with land in five Caribbean countries that in 1900 shipped more than a million bananas to the United States. Banana boats were technological marvels, refrigerated to allow the fruit to reach far-flung ports still not quite ripe.[131]

Recipes for coconut custard pies showed up in small towns like Pidcoke, Texas (population sixty-five), without any instructions on how to prepare the coconut. Most likely, after centuries of breaking and grating fresh coconut, many cooks began using the dried, sweetened variety. Confusingly, the American who hit on the idea of producing shredded coconut meat of uniform size and quality was Philadelphia flour miller Franklin Baker, who was not a baker and was a different Baker from the one who gave his name to the brand of chocolate.[132] Canned coconut, kept moist with coconut cream, quickly became a staple of southern bakers.[133]

Southerners continued to love homely, simple fried pies. Genevieve Sadler recalled young men from the Ozark Mountains politely refusing her unfamiliar pumpkin pie but eagerly eating fried pies made from dried peaches. Sadler prepared the pies from round pieces of dough, topped with stewed fruit or applesauce. She folded the circles in half, crimped the edges, and fried the pies in a skillet of grease "on top of the stove, each side being well browned as they were turned over in the smoking fat." Sadler observed that dried apples and dried peaches made the best fried pies but that the cooking required a large amount of grease.[134] Georgian Nora Garland remembered apple pies, fried in lard, which went by the names of tarts and half-moon pies, as holiday treats that her mother whipped up: "At Christmas she'd make a *big stack* of them pies."[135]

Cobblers, still humble and beloved, fed diners amply, as African American Texan Ora Lee Degrate recalled: "That was every day, some type of a cobbler. Our family was large, and the cobbler would always go further than a cake."[136] Cobblers could be made from gathered or homegrown fruits. White Alabaman Tommie Bass remembered, "Mother made them out of anything—apples, blackberries, huckleberries, peaches, and plums. We grew or gathered all these things in our homeplace."[137] Others recalled using wild grapes and dewberries. Sweet potatoes, sliced or mashed, also made good cobbler.[138]

Most cobblers started with a batch of biscuit dough, rolled and cut into strips.[139] Sometimes cooks stewed the fruit with water and sugar, and sometimes they put it into the pastry raw. A baker could start with crust or fruit on the bottom.[140] Ora Degrate detailed her method of making cobbler:

> I would get my flour into the bowl that I was going to mix it up in. And I would get my shortening, and take my spoon, and cut it up into that flour. And I would put a little sugar in there so—in order to make the crust sweet, too. And I would mix that up and knead it, just like I would biscuits. And then I would put it on the cloth that I rolled it out on, and get the rolling pin. And at that time, I didn't have a rolling pin so I used a bottle—a round bottle—to roll that dough out with. And then I would cut it in strips the way that I would want it to go in the pan and put it in there. And then I would have my peaches, dewberries, whatever I made the cobbler out of. I would have it in an extra pot. And then I put that layer of dough in there, I would pour more peaches, put more peaches on top,

where they could be in between the layers of the dough. And the reason was for that, my family was large. And if you just put, just two crusts, you don't get very much. But when you put about three in there, then when you cut you got a thick, pretty thick piece.[141]

Degrate made sure that all thirteen of her children had their share.

Cookies were also easy sweets. For Black and white southerners alike, tea cakes remained the most popular cookie. People recalled them as "plain" and not overly sweet.[142] Novelist Zora Neale Hurston gave the name "Tea Cake" to one of the most likable characters in her 1937 novel, *Their Eyes Were Watching God*.

As people from Italy came to the southern United States, particularly Tampa and New Orleans, they brought precious recipes with them. Cookies formed an integral part of St. Joseph's Day altars, multitiered displays of food to honor the husband of Mary the mother of Jesus, whose feast day is March 19. Honoring San Giuseppe began in Sicily in perhaps the twelfth century, and in twentieth-century Louisiana, women like Angelina Caronna Accardo began planning their altars right after Christmas.[143]

Women heaped their home altars with all manner of good foods, including pasta and vegetables, but the centerpiece was a cookie called *cuccidati*. Cuccidati dough was a simple blend of flour, shortening, water, and sugar, while the filling consisted of dried figs, honey, cinnamon, orange zest, and black pepper, ground together. The assembled cookies looked something like Fig Newtons, with an icing made of milk or cream, almond extract, and powdered sugar. Cuccidati for the St. Joseph's altars could be two feet across, shaped as religious symbols with elaborate designs cut into them. "Mommie" Accardo brought her dough-carving tools with her from Sicily.[144] Cuccidati also appeared at the Feast of St. Lucy, December 13, and, in Tampa, on the Cuban Christmas Eve celebration known as Fiesta de Noche Buena.[145]

Chocolate and lemon cannoli, *sfinge* (cream puffs), meringues, sesame seed cookies, biscotti, and *pignolata* also commemorated St. Joseph's Day. Biscotti were small, crunchy cakes in a variety of shapes and sizes, tinted, and flavored with almond, vanilla, lemon, orange, or anise. They were made into a roll, baked, sliced, and baked again. *Pignolata* ("pine cones"), which people also made at Christmas and Easter, started with a dough of eggs and flour that was rolled, stretched, and cut into half-inch pieces. After the pieces dried, the nimble-fingered cook fried them in deep fat, poured melted sugar over them, and then molded the hot, syrup-covered pieces into a pyramid shape. Some faithful cooks believed that the pain of fingers blistered by the hot sugar served as a penance.[146]

The items called cakes were by 1900 what we expect: large confections cut into individual portions. Although cakes became more common, they were still special, symbols of hospitality and abundance.[147] Plenty, not fancy, was the keyword in many southern families. When famed restaurateur Leah Chase was growing up in the African American community of Madisonville, Louisiana, in the 1920s, her family baked for two days before Christmas. Her mother wanted to have six or seven cakes on hand for visitors before midnight Mass. Chase recalled, "They were jelly cakes mostly, or butter cakes, fruitcakes, cakes with chocolate or jelly toppings, and plain pound cakes. . . . You had to make sure you had enough for everybody who came around."[148] Louisiana Cajuns ate *gâteau de sirop* (syrup cake) made in a single layer with homemade cane syrup and served with local fruits. The Steen Company began making cane syrup, "the color of gold in amber," in Abbeville, Louisiana, in 1910.[149]

Stack cakes, filled with dried apples, applesauce, or apple butter, were also simple but treasured, particularly in the southern mountains. The lore about wedding guests bringing and adding a layer is fictitious, however. Such a practice would make for a disappointing offering. As baker and writer Elizabeth Sims observes, the best stack cake cures for two to seven days as "the aromatic blend of cake, fruit, mace, and sorghum melds into dense strata."[150] Tommie Bass recalled the eagerness for stack cake in his childhood: His mother "generally baked this cake about a week or ten days before Christmas and she'd add some of the apple juice, and oh, Lord, that cake would just get as moist and it'd be just as soft, and you're talking about real eating when you hadn't had no cake or nothing since the Christmas before. We'd all crowd around, you know, and just wait for the time for her to start cutting that cake."[151]

Stack cakes could be made from cake, biscuit dough, or pie crust. They might be rolled or patted, and some people baked theirs on the stove rather than in the oven. North Carolinian Fredda Davis remembered her grandmother making stack cake with dried apple filling: "What you did, you made up a dough similar to making biscuits except you put some molasses in there, some shortening and spices like cinnamon and cloves—and in those days you had to chop up your cloves and cinnamon, you know, grind it up. Then you baked it in layers."[152] The layers usually were baked thin, although they could be made thicker and then split. Height counted: Alabamian Franklin Peacock commented, "Three or four weren't nothing to brag about. Five or six is about where you'd want to start talking about your cake."[153] Overachievers might have as many as fifteen layers.[154]

Other traditional favorites abounded. Fruitcakes were still a chore to make, with hours of chopping and difficult stirring. Emma Jane Christian, who cooked for the Moncure family in Williamsburg, observed (in a dialect ascribed to her by her employer), "You better not try dat by yo'self de fus time, ennways. 'Less you have one of dese here new fangled 'lectric aig beaters, yo' got some powful arm beatin' to do, fur dat cake sho' needs some excise [sic] behind de makin' of it!"[155]

The "electric egg beaters" to which Christian referred were likely the electric mixers introduced to the American public in the 1920s. In 1922, the Hobart Company introduced the KitchenAid H5, a stand mixer with a wire whip suspended above a bowl. An electric motor turned the whip at varying speeds. In 1937, KitchenAid developed the enamel-finished K model that has been the standard for more than eighty years.[156] In 1930, the Sunbeam Company launched its Mixmaster, with two interlocking detachable beaters. The Mixmaster could be bought on credit through local companies. In 1935, for example, Georgia Power offered the Mixmaster, which cost $24.50, for $1.95 down and payments of $2.00 per month.[157] Most home cooks, however, still used their eggbeaters or sturdy spoons.

In the 1930s, the Hills Brothers Company of New York, importer of Dromedary brand dates, developed a fruitcake mix that it called "Dixie-Mix, Fruit Cake Mixture from an Old Southern Recipe"—again, like its gingerbread mix, trading on "Old South" imagery. The mix contained fruit and nuts, and the cook added an egg and a third of a cup of fruit juice. Hills even included a baking tin with every package of mix.[158] It seems too good to be true. We don't have any reviews.

Jam cakes, not to be confused with jelly cakes, actually had jam in the batter rather than as a filling. Blackberry was the hands-down favorite, though strawberry jam could suffice. The cakes were sturdy, made with sour cream or buttermilk, spiced with nutmeg, cinnamon, cloves, and allspice, and filled and iced with sugar, butter, and cream or "canned milk." Although they were traditional in the Appalachians, by the early twentieth century jam cakes held favor across the South.[159]

Sponge cakes remained in heavy rotation among southern cooks. Writer James Agee noted that even desperately poor white southerners occasionally had "plain sponge cake with cocoa-chocolate frosting."[160] Angel food cake, introduced in the 1870s, became common after 1900. The delicate cake consisted only of sugar, flour, egg whites, and cream of tartar, sometimes flavored with vanilla. Cooks who used newly invented tube pans benefited from the structure in the center to give the cake extra loft.

And then there were the fancy layer cakes. Coconut cakes often towered at three or four layers.[161] Southerners loved coconut cakes of several kinds: those in which the cake and the frosting both had coconut; those with coconut only in the frosting; those with or without lemon or orange filling; those made with fresh coconut and those made with canned or dried. White and Black southerners Myrtle Dodd and Edna Lewis both remembered fresh coconut as a seasonal specialty. Dodd recalled, "And Christmas, my daddy would find us a coconut. And they'd cut that coconut up and she [her mother] always had a fresh coconut cake and it was so good."[162]

One may well be wondering, what about chocolate? A surprising number of bakers still referred to white layer cakes filled with chocolate frosting as chocolate cakes.[163] But most twentieth-century bakers put chocolate into the cake itself as well as into the frosting, and apparently the darker, the better. Among the first dark-chocolate cakes were fudge cakes, often with cooked chocolate fudge icings, from recipes developed in New England.[164]

Devil's food cake appeared around 1910 and rapidly became adored. Although some recipes included cocoa powder, which was becoming widespread as a baking ingredient, southern cooks called any rich chocolate cake devil's food. Often a devil's food cake sported caramel or white icing instead of chocolate.[165] Chocolate also started showing up as the dark portion of marble cakes, in place of the older spiced cake.[166]

Sometimes frostings eclipsed the cakes. Marshmallows—the soft, pillowy confections made of gum arabic (derived from tree sap), sugar, and egg whites—had been sold in sweet shops since the 1870s, but they became available in cans after 1900, with inexpensive gelatin substituted for the pricey gum.[167] Marshmallow cakes became all the rage. The marshmallows were used in the filling and frosting, not in the actual cake, which was generally a light white layer cake.[168] For her version, Kentuckian Emma Allen Hayes melted marshmallows and water together, added orange juice and chopped fruits and nuts, and beat the mixture until cold before spreading it on the cake.[169]

Caramel cake also took its name from the frosting rather than the cake. Most recipes for caramel cake called for a plain yellow cake, topped with cooked caramel icing. Edna Lewis's kin made their caramel icing by cooking cream and light brown sugar together, adding butter and vanilla, and stirring until the icing thickened.[170] Maya Angelou remembered that her grandmother Annie Henderson of Stamps, Arkansas, added caramel syrup to the cake batter. Mrs. Henderson's version of caramel cake took four to five hours to make.[171]

Fillings could dress up any cake. They of course always began with sugar and occasionally egg whites. Sometimes they were cooked and sometimes they were not. Chocolate filling was the most popular, but lemon remained a strong favorite as well.[172] Nuts could include almonds or pecans, and tropical fruits might be pineapple or coconut.[173]

The Lane cake continued to grow in popularity, with new cooks fancying up the filling with a combination of orange rind, mace, pecans, shredded coconut, or candied cherries and frosting the outside of the cake with white icing.[174] Another icon during this time was the Lady Baltimore cake, a plain cake made with egg whites, with a sumptuous filling usually consisting of sugar, egg whites, raisins, and English walnuts. Other versions included almonds, lemon juice, vanilla, or sherry. The originators of the cake were probably sisters Florence and Nina Ottolengui, managers of the Women's Exchange Tearoom in Charleston, which opened in 1885. After Owen Wister published his novel *Lady Baltimore*, in which the cake played an essential role, in 1907, recipes proliferated across the United States, many of them claiming to be the formula that Wister enjoyed in Charleston.[175] An Atlanta writer in 1912 twitted the "distinguished cookery writer" who "gathered seven 'original Lady Baltimore cake' recipes."[176]

"Japanese fruit cake" didn't resemble a traditional fruitcake in any meaningful way, nor was it Japanese, but it certainly had its admirers. Tennessean Kate Brew Vaughn traveled the United States for Procter and Gamble, demonstrating how to use Crisco. Her concoction, which she styled as the "Mikado Cake," likely named for Gilbert and Sullivan's comic opera, had twenty-seven ingredients, including oddities like apricot cordial, crystallized "angelique" (the candied stems of the herb angelica), kumquats, and pistachio extract, with two types of icing, "golden" and marshmallow.[177] Most "Japanese" cakes weren't that fancy, but they were still elaborate. Typically, one layer was plainer, sometimes spiced with cinnamon and cloves. The swankier layer might have spices and chunky ingredients like raisins, orange peel, dried figs, or nuts. In most instances the two layers were split into four and then filled with sugar, orange or lemon juice and rind, and coconut.[178]

Dates became increasingly important in southern cooking in the early twentieth century. American companies began importing dates from the Middle East in large quantities in the 1890s. In 1912, botanists from the U.S. Department of Agriculture transplanted date palms from present-day Iraq to California, where they thrived. With clever marketing, the sweet dried fruits became a must-have ingredient for bakers.[179] Date cakes could be baked in loafs or in layers, but in any case, they all had nuts—usually pecans or English walnuts—and could be guaranteed to require a long time of sticky chopping.[180]

For middle- and upper-class southerners, regardless of race, cakes formed the center of their choicest birthday, wedding, and anniversary celebrations. African Americans in Washington, D.C., for example, served cake with elaborate decorations: cut flowers for the wedding of Grace Louise Thomas and William Palmer; a "pyramid of fruit" holding the "wedding cake" for the silver anniversary of Mr. and Mrs. W. O. Fearing; and eighteen candles on the birthday cake for attorney Henry Heath.[181]

For ritzy white southerners, cakes for marriage festivities evolved into three distinct types. The "wedding cake" was still a fruitcake, boxed to give to guests as souvenirs.[182] Social referees insisted that it was wrong to call a white cake "wedding cake." The correct title, they announced, was "bride's cake."[183] An unnamed etiquette expert wrote, "The bride's cake is a white loaf, flavored with almond and distributed only to the attendants of the bride. It usually contains a ring, which falls to one of the attendants when the cake is cut."[184] Getting the ring meant that the recipient would marry. Sometimes the cake also held a thimble, predicting that the recipient would remain single. Bride's cakes often featured elaborate icing and ornamentation, and the practice of having a miniature bride and groom on the top began in the late nineteenth century.[185]

Groom's cakes varied more than bride's cakes, "surpass[ing] in richness and substance the airy nothingness which is the bride's own cake."[186] They were often light fruitcakes, but the Prince of Wales—a spicy butter cake, sometimes marbled and sometimes layered—also served nicely.[187] Groom's cakes might also have tokens. At a "miscellaneous shower" for a Georgia bridegroom in 1915, the cake contained a dime, forecasting financial prosperity; a penny, predicting poverty; a ring, indicating a future marriage; and a "bachelor's button," projecting an unwed future.[188]

At the opposite extreme from fancy layer cakes, fried wheat dough took many forms. Ray Hicks remembered that, in rural North Carolina, "God's Country" was where "flitters grew on bushes": "A flitter came after they got the pan to fry in and then getting wheat flour, after wheat flour came into the mountain. And they took and made up a thin dough and fried flitters, they called them. . . . It'll melt in your mouth."[189] As in the past, fritters/flitters could also be battered fruit, but the fruit was sometimes tropical and therefore more luxurious: bananas or pineapple instead of homely apple or peach.[190] Southerners kept making doughnuts and crullers at home, raised with baking powder and fried in deep fat. The primary difference between the two was their shape: doughnuts were formed in rings, and crullers were long and twisted.[191]

Charlottes, particularly of the russe variety, remained very popular, but they began to lose their base of ladyfingers or sponge cake as gelatin came into wider use and cooks simply poured the custard into molds. "Barrowsa Charlotte," the self-named invention of Annie Barrow of Pine Bluff, Arkansas, incorporated marshmallows and pecans.[192] Other dishes based on ladyfingers and sponge cake proliferated as trifles and puddings. Tipsy squire, previously called tipsy cake, became the in thing in the 1920s. The cake base was moistened with sherry and topped with a custard made of milk, eggs, cream, and vanilla. One version bristled with blanched almonds stuck "full" across its surface. A prohibitionist version, without alcohol, was called "Gypsy Squire."[193]

Low Country residents continued to eat rice. In 1901, Louisa Cheves Smythe Stoney edited a pamphlet titled the *Carolina Rice Cook Book* for a local exposition. A large portion of her bread recipes came directly from Sarah Rutledge's 1847 *Carolina Housewife*, but some were attributed to women still living around Charleston, including "Maum Peggy," mostly likely the African American cook for a white Charleston family. Her breakfast fry bread included boiled rice, wheat flour, egg, and milk, fried in boiling lard.[194]

WHILE HOME BAKING of sweets and quick breads continued unabated, commercial bakeries provided increasing shares of baked goods, particularly loaf bread. Though peddlers were almost gone in many places, in New Orleans, cala vendors still hawked their wares at the French Market.[195] Successful home bakers bridged the commercial divide, beginning small businesses to sell bread and sweets to individual customers. Mary Elizabeth Badders, for example, took seasonal orders for fruitcake in Silsbee, Texas, and Fannie Holt Teague did the same in Burlington, North Carolina. Badders's customers included the richest men of the area, while Teague baked for and shipped to "a select clientele," including members of the Duke family.[196]

Maggie Manning Thomas, who was African American, made and sold bread to her neighbors in Muskogee, Oklahoma. Her daughter Cleora Butler remembered, "Starting on Friday evenings and throughout most of Saturday, we'd all pile into the wagon and make deliveries. As we pulled up to each house, my brothers and I would run up to the door, make the delivery, and collect twenty-five cents for each loaf. This, mind you, was when a loaf of bread could be purchased for a nickel at the store."[197] Butler didn't comment on who their customers were, but they were obviously people who could buy expensive, handmade bread. In Fort Worth, Texas, Ninia Harrison Baird began selling her bread in 1908 when her husband's health failed. So much in demand was Mrs. Baird's bread that she bought a commercial oven in 1915, paying twenty-five dollars in cash and bartering seventy-five dollars' worth of bread and rolls. By the early 1920s, her homemade products were evolving into the enterprise that would dominate the bread market in North Texas for more than a century.[198]

In the years following World War I, the earnest women employed by the U.S. Department of Agriculture known as home demonstration agents set out to increase cash incomes for rural women. One of the ways that farm women could earn money was to make and sell baked goods. Improved roads and cars made it possible for women to make weekly treks to town to vend their wares.

The efforts started on a small scale, but they could yield healthy profits. One of the best examples is from Augusta County, Virginia, where white farm women established their so-called curb market in Staunton with baked goods, dressed chickens, and other homemade products. Many women developed followings for their specialties: layer cakes, pound cakes, pies, and so on.[199] Getting everything ready and then to Staunton by seven o'clock Saturday morning required intense effort. Hazel Van Lear remembered, "I made my pound cakes on Thursday, because it didn't hurt them to stand like it does the layer cakes." On Friday, she continued, "I baked the layer cakes and iced them, and . . . bake the bread and half a dozen other things. . . . You had to wrap all your cakes and your baked stuff."[200] The efforts paid off for many women: in 1930, one vendor reported selling forty-eight pies on a single Saturday; another claimed to have sold $475 worth of cakes in one summer.[201] The investments of time and ingredients brought in much-needed cash.

Individuals and groups also baked to raise money for causes they cared about. Pioneer educator and civil rights leader Mary McLeod Bethune opened Bethune-Cookman College in Daytona Beach, Florida, in 1904. Dr. Dorothy I. Height, Bethune's successor as president of the National Council of Negro Women, remembered, "I loved to hear Mary McLeod Bethune tell the story of the school she founded in 1904 with five little girls, $150 and faith in God. Times were hard. When she needed money to keep the school doors open, Mrs. Bethune would bake and sell sweet potato pies."[202] Mrs. Bethune used her culinary skills to keep her precious school afloat. Groups of all kinds, from the Woman's Christian Temperance Union to the Girl Scouts to every type of church auxiliary, held bake sales with doughnuts, "home made bread," cookies, and cakes.[203]

Although bread remained the most important food for Americans, the site of production shifted dramatically. In 1890, 90 percent of the loaf bread in the United States was baked at home, usually by women. By 1930, 94 percent of it was baked outside the home, usually by men, in factories of ever-growing size and complexity.[204]

Why did women give up baking bread at home? Much of their decision likely had to do with convenience. Even with standardized ingredients and ovens, bread baking was never easy. A second reason might be perceived quality. Bread factories, with their mechanized and repetitive processes, produced standardized loaves. So-called sandwich bread was perfectly shaped, with thin, tender crusts. And there was the perception that bakers' bread was more sanitary than home-baked. Waco, Texas, housewife Estelle J. Wallace Dupree, speaking to a bakers' convention in 1916, outlined her beliefs: "First and mainly, baker's bread well-made surpasses in my opinion the bread baked in the home. Second, I believe it is more economical and certainly less trouble. The third reason is that fresh bread can be had each day, which is not possible unless bread baked in the home is made each day."[205] You could buy fresh bread every day, but you likely couldn't bake it.

Increasingly, almost all southerners ate some store-bought loaf bread to supplement their cornbread and biscuits. It was more common in cities but wasn't unheard of in the country. Rural southerners often considered store-bought bread a treat. Lawrence Ridgle remembered "a loaf of bread in this house, maybe at somebody's birthday or something." Myrtle Calvert Dodd enthusiastically recalled the bread that her father brought from Waco on the weekends: "I could just make out my meal on light bread and butter."[206]

At the opposite extreme, some upper-class white southerners, who could afford the best and had domestic workers to bake for them, thought bakery bread an abomination. Virginia Foster Durr remembered, "Well, I had a cousin [who] married a lady from Minnesota, a Yankee lady. . . . And the cousin, one day he just disappeared. . . . I was very much puzzled by this . . . so I said to my father, 'Why in the world did he leave?' And Daddy said in a patronizing way, 'Well darling, that Yankee wife of his never fed him anything but cold store-bought light bread and that was enough to make a man leave a woman.'"[207] Bread reminded well-off southerners of long-held regional prejudices and the duties of a proper housewife.

The baking industry grew rapidly and became complex. In 1890, most commercial bakeries were small, one-oven shops with a handful of employees, located near neighborhoods. In the late 1920s, a large bakery could turn out 100,000 loaves a day. Changes in wheat growing and bakery mechanization made possible these enormous leaps in scale.[208] By 1940, the transition to store-bought loaf bread was almost complete.[209]

Wholesale bakeries stocked stores across the South, delivering bread every day and picking up unsold stale products. While many bakeries remained independently owned, others chose to align with national franchises, which furnished uniform recipes, distinctive packaging, and vigorous marketing. Butter-Nut, ButterKrust, and other national companies all had branches across the South by 1920. The Purity Bakery in Graham, North Carolina, for example, was a franchise of Holsum, based in Chicago. In 1915, it advertised, "Made clean, delivered clean, sold clean. . . . Never varies, never disappoints, never tired." A ten-cent loaf of bread modeled both sanitation and consistency.[210]

Commercially made doughnuts increased their fan base even during the Depression. Many doughnut enterprises were individually owned, but doughnuts, like bread, quickly became franchises.[211] Most famously, in 1937, Joe

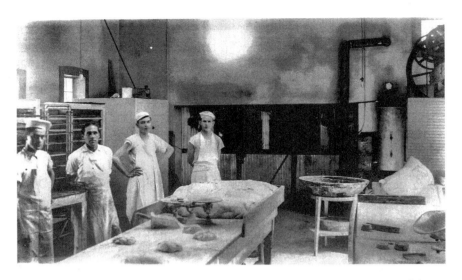

City Bakery, New Braunfels, Texas, 1913. A pre-industrial bakery. Owner Alvin Charles Plumeyer, son of German immigrants, may be second from the left. Courtesy Texas Historical Commission.

Krispy Kreme bakery and delivery vehicles, Salem, North Carolina, about 1938. Courtesy of Old Salem Museum and Gardens.

LeBeau sold his New Orleans recipe to grocer Ishmael Armstrong of Paducah, Kentucky. The Armstrong family opened doughnut shops in five states, using LeBeau's recipe. In North Carolina, Armstrong's nephew Vernon Rudolph and two friends called their shop Krispy Kreme. By 1940, the company had eight shops in five states, well on its way to becoming a southern icon.[212]

Immigrants to the United States brought distinctive styles of commercial baking with them. Cubans came to Tampa to work in the thriving cigar-making industry. A cooperative opened three bakeries in 1915, making thirty-six-inch-long loaves of Cuban bread, each with a strip of palmetto baked along the top. Tampeño homes had nails beside the front doors for delivery people to stick loaves of bread onto each morning.[213]

German immigrants continued to establish bakeries with the rich bread traditions of their native country, and many also quickly adapted to the American palate. George Leidenheimer founded his New Orleans bakery in 1895 and made his reputation by baking crisp-crusted New Orleans–style French bread.[214] Italian bakeries likewise thrived, particularly in New Orleans. Giuseppe Ruffino came to the Crescent City in the 1890s and began baking muffuletta loaves, the dense, round breads topped with sesame seed that could stand up to fillings soaked in olive oil. By 1909, fourteen Italian bakeries operated on Ursuline and St. Philip Streets.[215] Eastern European bakeries in Charleston and Savannah turned out "schvartzer" bread (rye and pumpernickel) and challah for their Jewish customers. African American bakers working in those shops learned to make traditional Jewish foods.[216] The New York Bakery in Atlanta, opened in 1930, may have offered the first bagels in the South.[217]

Commercial bakeries also made sweets for their customers, and by 1939, southerners bought more ready-baked treats than bread.[218] Examples abound: In Richmond, Everett Perkinson sold "wine cake," jelly rolls, pound cake, nine different kinds of layer cakes, and "small cakes in abundance."[219] John H. Hutcheson, the African American owner of the Idlewood Bakery in Richmond, offered fruitcake, four kinds of layer cake, pound cake, raisin cherry cake, and mincemeat pies for Christmas in 1930.[220] In Charleston, the most popular product of the Beckroge Bakery was the "vanilla," a jelly-filled sponge cake about the size of a biscuit, topped with vanilla icing.[221] Eastern European favorites like stollen (fruit bread), honey cake for Passover, tortes, rugelach (filled cookies), strudel, babka (braided sweet bread), teiglach (boiled pastries in honey syrup), twice-baked mandelbrot, and hamantaschen (triangular shaped cookies especially for Purim) came from bakers in several southern cities.[222]

One enterprising baker franchised his pies. Simon "the Pie Man" Hubig established pie-making plants in Dallas and Fort Worth in 1919, offering both baked and fried hand-sized fruit pies. Brothers R. Milton and Windsor Jones opened a Hubig's in New Orleans in 1922. By 1935, the other locations had closed, but the New Orleans location gained a fanatical following that continued into the twenty-first century.[223]

While king cakes had been around since the medieval period, in the twentieth century they became a popular product for commercial bakeries in New Orleans. The cake originated as part of the Roman Catholic celebration of the Feast of the Epiphany, January 6, to commemorate the visit of the magi, or kings, to the Christ Child. French colonists brought *galette des rois* to New Orleans. By the 1870s, the bread-like cakes contained beans made of gold and silver to bring good fortune to the recipients. By the 1910s, New Orleans dwellers consumed king cake from Epiphany to Mardi Gras, six weeks of carnival preceding the austerity of Lent.[224]

Another southern staple, the Moon Pie, started in 1917. The Chattanooga Bakery opened in the early twentieth century and quickly developed a large selection of goods.[225] Earl Mitchell, the bakery's Knoxville branch manager, asked Kentucky coal miners what they wanted in baked goods, and they replied that they craved something large and filling. When Mitchell got back to Knoxville, he saw bakery workers dipping graham cookies in marshmallow for their own snacks. Mitchell remembered the miners' request and had the idea "to stack one graham cookie on top of another, sandwich marshmallow in between, and top the concoction with a thick layer of creamy chocolate." The original Moon Pie was four inches in diameter and cost a nickel. It quickly became a "volume leader" for the company.[226]

Bakeries came in for their share of well-deserved criticism by food reformers. Michigan-based crusader Caroline Bartlett Crane made several trips to the South around 1910, and she found conditions almost universally awful, despite state laws. At six bakeries in Nashville, Crane discovered unscreened windows, dead flies, grungy towels, and unwashed hands. The bakeries were all poorly ventilated, and spiders (with flour-covered cobwebs), dogs, and cats made themselves at home. Racks, pans, and rolling pin handles all had "incredible accumulations of filth."[227] In 1912, Crane visited eight bakeries in Montgomery, Alabama, at the invitation of local women's clubs. Even in the cleanest bakery, she "found families of roaches occupying the closets for raising the dough." After Crane's visit, the Montgomery commissioner of health and sanitation agreed to appoint a food inspector, while the clubwomen of the city instigated a boycott of bakery bread until conditions improved.[228]

Playing off these conditions, bakeries of all sizes used cleanliness to market their goods. In Norfolk, C. T. Fernbaugh named his establishment the "Purity Bakery," while in Fort Worth, Austrian immigrant Francis Schaefer called his the "Sanitary Bakery."[229] Larger bakeries hopped on the sanitary bandwagon to exclude smaller competitors. An ad for the Eagle Steam Bakery in Fort Worth sneered in 1918, "In those jump-up bakery shops, without machinery, where men work long hours, mix and scale bread by hand, being both tired and often careless, such bread cannot be sanitary, no matter by what name they may call it. . . . Working the bread by hand it becomes contaminated by absorption of the perspiration from the arm[s] and face[s] of the workmen."[230]

The baking industry's move to mechanize and purify baking led to the de-skilling of an ancient art. Fort Worth bakery owner W. J. Doherty installed new equipment in his bakery in 1918 with a capacity of 25,000 loaves of bread and "thousands of cakes, pies and other bakery products" each day, with a payroll of only thirty-five men. Every step was mechanized except the last, the wrapping of the finished loaves.[231]

With improved transportation and packaging, national brands also brought standardization to the South. In towns large and small, from the turn of the twentieth century, the New York–based conglomerate Nabisco sold products that we know today, including ginger snaps, vanilla wafers, Fig Newtons, and the "creme"-filled chocolate sandwich cookies called Oreos.[232] Competitors such as Sunshine Biscuit, from Boston, also sold in southern markets.[233] Southerners with money could eat the same foods as their cousins in Oregon and Maryland. Homogenization was happening.

IN THE EARLY TWENTIETH CENTURY, the people of the South both caused and endured racial violence, Jim Crow, and old and new forms of businesses that exploited the poor and benefited the rich. On the surface, many foods stayed the same. Cornbread still appeared at mealtime, and women baked batch after batch of biscuits. But change was happening. Urbanization and transportation increased people's access to old and new ingredients and products, home-baked and commercially produced. In 1940, the South was part of a nation on the cusp of a war that brought dramatic transformation to the region. And baking would be a part of those new developments.

Chapter 8

CHIFFON PIE

....

Civil Rights and Sameness

World War II, the Cold War, and the civil rights movement all drew the South closer to the American mainstream. So did interstate highways, airplanes, and military bases that brought people and their foods from around the country and around the world to the region. From 1940 forward, the South grew ever more urban: during the war, more than 3 million southern farm people moved to town, drawn by better jobs. Incomes rose across the region, but in the poorest areas, food supplies remained precarious.

Deprivation continued, as more than a third of all southerners lived below the poverty line in 1960. Poor Black people and poor white people ate more alike than differently. Civil rights activist Anne Moody's mother, a domestic worker, for example, fed her family mostly on cornbread and beans as well as on the leftovers that her employer permitted her.[1] Commodity distribution from the U.S. government, which began during the Great Depression, included flour, canned goods, and staples. The program shifted to food stamps in 1964, intended to give poor families more choice in their foods. But the bureaucracy overseeing the program became a nightmare for many poor southerners.[2]

Baking—ingredients and finished baked goods alike—showed the different sides of oppression and resistance to racism more bluntly than ever. Simply put, white supremacists tried to starve the civil rights movement into submission. In Leflore County, Mississippi, an all-white board of supervisors administered the federal surplus commodities program, which distributed cornmeal, flour, and powdered milk to 5,000 residents, 90 percent of whom were African American. The Student Nonviolent Coordinating Committee (SNCC) established a voting rights campaign in Leflore County in 1962, and that winter, the board of supervisors halted the distribution of commodities as retribution. The Friends of SNCC organization in Chicago held a food drive for needy Mississippians, gathering donations of flour, cornmeal, rice, sugar, cereals, dried beans, cooking oils, and canned meats and delivering the food to Mississippi.[3] The movement nourished the poor people of Leflore County despite the cruelty of the whites in power.

When the bus boycott began in Montgomery, Alabama, in 1955, Georgia Gilmore joined the movement by baking pies and cakes. She enlisted friends to sell them door to door and to "black and white customers alike at beauty shops, laundries, cabstands, doctors' offices, stores, churches, and outside downtown cafeterias." Gilmore recalled, "We started selling sandwiches and went from there to selling full dinners in our neighborhoods and we'd bake pies and cakes for people." All the money that they raised—often $100 to $150 a week—went to the Montgomery Improvement Association to buy gasoline and service for the station wagons that ferried people through town to keep them off buses. Gilmore and her friends called themselves "the Club from Nowhere" so that the association's records would show that the money came from "nowhere," lest club members be found out and fired from their jobs. Gilmore began serving meals at her modest home, including cornbread and, for dessert, pineapple upside-down cake, 7-Up cake, peach cobbler, and sweet potato pie with coconut in the filling. With her baking, Georgia Gilmore fed the civil rights movement, literally and financially.[4]

WITHIN THE WEB of wealth, poverty, racism, and resistance, southern baking changed along with southern society. In the late 1930s, the United States wheeled from the Great Depression into World War II, bringing different kinds of challenges to bakers. Rationing was the most pronounced change. After war began in Europe in 1939, sugar prices started to rise worldwide.[5] When the United States declared war on Japan in December 1941, the government initiated its first price ceiling on sugar to foil speculators.[6] The sugar shortage, when it came, occurred largely because of logistics. Few ships were available to bring sugar to the United States from Puerto Rico and Cuba, and the Japanese controlled the Philippines.[7] Government-mandated rationing began in April 1942, with sugar limited to twenty-six pounds per person per year—about half the consumption in 1941.[8]

Georgia Gilmore adjusts her hat after appearing as a defense witness in the racial bus boycott trial of Rev. Martin Luther King Jr., March 21, 1956, in Montgomery. Gilmore testified, "When you pay your fare and they count the money, they don't know the Negro money from white money." Associated Press 5603210211.

Rationing boards functioned at the county level, and they often discrim- inated against African Americans, particularly domestic workers. Their employers frequently received the workers' ration books and removed stamps to cover the meals that the employees ate at the employers' homes. A domes- tic worker could never be sure how many stamps she would have with which to feed her own family.[9] World War II also signaled the beginning of the end of domestic work for African American women. As the war effort improved job opportunities for Black women, they took them. The percentage of African

American women working as domestics dropped from 60 percent in 1940 to 36 percent in 1960 and 7 percent in 1980.[10] Increasingly, affluent white women had to learn to cook for themselves or to eat out.

Women hoarded sugar for canning and desserts. Texan Mary Cimarolli remembered that her mother stored up sugar "and we always had desserts of one kind or another—sugar rationing or not."[11] Others substituted corn syrup, which wasn't rationed, for their sweet treats.[12] Mildred Council recalled, "During World War II, sugar was rationed or unavailable, but we always got Karo syrup for the babies." She invented something she called "Thin Man Pie" using brown sugar, Karo syrup, butter or margarine, eggs, and vanilla.[13] Rural southerners made out just fine with honey and syrup—cane and sorghum— which remained readily available and inexpensive throughout the war.[14]

Dairy products also shrank in supply. Shortages of fresh milk were acute in some locations, and cooks substituted canned or dried milk for fresh.[15] Canned milk and butter were rationed in March 1943. As oleomargarine became the butter substitute of choice, Atlanta columnist Clementine Paddleford urged readers to "use it just as butter is used, spoonful for spoonful, in any type of recipe."[16] The ever-vigilant dairy lobby still ensured that margarine could not look like butter. Mary Cimarolli commented, "I remember a margarine that came in a solid, colorless block. It looked as unappetizing as lard until Mama mixed it with the capsule of red coloring that came with it. After the white margarine was properly tinted, it had a more appetizing appearance—approximately the color of butter."[17]

Bread, flour, and cereals remained plentiful, often used as substitutes for meat. Industrial bakers retained 70 percent of their sugar allotments, and they touted their ability to waste fewer ingredients than home users and to produce baked goods for women working in the war effort. The number of commercial bakers in the United States increased significantly, supplying both bread and sweets. Wartime conditions accelerated the movement of baking from the home to commercial producers.[18]

Rationing was temporary, of course. Butter and milk came off the rolls in 1945, while sugar, the last item to become unrestricted, did so in June 1947.[19] Although southerners didn't storm the grocery stores after the curb lifted, they did dive into baking with new enthusiasm and a slew of shortcuts to help them.

As electricity spread throughout the rural South, kitchens evolved. Mary Cimarolli remembered with delight the used Westinghouse refrigerator that her father bought about 1942: "It had four claw-footed legs and a new round motor that sat on top, outside the box. By today's standards, the refrigerator would be considered tiny and completely inadequate, but how we all loved it."[20] Into the 1950s, however, southerners were less likely than other Americans to own refrigerators. While 70 percent of all Americans had refrigerators by 1947, by 1954 only 58 percent of the farm people around Kosciusko, Mississippi, had them.[21] Rural poor southerners remained without electricity and appliances longer than other citizens.

After World War II, stove ovens grew larger, and manufacturers advertised their dependability.[22] Vertically stacked double ovens, separate from the cooktop, became more common. Frigidaire's "Double Wall Oven" went on the market in 1960, in six exterior finishes: satin chrome, Aztec copper, turquoise, Mayfair pink, sunny yellow, and charcoal gray.[23] Dependability and efficiency didn't have to be boring.

Still, some woodstoves kept their places, whether through necessity—as on sharecroppers' farms, where owners had little motivation to improve kitchens—or by choice.[24] Some cooks, like Elma Lee Hall of Alabama, preferred their woodstoves over newer styles. In the late 1970s Hall complained, "Hit's this damn stove that burnt up my biscuits. Hit's the aggravatingest stove I ever cooked on! You can see I still got my old wood stove set up, and I can use it any time I want to. Hit still cooks better'n this new thing. I told Nathan I didn't want no 'lectric stove, but he went up to Mr. Jackson at the Western Auto Store and bought it anyhow. I told him it was sorry enough to make a preacher cuss."[25]

In another change, milling vanished from the home. Freedman Charles Alexander, born in 1861 on St. Simons Island, in the mid-1950s showed a visitor the grinding stones from the hand mill that his family had used for four generations. "He explained, however, that he did not use it any more for now he bought his meal and grits at the store."[26] A few small crossroads mills still ground corn but only rarely wheat. Some recipe writers began to specify stone-ground cornmeal to distinguish it from industrially produced meal.

Regional flour mills continued, particularly favorites such as White Lily and Martha White. Mills contributed greatly to southern culture by sponsoring radio shows. The Burrus Mill in Fort Worth Texas started the trend in 1931, engaging the Light Crust Doughboys and their distinctive western swing style, mixing country music with jazz, to entertain on the mill's behalf. Singer Ernest Tubb got his start as the "Gold Chain Troubadour" for Universal Mills in Fort Worth. In Helena, Arkansas, in 1941, the *King Biscuit Time* radio show showcased blues players, including Muddy Waters.[27] And in 1948, Martha White Flour began sponsoring the Grand Ole Opry in Nashville, with famous bluegrass pickers Lester Flatt and Earl Scruggs belting out the company's jingle. Increasingly, however, national brands of flour, like Pillsbury and Gold Medal from General Mills, dominated the grocery scene. The growth of national chain supermarkets such as Safeway and A&P accelerated the move toward standardized brands.

MARION FLEXNER summed up the situation pretty well in 1941 when she wrote about "Peggy Gaines's Kentucky Pecan Bourbon Cake": "This cake isn't a native Kentuckian at all, and Dame Rumor asserts with authority that a certain Frankfort matron (about 25 years ago) coaxed a famous New York maître d'hôtel to give her the recipe by crossing his palm with a lot of silver. But if it wasn't born here, it has become a Kentuckian by adoption and certainly deserves a place in any collection of the State's most delicious dishes."[28] And so it was: recipes not created in the South became southern because of the frequency with which they appeared on southern tables. Southern food, it seemed, was becoming as much a state of mind as a reality.

Two eternals remained, however: cornbread and biscuits. They were not as widespread as they had been before World War II, and some cooks took shortcuts, but they still mattered. As southerners moved to town, cornbread continued to be a way of life for many—by choice for some and by necessity for others, because cornmeal remained cheaper than flour.[29] The younger generation of affluent housewives needed a little coaxing, however. The first issue of *Southern Living* magazine, which spun off from *Progressive Farmer* in 1966, had an article sentimentally (and incorrectly) titled "Cornbread: The South's Own Creation." Its recipe for "Southern Cornbread" contained no flour and no sugar, and it did not specify white or yellow cornmeal.[30] Four years later, an anonymous *Southern Living* writer straddled all the divides, commenting, "There are great controversies about white versus yellow cornmeal, whether sugar should be added, and whether the bread should be made with sweet milk or buttermilk. And there are strong arguments for every side."[31] Perhaps half of the southern cornbread recipes after World War II called for sugar, which critics vehemently decried as a "Yankee" practice.[32]

As African Americans moved from the South to the cities of the North, they took cornbread with them. Helen Mendes, who grew up in New York eating the foods of her mother's South Carolina home, included six cornbread recipes in her exploration of West African and American cooking. Three of the recipes had no sugar, and two had only small amounts. Clarence McKennon of Jamaica, Long Island, however, included a third of a cup in his. Mendes observed, "It tastes like cake and stays moist for days."[33]

Soft, rich spoon breads and batter breads were still served at special meals.[34] While spoon bread rarely had sugar, batter bread often did.[35] Cornbread muffins and sticks usually included sugar, and they were always leavened with baking powder. They could be doctored up with onion, sage, or bacon grease.[36] Hushpuppies became common after World War II, popping up at homegrown fish fries and reputedly historic "taverns." Most recipes called for onions, a few for sugar, and some for garlic salt, and a few specified white cornmeal. Purists continued to fry their hushpuppies in the same fat in which fish had been cooked.[37] Other cakes of fried cornmeal, including hot-water cornbread, still appeared at dinner and supper.[38]

Crackling cornbread also persisted, long after most southerners had left hog slaughtering behind. But rather than bits left from rendering lard, the new cracklings might be crumbled crisp bacon or fried salt pork.[39] One Alabamian recommended adding cracklings to "ready-prepared corn-bread mix."[40] In the 1950s, Helen Corbitt of Texas began putting green peppers, onions, and pimentos into her corn muffins, a nod to the Mexican cuisine that was beginning to spread north and east from the Rio Grande. By the 1970s, cornbread with jalapeño peppers, often with grated cheese, became fashionable, particularly on the western end of the South.[41]

By 1950, cornbread mixes abounded, many the products of local or regional companies. The Chicago-based giant Jiffy, with its sweet flavor, began to make inroads into southern pantries. The market gradually consolidated, and by the 1970s most mixes came from national giants such as General Mills and Pillsbury.[42]

Southern cooks certainly availed themselves of biscuit mixes and canned biscuits. Food writer Sallie Hill even urged homemakers to create their own mixes of flour, baking powder, powdered milk, salt, and lard, "cover[ed] tightly and store[d] until ready for use."[43]

But, as Steve Yarbrough observed of the Mississippi Delta, "When I was growing up, in the late 1950s and early 1960s, country people made their cakes and breads and biscuits from scratch."[44] Biscuit making remained as much an art as ever.[45] Kentuckian Polly Rideout, born in 1928, recalled, "It took me a long time to learn how to make good biscuits but I'm glad I did."[46] But for those who didn't know, the editors at Southern Living announced in 1970 that biscuits should be served piping hot from the oven, crisp on the outside and tender on the inside.[47]

Most homemade biscuits still consisted of the same formula that had been around for almost a century: flour, baking powder, and fat, and sometimes sugar, salt, or milk. While many cooks had switched to vegetable shortening, others continued to use lard.[48] Southern cooks made all kinds of additions to ordinary biscuits: herbs, orange juice, nuts, cooked sausage or bacon.[49] Cheese, sometimes with cayenne pepper, was the most favored add-in, and the cheese most often stipulated was American, soft and mild flavored.[50]

The "angel biscuit," which used baking powder, baking soda, and yeast to attain new levels of airiness, became an immediate smash in the 1950s. With three leavens, the biscuits were supposedly foolproof even for beginners, earning them the name "bride's biscuits." No one knows for sure whether they came from the test kitchens of White Lily Flour or from those at Martha White Flour, but everyone thought they were great.[51]

Biscuit dough also served as the basis for sweet treats. Orange biscuits were spread with a paste of butter, flour, orange juice, orange rind, and sugar, rolled like a jelly roll. and sliced before baking.[52] Butter rolls followed the same process but with brown sugar and cinnamon. Jam windmills were rolled, cut into three-inch squares, and then spread with jam. The cook cut the roll diagonally from each corner to the center and folded the corner in to make a pinwheel.[53] Biscuit dough might be ordinary, but its variations didn't have to be.

As the postwar baby boom took hold in the United States, middle-class women believed that they needed to cook hot breakfasts for their kids. The unnamed author of a cookbook from Columbus, Georgia, wrote in 1957, "Skimpy breakfasts are out of date—and a stick to the ribs sort of breakfast spells pancakes to the American appetite. Clever mother who keeps a box of pancake mix within arm's reach—and clever the mother, too, who can go creative and take a whirl at a batch of her own, sometimes adding variations such as pecans, bacon, and the like."[54] Clever Mother could even use her newly affordable electric griddle instead of heating up the stove. Cooks could also fix pancakes for meals besides breakfast. With a recipe that jars our sensibilities, Claudia Reese of West Palm Beach, Florida, fashioned them from turtle eggs and cane syrup to serve with seafood.[55]

Fancy pancakes still became desserts. The famous Antoine's Restaurant in New Orleans shared its recipe for crêpes spread with red currant jelly ("a la Gelee"). Home cooks could serve crêpes suzette, flambéed with a sauce of butter, cognac, and orange liqueur. As the hostess ignited the sauce, warming each pancake in it, she could enjoy watching "the enraptured expressions around the table."[56]

Electric waffle irons increased in number in southern homes. In 1949, Montgomery Ward offered a chrome model with a ready light for pouring batter for $5.97.[57] Another indication of the growing use of appliances came from Columbus, Georgia, where a housewife observed that leftover waffles could be wrapped in aluminum foil and stored in the "deep freeze"—a sure sign of postwar abundance.[58]

Loaves of sweet quick bread, heavy with fruit and nuts, usually leavened with baking powder, continued to gain favor after World War II. Fast and easy to assemble, they provided satisfying snacks. The darling was banana bread, made with mashed ripe bananas and usually pecans, sometimes black walnuts.[59] Loaves flavored with orange juice and orange rind appeared often, loaded with pecans, dates, raisins, or candied orange rind.[60] Dried fruit—dates, apricots, or cranberries—filled nut breads.[61] Really, a cook could whip up a loaf of sweet quick bread with anything from peanut butter to grated zucchini.[62] They could even be made from biscuit mix, according to Sallie Hill: "If you're in a hurry, check your pantry for biscuit mix, and you're on your way!"[63] Muffins were made identically but in individual servings rather than loaves. Bran muffins began losing their medicinal quality after World War II, becoming more of a treat than a treatment.[64]

The old standbys—gingerbread, popovers, quick Sally Lunns—stayed in the southern bakers' repertoire, but the new kid on the block was coffee cake. While sweet breads topped with streusel had around for decades, particularly in German families, as we learned from Howard Matthies, the form took on new life in the 1950s.[65] Coffee cake in the South was generally a dense cake leavened with baking powder, often containing sour cream, and topped with streusel—a crumbly mixture of butter, nuts (often pecans), brown sugar, and cinnamon.[66] It is easy to imagine a gathering of stereotypical 1950s house-wives, enjoying the cake with their midmorning coffee.

Although most doughnut-eating southerners bought theirs at shops, some die-hard home cooks still fried their own. The most tenacious continued to use yeast to raise their rings, but others took a quicker route with baking pow-der.[67] Other workarounds existed, too. Mrs. William E. Wallace from Lafay-ette, Louisiana, recommended frozen bread dough, fried and sprinkled with powdered sugar.[68] Even canned biscuits, cut in half, pulled into oblongs, and twisted together, could be fried as doughnuts.[69]

A traditional Cajun fried specialty, *oreilles de cochon*, or pig's ears, received new attention. Two recipes were published in the 1967 *Talk about Good!* cook-book from Lafayette, one finished with confectioners' sugar and the other bathed in cane syrup, sugar, and salt. In 1971 a camera crew from Time-Life Books documented Mrs. Pline De Blanc making them at her home in St. Martin Parish, Louisiana. She mixed the dough from flour, baking powder, salt, eggs, and butter, then broke it into small pieces. She rolled each piece between her hands into a one-inch ball, then flattened it with a rolling pin into a "paper-thin round" eight or nine inches in diameter. De Blanc then fried each round individually in a cast iron skillet, twisting it with a long fork in the center to give it the "pig's ear" shape. After draining the "ears" on paper towels, she then covered them with warm cane syrup and chopped pecans.[70]

Sometimes people paid attention to the old ways, but home baking of loaf bread continued to decline. Kentuckian Ronni Lundy recalled three kinds of bread in her home when she was growing up in the 1950s: homemade bis-cuits and cornbread and store-bought "light bread," wrapped in cellophane.[71] Helen Corbitt, Texas tastemaker, observed in 1957, "Homemade breads have gone with the wind in the majority of homes."[72] By the 1970s, yeast bread was enough of a lost art that one cookbook included an entire page of directions, and a *Southern Living* writer assured readers, "Of course you can cook yeast breads!"[73] Would-be bread bakers needed instruction and encouragement. Those home cooks who went to the trouble of making yeast bread often made them fancy with Romano or Parmesan cheese and savory flavors like sage, marjoram, and chives.[74] Yeasted Sally Lunn recipes, both muffins and loaves, flourished through the 1960s.[75]

Although most home cooks stopped making yeasted loaf bread, some continued to make rolls. Yeasted rolls also traveled to the North with Black women like Louise Dow Davenport. Davenport's recipe, which evoked South Carolina in a New York home, could have stood in for thousands of others: yeast, water, milk, vegetable shortening, salt, sugar, egg, and flour.[76] These flexible doughs could be shaped into various forms: pocketbook, Parker House, cloverleaf, crescent, or bowknot.[77]

Icebox rolls remained popular, even as their name changed to "refrigerator rolls."[78] In 1941, Louisville writer Marion Flexner attested to the life-changing impact of icebox rolls, courtesy of a domestic worker named Ollie, for whom Flexner did not give a family name: "Since Ollie, our substitute cook, confided to me the recipe for her ice box rolls, I have practically discarded all other roll recipes. For this is without a doubt the greatest boon to housekeeping I have had in years. The dough will keep for several weeks in the electric refrigerator."[79] As always, white women had much to learn from African American women.

Rolls could be made savory with the additions of garlic salt, poppy seeds (long a fixture in Eastern European cuisine but relatively new in the South), caraway seeds, onions, or grated cheese.[80] For her onion rolls, Cleora Butler favored onion soup mix, which the Lipton company introduced in 1952.[81] Yeasted sweet rolls were served for breakfast and special occasions, topped with some combination of cinnamon, orange rind, lemon extract, white and brown sugar, dark corn syrup, raisins, and pecans, rolled like a jelly roll and sliced.[82] Perhaps because of marketing like the recipe competitions sponsored by the Florida Citrus Council, orange rolls appeared frequently.[83]

For housewives on tight schedules, the 1949 invention of brown-and-serve rolls was a game changer. Joseph Gregor served as a mess sergeant during World War II and, upon his discharge, established a bakery in Avon Park, Florida. Like all bakers, he and his partner faced a challenge in keeping yeast rolls fresh and hot for their customers. In June 1949, Gregor had to make a run with the local volunteer fire department, and he pulled a pan of partially cooked rolls from the oven. When he returned, he discovered that the half-baked dough had kept its form. He returned the rolls to the oven and they turned out perfectly. Gregor had accidentally discovered the process that came to be known as "interrupted baking." As he experimented, he learned that partially baked rolls would keep in the refrigerator for up to two weeks. Only three months later, General Mills bought the process for $43,000 and began using it for buns, breads, and sweet rolls as well as dinner rolls.[84] Now a home cook could buy dough at the grocery store and finish baking it at home, serving her family freshly baked, hot breads. By 1954, Dallas cooks could buy brown-and-serve bagels. Whether they should have, of course, is another question.[85]

As the United States entered the space age, housewives still labored to come up with solutions for pie crust. They tried varying proportions of lard and shortening. One woman merely commented, "I prefer [the] recipe on [the] Crisco label."[86] Crust mixes lured bakers with limited time or confidence. Even experts like African American cookbook author Jesse Willis Lewis of Bay St. Louis, Mississippi, embraced pie crust mix, adding extra water to the mix to ensure that it was moist enough.[87] By the late 1950s, those truly in despair over their crusts could buy them frozen at the grocery store.[88] By 1966, frozen goods included puff pastry and sheets of pie dough.[89]

Although graham cracker crusts had been around since the 1920s, they gained new users in the 1950s. Most cooks made their own from graham cracker crumbs, sugar, and melted butter, but those pressed for time could buy crushed graham crackers and even boxed mixes.[90] Prepared graham cracker crusts, in their own aluminum pans, appeared in the mid-1960s.[91] Both frozen and premade crusts made pie baking easier, faster, and less stressful.

Fruit pies stayed in the southern repertoire. Peach pie recipes often carried the name "Fresh Peach Pie," marking it as a seasonal delight, although with their new kitchen appliances, some home cooks could prolong the bounty by freezing or canning peaches.[92] Fresh strawberries brought pleasure in the spring, usually in a single crust, often glazed with sugar, water, and cornstarch, sometimes with cream cheese on the bottom.[93] Fresh blackberries and dewberries came reliably in the early summer. Dewberries had a shorter season, recalled Mildred Council, and they got only one or two dewberry pies or cobblers in a year. Blackberries grew "most everywhere," she said, though some were sweeter than others. Council and her sisters canned blackberries and made jam to tide them through the winter. As a result of efforts like theirs, cooks could substitute jam in turnovers and use home-canned blackberries in pies year-round.[94] Although canned pie filling began making inroads into southern markets in the early 1950s, recipe writers for the most part chose to use fresh, frozen, or canned fruit and add their own sweetener, thickener, and spices.[95]

Apple pie bakers became pickier about their ingredients, one cook specifying, "First choice: Jonathan; second choice: Winesap."[96] Family recipes for pear pie traveled north with African American cooks: fresh pears spiced with sugar, cinnamon, nutmeg, and perhaps even brandy, baked in a double crust.[97] Almost all cherry pie bakers, however, used canned cherries, specifying that they be both sour and pitted.[98]

Raisins were the dried fruit used most often in pies. No one knows for sure where the so-called Osgood pie came from, but the sweet, tangy filling—raisins combined with sugar, eggs, nuts (usually pecans), butter or margarine, and sometimes vinegar, often spiced with cinnamon and cloves, baked in a single crust—delighted diners across the South and the United States.[99]

Long after marshmallows made their debut, other commercially made candy became parts of pie recipes. Hershey's chocolate bars, from Hershey, Pennsylvania, marshmallows, and whipped cream could fill a pie crust made of crushed chocolate cookies or graham cracker crumbs.[100] Caramel, a cooked mixture of sugar and milk, had been in industrial production since the early twentieth century, and companies such as Chicago-based Brach's had taken their products national by the 1950s. Pies made with caramels could be dense, with only eggs, milk, and cornstarch, or light, with gelatin, whipped cream, and nuts.[101] "Red Hots" were small, cinnamon-flavored candies introduced by another Chicago company, Ferrara, in the 1930s. An inventive cook melted them with water to form a syrup for a deep-dish apple pie.[102]

Most recipes for pecan pie varied only in proportions of pecans, sugar, and eggs and in whether they used dark or light corn syrup.[103] To give a uniquely southern twist, some cooks deployed cane syrup in place of corn syrup, and some heretics suggested adding black walnuts or hickory nuts in place of the pecans.[104] By the late 1960s, chocolate appeared in some recipes, creating the wonderfully rich fudge version. Cooks also used muffin tins to create bite-sized pies, sometimes called pecan tassies (from the Scottish word for a small cup).[105]

Chess pie remained dear in southerners' hearts.[106] Coconut, vanilla, and chocolate dominated the realm of cream pies, while custard pies appeared in many guises: rum, apple, banana, coconut, buttermilk, pumpkin, sweet potato. Mildred Council proudly remembered cooking her first custard pie with eggs robbed from her family's guinea hens.[107] Sweet potato and pumpkin pie occupied common ground, fancied up with ingredients such as evaporated milk or fresh cream and candied ginger.[108]

Coconut held a proud place in southern pie-dom, usually as a cooked custard in a single crust. Some traditionalists still grated their own coconut, but most cooks bought theirs already grated and usually sweetened.[109] And, oh, the chocolate pies. Cooks used names like "Velvet" and "Heavenly" to describe them. The fillings could be made with gelatin, egg yolks, egg whites, butter, or cream and could be cooked or uncooked, topped (or not) with meringue or whipped cream. They could have milk, sweetened condensed milk, or no liquid at all. The chocolate could be solid or cocoa.[110]

But perhaps the most loved cold pies were lemon. In addition to fresh lemon juice and grated rind, sugar, and eggs, they might contain some varieties of corn syrup, gelatin, butter, milk, or sour cream. Almost all were topped with meringue.[111] The lemon pie that swept the South, though, was an uncooked version in a graham cracker crust. In 1931, recipe developers at the Borden Company came up with the idea of mixing lemon juice with their Eagle Brand sweetened condensed milk and calling it "Magic Lemon Cream Pie." The "magic," that the two ingredients thickened into pie filling, was the result of casein, a milk product that coagulates in the presence of acidity. It takes about three parts lemon juice to seven parts condensed milk for the coagulation to occur. The recipe became an instant standard, with a variety of names, including the dubious "Deep South Lemon Pie."[112] It was equally good topped with meringue or whipped cream or just left plain.

Close behind uncooked lemon pie came key lime pie, whose origins remain a mystery. Key limes—smaller and tarter than regular "Persian" limes—grew wild in the Florida Keys and then commercially between 1905 and 1935.[113] Who decided to mix them with sweetened condensed milk? One theory is that sponge divers working from Key West, who provisioned their months-long voyages with sweetened condensed milk and key lime juice, with ready access to bird and turtle eggs, came up with the concoction. Another possibility credits an "Aunt Sally" who supposedly cooked for Key West entrepreneur William Curry. But Aunt Sally can't be authenticated.[114] The least romantic but most probable answer is that somewhere in South Florida, someone simply decided to substitute key limes for lemons in the Borden Company recipe.[115]

According to Key West historian Tom Hambright, the first written reference to key lime pie appeared in a 1930s guidebook, which called it "world-famous." A recipe for "Key West Lime Pie" was published in, of all places, Brattleboro, Vermont, in 1945: condensed milk, egg yolks, and lime juice in a baked shell—not a graham cracker crust—topped with meringue.[116] Soon, like other legendary sweets, key lime pie had many "original" versions, with gelatin, grated lime rind, Angostura bitters, and so on.[117] Eventually the graham cracker crust nosed out the traditional baked crust.

Another happy invention in the early 1950s, probably by a home economist but enthusiastically adopted by southern cooks, was "angel pie." The shell was a basic meringue of sugar and egg whites, put into a pie pan and baked in a slow oven. The filling, sometimes cooked separately and sometimes baked with the crust, was often lemon. But chocolate, either plain or German's sweet, was the crowd favorite, occasionally gussied up with marshmallows, walnuts, coconut, or coffee. (More about German's chocolate in a bit.)[118]

Chiffon pie, a combination of gelatin and whipped egg whites in a graham cracker or cookie crust, came about in the 1920s, and its popularity grew with assistance from the Knox Gelatin company kitchens. After World War II, southern cooks took to the light, fluffy pie in throngs. The pie started with a baked crust or one made from crushed cookies or graham crackers. The cook usually softened gelatin in liquid. She then made a custard of egg yolks, sugar, and more milk or substituted sweetened condensed milk for the custard. She next added the gelatin and flavorings to the custard and let the mixture cool. Finally, she added beaten egg whites, giving the pie extra airiness and loft. She put the filling into the pie shell and chilled it before serving.[119] The pie could be topped with meringue or whipped cream.

The most loved chiffon pies were fruit, and the most loved fruits were citrus. Lime had a particular following, sometimes further enhanced with lime-flavored gelatin, green food coloring, or crème de menthe.[120] Orange juice and grated orange rind made another citrusy version of chiffon pie, and of course lemon had its devotees.[121] Strawberries could be used fresh or frozen.[122]

Pumpkin chiffon pie took its place on southern holiday tables, lighter and airier than a usual pumpkin pie. It began with cooked pumpkin plus gelatin, egg yolks, brown or white sugar, and beaten egg whites.[123] Other fruit chiffon pies were made with crushed pineapple or cranberry sauce.[124] Spirits—sherry or rum—also invigorated chiffon pies. One particularly opulent version featured a crust of Brazil nuts and sugar, then added candied cherries and rum just before the beaten egg whites.[125]

Chiffon pie mixes, complete with ingredients for the crust, came on the market in 1955 and then appeared in all sorts of dessert recipes across the South and the United States.[126] One recipe for "Rocky Road Chiffon Pie" shows how recipes spread across the nation. Using chocolate chiffon pie filling mix, scalded milk, sugar, marshmallows, and pecans, the recipe ran in California newspapers in 1958 and identically in the *River Road Recipes* cookbook from Baton Rouge the next year.[127] Good recipes traveled fast.

Small pies also had their fans. Fried pies, sometimes called hand pies, made people nostalgic. *Southern Living* magazine called them "Fried Pies Like Grandma Made," produced from rounds or squares of pie crust or biscuit dough, filled with a pulp made from dried or canned apples, apricots, or peaches. As always, the cook folded the dough over the filling and fried the pies to a golden brown.[128]

Tarts could be made the same way, with crusts folded around fillings of cooked sweet potatoes, rehydrated dried apricots, or raisins and nuts, but baked rather than fried.[129] A cook could also use special tart pans or muffin tins to shape the crusts for their small pies. Cooks preferred lemon over other kinds. Lemon tarts, unlike pies, generally had no milk products in them. The tangy, rich filling consisted mainly of lemon juice and rind, sugar, butter or margarine, and eggs—basically lemon curd.[130]

While fancy people shunned the humble cobbler, they served more short-cakes than ever. The American shortcake came into being in the late nine-teenth century. It was basically a biscuit, split and layered with fruit and whipped cream. Strawberries were the most popular shortcake fruit, although peach had its enthusiasts. Florida cooks developed a recipe for grapefruit shortcake with a dough of Bisquick, milk, and butter.[131] Dumplings, too, especially those made with apples, held their own with southern hearts. They cooked up fast and tasty on top of the stove for a family in a hurry.[132]

Tea cakes maintained their position as favorite cookie.[133] Rolled or dropped, with many variations on the original theme, what these cookies had in common was that many southerners adored and attached family memories to them. According to Elbert Mackey of Austin, Texas, creator of "The Tea Cake Project," they became "the national cookie of African-Americans." Tina Faye Luckett's grandmother included tea cakes in Luckett's box of food for the segregated bus trip to her aunt's home in Atlanta. Other people remembered them as special Sunday or holiday treats. For Yvonne Jackson, from Tyler, Texas, they were a reward for behaving in church. And so on.[134]

Inventive bakers created new cookies. One new twist was the use of store-bought candy: lemon drops, gumdrops, and the confection known as orange slices, which were large gumdrops shaped like citrus segments.[135] Dry, boxed cereals added texture to cookies of many kinds.[136]

The biggest splash on the cookie front was bar cookies. While they had been around since the 1920s, bar cookies gained popularity in the postwar years. They were a snap to make, with a variety of ingredients spread into a single pan, baked, cooled, and cut into squares for easy serving.

The favorite bar cookie in the South was the chocolate brownie. Most brownies had no leavening and so were dense and chewy, while some made with baking powder were more like cake. But they all featured deep chocolate, white or brown sugar (sometimes both), butter (usually), and vanilla. Many used nuts, usually pecans.[137] Some were frosted, but most were not.[138]

Almost as popular as brownies were date squares, sometimes given the mysterious name "Chinese chews." Although they seem to have originated in the date craze earlier in the century, these bar cookies with chopped dates and nuts (usually pecans) gained a wide following after World War II. The ingredients always included flour, white or brown sugar, soda or baking powder, and eggs and might also include milk, butter, cinnamon, or vanilla. After cutting the warm cookies into squares or sticks, the cook rolled them in powdered sugar.[139]

Other bar cookies included butterscotch and the closely related caramel, usually made with brown sugar and butter or margarine. Sprinkling chocolate chips and nuts over the hot cookies made them "toffee squares."[140] Bar cookies made with dried apricots or, more commonly, apricot jam filled recipe boxes across the South.[141] Pecans and black walnuts could be main ingredients in bar cookies, and so could coconut.[142]

While lemon "cheese" or curd—a sweet, rich filling made from lemons, eggs, and sugar—had been around since the 1850s, lemon bars as we know them didn't develop until the 1960s, courtesy of the researchers at Betty Crocker. A cook could use either fresh or bottled lemon juice in cooking the curd to top the cookie layer made of sugar, butter, and flour.[143]

Southern cooks made other layered cookies, most with a crust of flour and nuts or graham cracker crumbs. The toppings could be anything from crushed pineapple to coconut to chocolate chips. Sometimes a meringue or a frosting made from confectioners' sugar formed a third layer. Condensed milk, poured on last, often bound the entire confection. The quintessential layered cookie had various names—magic bar, seven-layer, Hello Dolly—and included butter, coconut, chocolate chips, graham cracker crumbs, and pecans, all lacquered together with sweetened condensed milk. The Hello Dolly cookie might have been the invention of Alecia Leigh Couch's grandmother. Couch, a precocious eleven-year-old from Dallas, gave the recipe to Atlanta food writer Clementine Paddleford in 1965.[144]

Dropped cookies required more work than bars did, but they were still easy, and they could accommodate a wide variety of flavors, from lemon to peanut butter and everything in between. Many American favorites circulated widely in the South. Oatmeal cookies, for example, became a southern staple.[145] Date cookies also had a strong following. Sometimes they were airy confections made with powdered sugar and egg whites, but they also could be substantial, with raisins, whole eggs, and butter or margarine, spiced with cinnamon and nutmeg.[146] Pecan cookies could also be made in the exact same two ways, leaving out the dates.[147]

Cookies made with candied fruit had many fans. Fruitcake cookies, sometimes called Lizzies, had candied fruit, pecans, allspice, cinnamon, and nutmeg as well as whiskey, wine, or fruit juice.[148] Fruit cookies used only raisins and nuts.

A couple of old-style dropped cookies from the North found their ways into southern homes, showing how regional changes occurred. Hermits were lumpy, chewy mounds of brown sugar, butter, sour cream, eggs, flour, and baking soda that could contain mincemeat or candied fruits. Cookbook compiler Marion Brown observed, "No Christmas, at least no Southern Christmas, is complete without them."[149] Similarly, the cookies often known as rocks circulated widely. Alabamian Ruth Lutken's recipe, which came from her grandmother, had butter, sugar, eggs, flour, cloves, allspice, ginger, cinnamon, baking soda, salt, raisins, currants, pecans, Brazil nuts, dates, watermelon rind preserves, and orange zest. Some cooks added cocoa or strong coffee to theirs.[150]

Cookies in which the dough was rolled out and then cut could be many flavors, but those that continued their favored status were ginger and molasses cookies and sugar cookies. Paper-thin Moravian Christmas cakes remained a tradition, particularly in North Carolina. Editor Sallie Hill observed that "the best way to roll cookies extra thin is on a cloth or covered board with a rolling pin tightly covered with a child's new white sock."[151]

A new, easy alternative to the tedium of rolling and cutting dough was icebox or, more modernly, refrigerator cookies, for which the cook made the dough, rolled it into a log, refrigerated or froze the log, and sliced the chilled dough into rounds before baking. In addition to the ease of slicing versus rolling and cutting, these cookies also had the benefit of keeping in their unbaked state, available to cook up hot and fresh at a moment's notice. The basic formula featured butter or margarine, white or brown sugar, eggs, vanilla, flour, and salt, but the variations were endless. Many cooks added pecans, and the cookies could be seasoned with cinnamon, lemon juice and rind, or orange juice and rind. Almonds, peanuts, or sesame seeds added flavor and crunch, and raisins and coconut provided taste and texture.[152]

The most popular shaped cookie went by various names: sand tarts, Mexican wedding cakes, snowballs, and even mothballs and cocoons. The small cookies, which had been around since the late nineteenth century, were made from flour, baking powder, butter or margarine, confectioners' or granulated sugar, egg, vanilla, and finely chopped pecans. The cook fashioned them by hand into balls or crescents and, after baking, rolled the warm cookies in more confectioners' sugar.[153] The thumbprint cookie, apparently a postwar creation, also went by several names—butter jewel, thimble cookie, maid of honor—but the idea was the same: a round cookie with a dent in its center

Bake sale, Mosier Valley, Texas, probably 1940s. Note the differences in cakes: some single-layer, some multilayer, some baked in tube pans. Heritage Room, Tarrant County College Northeast.

filled with jelly. The jelly could be currant, crab apple, strawberry, "the new cinnamon-flavored apple jelly," or the cook's choice.[154]

As Americans returned to the kitchen after World War II, some needed to be taught or reminded how to bake properly. Ethel Farmer Hunter told her readers in 1948, "The basis of a good cake is a dependable recipe. When the cook begins to cheat on the recipe—more or less shortening, more or less flour . . . fewer eggs—results are consequently uncertain. We must respect cake making rules by starting with a good recipe, and following it exactly."[155]

Thought postwar cooks had access to a variety of industrially made ingredients, some clung to their old ways. In Columbus, Georgia, for example, in 1957, one cook insisted on "butter (not margarine)" and Gayety Flour, produced by the local company, City Mills, for a white layer cake.[156]

Many cooks embraced new technologically produced shortcuts and flavors, however. Cake mixes developed more slowly than gingerbread and biscuit mixes, but by 1947, more than 200 regional companies offered them. General Mills and Pillsbury launched their versions in 1948.[157] The first cake mixes had uneven quality. The dried egg in them made them stick to the pan and taste eggy, and their shelf life was brief. Despite these shortcomings, sales of cake mixes doubled between 1947 and 1953.[158] In 1952, General Mills removed the egg and other companies followed suit. By 1954, General Mills offered five kinds of cake mix, including devil's food and angel food.[159]

Despite the volume of cake mix sales—more than $160 million in 1953—it's impossible to know how many women used them. Many housewives may have baked both "box cakes" and from scratch. Mixes didn't save that much time, and they often tasted "off," with too much sugar and too much artificial vanilla.[160] A middle way was the cake based on a mix and adding or substituting other ingredients. For example, an apricot cake from Lafayette, Louisiana, started with a "lemon supreme cake mix" and then replaced water with apricot nectar, a puree thicker than juice.[161] Gelatin, particularly Jell-O made by General Foods, could also lend fruit flavor. One strawberry cake recipe that circulated around Louisiana started with white cake mix and strawberry gelatin, frosted with a mixture of confectioners' sugar, butter, and frozen strawberries.[162] Lemon Jell-O and lemon juice flavored a white cake mix, while a yellow cake mix was enhanced with lemon or orange Jell-O and apricot nectar. Both citrus cakes had icing made of confectioners' sugar, butter or margarine, and lemon or orange juice, mixed and poured over the warm cake.[163] Jell-O lemon pudding mix (which debuted in the 1930s) and lemon extract combined with yellow cake mix for a lemon pudding cake.[164]

Commercially made candy and sweets formed parts of cake recipes just as they did in pies and cookies. Chocolate syrup, chocolate bars, and toffee bars all flavored cakes.[165] Chopped orange slice gumdrops provided a sweet, citrusy taste to a cake that also included coconut, chopped pecans, chopped dates, and buttermilk, frosted with orange juice and rind and powdered sugar.[166] Baker extraordinaire Nancie McDermott traces the orange slice cake over several generations to North Carolina and the Appalachian region.[167]

Many cakes stayed the same, even with the onslaught of new influences. Beloved types still included apple, spice, date, pecan, jelly roll, and coconut. Pound cake, the old, comforting friend, remained just as reliable as ever. Which is not to say that people didn't jazz it up—they did, adding chocolate chips, sour cream, German's sweet chocolate, orange juice, or dates.[168] Electric mixers helped with pound cakes. One cake recipe required one hour of beating but "less time" if using an electric mixer, while another needed "15 minutes with rotary beater, or 5 minutes with electric beater."[169]

The biggest change in pound cakes was the introduction of the Bundt pan in the late 1940s. A Bundt pan had a curved or fluted bottom and a tube in the middle, which produced a decorative pattern in the finished cake. In the late 1940s, Jewish bakers in Minneapolis asked officials of the Nordic Ware Company to produce a modern pan for *gugelhupf*, an Eastern European yeast bread. Nordic Ware introduced a cast aluminum version in 1950 that southern bakers quickly embraced for pound cake as well as other treats.[170]

As immigrants moved to the South, they adopted southern foodways into their family celebrations. Bertha Malacara Chavarría was born in 1931 in San Antonio to a Mexican American family. Her daughter Becky Chavarría-Cháirez remembered her seriousness about her product: "She'd often begin her fruitcake mission in late October when little by little she'd buy the ingredients, always hunting for bargains and the best of everything. Many years we'd spend a Friday evening or Saturday morning shelling pecans from our backyard until she had enough nuts for cooking. From year to year, her fruitcakes were a little different, like the vintner's annual fruits of his labor." Like her predecessors for hundreds of years, Chavarría made the cakes ahead, wrapping them in gauze and then soaking the gauze with brandy for at least two weeks before serving.[171]

Dark fruitcake still had its fans. Victoria Grady of New York City, child of the Great Migration from the South, used dark rum and brown sugar in hers.[172] Like other types of cakes, fruitcakes became the subject of experimentation with new ingredients: cane syrup for an "Acadian" version; cherry, apricot, and pineapple preserves for a "German" one.[173] Sweet potatoes, "grated oranges," and dates also had their uses. The writer of the recipe for "Big Mamma's Fruit Cake" specified that the bourbon for soaking the cake be a "good brand"—no cheap stuff accepted.[174]

Two new fruitcake fashions were to divide the batter into tiny paper cups for individual servings or to spread the batter thin and slice it into bars once it cooled after baking.[175] Mrs. J. K. Robertson of Spartanburg, South Carolina, baked small fruitcakes in "miniature aluminum cake pans that may be bought at the five-and-ten-cent stores" and gave them, along with "a tiny bottle of wine to pour on the cake," as Christmas gifts.[176]

Fruitcakes finally lost their place as wedding cakes. Even modest home weddings featured white cakes of at least three tiers, often topped with miniature statues of a bride and groom.

Angel food cakes could be flavored simply with vanilla or almond extract, frosted or unfrosted.[177] Other new formulas added lemon juice or extract.[178] Helen Corbitt, proprietor of the Zodiac Room restaurant at the fanciest department store in Texas, observed that "the most talked about cake at Neiman Marcus is the Coffee Angel Food," made with powdered instant coffee and frosted with butter icing with powdered coffee added.[179] But perhaps the new favorite was chocolate, flavored with cocoa, left plain or frosted with chocolate icing.[180]

Twentieth-century southerners baked two types of "cheese" cakes: the old-fashioned type in which the "cheese" was a sweet, thick custard filling, almost always flavored with lemon; and the New York style baked in a springform pan. After World War II, lemon cheese layer cakes popped up all over

The wedding of Helen and Garland Sharpless, Waco, Texas, October 25, 1947, with the requisite bride and groom figures atop the cake. Photo by Jimmie Willis.

the South: butter cakes with a filling of eggs, lemon juice and rind, butter or margarine, and sugar and frosted with a white frosting.[181] The New York–style cheesecake, which had been popular in the northeastern United States since the 1920s, made its way south beginning in the early 1960s: a crust of graham or zwieback cracker crumbs and a filling of cream cheese, eggs, and sugar, sometimes flavored with lemon. (Although cream cheese had been sold in southern stores since the late nineteenth century, southerners didn't bake with it much until later.) Sour cream topping also won favor. A cook from Lafayette, Louisiana, commented, "This was very popular at our League Bazaar."[182]

Lane and Lady Baltimore cakes still appeared for special occasions. The Lane cake reached its literary high point when, in the best-selling novel *To Kill a Mockingbird* by Harper Lee, Scout observed, "Miss Maudie Atkinson baked a Lane cake so loaded with shinny it made me tight." Sallie Hill remarked, "This cake, which was going great guns in Georgia and Alabama early in the century, has now breezed across the whole South," and *Southern Living* gave it a full-page color photograph in its second issue, the filling with candied cherries and raisins contrasting vividly with the white cake layers.[183] People continued to make up stories about the origins of Lady Baltimore cake. In 1948, Mary Agnes Harris wrote, "This is the original Lady Baltimore cake— has been in this family over one hundred years," a questionable claim, since that type of cake existed only after the Civil War.[184] To such assertions, Marion Brown observed that since the day Owen Wister first saw a Lady Baltimore cake, "every cake of similar ingredients and form bearing this name is said to be from the original recipe."[185]

In one more twist of chocolate names, in 1956, Charlotte Ulfers of El Reno, Oklahoma, published the recipe for a cake that she called "German Sweet Chocolate Cake." The cake, flavored with "German Sweet Chocolate," was baked in three layers and filled with a mixture of cream, coconut, and pecans.[186] The chocolate was in fact "German's Chocolate"—invented by Samuel German when he worked for the Baker Chocolate Company in the 1850s. General Foods, which owned Baker's Chocolate at the time, dropped the apostrophe from "German's," and thus the German chocolate cake was born.[187]

The cake that has come to be known as the Texas sheet cake has mysterious roots, but I have traced it to the Panhandle city of Amarillo in 1960. Bette Thompson, the food editor of the *Amarillo Globe-Times*, published the recipe in her "All Around the Town" column, saying, "Alrighty . . . another one of our tried and true Amarillo cooks has come forth with this recipe for what is called a Sheath Cake. . . . I haven't had a chance to try it, myself, but I'll take her word for its being delicious. . . . Here 'tis." The recipe that follows is exactly the same as today's: the cake of buttermilk, eggs, vanilla, baking soda, flour, sugar, cinnamon, and salt combined with a boiled mixture of shortening, cocoa, and water, baked on a sixteen-by-eleven-inch pan, with an icing of melted butter, milk, cocoa, confectioners' sugar, and pecans poured over the warm cake. The recipe spread like wildfire across the country, within a couple of years getting renamed "sheet cake" rather than "sheath cake." (No one knows where "sheath" came from except for maybe the dresses with that name that were popular in the early 1960s, and the cake that I made recently did look like a shimmer of brown satin.) One of my favorite baking memories is, as a senior in high school, sitting in front of a dying fire after one of my parents' parties, catching up with my mother on recent events and downing a big piece of what she called "chocolate sheath cake."[188]

Despite decades of myth-making, other storied cakes of the South aren't southern at all. Red velvet cake, for example, is actually just a dark chocolate cake with red food coloring added to the batter. It may have begun its life in the 1930s as a devil's food cake served at the Waldorf-Astoria Hotel in New York.[189] It was, however, a Texan who made it truly red. According to the Adams Extract Company in Austin, John and Betty Adams ate the cake at the Waldorf and decided to bring it back to Texas as a vehicle to sell food coloring. The company—possibly Betty Adams herself—added the color to the cake recipe and printed the recipe on cards. The white frosting, a combination of milk, flour, butter, and sugar, created a remarkable contrast to the red cake.[190] The red velvet cake became a staple of southern special occasions. Juneteenth, with its celebration of red foods (including watermelon and Big Red soda), was a special time for bakers to showcase their red velvet talents.[191]

Two other cherished cakes are rumored to have started in the South, but no one has been able to verify their origins. One is the Coca-Cola cake, which uses the much-loved southern soda to add sweetness to a chocolate cake. It has at least two origin stories. The first comes from the sugar-deprived days of World War II, when Coca-Cola was exempt from rationing and cooks could obtain it more easily than sugar. Another possible origin is the Coca-Cola test kitchens, with home economists looking for ways to sell more product. At any rate, *Southern Living* magazine published a recipe for "Cola Cake" in its first cookbook, *Our Best Recipes*, in 1970. The cake had flour, sugar, chopped marshmallows, shortening, margarine, cocoa, "cola drink," buttermilk, soda, and eggs, baked in a tube pan. The frosting featured margarine, cocoa, cola drink, confectioners' sugar, and pecans.[192]

A second cake of mysterious pedigree is the Italian cream cake, its three layers made with buttermilk, coconut, chopped pecans, and vanilla and frosted with cream cheese, margarine or butter, confectioners' sugar, and vanilla.[193] Although it is rumored to have originated in Texas, no evidence holds up that claim. Nevertheless, it became wildly popular, included by *Southern Living* magazine in *Our Best Recipes*.[194]

Charlotte russe again became the rage after World War II. Cooks alternated layers of ladyfingers—likely store-bought—with rich custards of eggs, cream, and gelatin and chilled them. After they turned out the chilled mixture, they frosted it with a layer of whipped cream. Sallie Hill called charlotte russe "a 'must' dish at Christmastime."[195]

In the 1950s, the charlotte morphed into the icebox cake, and southerners apparently couldn't get enough. The baked part was ladyfingers, sliced or cubed cake, or cookie crumbs, alternated with a soft, sweet filling. The mixture could be cooked, like a custard, or it could be an uncooked blend of heavy cream, gelatin, sugar, and a variety of other ingredients. Marshmallows, which derived from gelatin, could substitute. Chocolate was the hands-down favorite. The cake bases were usually angel food, but they might also be devil's food. The chocolate filling could be made from regular or German's chocolate. Other common ingredients included rum, coffee, and pecans. After the cake was unmolded, it was then covered with more whipped cream.[196]

Fruit flavors, particularly orange and lemon, also figured into the icebox cake phenomenon: fresh fruit, juice, or rind added to the gelatin/cream mixture. Coconut seemed a good flourish for the custard. Of course, whipped cream covered the entire enterprise.[197] Crushed pineapple also won favor, evoking such fanciful names as "Honolulu Pineapple Cake," perhaps an homage to the recently added fiftieth state.[198]

Icebox cakes flavored with alcohol had their fans, too, although they probably never made it to Baptist church suppers. For "eggnog" cake, eggs and bourbon joined the gelatin and whipped cream.[199] And sherry could both soak the cake base and flavor the custard that was poured over the sodden cake. Toasted almonds made a fine addition to the sherry as well.[200]

Split or hollowed whole angel food cakes provided another base for sweet fillings. One recipe gave careful instructions for removing the insides of a cake: "Cut entire top from cake one inch down. Cut trough in bottom section, leaving 1 inch wall outside, center and bottom of cake." The cake shell held mixtures of whipped cream and a variety of other possible ingredients: cocoa and almonds, for example, or maybe marshmallows, bananas, pecans, crushed pineapple, and maraschino cherries. As Anne Cole Boyd of Greensboro, North Carolina, urged, "Let your imagination run wild."[201] When all else failed, there was always "desperation dessert": an angel food loaf, frosted with sour cream, sprinkled "rather heavily" with brown sugar, and chilled.[202]

If the reader would like to get confused, then go no further than trying to figure out the word "torte" in the 1950s and 1960s. While a traditional Eastern European torte was most typically a layer cake, southern Americans used the name for all sorts of sweets.

Layered tortes could start with cake, topped with luscious sauces or with meringues, filled with whipped cream and fruit. For example, Cleora Butler's coconut torte was made with butter, sugar, egg whites, coconut, and vanilla. She topped that with ice cream and a sauce made of butter, sugar, eggs, vanilla, brandy, and nutmeg.[203] Some cooks made their torte layers from nuts and bread or cracker crumbs.[204]

Other "tortes" were more like pie: a crust made from graham cracker crumbs or from sugar, butter, and flour. Their fillings sometimes used gelatin and other times resembled cooked custard. They could have chocolate chips, lemon or orange juice, or nuts, almost always finished with whipped cream.[205]

But perhaps the most confounding torte of all was the one named "Huguenot": a mix of flour, baking powder, salt, eggs, vanilla, sugar, pecans, and chopped tart apples. According to chef and sleuth John Taylor Martin, the dish with the fancy Charleston name started out as "Ozark pudding"—which was not a pudding. Ozark pudding may have begun in the 1920s with an apple torte recipe combining flour, baking powder, salt, eggs, vanilla, sugar, pecans or walnuts, and chopped firm, tart apples.[206] The dish first debuted as "Huguenot Torte" in a 1950 cookbook, as the contribution of Evelyn Anderson Huguenin, who recalled that she first ate Ozark pudding at a church dinner in Galveston, Texas, in the 1930s. Once back home in Charleston, she tinkered with the recipe and in 1942 renamed it after the Huguenot Tavern, a Charleston restaurant where she made desserts. It was a smash hit, making the reputation of the tavern.[207]

Not to be confused with tortes, a dessert called tortoni gained wild admiration after World War II. A tortoni had a base of the almond cookies known as macaroons (not macarons, which are filled sandwich cookies), which had been available commercially for half a century. The cook crumbled the macaroons into a mixture of egg whites, whipping cream, and confectioners' sugar. She could next add a wide variety of other ingredients, from sherry to pistachio nuts. The combination then went into a fluted paper cup, a new postwar invention, and from there into the freezer.[208]

Frostings, fillings, and sauces have always had a mix-and-match quality. Any cake could have any frosting, any filling, and any sauce, providing limitless combinations. Frostings were the most typical finish for a cake, but fillings and sauces still had use.

Helen Corbitt took a swipe at cake in 1957: "Surely everyone has a *Betty Crocker Picture Cookbook*. I use its cake recipes." The special part, she averred, was the icing: "It is the icing that makes a cake popular."[209] And while Corbitt might have been minimizing cake's role as only a carrier of icing (although I largely agree with her), some striking icings developed after World War II.

Old-fashioned boiled icing, which Nancie McDermott calls "the great-grandmother" of frosting, was still around, and electric mixers made easier the challenging task of combining egg whites with boiled sugar syrup.[210] The new go-to was the so-called seven-minute icing, made of egg whites, sugar, light corn syrup or cream of tartar, and salt, cooked and beaten, usually with a rotary eggbeater, until it stood in peaks—theoretically seven minutes—and then flavored with vanilla extract and beaten some more until it was spreading consistency. Many cooks considered it a kitchen staple.[211]

Still a third variation of white icing was divinity frosting. The cook made a syrup of sugar and light corn syrup and then combined it with beaten egg whites, beating the combination over boiling water until the mixture stood in peaks—perhaps twenty minutes.[212] The cooks of Columbus, Georgia, made theirs with local Eelbeck cane syrup, which humorist Roy Blount described as looking like motor oil and being "the strongest thing I had ever put in my mouth."[213] The ingredients for the three types of icing were similar, but the manner of cooking and the finished texture differed for each.

Sauces remained consistent to their forebears. Lemon sauce, usually made with sugar, butter, and lemon juice, was the most popular. Newer ingredients began showing up, however, such as "ReaLemon," a bottled lemon juice concentrate invented in 1934. ReaLemon kept indefinitely in the refrigerator and had a consistent strength. Lemon sauce might also contain egg yolks, evaporated milk, or light corn syrup.[214] Orange sauces often had similar bases and might have whipped cream added at the end.[215] Caramel sauce, made with cooked white or brown sugar, could be served hot or cold.[216] And the list went on: fresh peaches, vanilla, wine—all sorts of good things made to be poured over baked goods.[217]

WHILE COOKING COMPETITIONS were nothing new, the battles heated up after World War II. As had long been the tradition, county and state fairs gave bakers chances to strut their stuff.[218] Local companies began sponsoring cooking contests, establishing bakers' reputations. In 1951, Lucile Plowden Harvey won second place and five dollars with her fruitcake recipe in a contest sponsored by the *Tampa Tribune*. The newspaper published Harvey's recipe—pecans, candied cherries, candied pineapple, flour, butter, sugar, eggs, baking powder, vanilla, and lemon extract—annually until 2010: a run of fifty-nine years.[219]

Communities created local food festivals and made cooking contests part of the celebrations. In 1958, for example, Ann Coit won the Yam Cooking Contest at the Louisiana Yambilee with her yam pecan pie and its streusel topping.[220] Corporate growers also sponsored cooking contests. The Florida Citrus Council gave awards to baked goods using its products: orange bread pudding, sponge roll with orange filling, orange-lime-nut pie, yeasted orange bowknot rolls, an orange fruit cake ("modern and refreshing").[221]

Baking contests also went national. In 1954, the "Mrs. America" pageant became a homemaking contest.[222] Mrs. Louisiana, Ann LeJeune of Lafayette, won the grand title in 1963. She declared her "Confetti Pudding"—made of crushed macaroons, Taylor's cream sherry, vanilla pudding mix, eggs, milk, sugar, butter, whipping cream, vanilla extract, chopped pecans, and pineapple—to be a "very important reason" for her victory.[223]

The largest and most prestigious competition, the Pillsbury Bake-Off, began in 1949. Each recipe had to use at least half a cup of Pillsbury's Best Family Flour and be made from scratch. For Ella Rita Helfrich of Houston, the bake-off meant fame and a modicum of fortune: a $5,000 prize, which she and her husband, Carl, used to buy a Chevrolet Impala. Her "Tunnel of Fudge" cake took only second place at the bake-off in 1966, but it soon gained a massive following. The batter of sugar, margarine, eggs, powdered sugar, flour, unsweetened cocoa, and chopped nuts baked up in a Bundt pan with a center of "soft, creamy chocolate." The recipe became the most requested in Pillsbury history, and the Nordic Ware company had to run extra shifts to keep up with the demand for Bundt pans. Helfrich became one of the first inductees into the Pillsbury Bake-Off Hall of Fame.[224]

THE TRANSITION from home cook to professional was still possible even as large businesses dominated the baking industry. Entrepreneurs created businesses, sometimes from their homes and sometimes from storefronts. Charlestonians Mildred Bernstein and Minnie Weinberg opened their kosher catering business in the 1940s, with goods including German babkas—sweet yeasted breads filled with cinnamon or chocolate—that took two days to prepare. African American employee Mary Stokes learned to make kosher specialties such as schnecken, sweet yeasted rolls in a spiral shape.[225] In New Orleans, Beulah Levy Ledner first baked and sold pastries from her home. Her signature product was a "doberge" cake, an adaptation of the Eastern European *dobos torta*. She changed the filling from buttercream to a lighter custard and gave the cake a "Frenchified" name. The cake had eight thin layers of lemon cake, filled with chocolate custard and frosted with chocolate buttercream.[226] The cake produced an army of imitators, some of whom changed the cake flavor to chocolate.[227] Ledner operated her own bakery until 1981, when she was eighty-seven years old.

Cleora Butler, in Tulsa, began cooking for the public by baking each night, with her mother, 150 small pies to sell at her father-in-law's billiard parlor for five cents each. She also made tarts for a lunchroom in south Tulsa. In 1961, Butler applied for and received one of the first Small Business Administration loans in North Tulsa, the segregated African American neighborhood. She opened Cleora's Pastry Shop and Catering in April 1962. She and her assistant baked pies and cakes in the kitchen at the rear of the shop. "After all these years I was now employer, rather than employee," she observed. "At the insistence of customers," they began to bake bread daily. Butler's career was cut short when her husband developed diabetes, and they closed the shop in 1967.[228]

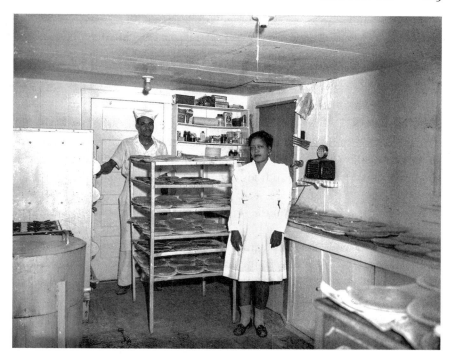

Fred Eugene Denman, proprietor of Denman's Pies, Dallas, 1946. Marion Butts Collection, Dallas Public Library, PA2005–4/92.

Lucille Bishop Smith, also African American, was a fine professional cook, but she made her business venture with a mix rather than a finished product. In 1943, she developed a hot roll mix and set up a business, Lucille B. Smith's Fine Foods, Inc. In addition to years of expertise as a teacher and a professional cook, Smith also closely aligned with local Bewley Mills, contributing to and endorsing its company cookbook. Bishop marketed her roll mix by demonstrating it in local grocery stores to both African American and white customers.[229]

The small bakery business had always been volatile, and the numbers of bakeries declined in the years after World War II. In Dallas, for example, there were fifty-eight retail bakeries in 1941 but only forty in 1955. Of the fifty-eight, only ten were still in business in 1955—an attrition rate of 83 percent.[230] World War II veteran Fred Denman, for example, opened a pie bakery in Dallas in 1946, but it lasted only briefly.

Like Denman's, many bakeries had their specialties. Jewish bakeries, such as the Shalom Bakery in Memphis, made bagels and strudel until the 1960s.[231] In Dallas, the number of Mexican bakeries rose from one to three between 1940 and 1960.[232] They likely made and sold corn and flour tortillas and pan dulce: cookies, empanadas (fried pies), cakes, and so on. In Cecilia, Louisiana, Pete and Della Patin baked French bread that writer Rick Bragg described as "chewy, buttery, comforting."[233] George Bullwinkel of Charleston specialized in a sponge cake layered with raspberry jam and whipped cream, sometimes selling more than a thousand of them in a single Christmas season.[234] And so it went, for hundreds of southern bakeries and their delighted customers.

Doughnut shops thrived in the postwar era, a product of the new car culture. They became "a short-distance commuter food," easy for a driver to eat with one hand while steering with the other.[235] By 1947 Krispy Kreme had branches in seven southeastern cities, and regional exclusivity added prestige to the product. Additionally, Krispy Kreme gained favor by helping youth and civic groups raise money.[236] By 1955, a quarter of the bakeries in Dallas sold only doughnuts.

In New Orleans, restaurants picked up where the street vendors left off. In 1971, writer Peter Feibleman observed, "The cala women have disappeared, but these unique deep-fried rice balls are still available, fresh and hot, at Maxcy's Coffee Pot Restaurant in the heart of the Quarter."[237] Likewise, the New Orleans doughnuts known as beignets became ever more popular. They were available from corner stands and from time-honored cafés such as the Morning Call and the Café du Monde, which began calling its doughnuts by their French name in 1958.[238]

Italian bread—Sicilian-style muffuletta loaves and twist bread with a hard crust and firm interior—came from a variety of sources, notably the United Bakery. New Orleans residents delighted in filling twist bread with lemon ice cream, particularly for breakfast. John Gendusa, a baker at United, observed that twist bread took an enormous amount of hand labor, running it through a dough break fifty-four times "to make it tight . . . like an Italian bread should be."[239] St. Joseph's altars became more public, with restaurants servings as hosts. The elements remained largely the same, though Faye Zuppardo added "fluffy coconut bars and lambs, Bible-shaped layer cakes, *cannoli* and *sfingi* (Italian-style beignets)." For this celebration in the middle of Lent, all restraints came off, and baked sweets took center stage, if only for a day.[240]

King cakes, also theoretically tied to the church year, grew in demand and audience, becoming sweeter and fancier. Increasingly, bakers used sweet-roll dough instead of bread and added icing to make the cake even more sugary.

The colors of Carnival—purple, green, and gold—became standard. The practice of inserting dolls—first porcelain, then plastic—into the cake spread in the 1960s.[241]

Tampeños still had their love affair with *pan Cubano*. An unnamed writer proclaimed in 1961, "One bread particularly typical of Tampa, the amazing Cuban bread, stands in a bin at the side of the counter because it's too long to lay flat. Cuban bread is one yard long! It's a crusty beige on the outside and 36 inches of delicate white fluff on the inside. . . . As long as a Tampan remains alive, there will always be a fierce demand for this marvelous bread."[242]

Other Americans, however, hid their native breads and ate white bread instead. Irene Palacios Robles remembered her immigrant parents' decision to give up tortillas: "The one thing that Daddy always did—he would always buy a lot of bread for us to take sandwiches because he didn't want the white kids to make fun of us if we took tortillas. So Mom always bought—I don't know how many loaves she bought for the whole week to make the sandwiches."[243] Racists still used baked goods to discriminate.

Although small bakeries still sold bread, large companies and franchises increasingly controlled both grocery store supply and home delivery. Richard Bielamowicz's family had a grocery store in the small Polish town of Bremond, Texas, and he recalled that in the 1960s, they sold bread from a wholesale bakery in large quantities: "These bread boys, they would bring in—it'd be a box with sixteen loaves in each box. . . . And they'd set them out in front of the store, and you might have five, six boxes of that out there. . . . And you'd sell practically all of it."[244]

The consumption of bread continued to grow in the United States. Industrial bakeries had an ever-increasing share of the market, as additives like calcium propionate extended the shelf life of baked goods by inhibiting mold.[245] In 1955, there were twenty-four wholesale bakers in Dallas, only six of which had existed before World War II. They included regional favorite Mrs. Baird's as well as national companies like Nabisco and Continental Baking, maker of Twinkies and Wonder Bread.[246] In 1968, one Dallas grocery store sold four different brands of bread, all priced identically and all made locally.[247] Commercial bakeries helped battle pellagra as federal and state law mandated increased nutrition of bread. By 1953, the American Institute of Baking estimated that 85 percent of all the bread sold in the United States was enriched.[248] Cases of pellagra declined dramatically, although they never completely vanished.

The wave of the future began as grocery stores turned into supermarkets and included in-house bakeries. Publix, based in Lakeland, Florida, was one of the early adopters of the trend, having a local bakery deliver fresh baked goods every day and then eventually acquiring the bakery.[249] (In 1984, Publix built a water tower in the shape of a three-tiered cake at its headquarters.) Some grocery-store baked goods lacked quality, but consumers valued the convenience enough to tolerate the dubious wares.

As we have seen with Helen Corbitt, department stores housed restaurants, and some of those employed in-house bakers. Callie Williams baked for the Magnolia Room at Rich's Department Store in downtown Atlanta. In 1948, Williams made 28,960 pecan pies. She later gave her recipe, which used dark corn syrup, to Clementine Paddleford for her *Great American Cookbook*.[250]

Americans, and southerners, began eating more store-bought packaged sweets. While many were nationally marketed products, such as Hostess, some had southern roots. In Chattanooga, O. D. and Ruth McKee started their bakery business in 1934. O. D. dreamed up a sandwich made of soft oatmeal-raisin cookies and marshmallow "creme" filling. In 1960, the McKees began wrapping individual sandwiches in cellophane and selling them by the dozen. They named the new line of products "Little Debbie" after their granddaughter. In the first ten months of production, the company sold more than 14 million cartons of Oatmeal Creme Pies. By 1964, Little Debbie had added thirteen more products, such as Swiss Cake Rolls (chocolate cake wrapped around marshmallow filling and covered with chocolate).[251]

Southern bakers added their touch to the national frozen pie market. Mrs. Smith's, from Pennsylvania, began selling frozen pies in 1952, and by 1953, Chicago-based Sara Lee was shipping its goods nationwide.[252] In Atlanta, Tom Edwards founded a small retail bakeshop, the Edwards Baking Company, eventually focusing on pies. In the 1960s, Edwards began selling frozen pies to grocery stores, starting with lemon meringue and then including key lime and pecan pies made exclusively with Georgia nuts.[253] By 1966, bakery goods were one of the fastest-growing segments of the frozen foods industry, largely because of the "excellent quality" of the goods, the "economy," and "the time-saving feature . . . an advantage every homemaker appreciates," according to an unnamed writer for the *Dallas Morning News*.[254]

THE CIVIL RIGHTS MOVEMENT, urbanization, growing (although still-limited) prosperity, and changing gender roles all affected the world of southern baking between 1940 and 1980. Many white women entered the paid workforce, and African American women left domestic work and found more gainful, if still constrained, employment. Recipes and ingredients increasingly resembled those in other parts of the United States. But if anyone feared that the old ways would die out, they need not have worried. Southern baking was on the cusp of a revival.

PASTEL DE TRES LECHES

....

The Cutting Edge of Southern Baking

After Michael Brown was murdered by police in Ferguson, Missouri, in 2014, Rose McGee packed up a load of sweet potato pies and drove 600 miles to deliver them to a hurting community. The next year, when nine people were murdered at Emanuel AME Church in Charleston, McGee took sweet potato pies to the church. She named them "Sweet Potato Comfort Pies," and she calls her work "baketivism": baking the pies, sharing them, and reflecting on the community built through eating pie together. As the people of the South and the United States struggle to deal with the racism and division that rend our country, McGee and her helpers believe that baked goods help, one slice of lovingly made pie at a time.[1]

Sweet Potato Comfort Pies reflect the tensions and the diversity of the twenty-first-century South. More urban, more multicultural, more affluent than ever before but perhaps just as racist and tense as ever, the South defies easy explanation. Baking can give us a lens through which to view the contemporary South.

In its September 2020 issue, *Southern Living* magazine detailed five innovative bakers, showcasing Lydia Faust's yeasted Czech kolaches, Jerrelle Guy's "Salted Irish Cream Apple Crostata," Melissa Martin's "Lagniappe Bread Rolls" made with whole-wheat flour and yeast, Vianney's Rodriguez's "Concha Tres Leches Cake," and Ashleigh Shanti's "Cracked-Corn Spoon Bread."[2] The women responsible for these pioneering yet traditional recipes are bloggers, chefs, cookbook writers. They are Black, Cajun, Czech, Latina. Like Rose McGee, they understand traditional southern baking—quick breads, yeasted breads, pies, cakes—but they are not bound by it. They represent a vanguard of southern baking going into the third decade of the twenty-first century.

The revival, adaptation, and social uses of traditional recipes show the striking transformation of southern baking that began in the late 1970s and continues vigorously today. After the repetitious sameness of many recipes in the 1950s and 1960s, some cooks began to seriously evaluate their roots. One of the pioneers was Edna Lewis, the revered Virginian who wowed New York with her southern food. Her first book, *The Taste of Country Cooking*, published in 1976, contained vignettes from her growing-up years in the all-Black hamlet of Freetown as well as recipes. As scholar Sara Franklin observed, the book presented an alternative history of the South—a prosperous community of African Americans—and a "new authoritative perspective on southern food."[3] Lewis genuinely appreciated the legacy of cooking in the South, and with her colleague Scott Peacock she founded the Society for the Revival and Preservation of Southern Food. (See chapter 7 for some of Lewis's baked goods.)

Chef Bill Neal, who was white, also had a huge impact on the renewal of attention to southern cooking. With his wife, Moreton Neal, he opened Crook's Corner, a restaurant in Chapel Hill, North Carolina, in 1982, using fresh, local ingredients in the same ways that chef Alice Waters did at Chez Panisse in California. *New York Times* food critic Craig Claiborne, a native of Sunflower, Mississippi, praised the new style of food as "an imaginative interpretation of southern cuisine focused on the freshest seasonal and local ingredients."[4] A former employee commented that Bill Neal "was the first person I knew of to claim that Southern food, the kind served at family reunions, deserved respect."[5] He served biscuits, cornbread made with black pepper, and sweet potato pie, among many other baked goods. Neal understood southern culture and southern food. In 1985, he insisted that southern food was "Western European, African, native American—meeting, clashing, and ultimately melding into one unique identity."[6] With guidance from Neal's cookbooks, including the baking-focused *Biscuits, Spoonbread, and Sweet Potato Pie*, chefs in other southern towns and cities began working purposefully with locally sourced foods.[7]

In 1999, John Egerton, author of *Southern Food: At Home, on the Road, in History*, convened a meeting in Birmingham to establish the Southern Foodways Alliance. Fifty people attended the meeting, which folded Lewis and Peacock's group and the American Southern Food Institute, led by Jeanne Voltz, into the new Southern Foodways Alliance. The primary purpose of the alliance is to "document, study, and explore the diverse food cultures of the changing American South."[8] Its work includes research, documentation, presentations, and publications, many of them featuring baking.

With this new attraction to southern food came an avalanche of southern cookbooks—hundreds of them, by local cooks and celebrities alike. Restaurateur and influential cooking teacher Nathalie Dupree hosted fifty episodes of *New Southern Cooking* on public television beginning in 1986 and published a cookbook of the same name with recipes like "Pecan Cookies Sandwiched with Fresh Peaches" and "Black Pepper Biscuits."[9] Southern cooking and baking were—pardon the pun—hot.

AS SOUTHERN BECAME FASHIONABLE, what were southerners actually baking? Cornbread, for sure. Craig Claiborne observed, "There are more recipes for corn bread than there are magnolia trees in the South."[10] Debates about yellow and white cornmeal and sugar versus no sugar continued just as strong as ever. Crescent Dragonwagon, whose wide-ranging *Cornbread Gospels* contains more than 200 recipes, observed that the best cornbread is that made by your mother or grandmother. Perhaps the most famous line in the debate came from Kentucky's Ronni Lundy: "If God had meant for cornbread to have sugar in it, he'd have called it cake."[11]

For many southerners, biscuits remained the highest attainment of the baker's art. Gig Smith, the mother of novelist Lee Smith, unimpressed with her first bagel in Chapel Hill, observed, "This may taste good to someone who has never eaten a biscuit."[12] (Though, to be fair, that southern version was likely nothing like the storied New York bagel.) In fact, biscuits became idolized and sentimentalized. People got downright mushy, talking about their grandmothers' biscuits.

Experienced cooks offered expert biscuit advice for those without family recipes. Bill Neal advocated using lard, vegetable shortening, and butter for perfect texture. Mixing the dough had to be done carefully, as each "iota" of flour must be "enrobed by fat." And the best biscuits were "never cut in half with a knife, but always split or pulled apart by hand to preserve the natural, delicate interior structure."[13] Like Neal, chef Virginia Willis cautioned against handling the dough too much: "You want to just barely activate the gluten, not overwork it," she warned.[14]

The food processor, introduced into the United States in 1973, became a tool for some biscuit makers. Chef and writer Martha Hall Foose observed, "I may be stoned for saying this, but I like to cut in the fat quickly with a food processor so my fingers do not warm the mixture."[15] Craig Claiborne offered a "modernized version" of beaten biscuits made in a food processor, which he proclaimed "fair."[16] In the 1990s, bread-making machines helped some bakers, but the results seldom compared favorably to oven-baked yeast bread.

Elaborate cakes continued to represent the South, even when they started elsewhere. The newest cake in the southern pantheon was the "Hummingbird Cake," which Eva Wiggins of Greensboro, North Carolina, contributed to *Southern Living* in 1978. A layer cake made with pecans or walnuts, mashed bananas, crushed pineapple, and cream cheese frosting, it became *Southern Living*'s most requested recipe of all time. The original recipe may have come from Jamaica, where the tourism board sent it to the American media as a "Doctor Bird cake."[17]

A genuine southern invention, the Ocracoke fig cake, has its own festival. Ocracoke Island clings to the Outer Banks off North Carolina, and figs are the only fruit that will grow in the wind-driven soil. In the late 1960s, local resident Margaret Garrish substituted preserved figs for dates in a date cake recipe, and thus the cake was born and quickly became a community favorite. The Fig Festival began in 2014, complete with a bake-off with categories of "traditional" and "innovative." The cakes are made with fig preserves, much like other jam cakes, and buttermilk and seasoned with nutmeg, allspice, and cinnamon.[18]

Local tourism agencies, like that on Ocracoke Island, have latched onto the idea of southern baking to create food festivals. Baked goods festivals are now a huge pull all over the region, for residents and tourists alike.

To name just a few, the King Biscuit Blues Festival started in 1986 in Helena, Arkansas, a spinoff of the *King Biscuit Time* radio show. The radio show began broadcasting in 1941, sponsored by the local King Biscuit Flour, and in 2021 is the longest-running radio show in the United States. While the festival focuses on music, it has a "Biscuit Bash" that includes gravy flowing from a fountain.[19] The National Cornbread Festival began in 1996 in South Pittsburg, Tennessee, home of the Lodge cast-iron cookware company. Competitors in the cooking competitions must use Martha White cornmeal and Lodge cookware.[20] Little Rock has its Arkansas Cornbread Festival, and Merritt Island, Florida, hosts a Key Lime Pie Festival, both established in 2011. In New Orleans, a King Cake Festival showcases entries from local bakeries, with the proceeds going to the Ochsner Children's Hospital.[21] All these festivals, and others, are designed to highlight baked foods, to encourage inventive home and professional bakers, and to bring people in to try various versions of them.

PROFESSIONAL BAKING has continued to evolve with tastes. The king cake is a prime example. In the 1980s, sweet fillings made the cakes even more decadent. One baker observed in 1985, "You wouldn't believe the fillings people ask for: blueberry, blackberry, cream cheese, lemon, pumpkin. Anything you

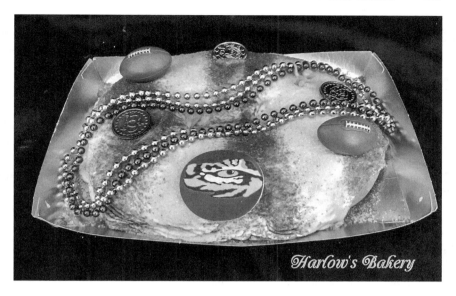

Louisiana State University national football championship king cake, 2020. Harlow's Bakery, Pineville, Louisiana. Courtesy of Harlow's.

can put in a pie they want in a king cake." In 1989, Haydel's Bakery partnered with Federal Express to ship king cakes nationwide, and the next year, more than 300,000 king cakes left New Orleans. Bakeries began recognizing the need for ethnic diversity in their cakes, with the grocery store Winn-Dixie offering a "Zulu Coconut" king cake in 1985. The plastic babies in the cakes began coming in a variety of colors. New residents in New Orleans altered the king cake to fit their customers' palates. Vietnamese king cakes, for example, are not as sweet as others.[22] Other types of customization flourished as well. Bakeries like Harlow's, in Pineville, Louisiana, offered Louisiana State University king cakes after the home team won the national football championship in 2020.

Changing demographics have resulted in shifts in southern baking, with new arrivals from around the globe bringing their specialties. As the Latinx population has spread across the South, so have *panaderias*. In August 2020, there were at least four in Charlotte, eight in Nashville, and twelve in Atlanta. Gaby's Bakery in Atlanta, for example, styles itself "La Casa del Pastel Tres Leches," the famous three-milks cake: a vanilla-flavored sponge cake soaked with evaporated milk, sweetened condensed milk, and cream and then frosted with whipped cream or meringue. It also sells pastries and pan dulce, several varieties of sweet bread, and cakelike muffins known as *mantecadas*.[23]

Increased immigration from Asia has brought Vietnamese, Chinese, and Indian bakeries, which often fuse into similar foodways. Vietnamese immigrants began arriving in Houston in the late 1970s, and in the next forty years the Southeast Asian population grew to more than 80,000 people. Vietnamese bakers brought Vietnamese-inflected wheat breads and French colonial baked goods. The Parisian Bakery, with three locations, sells *bánh da lon*, a layer cake made from rice flour and coconut milk, and *bánh tieu* (hollow doughnuts with sesame seeds) as well as traditional French breads such as croissants.[24] The Family Baking Company in Atlanta serves a variety of baked goods from Hong Kong, Taiwan, and Malaysia, such as buns and mochi (rice cakes) made with sweet red bean paste, and breads made with pandan, a Southeast Asian herb. The Family Baking Company's pandan is vegan.[25]

Nigerian bakeries in Houston and Dallas specialize in soft sweet bread known as *agege*, a fried flatbread called *bara*, and especially *chin-chin*, a beloved confection made of fried nuts, flour, and jelly. James and Jolly Onobun began their baking journey in Nigeria, where James worked for his uncle. After arriving in America, he worked in various commercial bakeries. The couple opened the Jolly Jolly Bakery ("House of Great Delicious and Soft Sweet Bread") in Houston and expanded north to Dallas. Another Nigerian bakery, Sammy's, opened in Houston in 2005.[26] Middle Eastern bakeries, like the Euro-Indo Bakery around the corner from me in Fort Worth, specialize in baked goods from the Mediterranean region: baklava, *znood alset* (cream-filled filo rolls), *awame* (fried dough coated with sugar syrup), and *zalabiya* (similar to a doughnut).[27]

Although dense, dark Eastern European breads can be hard to find in the South, kosher bakeries and caterers still sell them, and even some chain grocery stores offer bread that is "Pas Yisroel," or baked with the participation of an observant Jew. Scholar Marcie Cohen Ferris observes that it is easiest to locate "authentic challah" because non-Jews like the sweet flavor and light texture of challah.[28] Bagels have become common supermarket fare, although purists argue that a bagel that is baked without being boiled first is simply "a roll with a hole." It is possible to find good bagels in the South, however. BB's Bagels in Alpharetta, north of Atlanta, and Wholy Bagel in Austin made the list of the best bagels outside of New York from food website Epicurious.[29]

Even as baking reflects increasing diversity in the South, some far-flung visionaries are literally returning to their roots. Since the 1990s, the artisan baking movement, which regards baking as a craft rather than an industry, has surged. A synergy has grown between farmers, millers, and bakers, with locally grown and organic grains transforming into bread.

While the move toward heritage grains began in the 1970s, it took off in 1995, when South Carolinian Glenn Roberts began growing Carolina Gold rice. He then discovered and planted Carolina gourdseed white corn, one of several "landrace" grains from the South, and harvested his first crop in 1998. (Landrace grains are traditional domesticated species especially adapted to a local climate. Their producers focus on taste, not transportability, disease resistance, or other industrial concerns.)[30] Roberts and others established Anson Mills in Columbia, South Carolina, in 1998. In 2000, Anson Mills had its first "real harvest" of Carolina Gold rice and ten varieties of heirloom southern dent corn. In 2001, it produced organic Red May wheat.[31] Other farmers have followed suit on a small scale. Billy Carter of Eagle Springs, North Carolina, for example, began growing hard red wheat and rye as cover crops for his organic tobacco, and he found a ready market for his organic grains among bakers in the Asheville area. He acknowledges that the heat and the humidity in the Southeast make grain growing more of a challenge than in the Midwest. He and other farmers, however, grow patches of landrace grains with other crops to meet the increasing demand. Scientists at North Carolina State University have developed Carolina White, a soft wheat adapted to the climate.[32]

In a similar manner, Native Americans are reclaiming their agricultural heritage. Dave McCluskey, Mohawk (Kanien'kehá:ka) Haudenosaunee, specializes in teaching people about corn, squash, and beans—the "three sisters" of traditional Native American food. He grows heirloom corn in South Carolina, with a special fondness for the Cherokee gourdseed type. In North Carolina, Frank Cain oversees the Alliance of Native Seedkeepers, formed by members of the Monacan, Nottoway, and Tuscarora. The Alliance propagates and sells seeds for corn such as "Cherokee Tooth" and also a variety of beans.[33]

Millers have revived stone grinding. Except for a hiatus from 1975 to 1977, the Old Mill of Guilford in North Carolina has operated continuously since 1767, and Lindley Mills outside Asheville has been at work since 1755. The Lindley family restored the mill in 1975, installing millstones from a nearby mill that had fallen into disrepair. They grind organic wheat, amaranth, quinoa, millet, sorghum, and buckwheat.[34] Other millers have built powerful new stone mills through the South, particularly in North Carolina.[35] David Bauer of the Farm and Sparrow, in Mars Hill, North Carolina, proudly points out that his stones are made of Georgia granite.[36] Chefs in Arkansas depend on the organic cornmeal and flour ground with power from the historic waterwheel at the War Eagle Mill in Rogers.[37]

Many of the women and men who make artisan bread had formal culinary training and gradually made their way into their bread careers. In 2021, the Bread Bakers Guild of America has more than eighty members in the South.[38] Young bakers such as Allison and Ty Smith, from Bedford, Texas, bake carefully with a view to sustainability. They began their sourdough starter, which they named "Peach," in 2017. They sell sourdough bread in inventive flavors

Stenciled loaf made of Carolina Ground Flour by Chicken Bridge Bakery, Pittsboro, North Carolina. Courtesy of Chicken Bridge Bakery.

such as carrot and turmeric, chocolate and cherry, and goat cheese and rosemary to local restaurants and at farmers' markets.[39]

Jennifer Lapidus of Asheville shows the synergy between farmers, millers, and bakers. She trained with artisan bakers around the United States and moved to North Carolina in 1994. As a baker, she began working with the U.S. Department of Agriculture in the development of Carolina White wheat. About 2010, she opened her mill, Carolina Ground, which sells milled organic grains to bakers and food co-ops around the South.[40] In New Orleans, Graison Gill of Bellegarde Bakery ticks off the sources of his grains: Seashore Black Rye from South Carolina, durum wheat from Arizona, Aspen white wheat from Kansas. Like Lapidus, Gill works with agriculture schools at several universities. He also lobbies government to encourage organic agriculture.[41]

The makers of reliable old southern, soft-wheat flours have been taken over by national companies since the 1970s. New owner Smucker's moved White Lily from Knoxville to Toledo, Ohio, in 2003. Smucker's also bought Red Band and moved it from Johnson City, Tennessee, then discontinued it completely in 2009. Martha White is still based in Memphis. Southern cooks continue to swear by these low-protein, low-gluten flours.

Perhaps at the opposite end of the spectrum from artisan baking, fast-food biscuits have gained great followings. In 2018, Atlanta-based website Southern Kitchen evaluated seven chain biscuits, looking for a biscuit that was "flaky, flavorful, but not too salty or buttery with a moist, not gummy texture when you bite into it." They found the best to be Hardee's, founded in Greenville, North Carolina, in 1960, and Bojangles from Charlotte and Mrs. Winner's from Atlanta, both established in the late 1970s.[42] The writers at Southern Kitchen concede they are good alternatives for people who don't have time to bake. Another option is frozen biscuits, of which Mary B's brand is generally considered the best. The founder of Mary B's, retired beer sales-man Howard Burris, started manufacturing frozen rolled dumplings in 1984, then added buttermilk biscuits in 1997. He named the products after his wife, Mary B., and founded a company, Hom/Ade Foods, in Bagdad, Florida. In 2021 the company sells four kinds of biscuits: "butter taste," thin, buttermilk, and "southern made."[43]

Yeast rolls, too, are available in grocery store freezer cases. Patricia Schubert Barnes of Troy, Alabama, began selling frozen rolls made with her grandmother's recipe at her church in 1986. The rolls sold out three years in a row, and Barnes established a factory in 1991 to make "Sister Schubert's Homemade Rolls." The rolls are still made in Luverne, Alabama. In 2012, Sister Schubert's turned out 9 million rolls a day.[44]

Bakeries across the South ship their wares direct to consumers by mail, either fresh or frozen. In 1994, Dean Jacobs created Dean's Cake House in Andalusia, Alabama. Dean's manufactures, freezes, and ships seven-layer cakes across Alabama, Florida, and Mississippi. With a staff of older Alabamians, the company makes 400 seven-layer cakes and "several hundred" two-layer cakes each day.[45] Once limited to sturdy items like fruitcakes and cookies, mail-order baked goods now include elaborate layer cakes and cheesecakes, shipped from bakeries in every southern state. Although some are standard American fare, many are southern favorites such as paper-thin Moravian cookies and key lime pie.[46]

Baking continues to manifest in southern culture in multiple ways. The Montgomery Biscuits are a AA affiliate of the Tampa Bay Rays of Major League Baseball. The team colors are "butter and blue," and the team's entertainers shoot biscuits into the crowd with an air cannon. Country music still remembers. Alan Jackson evoked home in 2001, reminding listeners that "Where I come from, it's cornbread and chicken," while in 2015, Kacey Musgraves sang an anthem to independence, declaring, "Mind your own biscuits and life will be gravy."[47]

In the twenty-first century, southern baking culture is still evolving. Mardi Gras revelers in Mobile throw Moon Pies to spectators. And in 2019, Jerrelle Guy was a finalist for the revered James Beard Award for Baking and Desserts for her cookbook *Black Girl Baking*. Guy, founder of the food blog *Chocolate for Basil*, includes recipes such as the vegan, whole-wheat "Mango Lime Coconut Cake," five layers with "Mango Mousse Icing" between them, and strawberry shortcake made with olive oil and glazed with balsamic vinegar.[48] These recipes may be quintessentially southern, but they are not clichés. Creative young people like Guy and activists like Rose McGee will continue to make baking relevant to the South and to southerners.

As for me, I—like millions of other people—am baking my way through the pandemic, with the cobalt blue KitchenAid mixer that my brother gave me in 1994 and my gorgeous new double oven. I actually did just bake cornbread for supper: three parts yellow cornmeal (Lamb's, from Inez, Texas) to one part wheat flour, no sugar, in a cast-iron skillet that I ordered online (not having had the sense to keep my parents'—augh). There's a loaf of zucchini bread on the kitchen counter, and next up will be orange scones to get me through a batch of paper grading. Last week it was Irish soda bread (super easy) and before that, fabulous aniseed shortbread. Not southern, you say? Pooh. I'm a southerner, I live in the South, and if I bake it, it's southern.

If you're a southerner or you live in the South or you're baking a time-honored recipe from the South, it's southern. If your fire comes through a gas main or electric line, it's still fire. And no matter whether your grain is corn or wheat or spelt or a dozen other varieties, it's still grain. Y'all quit reading and go put some grain with some fire, share the result with somebody you care about or want to get to know, and enjoy.

Acknowledgments

First, to the millennia of bakers in the American South: thank you.

Great salutations go to the librarians and archivists who assisted me, in pandemic and not. At the Mary Coutts Burnett Library at Texas Christian University, I owe special gratitude to the circulation staff; to all the reference librarians, including their head, Linda Chenoweth; and especially to the good people in interlibrary loan. I literally could not have done this without them. Robyn Reid has been her usual information-goddess self. Sara Morris at the University of Kansas has provided all kinds of help from the goodness of her heart. Aaron Trehub and Greg Schmidt at Auburn University Libraries tracked down the original Lane cake recipe. The librarians at Texas Wesleyan University helped me access their rare complete run of *Southern Living* magazine.

I am also grateful to the army of unnamed, unsung folks who have scanned and digitized and uploaded tens of thousands of primary documents, especially cookbooks and newspapers, and those who have built and maintain the websites that make them available. Their efforts have made this project exponentially richer and deeper.

Several people generously read various drafts. Melissa Walker read the entire manuscript, and Alan Gallay checked the first chapters with his unbounded collegiality. Linda Civitello kept me straight on leavenings. Anne Sarah Rubin looked over the work on the Civil War. Thanks also go to the anonymous readers at the University of North Carolina Press. Any errors are, of course, my own.

Colleagues in the Department of History at Texas Christian University, including Gene Smith and Steve Woodworth, kept me from embarrassing myself when I moved beyond the boundaries of my knowledge. Jodi Campbell translated early Spanish for me and helped greatly with her understanding of early modern Spain and, as always, with love and good humor.

Brilliant graduate assistants sorted through sources and cheered me on. I owe a great debt to Codee Scott, Kendra DeHart, Meredith May, Leah LaGrone Ochoa, Jessica Webb, and Lisa Barnett. TCU supported the project with financial resources and a sabbatical, for which I thank department chair Bill Meier and Provost Teresa Abi-Nader Dahlberg very much.

Food-writing friends encouraged this newbie and unstintingly offered their expertise. They include Sheri Castle, Elizabeth Engelhardt, Marcie Cohen Ferris, Ronni Lundy, Paula Marcoux, Leni Sorensen, and Psyche Williams-Forson. Jane Aldrich and Allison Burkette kindly shared their work, and Sara Camp Milam of the Southern Foodways Alliance helped find sources. Rachel Laudan has been cheerleader and strong shoulder from early in the project.

Many historian friends have open-handedly shared sources and ideas. Many thanks go to Evan Bennett, Patricia Benoit, Angela Jill Cooley, Karen Cox, Rebekah Crowe, Mary Lenn Dixon, Megan Elias, Lesley Gordon, Debbie Linsley Liles, Chris Magra, Ann McCleary, Justin Nystrom, Susan O'Donovan, Philip Smith, Randy Sparks, Claire Strom, Keith Volanto, and Katherine Kuehler Walters. Colleagues in the Southern Association for Women Historians and the Texas State Historical Association—particularly the Wild Women of Texas History, Angela Boswell, Jensen Branscombe, and Nancy Baker Jones—have offered moral support, affection, and intellectual stimulation in person, via Zoom, and on social media. Ashley Rose Young and Kelly Kean Sharp gave me access to their excellent dissertations. Ben Vetter and Brady King bought and sent cookbooks from Washington to Texas.

Staff members at historic locations shared their detailed knowledge of their sites. They include Katrina Lawrence of the Heyward-Washington House; Joy MacMillan of the St. Augustine Foundation; Jamie May from Jamestown Rediscovery; and Danny Schmidt of Historic Jamestowne.

My cousin Jan Burr gave permission for the photo of the king cake from her bakery in Pineville, Louisiana, and Rob and Monica Segovia-Welsh of the Chicken Bridge Bakery, Pittsboro, North Carolina, provided images of their wonderful stenciled bread.

At the University of North Carolina Press, Chuck Grench kept gently asking what my next project was until I had an answer and then quickly turned me over to Elaine Maisner. Elaine has been guru, coach, and generous reader, and I am grateful for all that she brings to the project. Andreina Fernandez and Cate Hodorowicz have been wonderful readers and answerers of questions. It has been a pleasure to work with copyeditor Julie Bush and once again with Mary Carley Caviness, the embodiment of patience and style.

My friends have literally held me up in the past decade. They will forgive me as I list them together, as they all know that they are each special to me in a unique way. I have enormous gratitude for Candy Boxwell, Ann Short Chirhart, Carolyn Coke Reed Devany, Theresa Strouth Gaul, Sharon Grigsby, Brady King, Mary Larson, Debbie Linsley Liles, Theresa Furgeson McClellan,

Cathy Gawloski Montgomery, Sharlande Sledge, Linda Shopes, Kara Dixon Vuic, and Melissa Walker. My goddaughters, Amanda Sharpless and Bonnie Devany, are fantastic women of whom I am so very proud.

This project kept me engaged during the terminal illness of my husband, Tom Charlton, and my first years of widowhood. Tom helped make me a historian, and he delighted in my work with food, both in the kitchen and at the computer. In the words of e. e. cummings, "Whatever is done by only me is your doing, my darling." The book is dedicated to our blended family, who cherished him on earth and embrace me in his absence. I love you all.

Notes

INTRODUCTION

1. Cooper and Knotts, *Resilience*, 79.
2. Ferris, *Edible South*, 1.
3. Fuller and Gonzalez Carretero, "Archaeology of Neolithic Cooking Traditions," 111.
4. Campbell, *At the First Table*, 15.
5. Carney and Rosomoff, *Shadow of Slavery*, 19, 31, 52, 57; La Fleur, *Fusion Foodways*, 55.
6. Benét, *Western Star*, 116.
7. Neal, *Southern Cooking*, 5.

CHAPTER 1

1. Stevens, "Story of Plants," 206–7; Chapman and Shea, "Archaeobotanical Record," 69.
2. Sassaman, "Multicultural Genesis," 26; L. Thomas, "Gender Division of Labor," 32.
3. Ruhl, "Spanish Mission Paleoethnobotany," 566; Gremillion, "Human Ecology," 24.
4. Le Page du Pratz, *History of Louisiana*, 213; Messner, *Acorns and Bitter Roots*, 14, 16.
5. Adair, *History of the American Indians*, 409; Bartram, *Travels*, 38; Messner, *Acorns and Bitter Roots*, 14.
6. Hamor, *True Discourse*, 23; Lawson, *New Voyage*, 99.
7. Messner, *Acorns and Bitter Roots*, 17–18.
8. J. Smith, *Map of Virginia*, 12; Hariot, *Briefe and True Report*, [31].
9. Bourne, *Narratives of the Career of De Soto*, 123.
10. J. Smith, "Description of Virginia," 90. Pecans have thin shells that crack easily, so most of them were eaten raw rather than baked. McWilliams, *Pecan*, 8.
11. Scarry and Reitz, "Herbs, Fish, Scum, and Vermin," 349–50; Ruhl, "Spanish Mission Paleoethnobotany," 567; Milanich, "Life in a 9th Century Indian Household," 34.
12. Messner, *Acorns and Bitter Roots*, 17.
13. J. Smith, "Description of Virginia," 90.
14. Messner, *Acorns and Bitter Roots*, 16.
15. Milanich, "Life in a 9th Century Indian Household," 34; Hann, "Use and Processing of Plants," 94.
16. Laudan, *Cuisine and Empire*, 32.
17. J. Franklin, "Bedrock Mortar Hole Sites."
18. Messner, *Acorns and Bitter Roots*, 66; Milanich, "Life in a 9th Century Indian Household," 22.

19. Romans, *Concise Natural History*, 84; Stevens, "Story of Plants," 197.

20. Stevens, "Story of Plants," 197.

21. Strachey, *Historie of Travell*, 118; Romans, *Concise Natural History*, 84; Le Page du Pratz, *History of Louisiana*, 348–49.

22. Hann, "Use and Processing of Plants," 92, 94; Fontaneda, *Memoir*, 15; Romans, *Concise Natural History*, 84; Strachey, *Historie of Travell*, 121.

23. Laudan, *Cuisine and Empire*, 30, 31, 35.

24. Hann, "Use and Processing of Plants," 92; Messner, *Acorns and Bitter Roots*, 20.

25. J. Smith, *Generall Historie of Virginia*, 26.

26. Wright, "American Indian Corn Dishes," 160.

27. Walls and Keith, "Cooking Connects Them."

28. Marcoux, *Cooking with Fire*, 8, 10.

29. Balter, "Corn."

30. Mann, *1491*, 223.

31. Hardeman, *Shucks*, 6, 8; Kalm, Oxholm, and Chase, "Description of Maize," 112; Weatherwax, *Indian Corn*, 86.

32. McCann, *Maize and Grace*, 5.

33. Milanich, *Florida Indians*, 23, 26; Milanich, "Life in a 9th Century Indian Household," 15; Larsen et al., "Food and Stable Isotopes," 72; Weatherwax, *Indian Corn*, 49–50; Larsen, "Bioarchaeology," 29; Chapman and Shea, "Archaeobotanical Record," 79.

34. Ruhl, "Spanish Mission Paleoethnobotany," 560.

35. Perdue, *Cherokee Women*, 13–15.

36. Perdue, 18.

37. Le Page du Pratz, *History of Louisiana*, 328.

38. Martire d'Anghiera, *De Orbe Novo*, 263.

39. Hurt, *Indian Agriculture*, 15; "What You Need to Know about Corn"; C. Scarry, "Variability in Late Prehistoric Corn," 356, 365.

40. Adair, *History of the American Indians*, 407; Strachey, *Historie of Travell*, 73; Messner, *Acorns and Bitter Roots*, 36.

41. Le Page du Pratz, *History of Louisiana*, 321–24.

42. Perdue, *Cherokee Women*, 26.

43. Fussell, *Story of Corn*, 218.

44. Kalm, Oxholm, and Chase, "Description of Maize," 111; Usner, *Indians, Settlers, and Slaves*, 172.

45. Kalm, Oxholm, and Chase, "Description of Maize," 112.

46. Lawson, *New Voyage*, 207.

47. Adair, *History of the American Indians*, 416; Wright, "American Indian Corn Dishes," 156.

48. Kalm, Oxholm, and Chase, "Description of Maize," 113; Wright, "American Indian Corn Dishes," 156.

49. Wright, "American Indian Corn Dishes," 156; Newcomb, *Indians of Texas*, 294.

50. Adair, *History of the American Indians*, 407.

51. Hamor, *True Discourse*, 22; Kalm, Oxholm, and Chase, "Description of Maize," 113.

52. Lawson, *New Voyage*, 97; Beverley, *History of Virginia*, 107.

53. Lawson, *New Voyage*, 105; Beverley, *History of Virginia*, 107–8.

54. J. Smith, "Description of Virginia," 96.

55. Adair, *History of the American Indians*, 407; Swanton, *Indian Tribes*, 75; Le Page du Pratz, *History of Louisiana*, 348; Percy, "Observations," 18; Hann, *History of the Timucua Indians*, 98; J. Smith, "Description of Virginia," 96.

56. Fussell, *Story of Corn*, 226.

57. E. N. Anderson, *Everyone Eats*, 172.

58. Sassaman, "Multicultural Genesis," 26; Sassaman, *Early Pottery*, 118.

59. Rangel, "Account of the Northern Conquest," 259.

60. Campbell, *At the First Table*, 14, 18.

61. See Earle, *Body of the Conquistador*, for an excellent discussion of the European theory of humoral health, which required proper nutrition.

62. Bushnell, *Situado and Sabana*, 75.

63. Crosby, *Columbian Exchange*, 67.

64. Crosby, 70.

65. Milanich and Hudson, *Hernando de Soto*, 96.

66. Milanich and Hudson, 144.

67. Laudonnière, *Three Voyages*, 73.

68. Campbell, *At the First Table*, 16.

69. McGee, *On Food and Cooking*, 539.

70. Laudonnière, *Three Voyages*, 123; Milanich and Hudson, *Hernando de Soto*, 190, 209; Milanich, *Florida Indians*, 146.

71. Laudonnière, *Three Voyages*, 142, 145; Milanich, *Florida Indians*, 146.

72. Sparkes, "Voyage," 125.

73. Lyon, *Santa Elena*, 2.

74. Lyon, 3–4; Lyon, "Richer Than We Thought," 7.

75. Lyon, "Richer Than We Thought," 21–22, 38, 46, 47.

76. Lyon, 68.

77. Lyon, 81.

78. Manucy, *Sixteenth-Century St. Augustine*, 52.

79. Lyon, "Richer Than We Thought," 45.

80. Lyon, 59, 61; Milanich, *Florida Indians*, 44, 201.

81. E. Crane, *World History of Beekeeping*, 308.

82. Milanich, *Florida Indians*, 44, 201.

83. Kohler, "Corn, Indians, and Spaniards," 4.

84. Lyon, "Richer Than We Thought," 41, 51–65, 68.

85. Lyon, 22, 89–90.

86. Connor, *Colonial Records*, 147–49.

87. Lyon, *Santa Elena*, 6.

88. Otto and Lewis, "Formal and Functional Analysis," 108.

89. Manucy, *Sixteenth-Century St. Augustine*, 38–39.

90. Manucy, 57.

91. Manucy, 38–39.

92. Manucy, 52.

93. Manucy, 55; Hoffman, "Development of a Cultural Identity," 71.

94. Arnade, *Florida on Trial*, 9, 67, 74.

95. Arnade, 27.

96. García, "Relación de los trabajos," 191–92.

97. Vega, "La Florida," 2:353–54.

98. Bushnell, *Situado and Sabana*, 57.

99. Worth, "Spanish Missions," 58; Milanich, "Franciscan Missions," 295; Hann, *History of the Timucua Indians*, 143, 355; Francis and Kole, *Murder and Martyrdom*, 37.

100. Ruhl, "Spanish Mission Paleoethnobotany," 556–57, 569; Ruhl, "Archaeobotanical Data," 282; Crosby, *Columbian Exchange*, 74.

101. Hariot, *Briefe and True Report*, [21].

CHAPTER 2

1. "First Africans"; Wolfe, "Angela."

2. Wolfe, "Peirce, William."

3. Hoffman, "Development of a Cultural Identity," 74–75, 78–80.

4. Cumbaa, "Patterns of Resource Use," 204.

5. Hoffman, "Development of a Cultural Identity," 81.

6. Milanich, *Laboring in the Fields*, 146.

7. Milanich, 40, 146.

8. Hoffman, "Development of a Cultural Identity," 87.

9. Larsen, "Bioarchaeology," 30.

10. Ruhl, "Spanish Mission Paleoethnobotany," 569.

11. Ruhl, 561–62.

12. Cumbaa, "Patterns of Resource Use," 204.

13. Milanich, *Florida Indians*, 211.

14. Cumbaa, "Patterns of Resource Use," 204, 206.

15. Cumbaa, 204, 206.

16. Hoffman, "Development of a Cultural Identity," 103.

17. Francis, Mormino, and Sanderson, "Slavery."

18. Landers, "Spanish Sanctuary," 297–98.

19. Hann, "Apalachee Counterfeiters," 53, 55.

20. J. Scarry, "Resistance and Accommodation," 48.

21. Milanich, *Florida Indians*, 57–58.

22. Parent, *Foul Means*, 13.

23. J. Smith, "Description of Virginia," 96–97.

24. Percy, "Discourse," 931.

25. J. Smith, "Description of Virginia," 96–97.

26. G. Thomas, *Foods of Our Forefathers*, 17.

27. Percy, "Discourse," 934.

28. J. Smith, *Generall Historie of Virginia*, 86.

29. W. Harrison, *Elizabethan England*, 96.

30. J. Smith, "Description of Virginia," 185.

31. Percy, "Trewe Relacyon," 1097–98.

32. Strachey, *For the Colony in Virginea*, 14.

33. Strachey, 18–19.

34. Ransome, "'Shipt for Virginia,'" 448.

35. Ransome, "Wives for Virginia," 15.

36. Hamor, *True Discourse*, 45.

37. Cave, *Lethal Encounters*, 83, 91.

38. Stith, *History of the First Discovery*, 140; Rolfe, *True Relation*, 36.

39. Stith, *History of the First Discovery*, 140.

40. Kingsbury, *Records of the Virginia Company*, 1:423.

41. Kukla, "Order and Chaos," 284; Parent, *Foul Means*, 18.

42. Hecht, "Virginia Muster," 75; "Jamestown 1624/5 Food Records."

43. Kingsbury, *Records of the Virginia Company*, 4:58–59.

44. Hening, *Statutes at Large*, 2:118.

45. Durand, *Huguenot Exile*, 116; Walsh, "Wider Context," 17; McCartney, *Study of the Africans and African Americans on Jamestown Island*, 45; Walsh, *From Calabar to Carter's Grove*, 290.

46. Carney and Rosomoff, *Shadow of Slavery*, 19, 31, 52, 57; La Fleur, *Fusion Foodways*, 55.

47. McCann, *Maize and Grace*, 24; Warman, *Corn and Capitalism*, 62; Dow, *Slave Ships*, 53, 66; R. Hall, "Food Crops," 29–30.

48. La Fleur, *Fusion Foodways*, 119.

49. Opie, *Hog and Hominy*, 5; La Fleur, *Fusion Foodways*, 121–22.

50. *Perfect Description of Virginia*, 6.

51. Carr, Menard, and Walsh, *Robert Cole's World*, 52, 56–57, 58.

52. W. Bullock, *Virginia*, 9.

53. L. Gray, *History of Agriculture*, 1:161–63.

54. Hinke, "Report of the Journey of Francis Louis Michel," 114.

55. "Jamestown 1624/5 Food Records."

56. Carr, Menard, and Walsh, *Robert Cole's World*, 36, 286.

57. Ashe, *Carolina*, 182–83.

58. Spencer, "Food in Seventeenth-Century Tidewater Virginia," 108, 110, 111.

59. Carr, Menard, and Walsh, *Robert Cole's World*, 71, 177, 185; Breen and Innes, "*Myne Owne Ground*," 54; Spencer, "Food in Seventeenth-Century Tidewater Virginia," 180, 181, 185.

60. Danckaerts, *Journal*, 133.

61. Carr and Menard, "Immigration and Opportunity," 215.

62. "Jamestown 1624–25 Building Records"; C. Hatch, *First Seventeen Years*, 72.

63. *Perfect Description of Virginia*, 4.

64. Stephenson, "Mills in Eighteenth Century Virginia," 4.

65. Hening, *Statutes at Large*, 1:301, 348.

66. D. Brown, "Enslaved Landscape," 105–6, 226.

67. Upton, "Early Vernacular Architecture," 315; Carr, Menard, and Walsh, *Robert Cole's World*, 105.

68. T. Snyder, "Berkeley, Frances Culpeper Stephens."

69. Hess, *Martha Washington's Booke of Cookery*, 447, 463. Although the book is titled *Martha Washington's Booke*, historian Karen Hess believes that Lady Berkeley passed it to her stepdaughter Jane Ludwell Parke (1668?–1708, daughter of Lady Berkeley's third husband), who then gave it to her daughter Frances Parke Custis (1685–1714), Martha

Dandridge Custis Washington's first mother-in-law. The book came at some point to Martha Washington, and she gave it to her granddaughter Eleanor Parke Custis in 1799. Custis descendants gave it to the Historical Society of Pennsylvania in 1892.

70. Billings, *Sir William Berkeley*, 74.

71. La Fleur, *Fusion Foodways*, 116.

72. Hess, *Martha Washington's Booke of Cookery*, 120, 121.

73. Hess, 154–55.

74. Spencer, "Food in Seventeenth-Century Tidewater Virginia," 123; Hess, *Martha Washington's Booke of Cookery*, 10.

75. Kingsbury, *Records of the Virginia Company*, 3:473, 545; V. Anderson, *Creatures of Empire*, 112; Steiner, *Beginnings of Maryland*, 58.

76. Neill, *Virginia Carolorum*, 69.

77. Carr, Menard, and Walsh, *Robert Cole's World*, 177; Spencer, "Food in Seventeenth-Century Tidewater Virginia," 177, 178.

78. Hess, *Martha Washington's Booke of Cookery*, 316.

79. David, *English Bread*, 98–99.

80. Hess, *Martha Washington's Booke of Cookery*, 10, 11, 104, 295.

81. McGee, *On Food and Cooking*, 424.

82. McGee, 425, 426.

83. Kingsbury, *Records of the Virginia Company*, 3:238, 386, 387.

84. Spencer, "Food in Seventeenth-Century Tidewater Virginia," 108, 111, 128; Wheeler, "Lancaster County," 76; Carr, Menard, and Walsh, *Robert Cole's World*, 180.

85. Marcoux, *Cooking with Fire*, 211, 215.

86. "From Metal Working to Food Production"; "Jamestown Rediscovery"; email correspondence from Danny Schmidt, Historic Jamestowne, February 22, 2017.

87. G. Stone, "St. John's," 149.

88. Carson et al., "New World, Real World," 64.

89. G. Stone, "St. John's," 168; Carson et al., "Impermanent Architecture," 185–86.

90. Hess, *Martha Washington's Booke of Cookery*, 117.

91. Hess, 117, 199, 350.

92. G. Stone, "St. John's," 160; C. Carson, "Banqueting Houses," 737; Bragdon, Chappel, and Graham, "Scant Urbanity," 227; Durand, *Huguenot Exile*, 119–20; Epperson, "Constructing Difference," 166.

93. C. Carson, "Banqueting Houses," 738, 753, 761.

94. Chappell, "Accommodating Slavery," 72; C. Carson, "Banqueting Houses," 743.

95. Bragdon, Chappell, and Graham, "Scant Urbanity," 227, 229.

96. Chappell, "Accommodating Slavery," 80.

97. Henry Miller, "Colonization and Subsistence," 240.

98. Spencer, "Food in Seventeenth-Century Tidewater Virginia," 133, 135, 166, 216.

99. Hess, *Martha Washington's Booke of Cookery*, 334–35, 337.

100. McGee, *On Food and Cooking*, 413, 414.

101. Hess, *Martha Washington's Booke of Cookery*, 334–35, 337, 340.

102. Hess, 338.

103. Hess, 338–39.

104. Mintz, *Sweetness and Power*, 37; Spencer, "Food in Seventeenth-Century Tidewater Virginia," 108; Hess, *Martha Washington's Booke of Cookery*, 11.

105. Spencer, "Food in Seventeenth-Century Tidewater Virginia," 126.

106. David, *English Bread*, 6; Hess, *Martha Washington's Booke of Cookery*, 17–18.

107. Hess, *Martha Washington's Booke of Cookery*, 117.

108. Hess, 115.

109. Neill, *Virginia Carolorum*, 69; Munro, "Consumption of Spices."

110. Hess, *Martha Washington's Booke of Cookery*, 113–15.

111. Spencer, "Food in Seventeenth-Century Tidewater Virginia," 135.

112. Hess, *Martha Washington's Booke of Cookery*, 339–40.

113. Hess, 312, 315.

114. Hess, 315–19.

115. Hess, 319.

116. Kingsbury, *Records of the Virginia Company*, 3:238, 386, 387.

117. Durand, *Huguenot Exile*, 103.

118. Hess, *Martha Washington's Booke of Cookery*, 342–48.

119. Spencer, "Food in Seventeenth-Century Tidewater Virginia," 108, 110, 127.

120. *Perfect Description of Virginia*, 2, 16.

121. Hess, *Martha Washington's Booke of Cookery*, 199–201.

122. Markham, *Countrey Contentments*, 95.

123. Durand, *Huguenot Exile*, 116, 118.

124. Hess, *Martha Washington's Booke of Cookery*, 161.

125. Hess, 91, 95–96, 97, 160.

126. Hamor, *True Discourse*, 23; *Perfect Description of Virginia*, 15; G. Stone, "St. John's," 163; Durand, *Huguenot Exile*, 103.

127. Hess, *Martha Washington's Booke of Cookery*, 121–22.

128. Kingsbury, *Records of the Virginia Company*, 3:238.

129. Hess, *Martha Washington's Booke of Cookery*, 91, 95–96, 97, 126–27.

130. Hess, 92.

131. Hess, 80–93.

132. Hess, 94, 97–99.

133. Hess, 309–11.

134. Hess, 349–51.

135. Hess, 313–14.

136. Hess, 320.

CHAPTER 3

1. Rowland and Sanders, *Mississippi Provincial Archives*, 32.

2. Hémard, "Madame Langlois."

3. "Slave Voyages."

4. Lawson, *New Voyage*, 67, 69, 70, 71, 92.

5. M. Franklin, "Out of Site," 181; M. Franklin, "Archaeological and Symbolic Dimensions," 94; Mrozowski, Franklin, and Hunt, "Archaeobotanical Analysis," 710, 712; Samford, *Subfloor Pits*, 128, 133.

6. Perttula, "Caddo Agriculture," 82, 86, 98; B. Smith, "Eastern North America."

7. Dumont de Montigny, *Memoir of Lieutenant Dumont*, 368–69.

8. Brickell, *Natural History of North-Carolina*, 22, 38; Glen, *Description of South Carolina*, 67.

9. G. Hall, *Africans in Colonial Louisiana*, 218.

10. S. Parker, "Second Century of Settlement," 179.

11. Dumont de Montigny, *Memoir of Lieutenant Dumont*, 106.

12. Rutman and Rutman, *Place in Time*, 42, 235.

13. Hatley, *Dividing Paths*, 8.

14. Williams, *Early Travels*, 257, 479–80.

15. Le Page du Pratz, *History of Louisiana*, 165.

16. Kalm, Oxholm, and Chase "Description of Maize," 113.

17. Smyth, *Tour in the United States*, 1:99.

18. Dill, "Eighteenth Century New Bern, Part III," 299.

19. Swanton, *Indian Tribes*, 286; Usner, "Food Marketing," 280, 292.

20. Usner, "Frontier Exchange Economy," 181.

21. Galan, "Last Soldiers," 70–71, 130.

22. Deagan and MacMahon, *Fort Mose*, 34.

23. Kercheval, *History of the Valley of Virginia*, 361.

24. Williams, *Early Travels*, 257; Hatley, *Dividing Paths*, 33.

25. Kercheval, *History of the Valley of Virginia*, 360–61; H. Jones, *Present State of Virginia*, 53; Holt and Breazale, "Economic and Social Beginnings," 38.

26. Schoepf, *Travels*, 116; Kercheval, *History of the Valley of Virginia*, 361; McCartney, *Study of the Africans and African Americans on Jamestown Island*, 156.

27. Ferguson, *Uncommon Ground*, 98.

28. Kercheval, *History of the Valley of Virginia*, 328; Clayton, *History of Davidson County*, 19, 334.

29. Perttula, "Caddoan Area Archaeology," 311; Otto and Lewis, "Formal and Functional Analysis," 110; Shephard, "Spanish Criollo Majority," 75.

30. *South Carolina Gazette* (Charleston), December 15, 1739.

31. Le Page du Pratz, *History of Louisiana*, 165.

32. Smyth, *Tour in the United States*, 1:48; Cofield, "Hoe Cake," 6–7; Logan, "William Logan's Journal" [no. 1], 12; Fries, *Records of the Moravians*, 142, 144.

33. Galan, "Last Soldiers," 54; Morton, *Tortillas*, 13, 14.

34. Brickell, *Natural History of North-Carolina*, 363.

35. Miller Surrey, *Commerce of Louisiana*, 262, 289.

36. Dumont de Montigny, *Memoir of Lieutenant Dumont*, 343.

37. Hofstra and Geier, "Beyond the Great Blue Mountain," 225; M. Franklin, "Out of Site," 212; Mrozowski, Franklin, and Hunt, "Archaeobotanical Analysis," 710, 718–19.

38. B. Wood, *Women's Work*, 57; Hofstra, *Planting of New Virginia*, 223; Deagan, *Spanish St. Augustine*, 36.

39. Smyth, *Tour in the United States*, 1:44; Chamberlayne, *Vestry Book of Blisland Parish*, 16, 70, 120, 149, 175; A. Watson, "Public Poor Relief," 351.

40. Lawson, *New Voyage*, 75.

41. Smyth, *Tour in the United States*, 1:48; Weld, *Travels through the States of North America*, 183.

42. Schaw, *Journal of a Lady of Quality*, 171.

43. Beverley, *History of Virginia*, 237.

44. Beverley, 237.

45. Miller Surrey, "Development of Industries," 231–32.

46. Higginbotham, *Old Mobile*, 423; D'Artaguiette, "Journal," 22.

47. Fries, *Records of the Moravians*, 123, 209.

48. Quincy, *Memoir*, 128; Cresswell, *Journal*, 18, 47, 49, 197; Hazard, "Journal," 417; H. Gill, "Wheat Culture," 381, 387.

49. Schlotterbeck, "Plantation and Farm," 56.

50. Winters, *Tennessee Farming*, 157.

51. Grivno, *Gleanings of Freedom*, 43; *Virginia Gazette* (Williamsburg), September 22, 1768.

52. Hazard, "Journal," 415–16; L. Gray, *History of Agriculture*, 1:170–71.

53. Brickell, *Natural History of North-Carolina*, 40.

54. Brickell, 40.

55. Cresswell, *Journal*, 26.

56. Fries, *Records of the Moravians*, 209.

57. Dill, "Eighteenth Century New Bern, Part V," 74; Stephenson, "Mills in Eighteenth Century Virginia," 4, 5–15; Dill, "Eighteenth Century New Bern, Part II," 168, 171, 173.

58. Cresswell, *Journal*, 26; Feltman, *Journal*, 9; Stephenson, "Mills in Eighteenth Century Virginia," appendix, 1–3; Plater, "Building the North Wales Mill," 46–47.

59. Hockensmith, *Millstone Industry*, 202, 203, 204, 205, 210.

60. Hofstra, "Private Dwellings," 213.

61. Peterson, "Flour and Grist Milling," 100; Plater, "Building the North Wales Mill," 49; "George Washington's Gristmill."

62. Tailfer, Anderson, and Douglas, *True and Historical Narrative*, 79.

63. Hofstra, *Planting of New Virginia*, 154, 155, 157; H. Watson, "'Common Rights of Mankind,'" 22.

64. Fries, *Records of the Moravians*, 157; Harris, "Moravian Settlers during the Royal Period."

65. Hendricks, *Backcountry Towns*, 38.

66. Woods, "French and the Natchez Indians," 424; Pénicaut, *Fleur de Lys and Calumet*, 238.

67. Giraud, *History of French Louisiana*, 237–38, 247; Greenwald, *Marc-Antoine Caillot*, 108–9.

68. McCartney, *Study of the Africans and African Americans on Jamestown Island*, 154; Yost, "Ludwell-Paradise House," n.p.; Martin, *Buying into the World of Goods*, 179.

69. *Virginia Gazette*, October 18, 1770.

70. Galan, "Last Soldiers," 174.

71. Galan, 131, 135; McCorkle, "Los Adaes," 5–6.

72. Higginbotham, *Old Mobile*, 37; Pénicaut, *Fleur de Lys and Calumet*, 251; Miller Surrey, *Commerce of Louisiana*, 206–7.

73. Iberville, *Iberville's Gulf Journals*, 96.

74. Miller Surrey, *Commerce of Louisiana*, 213.

75. Higginbotham, *Old Mobile*, 423; D'Artaguiette, "Journal," 22.

76. Giraud, *History of French Louisiana*, 266; Dawdy, "'Wild Taste,'" 393; J. Clark, *New Orleans*, 59–60, 211–12; Vidal, "Antoine Bienvenu," 128.

77. Cuevas, *Cat Island*, 16–21.

78. *South Carolina Gazette*, July 29, 1766, and July 12, 1773; *Georgia Gazette* (Savannah), April 20, 1768; *Norfolk and Portsmouth Gazette*, September 23, 1789.

79. John, Visitor Services [no surname given], "Learning Experience."

80. Lawson, *New Voyage*, 36; Gallay, *Indian Slave Trade*, 338.

81. Dumont de Montigny, *Memoir of Lieutenant Dumont*, 350.

82. Burton and Smith, "Slavery in the Colonial Louisiana Backcountry," 144, 147.

83. Morgan, *Slave Counterpoint*, 244–45.

84. Dumont de Montigny, *Memoir of Lieutenant Dumont*, 275.

85. Burton and Smith, "Slavery in the Colonial Louisiana Backcountry," 160, 179.

86. *South Carolina Gazette*, May 1, 1749.

87. Rutman and Rutman, *Place in Time*, 166; MacLeod, "Doll"; McCartney, *Study of the Africans and African Americans on Jamestown Island*, 157.

88. *Williamsburg Gazette*, April 14, 1775.

89. Nicholls, "Aspects of the African American Experience," 5, 17, 18, 42.

90. Olmert, *Kitchens, Smokehouses, and Privies*, 31, 33; Rutman and Rutman, *Place in Time*, 154; Gregory et al., "Presidio Los Adaes," 71–72; Giraud, *History of French Louisiana*, 189, 223.

91. Chappell, "Housing Slavery," 165.

92. Herman, *Town House*, 121, 125; Epperson, "Constructing Difference," 168; Vlach, *Back of the Big House*, 43.

93. Upton, "White and Black Landscapes," 133.

94. "Heyward-Washington House"; email correspondence from Katrina Lawrence, Charleston, South Carolina, November 22, 2017.

95. Otto and Lewis, "Formal and Functional Analysis," 108.

96. S. Parker, "Second Century of Settlement," 89, 92; Cusick, "Ethnic Groups and Class," 75.

97. "Governor's House."

98. Dumont de Montigny, *Memoir of Lieutenant Dumont*, 259; Iberville, *Iberville's Gulf Journals*, 93.

99. *Virginia Gazette*, March 27, 1752; *South Carolina Gazette*, September 7, 1765; *Georgia Gazette*, September 10, 1766; J. Carson, *Colonial Virginia Cookery*, 18.

100. Burton, "Family and Economy," 93, 280.

101. Baine and De Vorsey Jr., "Provenance and Historical Accuracy," 803.

102. C. Jones, *History of Georgia*, 235.

103. *Virginia Gazette*, July 11, 1771.

104. *South Carolina Gazette*, May 21, 1763.

105. *South Carolina Gazette*, June 2, 1759, and November 17, 1766; "Appraisement of the Estate of Philip Ludwell," 396; Spruill, "Virginia and Carolina Homes," 337; Yentsch, *Chesapeake Family*, 158.

106. *South Carolina Gazette*, June 2, 1759; Martin, *Buying into the World of Goods*, 45.

107. Logan, "William Logan's Journal," [no. 1], 5, 11; Michaux, *Journal*, 88.

108. Clayton, *History of Davidson County*, 27.

109. M. Franklin, "Out of Site," 175; Burton and Smith, *Colonial Natchitoches*, 70; Mrozowski, Franklin, and Hunt, "Archaeobotanical Analysis," 710.

110. Jane Bolling Randolph was the wife of planter and legislator Richard Randolph and the mother of six living children at Curles Neck Plantation in Virginia. Eliza Lucas Pinckney was the daughter and wife of Charleston planters and mother of three but also an entrepreneur and planter in her own right. See Glover, *Eliza Lucas Pinckney*. Harriott Pinckney Horry, mother of two, maintained a household independent of her husband.

111. Harbury, *Colonial Virginia's Cooking Dynasty*, 204, 206, 208, 398.

112. Harbury, 204.

113. Harbury, 244.

114. H. Jones, *Present State of Virginia*, 52.

115. Harbury, *Colonial Virginia's Cooking Dynasty*, 408.

116. Hooker, *Colonial Plantation Cookbook*, 82.

117. Schoepf, *Travels*, 121.

118. Iberville, *Iberville's Gulf Journals*, 92.

119. Fries, *Records of the Moravians*, 269; Smyth, *Tour in the United States*, 1:161; Le Conte, "Germans in Louisiana," 82; Miller Surrey, *Commerce of Louisiana*, 263.

120. C. Jones, *History of Georgia*, 192–93; Miller Surrey, *Commerce of Louisiana*, 206.

121. Beverley, *History of Virginia*, 282; Burton, "Family and Economy," 286.

122. Cusick, "Ethnic Groups and Class," 64; Miller Surrey, *Commerce of Louisiana*, 186, 203, 206–7, 213, 289, 453; Yentsch, *Chesapeake Family*, 26.

123. B. Wood, *Women's Work*, 57; M. Wood, "Life in New Orleans," 671; Miller Surrey, *Commerce of Louisiana*, 260; Le Conte, "Germans in Louisiana," 82.

124. Harbury, *Colonial Virginia's Cooking Dynasty*, 298, 368, 376, 390.

125. Harbury, 210, 248, 382, 400; Hooker, *Colonial Plantation Cookbook*, 104–5.

126. Harbury, *Colonial Virginia's Cooking Dynasty*, 206, 210.

127. Fries, *Records of the Moravians*, 149, 158.

128. Cooke, *Cookery*, 199–200.

129. Harbury, *Colonial Virginia's Cooking Dynasty*, 402, 404.

130. Harbury, 212, 214, 246, 247.

131. Baudier, "Boss Bakers' Protective Association," 5.

132. Hooker, *Colonial Plantation Cookbook*, 95.

133. Glen, *Description of South Carolina*, 57, 73; *South Carolina Gazette*, January 21, 1751, and August 1, 1771.

134. Yentsch, *Chesapeake Family*, 162; *South Carolina Gazette*, January 20, 1733; *Georgia Gazette*, May 26, 1763; *Virginia Gazette*, December 17, 1767.

135. Sturtz, *Within Her Power*, 124; Martin, *Buying into the World of Goods*, 83, 150; Hofstra, *Planting of New Virginia*, 232.

136. Smyth, *Tour in the United States*, 2:23.

137. Galloway, *Sugar Cane Industry*, 108–9; *South Carolina Gazette*, August 1, 1771; Yentsch, *Chesapeake Family*, 163.

138. Martin, *Buying into the World of Goods*, 180.

139. Sturtz, *Within Her Power*, 123; Martin, *Buying into the World of Goods*, 45, 54, 56, 83, 85, 147; Hofstra, *Planting of New Virginia*, 192, 202, 32–33.

140. Harbury, *Colonial Virginia's Cooking Dynasty*, 208, 210.

141. David, *English Bread*, 213–13.

142. Lineback, *Preserving the Past*, 49.

143. Fries, *Records of the Moravians*, 80.

144. Fries, 233.

145. Tartan, *North Carolina and Old Salem Cookery*, 74, 79–80.

146. Fries, *Records of the Moravians*, 409.

147. Harbury, *Colonial Virginia's Cooking Dynasty*, 362.

148. Velden, "Yes or Noyaux"; Karp, "Case of the Tasty but Poisonous Nut"; Harbury, *Colonial Virginia's Cooking Dynasty*, 210; Hooker, *Colonial Plantation Cookbook*, 104.

149. Harbury, *Colonial Virginia's Cooking Dynasty*, 210; Hooker, *Colonial Plantation Cookbook*, 104.

150. Hooker, *Colonial Plantation Cookbook*, 81.

151. Harbury, *Colonial Virginia's Cooking Dynasty*, 372.

152. Harbury, 168, 210, 212, 246, 248, 336, 354, 366, 372, 406; Hooker, *Colonial Plantation Cookbook*, 72, 79, 80, 111, 119.

153. Harbury, *Colonial Virginia's Cooking Dynasty*, 398, 208, 214; Pinckney, *Recipe Book*, 18.

154. Harbury, *Colonial Virginia's Cooking Dynasty*, 230.

155. Harbury, 322.

156. Harbury, 150, 158.

157. Glen, *Description of South Carolina*, 74; Schoepf, *Travels*, 125; Schlotterbeck, "Plantation and Farm," 62; Calhoun, *Old Southern Apples*, 9.

158. Lawson, *New Voyage*, 108.

159. Williams, *Early Travels*, 479.

160. Catesby, "Catesby's Natural History," 108; Calhoun, *Old Southern Apples*, 9; Lawson, *New Voyage*, 109.

161. Harbury, *Colonial Virginia's Cooking Dynasty*, 240, 294.

162. Harbury, 242.

163. Harbury, 366, 410.

164. Harbury, 242, 366, 390, 410.

165. Brickell, *Natural History of North-Carolina*, 77; Fithian, *Journals and Letters*, 77, 142; Catesby, "Catesby's Natural History," 108; Lawson, *New Voyage*, 110.

166. Langhorne, Lay, and Rieley, *Virginia Family*, 97; Schlotterbeck, "Plantation and Farm," 62; Horn, *Adapting to a New World*, 278; Fithian, *Journals and Letters*, 171.

167. Brickell, *Natural History of North-Carolina*, 77.

168. Langhorne, Lay, and Rieley, *Virginia Family*, 97; *South Carolina Gazette*, August 11, 1733; *Virginia Gazette*, September 22, 1752, and September 16, 1766.

169. Glen, *Description of South Carolina*, 67; Brickell, *Natural History of North-Carolina*, 100.

170. Woods, "French and the Natchez Indians," 414; Brasseaux, *Founding of New Acadia*, 129; Glen, *Description of South Carolina*, 66; Lawson, *New Voyage*, 111.

171. Glen, *Description of South Carolina*, 28–29; "Introduction."

172. Langhorne, Lay, and Rieley, *Virginia Family*, 101; Sturtz, *Within Her Power*, 129.

173. Hussey, "Freezes, Fights, and Fancy," 83.

174. Miller Surrey, "Development of Industries," 230–31.

175. Hooker, *Colonial Plantation Cookbook*, 136.

176. Wood, *Black Majority*, 60–62; Carney, "African Rice," 384. Enslaved people also brought sesame, or benne, with them from Africa. While a few people baked it into bread, most used it in soup (Carney and Rosomoff, *Shadow of Slavery*, 140, 151).

177. Tuten, *Lowcountry Time and Tide*, 12–14.

178. G. Hall, *Africans in Colonial Louisiana*, 10.

179. Miller Surrey, "Development of Industries," 232.

180. Tuten, *Lowcountry Time and Tide*, 16–19.

181. Giraud, *History of French Louisiana*, 23.

182. Glen, *Description of South Carolina*, 7–8.

183. Miller Surrey, *Commerce of Louisiana*, 173; Dumont de Montigny, *Memoir of Lieutenant Dumont*, 169.

184. Hess, *Carolina Rice Kitchen*, 116.

185. Schoepf, *Travels*, 156.

186. Schoepf, 157.

187. "Interview with James Freeman," 44.

188. Logan, "William Logan's Journal (Continued)," 162.

189. Feltman, *Journal*, 35.

190. Hess, *Carolina Rice Kitchen*, 119.

191. Miller Surrey, *Commerce of Louisiana*, 170.

192. Baudier, "Boss Bakers' Protective Association," 4.

193. J. Clark, *New Orleans*, 258; Mizell-Nelson, "French Bread," 39.

194. Hooker, *Colonial Plantation Cookbook*, 120, 121.

195. Hess, *Carolina Rice Kitchen*, 118–19.

196. Sturtz, *Within Her Power*, 90; Richter, "Christiana Campbell."

197. *Georgia Gazette*, November 30, 1768.

198. Hatley, *Dividing Paths*, 96.

199. Dumont de Montigny, *Memoir of Lieutenant Dumont*, 191, 228, 360.

200. Elie, "Origin Myth," 217.

201. *South Carolina Gazette*, May 23, 1761.

202. *South Carolina Gazette*, September 30, 1766.

203. Morgan, *Slave Counterpoint*, 367.

204. Usner, *Indians, Settlers, and Slaves*, 197.

205. Martin, *Buying into the World of Goods*, 174–75.

206. B. Wood, *Women's Work*, 86.

207. Schaw, *Journal of a Lady of Quality*, 178.

208. K. Lewis, "Metropolis and the Backcountry," 8.

209. Warren Smith, *White Servitude*, 23.

210. *South Carolina Gazette*, August 5, 1766.

211. Mizell-Nelson, "French Bread," 39; Baudier, "Boss Bakers' Protective Association," 5; Greenwald, *Marc-Antoine Caillot*, 116.

212. Miller Surrey, *Commerce of Louisiana*, 267.

213. *South Carolina Gazette*, October 29, 1772.

214. *Georgia Gazette*, October 1, 1766; *Virginia Gazette*, August 8, 1766.

215. *Virginia Gazette*, July 11, 1771.

216. Coulter and Saye, *Early Settlers of Georgia*, 1, 4, 11, 15, 49, 64; B. Wood, *Slavery in Colonial Georgia*, 13.

217. *South Carolina Gazette*, May 1, 1736; September 9, 1745; December 29, 1746; April 1, 1767.

218. *South Carolina Gazette*, April 13, 1767. I have been unable to discover what several of these creations are.

219. *South Carolina Gazette*, July 19, 1768; February 7, 1769; April 18, 1769; May 16, 1769; August 1, 1769; December 11, 1770; May 28, 1771.

220. Baudier, "Boss Bakers' Protective Association," 7; Mizell-Nelson, "French Bread," 39.

221. Baudier, "Boss Bakers' Protective Association," 2, 4; Mizell-Nelson, "French Bread," 38–39.

222. Maduell, *Census Tables*, 18; Baudier, "Boss Bakers' Protective Association," 7.

223. Postlethwayt, *Universal Dictionary of Trade and Commerce*, n.p.

224. *Virginia Gazette*, September 19, 1751; *Georgia Gazette*, June 18, 1766; *South Carolina Gazette*, July 15, 1769.

225. Deagan and MacMahon, *Fort Mose*, 34.

226. Baudier, "Boss Bakers' Protective Association," 5–6.

227. Cooper and McCord, *Statutes at Large of South Carolina*, 3:715–16.

228. *South Carolina Gazette*, September 21, 1767, and March 1, 1776.

CHAPTER 4

1. Douglass, *Life and Times*, 118.

2. Ethridge, *Creek Country*, 154–55; Saunt, *Black, White, and Indian*, 18, 21.

3. Saunt, *Black, White, and Indian*, 30.

4. *Cherokee Phoenix and Indians' Advocate* (New Echota, Ga.), April 30, 1831.

5. Bolton, *Poor Whites*, 17, 36, 103–4.

6. Olmsted, *Journey in the Seaboard States*, 108, 680, 700; Padgett, "Journal of Daniel Walker Lord," 188; Northrup, *Twelve Years a Slave*, 168–69.

7. Ball, *Slavery*, 96–97.

8. Northrup, *Twelve Years a Slave*, 168–70; Breeden, *Advice among Masters*, 90; Grandy, *Narrative*, 29; Jackson, *Experience of a Slave*, 12.

9. Bernhard, *Travels through North America*, 2:9–10.

10. *Mobile Gazette and Commercial Adviser*, April 6, 1819.

11. Edmondston, "Journal of a Secesh Lady," 19.

12. *Charleston City-Gazette and Daily Advertiser*, June 21, 1800; *Richmond Enquirer*, February 13, 1810; *Dallas Weekly Herald*, September 29, 1858; *Augusta Daily Chronicle and Sentinel*, January 7, 1857.

13. Chaplin, *Anxious Pursuit*, 291–92, 297; Grivno, *Gleanings of Freedom*, 29–30; L. Gray, *History of Agriculture*, 2:816.

14. Rood, "Bogs of Death," 25; Brush, *Small Tract*, 27–28.

15. Fields, *Slavery and Freedom*, 5, 19; Schlotterbeck, "Plantation and Farm," 171, 195.

16. Grivno, *Gleanings of Freedom*, 43.

17. Grivno, 4, 100; Bolton, *Poor Whites*, 15.

18. Hansen, "How a Threshing Machine Works"; Peterson, "Flour and Grist Milling," 103.

19. Grivno, *Gleanings of Freedom*, 161, 175.

20. Perdue, Barden, and Phillips, *Weevils in the Wheat*, 215–16.

21. Schlotterbeck, "Plantation and Farm," 65, 214.

22. Hofstra and Geier, "Farm to Mill to Market," 57, 58, 59; Bernhard, *Travels through North America*, 1:193.

23. M. Hayes, "Brief History of Temperance Hall."

24. Abernethy, *Formative Period*, 15.

25. Rood, "Bogs of Death," 19, 20; Kirby, *Poquosin*, 132, 135, 137.

26. Kirby, *Poquosin*, 177.

27. Hopley, *Life in the South*, 1:221–22; Bruce, *New Man*, 24–25; McCartney, *Study of the Africans and African Americans on Jamestown Island*, 174; Rivers, "'Dignity and Importance,'" 416, 417.

28. O. Evans, *Young Mill-wright*, 97–99.

29. Sharrer, "Merchant-Millers," 144–45; Bernhard, *Travels through North America*, 1:166.

30. Rood, "Bogs of Death," 29; Peterson, "Flour and Grist Milling," 104; Berry, "Rise of Flour Milling," 388.

31. Storck and Teague, *Flour*, 153.

32. Takagi, *Rearing Wolves*, 77; Rood, "Bogs of Death," 26.

33. J. Clark, *Grain Trade*, 215; L. Gray, *History of Agriculture*, 2:817; Storck and Teague, *Flour*, 178.

34. M. Wood, "Life in New Orleans," 666, 669; Ingersoll, *Mammon and Manon*, 156–57; Mizell-Nelson, "French Bread," 39.

35. Cusick, "Ethnic Groups and Class," 64–65.

36. Rood, "Bogs of Death," 31.

37. *Chattanooga Gazette*, May 18, 1844; Hougland, "Mills of Washington County."

38. Holt and Breazale, "Economic and Social Beginnings," 31.

39. *Daily Morning News* (Savannah), March 21, 1850.

40. Ferguson, *Uncommon Ground*, 81–82.

41. Tyler and Murphy, *Slave Narratives*, 36.

42. "Pa Mac," "How'd They Used to Build a Fireplace"; E. Evans, "East Texas House," 3; DesChamps, "Early Days in the Cumberland Country," 198; Breeden, *Advice among Masters*, 121.

43. Cannon interview, 189.

44. E. Evans, "East Texas House," 3; DesChamps, "Early Days in the Cumberland Country," 198.

45. Vlach, "'Snug Li'l House,'" 118.

46. Singleton, "Archaeology of Afro-American Slavery," 130, 131, 135.

47. Perttula, "Material Culture of the Koasati Indians," 68.

48. Tyler and Murphy, *Slave Narratives*, 43.

49. Kniffen, "Outdoor Oven," 28–34.

50. Brooke, *Majesty of St. Augustine*, 63; Ximenez-Fatio House Museum, "Our Story."

51. McReynolds, "Family Life," 50, 69.

52. Vlach, *Back of the Big House*, 44.

53. "Rosegill."

54. Bullitt, *My Life at Oxmoor*, 56–57.

55. "Rosegill"; Otto, *Cannon's Point Plantation*, 134; Vlach, *Back of the Big House*, 50, 51.

56. Otto, *Cannon's Point Plantation*, 134.

57. Brewer, *From Fireplace to Cookstove*, 45, 66.

58. Brewer, 41, 71, 89; Marcoux, *Cooking with Fire*, 173–74, 210; David, *English Bread*, 167–68.

59. *Arkansas Weekly Gazette* (Little Rock), December 18, 1819.

60. *Savannah Daily Morning News*, January 17, 1850.

61. *Savannah Daily Morning News*, December 22, 1853; *San Antonio Ledger*, March 23, 1854; *The Standard* (Clarksville, Tex.), November 6, 1858.

62. *Augusta Daily Chronicle and Sentinel*, January 7, 1857; *State Gazette* (Austin, Tex.), August 13, 1859.

63. Jefferson, *Memoirs*, 1; A. Miller, *President's Kitchen Cabinet*, xx, 61, 75; Burwell, *Girl's Life*, 9.

64. Shields, *Southern Provisions*, 113–14.

65. C. Kennedy, *Braided Relations*, 149.

66. Burke, *Reminiscences of Georgia*, 123–24.

67. Srygley, *Seventy Years in Dixie*, 121–22.

68. Jacobs, *Incidents in the Life of a Slave Girl*, 22.

69. Covey and Eisnach, *What the Slaves Ate*, 189; Burr, *Secret Eye*, 133; Jacobs, *Incidents in the Life of a Slave Girl*, 22.

70. Tyler and Murphy, *Slave Narratives*, 24.

71. Perdue, Barden, and Phillips, *Weevils in the Wheat*, 274.

72. Perdue, Barden, and Phillips, 62.

73. Weiner, *Mistresses and Slaves*, 44.

74. M. Thompson, "Martha Washington's Cookbooks," 31; Hess, historical notes and commentaries, in Randolph, *Virginia House-wife*, xiii.

75. Herman, *Town House*, 34.

76. Gabaccia and Aldrich, "Recipes in Context."

77. Opie, *Hog and Hominy*, 37; Farrish, "Theft, Food, Labor," 155, 156–57.

78. Perdue, Barden, and Phillips, *Weevils in the Wheat*, 229; Joyner, *Down by the Riverside*, 94, 101, 102; Covey and Eisnach, *What the Slaves Ate*, 161, 193; Northrup, *Twelve Years a Slave*, 255.

79. Northrup, *Twelve Years a Slave*, 215.

80. Talley, *Negro Folk Rhymes*, 26; Hughes, *Thirty Years a Slave*, 15.

81. Breeden, *Advice among Masters*, 90, 92.

82. Perdue, Barden, and Phillips, *Weevils in the Wheat*, 181; Ball, *Slavery*, 149.

83. Covey and Eisnach, *What the Slaves Ate*, 146, 155, 156; Perdue, Barden, and Phillips, *Weevils in the Wheat*, 189, 227.

84. Hughes, *Thirty Years a Slave*, 10; Ball, *Slavery*, 96; M. Evans interview, 250; Beoku-Betts, "'She Make Funny Flat Cake,'" 217.

85. Perdue, Barden, and Phillips, *Weevils in the Wheat*, 268–69; Covey and Eisnach, *What the Slaves Ate*, 157.

86. Tyler and Murphy, *Slave Narratives*, 58.

87. Covey and Eisnach, *What the Slaves Ate*, 147; Hughes, *Thirty Years a Slave*, 16.

88. Joyner, *Down by the Riverside*, 91, 92, 93; Breeden, *Advice among Masters*, 102, 105, 107; Tyler and Murphy, *Slave Narratives*, 45.

89. Covey and Eisnach, *What the Slaves Ate*, 163.

90. Hughes, *Thirty Years a Slave*, 15.

91. Breeden, *Advice among Masters*, 102; Hundley, *Social Relations*, 343; R. McDonald, *Economy and Material Culture*, 259.

92. Tyler and Murphy, *Slave Narratives*, 46.

93. G. Wilson diary, October 19, 1853.

94. Covey and Eisnach, *What the Slaves Ate*, 152, 153; Breeden, *Advice among Masters*, 107.

95. Rutledge, *Carolina Housewife*, 119; Randolph, *Virginia House-wife*, 149; Crump, *Hearthside Cooking*, 263.

96. Ladies of the Guild of St. James' Parish Church, *Favorite Foods*, 73; Robert, "Lee the Farmer," 431, 432.

97. *North Carolina Journal* (Halifax), January 5, 1795; *Blakeley Sun and Alabama Advertiser*, December 18, 1818; *Augusta Chronicle*, November 13, 1824.

98. Shields, *Southern Provisions*, 255, 256; Sitterson, *Sugar Country*, 28.

99. Ballinger, *History of Sugar Marketing*, 7.

100. *Virginia Journal and Alexandria Advertiser*, April 21, 1785.

101. J. Thomas, *Old Days in Nashville*, 18.

102. Martin, *Buying into the World of Goods*, 182; McKee, "Plantation Food Supply," 130; R. McDonald, *Economy and Material Culture*, 54, 67, 81, 83, 84, 89, 243–51, 253–57.

103. Bernhard, *Travels through North America*, 2:69, 81.

104. Northrup, *Twelve Years a Slave*, 208–13. See also Sitterson, *Sugar Country*, 137–44.

105. Rutledge, *Carolina Housewife*, 28, 209; Randolph, *Virginia House-wife*, 171.

106. Rutledge, *Carolina Housewife*, 30, 35.

107. *City Gazette and Daily Advertiser* (Charleston), July 22, 1808.

108. Olmsted, *Journey in the Seaboard Slave States*, 478; Rutledge, *Carolina Housewife*, 14, 16, 17, 18, 19; Shields, *Southern Provisions*, 245.

109. Joyner, *Down by the Riverside*, 96–97; Beoku-Betts, "'She Make Funny Flat Cake,'" 211, 218; *Drums and Shadows*, 162, 167; Diouf, *Servants of Allah*, 63, 65.

110. Dimond and Hattaway, *Letters from Forest Place*, 165; Moore, *Plantation Mistress*, 61; R. McDonald, *Economy and Material Culture*, 89.

111. A. King, *Anna*, 118.

112. *Agriculture of the United States in 1860*, cviii.

113. Dimond and Hattaway, *Letters from Forest Place*, 156–57.

114. Burke, *Reminiscences of Georgia*, 26.

115. Hamilton, *Colonial Mobile*, 390; *Blakeley Sun and Alabama Advertiser*, March 16, 1819; *Mobile Gazette and Commercial Adviser*, April 7, 1832; *Civilian and Galveston Gazette*, October 19, 1838.

116. *Texian Advocate* (Victoria), May 18, 1848; *Transactions of the New-York State Agricultural Society*, 572.

117. Randolph, *Virginia House-wife*, 159, 163; Bryan, *Kentucky Housewife*, 290; Rutledge, *Carolina Housewife*, 198, 199, 200; "Lady of Charleston," *Carolina Receipt Book*, 35; N. Lewis, *Housekeeping Book*, 106.

118. E. Harrison, *Best Companions*, 227; Bryan, *Kentucky Housewife*, 292, 293; Randolph, *Virginia House-wife*, 158–59; "Lady of Charleston," *Carolina Receipt Book*, 33; Rutledge, *Carolina Housewife*, 208–9.

119. Rutledge, *Carolina Housewife*, 205; *Arkansas State Gazette* (Little Rock), May 29, 1839; *Thomson's Mercantile and Professional Directory*, 230; Salls, "Pamela Savage," 552–53.

120. Rutledge, *Carolina Housewife*, 205–6.

121. Perdue, Barden, and Phillips, *Weevils in the Wheat*, 80; Covey and Eisnach, *What the Slaves Ate*, 152, 153, 158, 159.

122. Alsen, "Alabama Food Frontier."

123. Randolph, *Virginia House-wife*, 170; N. Lewis, *Housekeeping Book*, 104.

124. Hughes, *Thirty Years a Slave*, 70–72.

125. Alsen, "Alabama Food Frontier"; Rutledge, *Carolina Housewife*, 33.

126. Randolph, *Virginia House-wife*, 157; "Lady of Charleston," *Carolina Receipt Book*, 32; Rutledge, *Carolina Housewife*, 19, 34, 206; Bryan, *Kentucky Housewife*, 304–7.

127. "Lady of Charleston," *Carolina Receipt Book*, 50; Gabaccia and Aldrich, "Recipes in Context," 206.

128. Hess, "Historical Glossary," in Randolph, *Virginia House-wife*, 280.

129. Bryan, *Kentucky Housewife*, 304, 306–7.

130. Civitello, *Baking Powder Wars*, 38.

131. Moore, *Plantation Mistress*, 53, 58.

132. *Blakeley Sun and Alabama Advertiser*, March 16, 1819; *Texian Advocate*, May 10, 1850.

133. *Arkansas State Gazette*, May 29, 1839.

134. Opie, *Hog and Hominy*, 33.

135. Ramsay, *Ramsay's History of South Carolina*, 566; E. Harrison, *Best Companions*, 36, 227.

136. Wiggins, *Journal*, 5, 6.

137. W. King, *Northern Woman*, 40.

138. Burwell, *Girl's Life*, 39–40, 71.

139. *New Orleans Times-Picayune*, January 16, 1844; *Arkansas Intelligencer* (Van Buren), December 27, 1845.

140. Randolph, *Virginia House-wife*, 168; and numerous others.

141. Bryan, *Kentucky Housewife*, 319; Rutledge, *Carolina Housewife*, 11.

142. Dimond and Hattaway, *Letters from Forest Place*, 191–92; Hunt, *First Forty Years*, 5.

143. Hess, "Historical Glossary," in Randolph, *Virginia House-wife*, 259–60.

144. Rutledge, *Carolina Housewife*, 28, 29; N. Lewis, *Housekeeping Book*, 70, 106; "Lady of Charleston," *Carolina Receipt Book*, 29; Randolph, *Virginia House-wife*, 170.

145. Bryan, *Kentucky Housewife*, 306; "Lady of Charleston," *Carolina Receipt Book*, 29; N. Lewis, *Housekeeping Book*, 84; Rutledge, *Carolina Housewife*, 12, 13, 14, 31, 32.

146. *Mobile Gazette and Commercial Adviser*, April 6, 1819; *Savannah Daily Morning News*, February 17, 1855.

147. Rutledge, *Carolina Housewife*, 207; "Lady of Charleston," *Carolina Receipt Book*, 30.

148. Calvert, *Mistress of Riversdale*, 9.

149. Moore, *Plantation Mistress*, 63, 102.

150. Bryan, *Kentucky Housewife*, 259–62.

151. McInnis, *Politics of Taste*, 253; M. Thompson, "'Served Up in Excellent Order,'" 40; Rutledge, *Carolina Housewife*, 114; "Lady of Charleston," *Carolina Receipt Book*, 41.

152. Bryan, *Kentucky Housewife*, 271–74.

153. Côté, *Mary's World*, 90; N. Smith, *History of Pickens County*, 92; Norton, "'Abundance of Every Thing,'" 79.

154. Calhoun, *Old Southern Apples*, 9.

155. Dimond and Hattaway, *Letters from Forest Place*, 3, 194; *Trinity Advocate* (Palestine, Tex.), April 22, 1857.

156. Wilstach, *Mount Vernon*, 151; N. Smith, *History of Pickens County*, 92.

157. Perdue, Barden, and Phillips, *Weevils in the Wheat*, 227.

158. J. Thomas, *Old Days in Nashville*, 39; Bryan, *Kentucky Housewife*, 262.

159. Otto, *Cannon's Point Plantation*, 150.

160. Bryan, *Kentucky Housewife*, 263, 264, 265; Stuart, *Three Years in North America*, 2:200; Dimond and Hattaway, *Letters from Forest Place*, 156; Padgett, "Journal of Daniel Walker Lord," 194.

161. B. Wood, *Women's Work*, 96; J. Claiborne, "Trip through the Piney Woods," 490; Ownby, *American Dreams*, 50.

162. Bryan, *Kentucky Housewife*, 265, 266.

163. Bullitt, *My Life at Oxmoor*, 64; N. Smith, *History of Pickens County*, 92; Jurney and Perttula, "Alibamu-Koasati Pottery," 19–20.

164. P. Hatch, "Thomas Jefferson and Gardening."

165. Bryan, *Kentucky Housewife*, 263, 302.

166. Norton, "'Abundance of Every Thing,'" 79; Bullitt, *My Life at Oxmoor*, 64; *Civilian and Galveston Gazette*, October 19, 1838; Padgett, "Journal of Daniel Walker Lord," 194.

167. Bryan, *Kentucky Housewife*, 266–67.

168. According to the *Oxford English Dictionary Online*, the term *cobbler* is American from the nineteenth century: "a pot lined with dough of great thickness upon which the fruit is placed." Bryan, *Kentucky Housewife*, 267–68; J. Thomas, *Old Days in Nashville*, 123.

169. Hughes, *Thirty Years a Slave*, 49.

170. Bryan, *Kentucky Housewife*, 270, 294.

171. Rutledge, *Carolina Housewife*, 134.

172. Norton, "'Abundance of Every Thing,'" 83; *Weekly Nashville Union*, January 14, 1846; *Arkansas State Gazette*, May 29, 1839.

173. *The Standard* (Clarksville, Tex.), October 29, 1853; Bernhard, *Travels through North America*, 2:7; Atherton, *Southern Country Store*, 80.

174. Rutledge, *Carolina Housewife*, 135.

175. Okihiro, *Pineapple Culture*, 87.

176. "Lady of Charleston," *Carolina Receipt Book*, 42; Rutledge, *Carolina Housewife*, 133.

177. Montgomery, *Sketches of Old Warrenton*, 53; Kennedy, *Memoirs of the Life of William Wirt*, 1:135.

178. Bryan, *Kentucky Housewife*, 287, 288; Rutledge, *Carolina Housewife*, 116, 117.

179. Bryan, *Kentucky Housewife*, 257.

180. Randolph, *Virginia House-wife*, 155; Bryan, *Kentucky Housewife*, 257; Rutledge, *Carolina Housewife*, 119.

181. Randolph, *Virginia House-wife*, 160.

182. Hess, "Historical Glossary," in Randolph, *Virginia House-wife*, 270–71.

183. N. Lewis, *Housekeeping Book*, 71; Randolph, *Virginia House-wife*, 160; Bryan, *Kentucky Housewife*, 298.

184. "Lady of Charleston," *Carolina Receipt Book*, 37.

185. Bryan, *Kentucky Housewife*, 298.

186. N. Lewis, *Housekeeping Book*, 78; Bryan, *Kentucky Housewife*, 298.

187. Côté, *Mary's World*, 88, 89, 160–61.

188. "Lady of Charleston," *Carolina Receipt Book*, 34; Randolph, *Virginia House-wife*, 159; Bryan, *Kentucky Housewife*, 296, 300, 301; Rutledge, *Carolina Housewife*, 197–98, 199–200; N. Lewis, *Housekeeping Book*, 66, 75.

189. Randolph, *Virginia House-wife*, 157; N. Lewis, *Housekeeping Book*, 78; "Lady of Charleston," *Carolina Receipt Book*, 36.

190. Bryan, *Kentucky Housewife*, 292–93.

191. N. Lewis, *Housekeeping Book*, 79; Rutledge, *Carolina Housewife*, 204–5; Randolph, *Virginia House-wife*, 173.

192. "Lady of Charleston," *Carolina Receipt Book*, 37; Bryan, *Kentucky Housewife*, 277, 278, 281–82; H. Bullock, *Williamsburg Art*, 173, 179, 183.

193. J. Thomas, *Old Days in Nashville*, 57.

194. Dimond and Hattaway, *Letters from Forest Place*, 211; Wiggins, *Journal*, 37.

195. Amy Young, "Risk and Material Conditions," 35.

196. Bryan, *Kentucky Housewife*, 274–75.

197. Covey and Eisnach, *What the Slaves Ate*, 160.

198. A. King, *Anna*, 323; Conrad, "Reminiscences," pt. 3, 255; Conrad, "Reminiscences," pt. 4, 359; Bullitt, *My Life at Oxmoor*, 57.

199. E. Harrison, *Best Companions*, 98.

200. W. King, *Stolen Childhood*, 148; Joyner, *Down by the Riverside*, 105.

201. Covey and Eisnach, *What the Slaves Ate*, 203.

202. Côté, *Mary's World*, 162.

203. "Lady of Charleston," *Carolina Receipt Book*, 36; Bryan, *Kentucky Housewife*, 283–85; N. Lewis, *Housekeeping Book*, 66, 80, 81; Randolph, *Virginia House-wife*, 161–62.

204. Rutledge, *Carolina Housewife*, 120, 151.

205. Bryan, *Kentucky Housewife*, 280, 281.

206. J. Thomas, *Old Days in Nashville*, 106.

207. Bryan, *Kentucky Housewife*, 277.

208. Edmondston, "Journal of a Secesh Lady," 19.

209. Ferris, *Edible South*, 45; Côté, *Mary's World*, 91.

210. Rutledge, *Carolina Housewife*, 118–19.

211. Rutledge, 117–18.

212. Rutledge, 136–37; Shields, *Culinarians*, 133.

213. E. Harrison, *Best Companions*, 30.

214. Buckingham, *Slave States*, 1:226, 512; Olmsted, *Cotton Kingdom*, 139.

215. Smyth, *Tour in the United States*, 1:77; Buckingham, *Slave States*, 2:155; Stuart, *Three Years in North America*, 2:158.

216. Bullitt, *My Life at Oxmoor*, 55.

217. *Floridian and Advocate* (Tallahassee), October 12, 1830.

218. Hale, *History of DeKalb County*, 100.

219. Schlotterbeck, "Plantation and Farm," 315.

220. B. Wood, *Women's Work*, 86.

221. Yentsch, "Excavating the South's African American Food History," 73; W. Johnson, *Black Savannah*, 69; Lichtenstein, "'That Disposition to Theft,'" 429–30; Singleton, "Slave Tag," 47, 49, 58.

222. Stuart, *Three Years in North America*, 2:200.

223. Ashley Young, "Nourishing Networks," 46, 101, 110.

224. Schlotterbeck, "Plantation and Farm," 238, 315.

225. Elizer, *Directory for 1803*.

226. Mizell-Nelson, "French Bread," 40.

227. *Thomson's Mercantile and Professional Directory*, 139.

228. *Richmond Enquirer*, November 28, 1806; and numerous others.

229. *Cahawba Press and Alabama Intelligencer*, July 10, 1819.

230. Mizell-Nelson, "French Bread," 45.

231. C. Kennedy, *Braided Relations*, 150.

232. *Tri-Weekly Flag and Advertiser* (Montgomery, Ala.), August 17, 1847.

233. Riley, "Ancient City," 308; Yentsch, *Chesapeake Family*, 246; "Capsule Summary of 156 Prince George Street."

234. Sumler-Edmond, *Secret Trust*, 18, 122.

235. Yentsch, "Excavating the South's African American Food History," 73; Fraser, *Savannah in the Old South*, 283.

236. C. Kennedy, *Braided Relations*, 129.

237. Shields, *Culinarians*, 85, 86; Shields, *Southern Provisions*, 112–14, 115.

238. Mizell-Nelson, "French Bread," 40; Bell, "Regional Identity," 12.

239. Mehrländer, *Germans of Charleston*, 56, 58, 60.

240. Mehrländer, 173; Bell, "Regional Identity," 19.

241. Myers, *Children of Pride*, 1468; Memorial page for Anton Christian Borchert, Find a Grave website.

242. Rockman, *Scraping By*, 175–76, 178; Bogin, "Petitioning," 392, 393, 397.

243. Mizell-Nelson, "French Bread," 39; J. Clark, *New Orleans*, 283.

244. Scroggs, "Assize of Bread."

245. Smith, *Reports of the Decisions of the Supreme Court of the State of Alabama*, 7:79.

CHAPTER 5

1. Ash, *Rebel Richmond*, 61; Craig, *Upcountry South Carolina*, 58.

2. *Charleston Mercury*, March 18, 1862.

3. *Daily Richmond Examiner*, November 4, 1863.

4. Hopley, *Life in the South*, 2:155.

5. Mehrländer, *Germans of Charleston*, 198.

6. Ross, *Visit to the Cities and Camps*, 109.

7. Glatthaar, "Confederate Soldiers in Virginia," 54–55.

8. Pember, *Southern Woman's Story*, 99.

9. Cumming, *Journal of a Confederate Nurse*, 15, 16, 43, 67, 93, 94–95.

10. Holmes, *Diary*, 43.

11. Scott, "Selma," 217.

12. Myers, *Children of Pride*, 1118–19.

13. Ash, *Rebel Richmond*, 70.

14. Duncan, *Beleaguered Winchester*, 28–29.

15. Hurt, *Agriculture and the Confederacy*, 102, 166.

16. *Charleston Mercury*, November 14, 1861; *Hinds County Gazette* (Raymond, Miss.), January 8, 1862.

17. Dimond and Hattaway, *Letters from Forest Place*, 290, 315.

18. *Daily South Carolinian* (Columbia), March 15, 1864.

19. Dimond and Hattaway, *Letters from Forest Place*, 325; *Charleston Tri-Weekly Courier*, January 10, 1863; *Charleston Mercury*, November 10, 1863.

20. Scott, "Selma," 217; Massey, *Ersatz in the Confederacy*, 66.

21. L. Anderson, *North Carolina Women*, 13, 89; Revels, *Grander in Her Daughters*, 59; Scott, "Selma," 217.

22. Hurt, *Agriculture and the Confederacy*, 35, 60, 76, 153, 192, 193; Clay-Clopton, *Belle of the Fifties*, 185.

23. *Chattanooga Daily Rebel*, July 3, 1863; Hale, *History of DeKalb County*, 32, 34, 91; T. Smith, *Mississippi in the Civil War*, 69, 70; Grimsley, *Hard Hand of War*, 152, 156.

24. "Rhea's Mill Ledger."

25. A. Smith, *Starving the South*, 130.

26. Koons, "'Staple of Our Country,'" 7, 8; Grimsley, *Hard Hand of War*, 166, 168, 178; Blair, *Virginia's Private War*, 108; Duncan, *Beleaguered Winchester*, 209–10.

27. Cashin, *War Stuff*, 54–81.

28. T. Smith, *Mississippi in the Civil War*, 69.

29. Myers, *Children of Pride*, 1190.

30. Hague, *Blockaded Family*, 22, 24.

31. Burge, *Woman's Wartime Journal*, 40–41.

32. Clay-Clopton, *Belle of the Fifties*, 185.

33. K. Stone, *Brokenburn*, 145.

34. Mehrländer, *Germans of Charleston*, 235, 238, 240.

35. Massey, "Free Market," 205, 209, 212; Brock, *Richmond during the War*, 343.

36. Escott, *Many Excellent People*, 56, 57.

37. McCurry, *Confederate Reckoning*, 175, 179, 182; Hurt, *Agriculture and the Confederacy*, 128.

38. McCurry, *Confederate Reckoning*, 182–83; Escott, *Many Excellent People*, 65–67; A. Smith, *Starving the South*, 50; Hurt, *Agriculture and the Confederacy*, 129.

39. A. Smith, *Starving the South*, 52.

40. Chesson, "Harlots or Heroines?," 139, 143, 144; Ambrose, "Bread Riots," 203; A. Smith, *Starving the South*, 49–50, 56–57.

41. Alsen, "Alabama Food Frontier"; A. Smith, *Starving the South*, 62–63.

42. A. Smith, *Starving the South*, 50, 51, 65; Hurt, *Agriculture and the Confederacy*, 200.

43. Hurt, *Agriculture and the Confederacy*, 101.

44. Hague, *Blockaded Family*, 25.

45. K. Stone, *Brokenburn*, 109.

46. Cumming, *Journal of a Confederate Nurse*, 269.

47. *Houston (Ga.) Tri-Weekly Telegraph*, September 8, 1862.

48. Revels, *Grander in Her Daughters*, 59.

49. Smedes, *Memorials*, 224; Revels, *Grander in Her Daughters*, 59.

50. L. Anderson, *North Carolina Women*, 97.

51. Pryor, *My Day*, 237.

52. Massey, *Ersatz in the Confederacy*, 67, 69.

53. Myers, *Children of Pride*, 632; Revels, *Grander in Her Daughters*, 59.

54. *Charleston Mercury*, October 16, 1862.

55. Cable, "Woman's Diary," 769.

56. Loughborough, *My Cave Life*, 77; Cable, "Woman's Diary," 772.

57. A. Smith, *Starving the South*, 102.

58. Massey, *Ersatz in the Confederacy*, 67.

59. Myers, *Children of Pride*, 1245.

60. Massey, *Ersatz in the Confederacy*, 67, 70, 188; Revels, *Grander in Her Daughters*, 59; L. Anderson, *North Carolina Women*, 13, 89.

61. Edmondston, "Journal of a Secesh Lady," 385.

62. Revels, *Grander in Her Daughters*, 59; L. Anderson, *North Carolina Women*, 13, 89; Scott, "Selma," 220; Massey, *Ersatz in the Confederacy*, 67, 70.

63. *Hinds County Gazette*, January 8, 1862.

64. Scott, "Selma," 220.

65. Burr, *Secret Eye*, 220.

66. G. Wilcox, "Interrupted Wedding." Groom's cakes apparently appeared around 1850 around the United States. Despite current belief, they were not uniquely southern.

67. Pickett, *Pickett and His Men*, 322. Historian Lesley Gordon finds it highly improbable that Mrs. Lee sent a cake, as the Lees and the Picketts were not friendly.

68. K. Stone, *Brokenburn*, 58.

69. Massey, *Refugee Life*, 196.

70. Myers, *Children of Pride*, 1154.

71. *Charleston Mercury*, November 14, 1861; *Daily South Carolinian*, July 20, 1861.

72. *Charleston Mercury*, October 16, 1862.

73. Hague, *Blockaded Family*, 47–48.

74. Scott, "Selma," 218.

75. *Confederate Receipt Book*, 6.

76. Cable, "Woman's Diary," 769.

77. Felton, *Country Life*, 273.

78. Hague, *Blockaded Family*, 161.

79. "Last Days of the Southern Confederacy," 330.

80. *Charleston Mercury*, November 10, 1863.

81. *Confederate Receipt Book*, 6, 21.

82. *Macon (Ga.) Telegraph*, January 1, 1862; Hurt, *Agriculture and the Confederacy*, 216.

83. Massey, *Ersatz in the Confederacy*, 69, 70; Hopley, *Life in the South*, 1:251.

84. *Charleston Mercury*, November 10, 1863.

85. Massey, *Ersatz in the Confederacy*, 67, 188; Holmes, *Diary*, 313; Myers, *Children of Pride*, 1139, 1161.

86. Massey, *Ersatz in the Confederacy*, 70.

87. *Daily Richmond Examiner*, October 27, 1864.

88. *Daily Morning News*, August 15, 1861.

89. *Fayetteville (N.C.) Observer*, April 30, 1863.

90. *Daily South Carolinian*, January 18, 1865.

91. Myers, *Children of Pride*, 632; "Nathan O. Tisdale"; *New Orleans Times-Picayune*, March 21, 1863.

92. *Daily Morning News*, January 25, 1862; Blackman, *Wild Rose*, 203, 208, 210; Greenhow, *My Imprisonment*, 172, 173, 210, 230.

93. Dimond and Hattaway, *Letters from Forest Place*, 239.

94. *Houston (Tex.) Telegraph*, June 17, 1864.

95. Edmondston, "Journal of a Secesh Lady," 386.

96. Pearce, *Pensacola during the Civil War*, 96.

97. Reed, "Woman's Experiences," 922.

98. Conrad, "Reminiscences," pt. 5, 409.

99. McGuire, *Diary of a Southern Refugee*, 48.

100. *Charleston Courier*, September 11, 1862; Dimond and Hattaway, *Letters from Forest Place*, 300; Cumming, *Journal of a Confederate Nurse*, 169.

101. Eppes, *Through Some Eventful Years*, 253.

102. *Daily True Delta* (New Orleans), April 26, 1862.

103. *New Orleans Times-Picayune*, July 28, 1863; *Daily Picayune* (New Orleans), December 7, 1863.

104. W. Vaughan, "Natchez during the Civil War," 340–41.

105. Govan and Livingood, "Chattanooga under Military Occupation," 26, 30; *Chattanooga Daily Gazette*, December 18, 1864.

106. *Daily Richmond Examiner*, September 19, 1863, and June 17, 1864.

107. *Daily True Delta*, September 21, 1864.

108. *New Orleans Times*, March 2, 1865; Tomblin, *Bluejackets*, 251.

109. Manning, *Troubled Refuge*, 55.

110. *Fayetteville Observer*, July 18, 1864.

111. Tomblin, *Bluejackets*, 147–48; Manning, *Troubled Refuge*, 54–55.

112. Duncan, *Beleaguered Winchester*, 145, 147.

113. W. Vaughan, "Natchez during the Civil War," 361.

114. Myers, *Children of Pride*, 1246.

115. *Fayetteville Observer*, February 9, 1863.

116. *Chattanooga Daily Rebel*, April 19, 1863.

117. *Daily Richmond Examiner*, November 4, 1863.

118. *Charleston Mercury*, March 16, 1864; *Daily South Carolinian* (Columbia), March 15, 1864.

119. Holmes, *Diary*, 258.

120. Hurt, *Agriculture and the Confederacy*, 199.

121. Ross, *Visit to the Cities and Camps*, 195.

122. *Daily Picayune*, August 8, 1863.

123. *Natchez Courier*, November 10, 1863.

124. *Natchez Courier*, October 13, 1863.

125. Cumming, *Journal of a Confederate Nurse*, 261.

126. Ross, *Visit to the Cities and Camps*, 195.

127. *Daily Selma Reporter*, January 28, 1865.

128. Perdue, Barden, and Phillips, *Weevils in the Wheat*, 163.

129. Perdue, Barden, and Phillips, 187.

130. Pearson, *Letters from Port Royal*, 69, 80, 114; Towne, *Letters and Diary*, 114; Cooper, "'Lord, Until I Reach My Home,'" 250.

131. Pearson, *Letters from Port Royal*, 52–53.

132. Swint, *Dear Ones at Home*, 23.

133. Click, *Time Full of Trial*, 135.

134. Manning, *Troubled Refuge*, 228; Cooper, "'Lord, Until I Reach My Home,'" 139.

135. Cimprich, *Slavery's End*, 65; Manning, *Troubled Refuge*, 55.

136. Click, *Time Full of Trial*, 122.

137. *Chicago Tribune*, June 9, 1864; Taylor, *Embattled Freedom*, 153, 154.

138. Pearson, *Letters from Port Royal*, 144–45; Swint, *Dear Ones at Home*, 130.

139. Swint, *Dear Ones at Home*, 117.

140. Duncan, *Beleaguered Winchester*, 125; L. Anderson, *North Carolina Women*, 80.

141. Pember, *Southern Woman's Story*, 175.

142. Duncan, *Beleaguered Winchester*, 245.

143. Pryor, *My Day*, 266.

CHAPTER 6

1. *Weekly Advertiser* (Montgomery, Ala.), November 3, 1868.

2. *Weekly Telegraph* (Macon, Ga.), November 13, 1888.

3. Adams and Smith, "Historical Perspectives," 318, 320.

4. Rodrigue, *Reconstruction*, 52; Perdue, Barden, and Phillips, *Weevils in the Wheat*, 311.

5. Fairbanks, "Plantation Archaeology," 8.

6. Atwater and Woods, *Dietary Studies*, 16–17, 21, 26, 33; Frissell and Bevier, *Dietary Studies of Negroes*, 15, 20.

7. Aldrich, "Kerosene Kitchen," 41.

8. *Macon (Ga.) Telegraph and Messenger*, March 7, 1873; *Atlanta Daily Herald*, February 22, 1874.

9. *Housekeeping in Alabama*, 116–17.

10. Sharpless, *Cooking in Other Women's Kitchens*, 5–9.

11. Edwards, *Twenty-Five Years in the Black Belt*, 5, 15–16.

12. Hockensmith, *Millstone Industry*, 58.

13. Frissell and Bevier, *Dietary Studies of Negroes*, 8; Atwater and Woods, *Dietary Studies*, 9, 20.

14. M. Smith, *Virginia Cookery-Book*, 21; and numerous other cookbooks of the period.

15. *Macon Telegraph*, February 11, 1866.

16. Weiner, *Mistresses and Slaves*, 212.

17. Eppes, *Through Some Eventful Years*, 310.

18. Eppes, 310.

19. *Texas Almanac*, 36.

20. White and Holland, *No Quittin' Sense*, 61.

21. Hall, "'Reliable Grocer,'" 277; *Macon Telegraph*, July 11, 1866; Jones and Willaford Grocery Account Book; Rodrigue, *Reconstruction*, 152.

22. B. Moss, "Dairy Industry in Alabama"; Cringan, *Instruction in Cooking*, ads.

23. *City Directory of Macon*, 567.

24. "Selling Goshen Butter," *New York Times*, November 14, 1886; Gibson, *Maryland and Virginia Cook Book*, 281; Shields, *Southern Provisions*, 260–61.

25. M. Smith, *Virginia Cookery-Book*, 286–87.

26. Rees, *Refrigeration Nation*, 121–22.

27. *Galveston Daily News*, January 2, 1867.

28. *Houston (Tex.) Post*, September 23, 1900.

29. McGee, *On Food and Cooking*, 37; Shurtleff and Aoyagi, "History of Soy Oil Shortening."

30. Westervelt, *American Pure Food and Drug Laws*, 485, 1361.

31. Frissell and Bevier, *Dietary Studies of Negroes*, 8.

32. White and Holland, *No Quittin' Sense*, 5–6.

33. Levine, *Black Culture*, 218.

34. Fisher, *What Mrs. Fisher Knows*, 62.

35. Gibson, *Maryland and Virginia Cook Book*, 20; Central Presbyterian Church, *Southern Housekeeper*, 21.

36. Tyree, *Housekeeping in Old Virginia*, 416; Mrs. H. Wilson, *Tested Recipe Cook Book*, 69.

37. Atwater and Woods, *Dietary Studies*, 21; Pretlow, *Calendar of Old Southern Recipes*, 89.

38. *Gulf City Cook Book*, 107.

39. Fussell, *Story of Corn*, 223.

40. Koons, "'Staple of Our Country,'" 3, 8, 9, 10, 14.

41. Fields, *Slavery and Freedom*, 170; Steen, *Flour Milling*, 103–4; Ayers, *Promise of the New South*, 7, 10, 11, 450.

42. Hale, *History of DeKalb County*, 34–35, 141, 143.

43. Berry, "Rise of Flour Milling," 407; "Richard Barton Haxall."

44. Clayton, *History of Davidson County*, 221.

45. Steen, *Flour Milling*, 47, 48.

46. Steen, 54.

47. Peterson, "Flour and Grist Milling," 106.

48. Hale, *History of DeKalb County*, 34, 92.

49. Steen, *Flour Milling*, 39.

50. Ferris, *Edible South*, 193.

51. *Denton [Tex.] Business Review*, n.p.

52. Parloa, *Miss Parloa's Kitchen Companion*, 92.

53. W. King, *Northern Woman*, 197.

54. Cringan, *Instruction in Cooking*, 14.

55. Tyree, *Housekeeping in Old Virginia*, 20.

56. Holt, *Making Freedom Pay*, 79, 90; Perdue, Barden, and Phillips, *Weevils in the Wheat*, 311; Frissell and Bevier, *Dietary Studies of Negroes*, 12, 13, 14–16, 18, 20–21, 24, 34; Atwater and Woods, *Dietary Studies*, 20, 21, 22.

57. Pickens, *Heir of Slaves*, 25.

58. *Richmond Dispatch*, quoted in "Why the Hoecake is Going," *Boston Daily Globe*, February 13, 1898; Rodrigue, *Reconstruction*, 36.

59. Manring, *Slave in a Box*, 60–74.

60. Rushing, "Stovetop Waffle Iron Patented."

61. Fisher, *What Mrs. Fisher Knows*, 10.

62. Du Bois, *Negroes of Farmville*, 27, 28; Frissell and Bevier, *Dietary Studies of Negroes*, 29.

63. Orrick interview, 11.

64. M. Smith, *Virginia Cookery-Book*, 6.

65. Ferris, *Edible South*, 143.

66. Tyree, *Housekeeping in Old Virginia*, 42; Hearn, *La Cuisine Creole*, 128–30; E. Glover, *Warm Springs Receipt-Book*, 211; Augusta, Ga., Second Presbyterian Church, *Choice Recipes*, 53.

67. Cierzniak, "Indianapolis Collected"; Cringan, *Instruction in Cooking*, ads; St. Paul's, *Household Manual*, 328.

68. Hearn, *La Cuisine Creole*, 150; St. Paul's Guild, *Household Manual*, 163.

69. A. Hill, *Mrs. Hill's Southern Practical Cookery*, 228, 230, 233; Ladies Aid and Sewing Society of New Orleans, *Up-to-Date Cookbook*, 94.

70. Hearn, *La Cuisine Creole*, 129.

71. St. Paul's Guild, *Household Manual*, 310, 316, 318.

72. Russell, *Domestic Cook Book*, 7; A. Hill, *Mrs. Hill's Southern Practical Cookery*, 233.

73. Augusta, Ga., Second Presbyterian Church, *Choice Recipes*, 53; Hearn, *La Cuisine Creole*, 128–29.

74. Russell, *Domestic Cook Book*, 7; and numerous others.

75. Hounihan, *Bakers' and Confectioners' Guide*, 31.

76. Civitello, *Baking Powder Wars*, 41–42, 70.

77. Adams and Smith, "Historical Perspectives," 318; M. Hall, "'Reliable Grocer,'" 272; Frissell and Bevier, *Dietary Studies of Negroes*, 13, 14, 31, 32, 34, 37.

78. McPhail, *F. F. V. Receipt Book*, 286; Central Presbyterian Church, *Southern Housekeeper*, 51, 101.

79. Gibson, *Maryland and Virginia Cook Book*, 171.

80. Jones and Willaford Grocery Account Book.

81. M. Smith, *Virginia Cookery-Book*, 13.

82. Page, "Baking Powder," 147.

83. *Savannah Republican*, August 22, 1865; *North Georgia Citizen* (Dalton), March 6, 1873; *Sandersville (Ga.) Herald*, January 1, 1875; Baudier, "Boss Bakers' Protective Association," 25.

84. *Morning News* (Savannah), November 26, 1875.

85. M. Smith, *Virginia Cookery-Book*, 7–8.

86. Egerton, *Southern Food*, 219; "Improvement in Dough-Kneading Machines."

87. A. Hill, *Mrs. Hill's Southern Practical Cookery*, 230; and numerous others.

88. Cringan, *Instruction in Cooking*, 250.

89. Mrs. H. Wilson, *Tested Recipe Cook Book*, 45.

90. Russell, *Domestic Cook Book*, 25; *Handy Housekeeping*, 7; Dennis and Wright, *Annie Dennis' Cookbook*, 254.

91. *Gulf City Cook Book*, 131; and numerous others.

92. Verstille, *Mrs. E. J. Verstille's Southern Cookery*, 119; *Gulf City Cook Book*, 102; Hearn, *La Cuisine Creole*, 157; Central Presbyterian Church, *Southern Housekeeper*, 112.

93. Lineback, *Preserving the Past*, 78.

94. Wallach, *How America Eats*, 144–48.

95. *Gulf City Cook Book*, 97–98; Hearn, *La Cuisine Creole*, 126, 127, 133.

96. *Handy Housekeeping*, handwritten on p. 111, University of Denver Penrose Library.

97. St. Paul's Guild, *Household Manual*, 86–87.

98. Wait, *Nutrition Investigations*, 19, 22.

99. *Housekeeping in Alabama*, 146–47.

100. Although salt-rising bread is, as Smith notes, associated with Appalachia, the first print references came from the Midwest around 1860. M. Smith, *Virginia Cookery-Book*, 17.

101. Russell, *Domestic Cook Book*, 6; M. Smith, *Virginia Cookery-Book*, 17.

102. E. Glover, *Warm Springs Receipt-Book*, 209.

103. Tyree, *Housekeeping in Old Virginia*, 19, 23.

104. *Housekeeping in Alabama*, 141.

105. *Handy Housekeeping*, 1; *Alexandria Gazette*, January 29, 1879; "History of Fleischmann's Yeast."

106. E. Wilcox, *New Dixie Cook-Book*, 9, 13.

107. *Handy Housekeeping*, handwritten on pp. 108–9, University of Denver Penrose Library.

108. Tyree, *Housekeeping in Old Virginia*, 20, 22.

109. Frissell and Bevier, *Dietary Studies of Negroes*, 20, 24, 31.

110. W. King, *Northern Woman*, 221 (emphasis in original).

111. Central Presbyterian Church, *Southern Housekeeper*, 48.

112. Russell, *Domestic Cook Book*, 24; and numerous others.

113. Hearn, *La Cuisine Creole*, 137, 235; Mrs. M. Moncure, *Art of Good Living*, 147; Russell, *Domestic Cook Book*, 28; St. Paul's Guild, *Household Manual*, 86.

114. Porter, *Mrs. Porter's New Southern Cookery Book*, 275–78.

115. Tyree, *Housekeeping in Old Virginia*, 404–5.

116. "Historical Review of the Rise of Mechanical Refrigeration."

117. Fisher, *What Mrs. Fisher Knows*, 24; Russell, *Domestic Cook Book*, 22, 25.

118. Hearn, *La Cuisine Creole*, 186.

119. Rodrigue, *Reconstruction*, 153; Edwards, *Twenty-Five Years in the Black Belt*, 16; Frissell and Bevier, *Dietary Studies of Negroes*, 31; Wait, *Nutrition Investigations*, 16.

120. M. Evans interview, 250.

121. Frissell and Bevier, *Dietary Studies of Negroes*, 31; Wait, *Nutrition Investigations*, 16.

122. Porter, *Mrs. Porter's New Southern Cookery Book*, 303–6.

123. Fisher, *What Mrs. Fisher Knows*, 27; and numerous others.

124. Porter, *Mrs. Porter's New Southern Cookery Book*, 303.

125. Harland, *Dinner Year Book*, 80.

126. Gibson, *Maryland and Virginia Cook Book*.

127. *Charleston Daily News*, December 25, 1869; *Macon Telegraph*, December 16, 1866.

128. Adams and Smith, "Historical Perspectives," 318.

129. Frissell and Bevier, *Dietary Studies of Negroes*, 31.

130. Verstille, *Mrs. E. J. Verstille's Southern Cookery*, 135; Russell, *Domestic Cook Book*, 23; St. Paul's Guild, *Household Manual*, 177.

131. Hearn, *La Cuisine Creole*, 206, 208; Fisher, *What Mrs. Fisher Knows*, 64.

132. Russell, *Domestic Cook Book*, 25; Tyree, *Housekeeping in Old Virginia*, 413; M. Smith, *Virginia Cookery-Book*, 177.

133. *Charleston Daily News*, December 25, 1869.

134. Augusta, Ga., Second Presbyterian Church, *Choice Recipes*, 99; and numerous others.

135. "Citrus Industry History."

136. Tyree, *Housekeeping in Old Virginia*, 407; Fisher, *What Mrs. Fisher Knows*, 26–27; Hearn, *La Cuisine Creole*, 191.

137. Russell, *Domestic Cook Book*, 23; Fisher, *What Mrs. Fisher Knows*, 26.

138. Harland, *Autobiography*, 412.

139. Olmsted, *Cotton Kingdom*, 337.

140. Elliott, *Mrs. Elliott's Housewife*, 257.

141. "Hints on Cooking," 865.

142. Russell, *Domestic Cook Book*, 30; Fisher, *What Mrs. Fisher Knows*, 65–66.

143. Burr, *Secret Eye*, 259.

144. Russell, *Domestic Cook Book*, 16–17, 23, 34; Augusta, Ga., Second Presbyterian Church, *Choice Recipes*, 89; Porter, *Mrs. Porter's New Southern Cookery Book*, 264; Hearn, *La Cuisine Creole*, 154, 234.

145. Ballinger, *History of Sugar Marketing*, 10, 17.

146. Sitterson, *Sugar Country*, 265, 275, 277, 317–18.

147. Sitterson, 260–61, 263, 281; Vogt, *Sugar Refining Industry*, 15–16.

148. Ballinger, *History of Sugar Marketing*, 16.

149. Adams and Smith, "Historical Perspectives," 318, 320; Ownby, *American Dreams*, 69, 71; Frissell and Bevier, *Dietary Studies of Negroes*, 11, 13, 15, 18, 20, 36.

150. Hearn, *La Cuisine Creole*, 141; Tyree, *Housekeeping in Old Virginia*, 304.

151. *Handy Housekeeping*, unpaged ad.

152. St. Paul's Guild, *Household Manual*, 297; *Housekeeping in Alabama*, unpaged ad.

153. Adams and Smith, "Historical Perspectives," 318; Frissell and Bevier, *Dietary Studies of Negroes*, 20.

154. "About Us," Sauer Brands website.

155. Young Men's Christian Association, Peterson, Va., Ladies' Auxiliary, *Old Virginia Cook Book*, unpaged ad; McPhail, *F. F. V. Receipt Book*, 278; Cringan, *Instruction in Cooking*, 22, 237.

156. Adams and Smith, "Historical Perspectives," 318; Frissell and Bevier, *Dietary Studies of Negroes*, 20.

157. "Cookie Cutters Have Intriguing History," *Orlando Sentinel*, February 9, 1990.

158. Tyree, *Housekeeping in Old Virginia*, 359.

159. St. Paul's Guild, *Household Manual*, 163; and numerous others.

160. Cringan, *Instruction in Cooking*, 265.

161. Hearn, *La Cuisine Creole*, 148.

162. Fisher, *What Mrs. Fisher Knows*, 33; Mrs. H. Wilson, *Tested Recipe Cook Book*, 140.

163. Fisher, *What Mrs. Fisher Knows*, 33; *Housekeeping in Alabama*, 155; and numerous others.

164. M. Smith, *Virginia Cookery-Book*, 188–89; Tyree, *Housekeeping in Old Virginia*, 354–55.

165. Hearn, *La Cuisine Creole*, 153; Mrs. H. Wilson, *Tested Recipe Cook Book*, 137.

166. St. Paul's Guild, *Household Manual*, 148; Ladies Aid and Sewing Society of New Orleans, *Up-to-Date Cookbook*, 104.

167. Du Bois, *Negroes of Farmville*, 36.

168. Verstille, *Mrs. E. J. Verstille's Southern Cookery*, 101–2; Porter, *Mrs. Porter's New Southern Cookery Book*, 264; *Gulf City Cook Book*, 126; Mrs. H. Wilson, *Tested Recipe Cook Book*, 57.

169. Mrs. M. Moncure, *Art of Good Living*, 154–55; and numerous others.

170. St. Paul's Guild, *Household Manual*, 156; and numerous others.

171. Porter, *Mrs. Porter's New Southern Cookery Book*, 195.

172. M. Smith, *Virginia Cookery-Book*, 184.

173. Porter, *Mrs. Porter's New Southern Cookery Book*, 197.

174. Burr, *Secret Eye*, 392.

175. Russell, *Domestic Cook Book*, 8; *Gulf City Cook Book*, 111–12; Hearn, *La Cuisine Creole*, 144.

176. Hearn, *La Cuisine Creole*, 143–44.

177. *Housekeeping in Alabama*, 116.

178. Tyree, *Housekeeping in Old Virginia*, 313–14; McPhail, *F. F. V. Receipt Book*, 165; Mrs. H. Wilson, *Tested Recipe Cook Book*, 115.

179. Hearn, *La Cuisine Creole*, 142.

180. Central Presbyterian Church, *Southern Housekeeper*, 144.

181. Russell, *Domestic Cook Book*, 7; Verstille, *Mrs. E. J. Verstille's Southern Cookery*, 11.

182. Helen [no surname given], "Early Rotary Egg Beaters."

183. Tyree, *Housekeeping in Old Virginia*, 304, 309.

184. Benedict, *Choice Collection*, unpaged ad.

185. Adams and Smith, "Historical Perspectives," 318.

186. Jones and Willaford Grocery Account Book; Atwater and Woods, *Dietary Studies*, 9.

187. Tyree, *Housekeeping in Old Virginia*, 304.

188. Porter, *Mrs. Porter's New Southern Cookery Book*, 227.

189. Fisher, *What Mrs. Fisher Knows*, 29.

190. Lineback, *Preserving the Past*, 71; and numerous others.

191. Hearn, *La Cuisine Creole*, 152; Porter, *Mrs. Porter's New Southern Cookery Book*, 220; Tyree, *Housekeeping in Old Virginia*, 337–39; Russell, *Domestic Cook Book*, 8.

192. Fisher, *What Mrs. Fisher Knows*, 30–31; and numerous others.

193. *Morning News*, November 23, 1896.

194. Augusta, Ga., Second Presbyterian Church, *Choice Recipes*, 72; and numerous others.

195. Tyree, *Housekeeping in Old Virginia*, 309; Russell, *Domestic Cook Book*, 9; Lineback, *Preserving the Past*, 71; Hearn, *La Cuisine Creole*, 144.

196. Gibson, *Maryland and Virginia Cook Book*, 175; and numerous others.

197. Tyree, *Housekeeping in Old Virginia*, 322–24; Hearn, *La Cuisine Creole*, 160.

198. M. Hall, "'Reliable Grocer,'" 277; M. Smith, *Virginia Cookery-Book*, 294.

199. Fisher, *What Mrs. Fisher Knows*, 28–29; Hearn, *La Cuisine Creole*, 157–59; *Gulf City Cook Book*, 110–11.

200. Central Presbyterian Church, *Southern Housekeeper*, 102.

201. *Gulf City Cook Book*, 110–11; and numerous others.

202. "Sweet History."

203. Gibson, *Maryland and Virginia Cook Book*, 200.

204. Tyree, *Housekeeping in Old Virginia*, 325–27; St. Paul's Guild, *Household Manual*, 99, 148; Hearn, *La Cuisine Creole*, 153–54.

205. *Handy Housekeeping*, 56, 59; and numerous others.

206. Hearn, *La Cuisine Creole*, 162.

207. St. Paul's Guild, *Household Manual*, 143; McPhail, *F. F. V. Receipt Book*, 160; Cringan, *Instruction in Cooking*, 259.

208. Lane, *Some Good Things*, 39–40.

209. I have been unable to determine how the switch from the term "icing" to "frosting" occurred. The earliest reference to frosting that I have found is in Child, *American Frugal Housewife*, 120.

210. Hearn, *La Cuisine Creole*, 140–41; Gibson, *Maryland and Virginia Cook Book*, 196.

211. McDermott, *Southern Cakes*, 152.

212. Hearn, *La Cuisine Creole*, 141.

213. McPhail, *F. F. V. Receipt Book*, 162.

214. A. Hill, Mrs. Hill's Southern Practical Cookery, 280; M. Smith, Virginia Cookery-Book, 180; Mrs. H. Wilson, Tested Recipe Cook Book, 75.

215. A. Hill, Mrs. Hill's Southern Practical Cookery, 279.

216. A. Hill, 281.

217. Tyree, Housekeeping in Old Virginia, 423–25; Uhler, Collection of Valuable Receipts, 33–34.

218. Savannah Morning News, December 20, 1895; Gibson, Maryland and Virginia Cook Book, unpaged ads; Cringan, Instruction in Cooking, unpaged ads.

219. Uhler, Collection of Valuable Receipts, 35; Gibson, Maryland and Virginia Cook Book, 154.

220. Verstille, Mrs. E. J. Verstille's Southern Cookery, 119.

221. S. Andrews, South since the War, 224.

222. Hale, History of DeKalb County, 87.

223. Cringan, Instruction in Cooking, unpaged ads.

224. New Orleans Times-Picayune, September 1, 1886, and November 29, 1882.

225. Newnan (Ga.) Herald, April 7, 1885; Columbus (Ga.) Enquirer-Sun, December 21, 1890; Jackson Economist (Winder, Ga.), June 1, 1899.

226. Burr, Secret Eye, 279; Harland, Autobiography, 414.

227. Frissell and Bevier, Dietary Studies of Negroes, 11, 29.

228. Stringer, "Collin Street Bakery."

229. Mizell-Nelson, "French Bread," 45, 46.

230. Washington Bee, February 4, 1888, and June 27, 1896.

231. Du Bois, Negro in Business, 7, 29, 31, 38; Du Bois, Negroes of Farmville, 18, 20.

232. Hounihan, Bakers' and Confectioners' Guide, 34, 83, 86.

233. "Preservation Society of Charleston"; "Historic Charleston Foundation."

234. Ferris, Matzoh Ball Gumbo, 42, 98–99.

235. Mullins, Race and Affluence, 81.

236. Baudier, "Boss Bakers' Protective Association," 22, 23, 25, 27.

237. Luck, "Finding Margaret Haughery," 7, 12–13, 15, 26–27.

238. "Beignet History and Recipe"; "Powdered Sugar Pillows."

239. Baudier, "Boss Bakers' Protective Association," 25, 26.

240. Ferris, Matzoh Ball Gumbo, 114.

241. Mizell-Nelson, "French Bread," 46.

242. Hounihan, Bakers' and Confectioners' Guide, 23.

243. "Fox's Steam Bakery."

244. Figoni, How Baking Works, 280.

245. True Citizen (Waynesboro, Ga.), December 30, 1893.

246. Hounihan, Bakers' and Confectioners' Guide, 27, 29.

CHAPTER 7

1. G. Johnson, "Double Meaning," 13–14.

2. Walker County (Ga.) Messenger, October 4, 1918.

3. Huse, From Saloons to Steak Houses, 131, 134–35.

4. Matthies and Matthies interview, 30; Dodd interview, 43.

5. Du Bois, Negro American Family, 68–79; U.S. Senate, Report on the Condition of Woman and Child Wage-Earners, 123–24.

6. Cast Iron Collector website; Cimarolli, *Bootlegger's Other Daughter*, 21.

7. Council, *Mama Dip's Kitchen*, 5.

8. Cimarolli, *Bootlegger's Other Daughter*, 89; Sadler, *Muzzled Oxen*, 147–48, 170.

9. Page and Wigginton, *Foxfire Book of Appalachian Cookery*, 14.

10. Folley interview, 15.

11. C. Snyder interview, 4.

12. *San Antonio Express*, March 5, 1922; "Corning Pyrex Bakeware"; Goldberg, "Why America Fell in Love with Pyrex."

13. Vlach, *Back of the Big House*, 60; S. Oates interview, 6–7.

14. Shell interview, 6.

15. Mormino and Pozzetta, *Immigrant World*, 244; Margavio and Salomone, *Bread and Respect*, 170.

16. Margavio and Salomone, *Bread and Respect*, 170.

17. Dodd interview, 79; Dickins, *Food and Health*, 13.

18. Sharpless, *Fertile Ground*, 137–38; Dull, *Southern Cooking*, 10–11.

19. Dickins, *Food and Health*, 13.

20. *Athens (Ga.) Banner-Herald*, August 31, 1924; *Union Recorder* (Milledgeville, Ga.), May 14, 1925.

21. Rees, *Refrigeration Nation*, 140–61; Cowan, *More Work for Mother*, 128–43.

22. *Jackson (Ga.) Progress-Argus*, September 12, 1940; *Southern Israelite* (Atlanta), July 19, 1940.

23. Saxon, Dreyer, and Tallant, *Gumbo Ya-Ya*, 413.

24. "Relief Flour Going to 10,000,000 Needy," *New York Times*, May 29, 1932.

25. Poppendieck, *Breadlines*, 165.

26. Relief order 4/7/34, Gov. B. M. Miller, Administrative Files, Alabama Department of Archives and History, https://archives.alabama.gov/teacher/dep/dep4/doc1.html; Ferris, *Edible South*, 161; Alsen, "Alabama Food Frontier."

27. Harvey, *Want in the Midst of Plenty*, 13–14, 16; Cooley, "Freedom's Farms," 204–5.

28. Burkette, "'Stamped Indian,'" 312, 315, 317, 318.

29. Sadler, *Muzzled Oxen*, 130.

30. C. Reynolds, "JIFFY," 64.

31. Dabney, *Smokehouse Ham*, 101.

32. Guderian interview, 15.

33. E. Lewis, *Taste of Country Cooking*, 21–22, 81, 189, 249.

34. Wright, "American Indian Corn Dishes," 163–64.

35. Wright, 166; Chiltoskey and Grant interview, 6.

36. Wright, "American Indian Corn Dishes," 160.

37. Wright, 163–64.

38. Wright, 165.

39. Wright, 165.

40. Butler, *Cleora's Kitchen*, 61; Malone interview, 26.

41. Dodd interview, 78; Council, *Mama Dip's Kitchen*, 36.

42. *Butler (Ga.) Herald*, February 25, 1937; *Jackson Progress-Argus*, June 1, 1939.

43. Hernandez and Hernandez interview, 48.

44. Almanza interview, 96–98.

45. Moreno interview, 10.

46. Dickins, *Nutrition Investigation*, 37.

47. Davis, Gardner, and Gardner, *Deep South*, 379, 382–83, 386; Ownby, *American Dreams*, 71; Granade, "Twilight of Cotton Culture," 270.

48. Engelhardt, *Mess of Greens*, 56, 58.

49. Moss, Moss, Moss, Moss, and Moss interview, 23.

50. Faucette interview, 10; Truitt interview, 20.

51. Kuykendall interview, 16.

52. W. Moss interview, 11; Jones and Park, "From Feed Bags to Fashion," 97.

53. Allen interview, 33.

54. L. Jones, *Mama Learned Us to Work*, 173; Cimarolli, *Bootlegger's Other Daughter*, 94.

55. Olive interview, 15.

56. Walker, *Country Women*, 31; L. Jones, *Mama Learned Us to Work*, 172.

57. *Butler Herald*, September 5, 1929, and October 22, 1931.

58. Faucette interview, 30; Snipes interview, 15.

59. Brown and Brown, "Discourse of Food," 324.

60. Dashiell, *General Laws*, 70.

61. Westervelt, *American Pure Food and Drug Laws*, 100, 440; Bobrow-Strain, "White Bread Bio-politics," 27, 31, 32.

62. Etheridge, *Butterfly Caste*, 217; Bollet, "Politics and Pellagra," 219.

63. Bollet, "Politics and Pellagra," 213, 216–17; Etheridge, *Butterfly Caste*, 211; Bishai and Nalubola, "History of Food Fortification," 42–43.

64. Abbott, *Composition and Food Value*, 13–14.

65. *Athens (Ga.) Daily Herald*, December 4, 1916; *Atlanta Georgian and News*, February 24, 1911; *Instructions to "Wear-Ever" Salesmen*, 92–96.

66. G. Vaughan, *Cotton Renter's Son*, 18.

67. Hurtado interview, 24, 43.

68. W. Hall, *Conecuh People*, 109.

69. Weir interview, 13–14.

70. Sadler, *Muzzled Oxen*, 54, 91, 227, 256.

71. MacDougall interview, 40.

72. Colquitt, *Savannah Cook Book*, 17; Breckinridge, *From Soup to Nuts*, 13.

73. Fox, *Blue Grass Cook Book*, 3–4; and numerous others.

74. Dabney, *Smokehouse Ham*, 114, 115; Ellis, *Biscuits*, 30. I have been unable to discover the origin of the name "cathead."

75. "Refrigerated Biscuits Part of Food History," *Toledo (Ohio) Blade*, November 10, 2008; Kleber, *Encyclopedia of Louisville*, s.v. "Lively Burgess Willoughby"; "Method and Means of Packing Dough."

76. J. Gray, *Business without Boundary*, 210–13; Civitello, *Baking Powder Wars*, 153–57.

77. *Brenham (Tex.) Banner-Press*, March 18, 1932.

78. Wallach, *Every Nation*, 55–56.

79. Joe interview, 7; Robinson interview, 5.

80. Wharton interview, 13.

81. *Butler Herald*, September 26, 1935; *Good Housekeeping* 99, no. 6 (December 1934), 138.

82. Jamison, *Tea Kettle*, 69; and numerous others.

83. Butler, *Cleora's Kitchen*, 45.
84. McWilliams, *Pecan*, 56–62, 77.
85. Carver, *How to Grow the Peanut*, 9–16.
86. Mormino and Pozzetta, *Immigrant World*, 244.
87. Bryant, *Athens Woman's Club*, 46, 51; Dull, *Southern Cooking*, 160; Knoxville Woman's Building Association, *Knoxville Cook Book*, 16.
88. Behr, "Eula Mae Doré," 146; Wattigny, "Food for Thought."
89. E. Lewis, *Taste of Country Cooking*, 11–13, 46.
90. Sadler, *Muzzled Oxen*, 65.
91. Folley interview, 19–20.
92. Landrey, *Boardin' in the Thicket*, 44; Pash interview, 11.
93. Butler, *Cleora's Kitchen*, 100; *Favorite Recipes of Alabama Housewives*, 12.
94. Circle of Service, *King's Daughters Cook Book*, 50–51; and numerous others.
95. Matthies and Matthies interview, 31.
96. McKey, *From Tea Cakes to Tamales*, 246–50; Skrabanek, *We're Czechs*, 135.
97. Vaughn, *Culinary Echoes from Dixie*, 139.
98. Dull, *Southern Cooking*, 167, 168.
99. Dickins, *Food and Health*, 14.
100. *Community League Cook Book*, 37.
101. Veit, "Eating Cotton," 398–99.
102. Shurtleff and Aoyagi, "History of Soy Oil Shortening."
103. Veit, "Eating Cotton," 404.
104. Westervelt, *American Pure Food and Drug Laws*, 270.
105. "From the Sweet Past," Karo Syrup website.
106. Richard, *New Orleans Cookbook*, 112.
107. Berenstein, "Making a Global Sensation," 399–400, 403.
108. L. Jones, "Gender, Race, and Itinerant Commerce," 77, 80.
109. L. Jones, *Mama Learned Us to Work*, 58; Walker, *Country Women*, 8.
110. Bomgardner, "Problem with Vanilla."
111. Westervelt, *American Pure Food and Drug Laws*, 186; Gorvett, "Delicious Flavour with a Toxic Secret."
112. Westervelt, *American Pure Food and Drug Laws*, 99.
113. Berenstein, "Making a Global Sensation," 416; Westervelt, *American Pure Food and Drug Laws*, 483.
114. Caufield interview, 68.
115. Kyle Baptist Church Ladies Aid and Missionary Society, *Kyle Baptist Church Cook Book*, 75; and numerous others.
116. Warren, *Mississippi Cook Book*, 107.
117. Westervelt, *American Pure Food and Drug Laws*, 469.
118. David Shields, "Pie Wars: Sweet Potato v. Pumpkin," Facebook, November 23, 2014; www.facebook.com/david.s.shields/; *Favorite Southern Recipes*, 87–88.
119. Landrey, *Boardin' in the Thicket*, 83; Truitt interview, 18–19.
120. Landrey, *Boardin' in the Thicket*, 83; Bass, *Plain Southern Eating*, 62–63.
121. *Favorite Southern Recipes*, 83–84.

122. Mormino and Pozzetta, *Immigrant World*, 279; Kohn, "Development of Dairy Farming," 188.

123. Mormino and Pozzetta, *Immigrant World*, 278–79.

124. Kohn, "Development of Dairy Farming," 192, 194; Hatcher, "Dairying in the South," 60; B. Moss, "Dairy Industry in Alabama."

125. Circle of Service, *King's Daughters Cook Book*, 2; *Calvary Church Circle Cook Book*, 12; Arlington County School Federation, *Washington Lee High School Cook Book*, inside front cover.

126. Sharpless, "'She Ought to Have Taken Those Cakes,'" 54–56.

127. Strom, "Problems Confronting the Dairy Industry"; *Lone Star Cook Book*, 60.

128. Dashiell, *General Laws*, 65–66.

129. Okihiro, *Pineapple Culture*, 132, 133.

130. Dull, *Southern Cooking*, 178; Lustig, Sondheim, and Rensel, *Southern Cook Book*, 38.

131. Hoganson, *Consumer's Imperium*, 115; Koeppel, *Banana*, 55, 60, 62.

132. "History," Franklin Baker website.

133. Parks, *Bravetart*, 161; *Atlanta Georgian and News*, June 27, 1911; *Favorite Southern Recipes*, 76–77.

134. Sadler, *Muzzled Oxen*, 91, 138.

135. Page and Wigginton, *Foxfire Book of Appalachian Cookery*, 300–301.

136. Degrate interview.

137. Bass, *Plain Southern Eating*, 62.

138. Folley interview, 25; Washington interview, 26; G. Vaughan, *Cotton Renter's Son*, 65.

139. Bass, *Plain Southern Eating*, 62.

140. Landrey, *Boardin' in the Thicket*, 137; E. Lewis, *Taste of Country Cooking*, 110–11; 140–41; Page and Wigginton, *Foxfire Book of Appalachian Cookery*, 222–23.

141. Degrate interview, 12–13.

142. Dodd interview, 80; B. Stone, *Roanoke Cook Book*, 88; and numerous others.

143. Juneau, *Celebrating with St. Joseph Altars*, 1.

144. Juneau, 102–3, 117–30.

145. Mormino and Pozzetta, *Immigrant World*, 245.

146. Margavio and Salomone, *Bread and Respect*, 245; Juneau, *Celebrating with St. Joseph Altars*, 27, 91–94.

147. U.S. Senate, *Report on the Condition of Woman and Child Wage-Earners*, 41, 45–46, 94–98, 109.

148. Chase, *Dooky Chase Cookbook*, 216.

149. Bienvenu, Brasseaux, and Brasseaux, *Stir the Pot*, 23; Feibleman, *American Cooking*, 152.

150. Sims, "Layers of Love."

151. Bass, *Plain Southern Eating*, 78–79.

152. Davis interview, 7–8.

153. Severson, "Festiveness."

154. Alsen, "Alabama Food Frontier"; McDermott, *Southern Cakes*, 128–29.

155. B. Moncure, *Emma Jane's Souvenir Cook Book*, 10.

156. "Our History," Hobart website; Kindy, "For 100 Years."

157. "History," Sunbeam website; *Jackson Herald* (Jefferson, Ga.), December 12, 1935.

158. *Good Housekeeping* 99, no. 6 (December 1934), 213; *Jackson Progress-Argus*, December 4, 1936.

159. Kyle Baptist Church Ladies Aid and Missionary Society, *Kyle Baptist Church Cook Book*, 15; and numerous others.

160. Agee, *Cotton Tenants*, 94.

161. Landrey, *Boardin' in the Thicket*, 168; Rhett and Gay, *200 Years*, 191–92.

162. Dodd interview, 43–44.

163. Dull, *Southern Cooking*, 227; and numerous others.

164. Knoxville Woman's Building Association, *Knoxville Cook Book*, 180; Bryant, *Athens Woman's Club*, 110; E. Hayes, *Kentucky Cook Book*, 9.

165. *Favorite Southern Recipes*, 156–57; *Community League Cook Book*, 51; Woman's Auxiliary, Second Baptist Church, *Second Baptist Church Cook Book*, 32; Dull, *Southern Cooking*, 257.

166. Fox, *Blue Grass Cook Book*, 253; Rhett and Gay, *200 Years*, 184; Lustig, Sondheim, and Rensel, *Southern Cook Book*, 42; E. Hayes, *Kentucky Cook Book*, 9.

167. Kawash, *Candy*, 146.

168. Huggins, *Tried and True*, 183, 214.

169. E. Hayes, *Kentucky Cook Book*, 12.

170. *Favorite Southern Recipes*, 130–32; E. Lewis, *Taste of Country Cooking*, 128–29.

171. Angelou, *Hallelujah!*, 13.

172. *Favorite Southern Recipes*, 172–74; B. Moncure, *Emma Jane's Souvenir Cook Book*, 51; and numerous others.

173. *Dalton Cook Book*, 53; and numerous others.

174. C. Claiborne, *Craig Claiborne's Southern Cooking*, 290.

175. Castle, "History behind the Legendary Lady Baltimore Cake."

176. Eddington, "Lady Baltimore Cake."

177. Vaughn, *Culinary Echoes from Dixie*, 203.

178. *Dalton Cook Book*, 53; Dull, *Southern Cooking*, 231.

179. "Forbidding Fruit"; Butterick, *Story of a Pantry Shelf*, 130–34.

180. Bryant, *Athens Woman's Club*, 128; Dull, *Southern Cooking*, 234.

181. *Washington Bee*, July 5, 1902; November 7, 1908; September 9, 1911.

182. *Richmond Dispatch*, April 28, 1900; Timlin, *Sandwiches*, 156; E. Hayes, *Kentucky Cook Book*, 10.

183. Eddington, "Bride's Cake."

184. "Cake for a Wedding," *Beaumont (Tex.) Enterprise*, June 3, 1905.

185. "Kinard—McCallum," *Jackson (Ga.) Argus*, October 29, 1896.

186. "No Wedding Complete without Groom Cake: Here's Nifty Recipe," *Beaumont Enterprise*, June 27, 1919.

187. Andrews and Kelly, *Hammond-Harwood House*, 287; S. Hill, *Progressive Farmer's Southern Cookbook*, 264; MacDonald, *Best from Helen Corbitt's Kitchens*, 338.

188. "Mr. Hammond John Entertained," *Gainesville (Ga.) News*, October 6, 1915.

189. Hicks interview, 2.

190. *Favorite Southern Recipes*, 101; and numerous others.

191. Woman's Auxiliary, Second Baptist Church, *Second Baptist Cook Book*, 66; and numerous others.

192. *YWCA Cook Book*, 183; and numerous others.

193. Fox, *Blue Grass Cook Book*, 234; *Dalton Cook Book*, 67.

194. Stoney, *Carolina Rice Cook Book*, 25.

195. Washburn, "French Market"; *Charleston Recipes*, 9.

196. Landrey, *Boardin' in the Thicket*, 40; M. Brown, *Southern Cook Book*, 256.

197. Butler, *Cleora's Kitchen*, 29.

198. Baird, "Baird, Ninia Lilla."

199. McCleary, "Shaping a New Role," 267; McCleary, "'Seizing the Opportunity,'" 122.

200. McCleary, "Shaping a New Role," 286–87.

201. McCleary, "'Seizing the Opportunity,'" 116.

202. Clark, "Mary McLeod Bethune"; National Council of Negro Women, *Black Family Reunion Cookbook*, 147.

203. *Beaumont Enterprise*, April 26, 1913; *The Standard* (Cedartown, Ga.), April 15, 1920; *Houston Post*, March 13, 1921.

204. Bobrow-Strain, "White Bread Bio-politics," 20.

205. "Sixteenth Annual Convention of the Texas Association," 76.

206. Ridgle interview, 10; Dodd interview, 82.

207. Durr interview, 42.

208. Bobrow-Strain, "White Bread Bio-politics," 20; Steen, *Flour Milling*, 123–24.

209. Du Bois, *Negro American Family*, 117–19, 135–42, 147–52; U.S. Senate, *Report on the Condition of Woman and Child Wage-Earners*, 51, 53, 55, 72, 81, 123–25; Dickins, *Study of Food Habits*, 22, 26–27, 31–37; Stiebeling and Phipard, *Diets of Families*, 25–26.

210. Werlin, "Tales of a Traveler," 93; Truitt interview, 16; *Alamance Gleaner* (Graham, N.C.), February 18, 1915.

211. "Shipley History."

212. McGehee, "Krispy Kreme," 191.

213. Peckenpaugh, "Más Cubano," 10.

214. Mizell-Nelson, "French Bread," 46; "Our Story," Leidenheimer Baking Company website.

215. Nystrom, *Creole Italian*, 84–85, 123.

216. Ferris, *Matzoh Ball Gumbo*, 45, 48–49.

217. *Southern Israelite* (Atlanta), October 15, 1930.

218. Stiebeling and Phipard, *Diets of Families*, 26.

219. *Richmond Planet*, March 10, 1906.

220. *Richmond Planet*, December 20, 1930.

221. Raskin, "Beckroge's."

222. Ferris, *Matzoh Ball Gumbo*, 45, 48–49.

223. *Fort Worth Star-Telegram*, August 12, 1918; *Dallas Morning News*, April 5, 1919, and February 10, 1926; Kolb, "'Hand-Held' before It Was Fashionable."

224. Stanonis and Wallace, "Tasting New Orleans," 7, 10, 12, 13, 14.

225. Magee, *MoonPie*, 22–23.

226. Magee, 29, 31, 32, 34.

227. C. Crane, *General Sanitary Survey of Nashville*, 12–13.

228. Bennett, "Cleaning Up the American City."

229. Circle of Service, *King's Daughters Cook Book*, 53; *Fort Worth Star-Telegram*, October 29, 1917.

230. Fort Worth Star-Telegram, July 2, 1911.

231. Fort Worth Star-Telegram, June 10, 1911, and December 4, 1918.

232. Brunswick (Ga.) News, January 19, 1902; Walker County (Ga.) Herald, March 28, 1913.

233. Waycross (Ga.) Evening Herald, September 15, 1911.

CHAPTER 8

1. Moody, Coming of Age, 34, 43, 45.

2. Cobb, Most Southern Place, 257–58.

3. Cooley, "Freedom's Farms," 206–7; Potorti, "'What We Eat Is Politics.'"

4. Blejwas, Story of Alabama, 212, 214; "Georgia Gilmore"; Nadasen, Household Workers Unite, 27–32; Edge, Potlikker Papers, 15–24.

5. Ballinger, History of Sugar Marketing, 48.

6. M. Thomas, Riveting and Rationing, 94.

7. Miller, Kitchen in War Production, 16.

8. Ballinger, History of Sugar Marketing, 50, 54; M. Thomas, Riveting and Rationing, 94.

9. M. Thomas, Riveting and Rationing, 97, 101–2.

10. Sharpless, Cooking in Other Women's Kitchens, 179.

11. Cimarolli, Bootlegger's Other Daughter, 129.

12. Pando, Stirring Up Memories, 81–82.

13. Council, Mama Dip's Kitchen, 193.

14. J. Parker, "Making Do," 15–16.

15. M. Thomas, Riveting and Rationing, 103; H. Miller, Kitchen in War Production, 21.

16. Paddleford, "Batting for Butter."

17. Cimarolli, Bootlegger's Other Daughter, 129–30.

18. Bentley, Eating for Victory, 107.

19. Ballinger, History of Sugar Marketing, 58.

20. Cimarolli, Bootlegger's Other Daughter, 115.

21. Dickins, Welch, and Christian, Industrialization, 7; Rees, Refrigeration Nation, 163–64.

22. Jackson Progress-Argus, September 29, 1949.

23. Houston (Tex.) Chronicle, May 8, 1960.

24. Dickins, "Food Patterns," 426.

25. W. Hall, Conecuh People, 103.

26. Wightman and Cate, Early Days of Coastal Georgia, 181.

27. "VIP Biscuit Bash," King Biscuit Blues Festival website.

28. Flexner, Dixie Dishes, 257.

29. M. Brown, Southern Cook Book, 209; S. Hill, Progressive Farmer's Southern Cookbook, 31; Andrews and Kelly, Hammond-Harwood House, 30, 31; Cook's Tour of Shreveport, 71.

30. Boddie, "Cornbread," 44.

31. "Breads Made with Cornmeal."

32. Strobel, Princess Pamela's Soul Food Cookbook, 149; Lundy, Shuck Beans, 238; and numerous others.

33. Mendes, African Heritage Cookbook, 189.

34. Meade, Recipes from the Old South, 18; and numerous others.

35. Pohick Cookery, 7; M. Brown, Southern Cook Book, 212; Andrews and Kelly, Hammond-Harwood House, 32; S. Hill, Progressive Farmer's Southern Cookbook, 28–29, 33.

36. Smart-Grosvenor, *Vibration Cooking*, 37; M. Brown, *Southern Cook Book*, 213; *Gasparilla Cookbook*, 26, 29; Andrews and Kelly, *Hammond-Harwood House*, 31.

37. *Victuals and Vitamins*, 89, 90; and numerous others.

38. S. Hill, *Progressive Farmer's Southern Cookbook*, 30, 31; *River Road Recipes*, 40; email correspondence from Libby Barker Willis, Fort Worth, Texas, June 6, 2019.

39. *River Road Recipes*, 40; Bowers, *Plantation Recipes*, 16; S. Hill, *Progressive Farmer's Southern Cookbook*, 29, 30.

40. M. Brown, *Southern Cook Book*, 213.

41. Corbitt, *Helen Corbitt's Cookbook*, 227; Junior League of New Orleans, *Plantation Cookbook*, 214; McLennan County Medical Auxiliary (hereafter MCMA), *Gingerbread*, 135.

42. S. Hill, *Progressive Farmer's Southern Cookbook*, 33.

43. S. Hill, 28.

44. Yarbrough, "Grandma's Table," 92.

45. *Victuals and Vitamins*, 77; *Cook's Tour of Shreveport*, 69.

46. Lundy, *Shuck Beans*, 257.

47. "Butter Two Biscuits While They're Hot," 101.

48. Lundy, *Shuck Beans*, 259–61, 264; *River Road Recipes*, 37; *Gasparilla Cookbook*, 27.

49. S. Hill, *Progressive Farmer's Southern Cookbook*, 25, 27; Andrews and Kelly, *Hammond-Harwood House*, 25; *Recipes Collected and Tested by the Junior League of Columbus, Georgia*, 124; *Cook's Tour of Shreveport*, 70.

50. *River Road Recipes*, 37; S. Hill, *Progressive Farmer's Southern Cookbook*, 27, 28; *Cook's Tour of Shreveport*, 70; M. Brown, *Southern Cook Book*, 220.

51. "Don't Call Me Angel Biscuits"; Ellis, *Biscuits*, 28; *Talk about Good!*, 27.

52. *Gasparilla Cookbook*, 28.

53. S. Hill, *Progressive Farmer's Southern Cookbook*, 27.

54. *Recipes Collected and Tested by the Junior League of Columbus, Georgia*, 121.

55. M. Brown, *Southern Cook Book*, 214.

56. M. Brown, 240, 241; Feibleman, *American Cooking*, 73.

57. *Kingsport (Tenn.) Times*, March 17, 1949.

58. *Recipes Collected and Tested by the Junior League of Columbus, Georgia*, 122.

59. *Recipes Collected and Tested by the Junior League of Columbus, Georgia*, 123; and numerous others.

60. *Gasparilla Cookbook*, 24; and numerous others.

61. MCMA, *Gingerbread*, 144; *River Road Recipes*, 39; *Cook's Tour of Shreveport*, 78; and numerous others.

62. S. Hill, *Progressive Farmer's Southern Cookbook*, 38, 39; and numerous others.

63. *Victuals and Vitamins*, 84; and numerous others.

64. *Victuals and Vitamins*, 78; MCMA, *Gingerbread*, 136, 138.

65. Grace W. Gray, "Successful Homemaking," *Houston Home Journal* (Perry, Ga.), December 4, 1930; *Forsyth (Ga.) County News*, September 12, 1940.

66. Corbitt, *Helen Corbitt's Cookbook*, 229, 231–32; *Cook's Tour of Shreveport*, 85, 86, 87; *Talk about Good!*, 39; S. Hill, *Progressive Farmer's Southern Cookbook*, 40.

67. *Cook's Tour of Shreveport*, 67; M. Brown, *Southern Cook Book*, 222; S. Hill, *Progressive Farmer's Southern Cookbook*, 40, 51–52.

68. Junior League of New Orleans, *Plantation Cookbook*, 215; *Talk about Good!*, 43, 44.

69. *Cook's Tour of Shreveport*, 67.

70. Feibleman, *American Cooking*, 138–40, 163.

71. Lundy, *Shuck Beans*, 248.

72. Corbitt, *Helen Corbitt's Cookbook*, 221.

73. MCMA, *Gingerbread*, 133; "Yeast Breads Rise to the Occasion," 69.

74. *Gasparilla Cookbook*, 22; *Cook's Tour of Shreveport*, 81, 82, 83, 84.

75. S. Hill, *Progressive Farmer's Southern Cookbook*, 43; and numerous others.

76. Mendes, *African Heritage Cookbook*, 195.

77. *Recipes Collected and Tested by the Junior League of Columbus, Georgia*, 125; and numerous others.

78. M. Brown, *Southern Cook Book*, 214; S. Hill, *Progressive Farmer's Southern Cookbook*, 44.

79. Flexner, *Dixie Dishes*, 13–14.

80. *River Road Recipes*, 44; *Gasparilla Cookbook*, 32, 33; S. Hill, *Progressive Farmer's Southern Cookbook*, 44; M. Brown, *Southern Cook Book*, 214.

81. Butler, *Cleora's Kitchen*, 111.

82. Andrews and Kelly, *Hammond-Harwood House*, 37; *Victuals and Vitamins*, 1962 supplement, 181; S. Hill, *Progressive Farmer's Southern Cookbook*, 50; *Cook's Tour of Shreveport*, 82, 85; *Gasparilla Cookbook*, 33.

83. M. Brown, *Southern Cook Book*, 221; *Cook's Tour of Shreveport*, 86; *Victuals and Vitamins*, 81–82.

84. Rod Arkell, "GIs Who Developed Rolls Battle over Dough," *Miami Herald*, August 13, 1950; J. Gray, *Business without Boundary*, 253; "Rolls You Buy, Then Bake," 119; William, "Quick-Bake Roll Pioneers' Suit."

85. *Dallas Morning News*, January 24, 1954.

86. *Talk about Good!*, 439; Hunter, *Secrets*, 237; *Victuals and Vitamins*, 101.

87. Watts and Watts, *Jesse's Book*, 153–54.

88. "Frozen Pie Crust Dough."

89. "Frozen Bakery Items Aid Dessert."

90. *River Road Recipes*, 204.

91. *Good Housekeeping* 162, no. 3 (March 1966): 53.

92. *Recipes Collected and Tested by the Junior League of Columbus, Georgia*, 139; *River Road Recipes*, 205; *Talk about Good!*, 439.

93. *Victuals and Vitamins*, 100; *River Road Recipes*, 207; *Cook's Tour of Shreveport*, 269; Andrews and Kelly, *Hammond-Harwood House*, 229, 232.

94. Council, *Mama Dip's Kitchen*, 8–9; Feibleman, *American Cooking*, 197; and numerous others.

95. *Dallas Morning News*, January 13, 1956; "About Us," Lucky Leaf website.

96. *Cook's Tour of Shreveport*, 258.

97. Bowers, *Plantation Recipes*, 142; Mendes, *African Heritage Cookbook*, 219.

98. *Cook's Tour of Shreveport*, 261; *Talk about Good!*, 431.

99. *Cook's Tour of Shreveport*, 267; *Talk about Good!*, 444; MCMA, *Gingerbread*, 161; S. Hill, *Progressive Farmer's Southern Cookbook*, 218, 227.

100. *Talk about Good!*, 441; Van Duzor, *Fascinating Foods*, 62.

101. *River Road Recipes*, 200; *Talk about Good!*, 447.

102. *River Road Recipes*, 200. My mom decorated sugar cookies with them in the 1960s. I still do.

103. Corbitt, *Helen Corbitt's Cookbook*, 275; *Victuals and Vitamins*, 94; *Recipes Collected and Tested by the Junior League of Columbus, Georgia*, 140.

104. M. Brown, *Southern Cook Book*, 296, 297; S. Hill, *Progressive Farmer's Southern Cookbook*, 225.

105. *Talk about Good!*, 438; M. Brown, *Southern Cook Book*, 296.

106. Landrey, *Boardin' in the Thicket*, 106; and numerous others.

107. Council, *Mama Dip's Kitchen*, 6–7; and numerous others.

108. *River Road Recipes*, 206; and numerous others.

109. *Victuals and Vitamins*, 96; *River Road Recipes*, 204; M. Brown, *Southern Cook Book*, 298, 299.

110. *Talk about Good!*, 440, 441; and numerous others.

111. *Lawrenceburg's Treasury*, 83; and numerous others.

112. *River Road Recipes*, 204; *Talk about Good!*, 435; Van Duzor, *Fascinating Foods*, 62.

113. Sloan, *Key West*, 38.

114. Sloan, 33–34.

115. Parks, *Bravetart*, 171–72.

116. S. Brown, "Key Lime Pie."

117. *Talk about Good!*, 432; and numerous others.

118. Butler, *Cleora's Kitchen*, 143; Strobel, *Princess Pamela's Soul Food Cookbook*, 213; *Talk about Good!*, 433, 440.

119. *Victuals and Vitamins*, 101.

120. *Victuals and Vitamins*, 99; *Talk about Good!*, 434; *Cook's Tour of Shreveport*, 266.

121. *Cook's Tour of Shreveport*, 266; Corbitt, *Helen Corbitt's Cookbook*, 275; *Victuals and Vitamins*, 99.

122. *Talk about Good!*, 435; M. Brown, *Southern Cook Book*, 305.

123. *Talk about Good!*, 435, 436.

124. S. Hill, *Progressive Farmer's Southern Cookbook*, 225, 229; *Victuals and Vitamins*, 97.

125. *Victuals and Vitamins*, 100, 101; *River Road Recipes*, 203.

126. *Fort Worth Star-Telegram*, April 22, 1955.

127. *River Road Recipes*, 203; *Cook's Tour of Shreveport*, 263.

128. Bowers, *Plantation Recipes*, 142; Woman's Club of South Jacksonville, *Cook Book*, 79; "Fried Pies Like Grandma Made," 61.

129. Mendes, *African Heritage Cookbook*, 220; and numerous others.

130. *Victuals and Vitamins*, 98; M. Brown, *Southern Cook Book*, 306; Andrews and Kelly, *Hammond-Harwood House*, 231.

131. *Gasparilla Cookbook*, 206; and others.

132. *Talk about Good!*, 341; *Cook's Tour of Shreveport*, 285; Lundy, *Shuck Beans*, 314.

133. City Federation, *Feastin' with the Federation*, 86; and numerous others.

134. Tea Cake Project website; Mackey, *Tea Cake Roundup*, 12, 20.

135. *River Road Recipes*, 195, 196; S. Hill, *Progressive Farmer's Southern Cookbook*, 288; Villas, *My Mother's Southern Kitchen*, 9–10.

136. *Cook's Tour of Shreveport*, 278; and numerous others.

137. *Victuals and Vitamins*, 144, 145, 146; *River Road Recipes*, 190, 191; *Cook's Tour of Shreveport*, 274, 275.

138. *Talk about Good!*, 399; *Favorite Recipes from Belle Haven Kitchens*, 42.

139. Hunter, *Secrets*, 296; and numerous others.

140. *Recipes Collected and Tested by the Junior League of Columbus, Georgia*, 154; and numerous others.

141. *River Road Recipes*, 194, 195; MCMA, *Gingerbread*, 151; S. Hill, *Progressive Farmer's Southern Cookbook*, 301.

142. *Recipes Collected and Tested by the Junior League of Columbus, Georgia*, 155; and numerous others.

143. *River Road Recipes*, 196; and numerous others.

144. *River Road Recipes*, 198; Locker, "How Hello Dolly Bars Got Their Funny and Magical Name"; *Cook's Tour of Shreveport*, 280.

145. *Victuals and Vitamins*, 151; and numerous others.

146. *Victuals and Vitamins*, 147, 153; *River Road Recipes*, 192; *Cook's Tour of Shreveport*, 278; *Talk about Good!*, 403, 409.

147. *Recipes Collected and Tested by the Junior League of Columbus, Georgia*, 154; and numerous others.

148. *Victuals and Vitamins*, 149; S. Hill, *Progressive Farmer's Southern Cookbook*, 294; *River Road Recipes*, 193, 194; *Talk about Good!*, 409, 410.

149. *River Road Recipes*, 197; M. Brown, *Southern Cook Book*, 286–87.

150. All Saints Episcopal Guild, *Inverness Cook Book*, 124; and numerous others.

151. S. Hill, *Progressive Farmer's Southern Cookbook*, 285; and numerous others.

152. *Victuals and Vitamins*, 149, 151, 152; and numerous others.

153. Andrews and Kelly, *Hammond-Harwood House*, 392; and numerous others.

154. *Talk about Good!*, 400, 404; and numerous others.

155. Hunter, *Secrets*, 256–57.

156. *Recipes Collected and Tested by the Junior League of Columbus, Georgia*, 148.

157. Shapiro, *Something from the Oven*, 72–73.

158. Shapiro, 73, 76.

159. J. Gray, *Business without Boundary*, 252.

160. Shapiro, *Something from the Oven*, 74–75.

161. *Talk about Good!*, 387.

162. *River Road Recipes*, 182; *Talk about Good!*, 387.

163. *Cook's Tour of Shreveport*, 234.

164. *Talk about Good!*, 387; "History of Gelatin, Gelatine, and JELL-O"; Erin Anderson, "Molded Magic," 53.

165. *Victuals and Vitamins*, 1962 supplement, 181, 182; *Cook's Tour of Shreveport*, 23.

166. MCMA, *Gingerbread*, 174.

167. McDermott, *Southern Cakes*, 78.

168. MCMA, *Gingerbread*, 172; *Cook's Tour of Shreveport*, 229, 239; *Talk about Good!*, 391.

169. M. Brown, *Southern Cook Book*, 260, 261.

170. Sterling, "Brief, Delightful History of the Bundt Pan."

171. Chavarría-Cháirez, "Bertha M. Chavarría," 65, 67–68.

172. Mendes, *African Heritage Cookbook*, 209.

173. Feibleman, *American Cooking*, 152; MCMA, *Gingerbread*, 173.

174. *River Road Recipes*, 184; *Cook's Tour of Shreveport*, 248; S. Hill, *Progressive Farmer's Southern Cookbook*, 260, 261, 263.

175. *Cook's Tour of Shreveport*, 249.

176. M. Brown, *Southern Cook Book*, 255.

177. *Victuals and Vitamins*, 125; *Cook's Tour of Shreveport*, 221; M. Brown, *Southern Cook Book*, 264.

178. S. Hill, *Progressive Farmer's Southern Cookbook*, 265; *Gasparilla Cookbook*, 228.

179. Corbitt, *Helen Corbitt's Cookbook*, 259.

180. *Talk about Good!*, 363; M. Brown, *Southern Cook Book*, 265.

181. *Gasparilla Cookbook*, 241; S. Hill, *Progressive Farmer's Southern Cookbook*, 250.

182. *Talk about Good!*, 372, 373, 374, 375; MCMA, *Gingerbread*, 173; *Gasparilla Cookbook*, 228, 229.

183. *Gasparilla Cookbook*, 240; M. Brown, *Southern Cook Book*, 240; S. Hill, *Progressive Farmer's Southern Cookbook*, 239; Sturges, "South Takes to Cakes," 42.

184. *Recipes of the Deep South*, 58.

185. M. Brown, *Southern Cook Book*, 250–51; Andrews and Kelly, *Hammond-Harwood House*, 285; S. Hill, *Progressive Farmer's Southern Cookbook*, 240.

186. "Recipe of the Day," *Dallas Morning News*, June 3, 1957.

187. Booke, "Did You Know?"

188. B. Thompson, "All Around the Town"; Bond, "Texas Sheet Cake"; Harbster, "Great Sheet Cake Mystery."

189. *Roxboro Baptist Church Cook Book*, 11; and numerous others.

190. Severson, "Red Velvet Cake: A Classic, Not a Gimmick," *New York Times*, May 12, 2014; Perry, "South's Most Storied Cakes."

191. Kayal, "Reviving the Tea Cake."

192. Sturges, *Our Best Recipes*, 59; York, "Classic Cola Sheet Cake."

193. MCMA, *Gingerbread*, 176; Butler, *Cleora's Kitchen*, 184.

194. Sturges, *Our Best Recipes*, 67.

195. S. Hill, *Progressive Farmer's Southern Cookbook*, 192; and numerous others.

196. "Favorite Recipes," *El Reno (Okla.) American*, July 12, 1956.

197. Booke, "Did You Know?," places the cake in Dallas in 1957.

198. *River Road Recipes*, 165; and numerous others.

199. *Cook's Tour of Shreveport*, 288; M. Brown, *Southern Cook Book*, 232; *Recipes Collected and Tested by the Junior League of Columbus, Georgia*, 138.

200. *Victuals and Vitamins*, 103; *Gasparilla Cookbook*, 217; M. Brown, *Southern Cook Book*, 241.

201. *Victuals and Vitamins*, 104; *Cook's Tour of Shreveport*, 286.

202. *Recipes Collected and Tested by the Junior League of Columbus, Georgia*, 131.

203. Butler, *Cleora's Kitchen*, 48–49; *Gasparilla Cookbook*, 212; *Cook's Tour of Shreveport*, 287, 289.

204. *River Road Recipes*, 172; *Talk about Good!*, 377.

205. Bowers, *Plantation Recipes*, 148; and numerous others.

206. McDermott, *Southern Cakes*, 43.

207. "Huguenot Torte History and Recipe"; *Victuals and Vitamins*, 108.

208. *River Road Recipes*, 167; *Talk about Good!*, 346, 347.

209. Corbitt, *Helen Corbitt's Cookbook*, 252.

210. McDermott, *Southern Cakes*, 152; and numerous others.

211. Darden and Darden, *Spoonbread*, 219.

212. Corbitt, *Helen Corbitt's Cookbook*, 252.

213. *Recipes Collected and Tested by the Junior League of Columbus, Georgia*, 153; Blount, "Raising Cane."

214. *River Road Recipes*, 188; S. Hill, *Progressive Farmer's Southern Cookbook*, 36; *Talk about Good!*, 397, 398.

215. *Cook's Tour of Shreveport*, 255; *River Road Recipes*, 188.

216. *Talk about Good!*, 398.

217. *River Road Recipes*, 189; *Talk about Good!*, 397; MCMA, *Gingerbread*, 143.

218. MCMA, *Gingerbread*, 167; M. Brown, *Southern Cook Book*, 255; McDermott, *Southern Cakes*, 27.

219. Memorial page for Lucile P. Plowden Harvey, Find a Grave website.

220. *River Road Recipes*, 207.

221. M. Brown, *Southern Cook Book*, 237, 244, 253, 265, 283, 302.

222. Aggarwal-Schifellite, "Long, Strange Career of the Mrs. America Pageant."

223. *Talk about Good!*, 349; "Mrs. Ann LeJeune Is Louisiana 'Mrs. America' Contest Entry," *Kaplan (La.) Journal*, April 4, 1963.

224. Feldman, "Houston Says Goodbye."

225. Ferris, *Matzoh Ball Gumbo*, 55.

226. Curry, "Lavishly Layered"; Mullenweg, "Houston Doberge Project."

227. McDermott, *Southern Cakes*, 107.

229. Butler, *Cleora's Kitchen*, 53–56.

229. Roark, "Cracking the Glass Ceiling," 251; Roark, "Cooking for a Living," 234; Stewart, "Fine Legacy," 48–55.

230. *Dallas City Directory*, 1941 and 1955.

231. Ferris, *Matzoh Ball Gumbo*, 246–47.

232. *Dallas City Directory*, 1941 and 1961.

233. Bragg, "Back to the Bayou," 249.

234. Raskin, "Bullwinkel's Whipped Cream Cake."

235. Mullins, *Glazed America*, 65.

236. Mullins, 65, 68; Mazzocchi, "Krispy Kreme Doughnut Corporation"; *Southern Israelite* (Atlanta), April 22, 1938; *Jackson Progress-Argus*, October 10, 1968.

237. Feibleman, *American Cooking*, 25.

238. Feibleman, 54; "Beignet History and Recipe"; "Powdered Sugar Pillows."

239. Nystrom, *Creole Italian*, 119, 123–25, 129, 132.

240. Orso, *St. Joseph Altar Traditions*, 12–13, 50, 53, 55.

241. Stanonis and Wallace, "Tasting New Orleans," 14, 15.

242. *Gasparilla Cookbook*, 19.

243. Robles interview, 38.

244. Bielamowicz interview, 15–16.

245. B. McDonald, *Food Power*, 56; Burk, "Pounds and Percentages," 593, 595, 598; Bobrow-Strain, "White Bread Bio-politics," 26.

246. *Dallas City Directory*, 1941 and 1955.

247. *Dallas Morning News*, February 7, 1968.

248. Etheridge, *Butterfly Caste*, 211–14; Bishai and Nalubola, "History of Food Fortification," 44; Roe, *Plague of Corn*, 133.

249. Aijana W., "Publix Bakery Beginnings."

250. McWilliams, *Pecan*, 122; Paddleford, *Great American Cookbook*, 271–72.

251. Parks, *Bravetart*, 231–32; "Who We Are: A Family Bakery."

252. Downey, "Robert C. Smith"; "Our Heritage," Sara Lee website, https://saraleedesserts .com/about/.

253. "About Us," Edwards Desserts website; Kessler, "Fun of Factory Visit Is Off the Pie Chart."

254. "Frozen Bakery Items Aid Dessert."

PASTEL DE TRES LECHES

1. Sweet Potato Comfort Pie website.

2. *Southern Living* 55, no. 8 (September 2020): 56, 60, 66, 70, 90, 97.

3. S. Franklin, "Introduction," 6.

4. Ferris, *Edible South*, 317–18.

5. M. Neal, *Remembering Bill Neal*, 104.

6. Neal, *Bill Neal's Southern Cooking*, 2.

7. B. Neal, *Biscuits, Spoonbread, and Sweet Potato Pie*.

8. "History and Founders," Southern Foodways Alliance website.

9. Dupree, *New Southern Cooking*, 213, 286–87.

10. C. Claiborne, *Craig Claiborne's Southern Cooking*, 243.

11. Dragonwagon, *Cornbread Gospels*, 7; Lundy, "Cooking Fresh."

12. L. Smith, *Dimestore*, 39.

13. B. Neal, *Biscuits, Spoonbread, and Sweet Potato Pie*, 42–43.

14. Willis, *Bon Appétit*, 204.

15. Foose, *Screen Doors*, 171.

16. C. Claiborne, *Craig Claiborne's Southern Cooking*, 254–55.

17. Purvis, "Mystery of the Hummingbird Cake"; McGough, "We Cracked the Case of the Hummingbird Cake."

18. Weigl, "Alongside Shrimp and Bluefish," 135; "Figs to Star at Ocracoke Fig Festival Aug. 17 and 18," *Ocracoke (N.C.) Observer*, August 7, 2018; Castle, "Ocracoke Fig Preserves Cake with Buttermilk Glaze."

19. "The History," King Biscuit Time website; "VIP Biscuit Bash."

20. "History," National Cornbread Festival website.

21. Stanonis and Wallace, "Tasting New Orleans," 19.

22. Stanonis and Wallace, 15, 16, 17–18.

23. Pack, "Got Milk?"

24. Parisian Bakery & Cafe Facebook page, https://www.facebook.com/pages/category/ Bakery/Parisian-Bakery-Cafe-202623776424570/.

25. Family Baking Bakery and Cafe website, https://www.familybakingchamblee.com.

26. Jolly Jolly Bakery website; "Enjoying the Sweet Life"; Sammy's Bakery website.

27. EuroIndo Mideast Market website, http://euroindomideastmarket.com/menu/.

28. Ferris, *Matzoh Ball Gumbo*, 79–80, 248; "Butchers, Caterers, Bakeries, and Groceries."

29. Ross and Rothkopf, "Best Bagel Shops in America."

30. Shields, *Southern Provisions*, xiii.

31. "Who We Are: Glenn Roberts."

32. Carter interview, 13–28; Lapidus interview, 3–4.

33. Patterson, "Kernels of Truth about Corn"; "Alliance of Native Seedkeepers."

34. Old Mill of Guilford website; "North Carolina Flour Mill since 1755." A number of historic stone mills exist in the South, and a handful still operate. See the Society for the Preservation of Old Mills website for a map.

35. Barton Springs Mill website.

36. "The Mill."

37. Christman, "Golden Goodness."

38. "Find Members," Bread Bakers Guild of America website.

39. Proof Bakery website.

40. Lapidus interview, 1–37. For a detailed description of her work and the bakers whom she supplies, see Lapidus, *Southern Ground*.

41. G. Gill interview, 1–8, 22–43.

42. "Our Definitive List."

43. Kaczor, "Salesman Spends Latest Career"; "About Us," Mary B's website.

44. Alsen, "Alabama Food Frontier."

45. "Meet Ms. Dean," Dean's Cake House website.

46. For just one example, see Castle, "Mrs. Hanes' Hand-Made Moravian Cookies."

47. "Where I Come From," written and sung by Alan Jackson, 2001; "Biscuits," sung by Kacey Musgraves; lyrics by Kacey Musgraves, Shane McAnally, and Brandy Clark, 2015.

48. *Chocolate for Basil* blog; Guy, *Black Girl Baking*, 58, 163–64.

Bibliography

ARCHIVAL SOURCES

Baudier, Roger. "Boss Bakers' Protective Association, New Orleans, Master Bakers Protective Association, New Orleans Master Bakers Association, Together with a General Review of Origin and Development of the Baking Industry in Old New Orleans, 1722–1892." Typescript, 1953, in Joseph Roger Baudier Papers. LaRC/Manuscripts Collection 805. Tulane University, Howard-Tilton Memorial Library Special Collections, Louisiana Research Collection, New Orleans.
Jones and Willaford Grocery Account Book, 1893–94. Middle Georgia Archives, Washington Memorial Library, Bibb County Library, Macon, Georgia.

NEWSPAPERS

Alamance Gleaner (Graham, N.C.)
Alexandria (Va.) Gazette
Amarillo Globe-Times
Arkansas Intelligencer (Van Buren)
Arkansas State Gazette (Little Rock)
Arkansas Weekly Gazette (Little Rock)
Athens (Ga.) Banner-Herald
Athens (Ga.) Daily Herald
Atlanta Constitution
Atlanta Daily Herald
Atlanta Georgian and News
Augusta Chronicle
Augusta Daily Chronicle and Sentinel
Beaumont (Tex.) Enterprise
Blakeley Sun and Alabama Advertiser
Boston Daily Globe
Brenham (Tex.) Banner-Press
Brunswick (Ga.) News
Butler (Ga.) Herald
Cahawba Press and Alabama Intelligencer
Charleston Courier
Charleston Daily News
Charleston Mercury

Charleston Tri-Weekly Courier
Chattanooga Daily Gazette
Chattanooga Daily Rebel
Chattanooga Gazette
Cherokee Phoenix and Indians' Advocate
    (New Echota, Ga.)
Chicago Tribune
City Gazette and Daily Advertiser
    (Charleston)
Civilian and Galveston Gazette
Columbus (Ga.) Enquirer-Sun
Daily Iberian (New Iberia, La.)
Daily Morning News (Savannah)
Daily Picayune (New Orleans)
Daily Richmond Examiner
Daily Selma Reporter
Daily South Carolinian (Columbia)
Daily True Delta (New Orleans)
Dallas Morning News
Dallas Weekly Herald
El Reno (Okla.) American
Fayetteville (N.C.) Observer
Floridian and Advocate (Tallahassee)

Forsyth (Ga.) County News
Fort Worth Star-Telegram
Gainesville (Ga.) News
Galveston Daily News
Georgia Gazette (Savannah)
Hinds County Gazette (Raymond, Miss.)
Houston (Ga.) Tri-Weekly Telegraph
Houston (Tex.) Chronicle
Houston (Tex.) Post
Houston (Tex.) Telegraph
Houston Home Journal (Perry, Ga.)
Jackson Economist (Winder, Ga.)
Jackson (Ga.) Argus
Jackson (Ga.) Progress-Argus
Jackson Herald (Jefferson, Ga.)
Kaplan (La.) Journal
Kingsport (Tenn.) Times
Macon (Ga.) Telegraph
Macon (Ga.) Telegraph and Messenger
Miami Herald
Mobile Gazette and Commercial Adviser
Morning News (Savannah)
Natchez Courier
Newnan (Ga.) Herald
New Orleans Times
New Orleans Times-Picayune
New York Times
Norfolk and Portsmouth Gazette
North Carolina Journal (Halifax)
North Georgia Citizen (Dalton)
Ocracoke (N.C.) Observer
Orlando Sentinel

Richmond Dispatch
Richmond Enquirer
Richmond Planet
San Antonio Express
San Antonio Ledger
Sandersville (Ga.) Herald
Savannah Daily Morning News
Savannah Morning News
Savannah Republican
South Carolina Gazette (Charleston)
Southern Israelite (Atlanta)
The Standard (Cedartown, Ga.)
The Standard (Clarksville, Tex.)
State Gazette (Austin, Tex.)
Tampa Tribune
Texian Advocate (Victoria)
Toledo (Ohio) Blade
Trinity Advocate (Palestine, Tex.)
Tri-Weekly Flag and Advertiser (Montgomery, Ala.)
True Citizen (Waynesboro, Ga.)
Union Recorder (Milledgeville, Ga.)
Virginia Gazette (Williamsburg)
Virginia Journal and Alexandria Advertiser
Walker County (Ga.) Herald
Walker County (Ga.) Messenger
Washington Bee
Waycross (Ga.) Evening Herald
Weekly Advertiser (Montgomery, Ala.)
Weekly Nashville Union
Weekly Telegraph (Macon, Ga.)
Williamsburg Gazette

PUBLISHED PRIMARY SOURCES

Adair, James. The History of the American Indians, Particularly Those Nations Adjoining to the Mississippi, East and West Florida, Georgia, South and North Carolina, and Virginia. London: Edward and Charles Dilly, 1775.

Ambrose, Stephen E. "The Bread Riots in Richmond." Virginia Magazine of History and Biography 71, no. 2 (April 1963): 203.

Andrews, Sidney. The South since the War: As Shown by Fourteen Weeks of Travel and Observations in Georgia and the Carolinas. Boston: Ticknor and Fields, 1866.

"Appraisement of the Estate of Philip Ludwell Esqr Decd." Virginia Magazine of History and Biography 21, no. 1 (1913): 395–416.

Ashe, Thomas. *Carolina, or a Description of the Present State of That Country, 1682.* London, 1682. Reprint, Tarrytown, N.Y.: William Abbatt, 1917.

Ball, Charles. *Slavery in the United States: A Narrative of the Life and Adventures of Charles Ball, a Black Man.* New York: John S. Taylor, 1837.

Bartram, William. *Travels through North and South Carolina, Georgia, East and West Florida, the Cherokee Country, the Extensive Territories of the Muscogulges, or Creek Confederacy, and the Country of the Chactaws.* Dublin: J. Moore, R. Jones, R. McAllister, and J. Rice, 1793.

Bass, Tommie. *Plain Southern Eating: From the Reminiscences of A. L. Tommie Bass, Herbalist.* Compiled and edited by John K. Crellin. Durham: Duke University Press, 1988.

Bernhard, [Karl], Duke of Saxe-Weimar Eisenach. *Travels through North America during the Years 1825 and 1826.* 2 vols. Philadelphia: Carey, Lea, and Carey, 1828.

Beverley, Robert. *The History of Virginia in Four Parts.* London, 1722. Reprint, Richmond: J. W. Randolph, 1855.

Bourne, Edward Gaylord, ed. *Narratives of the Career of Hernando De Soto in the Conquest of Florida.* Vol. 2. New York: A. S. Barnes, 1904.

Breeden, James O. *Advice among Masters: The Ideal in Slave Management in the Old South.* Westport, Conn.: Greenwood Press, 1980.

Brickell, John. *The Natural History of North-Carolina; with an Account of the Trade, Manners, and Customs of the Christian and Indian Inhabitants.* Dublin: J. Carson, 1737.

Brock, Sally A. *Richmond during the War: Four Years of Personal Observation.* New York: G. W. Carleton, 1867.

Bruce, Henry Clay. *The New Man: Twenty-Nine Years a Slave; Twenty-Nine Years a Free Man.* York, Pa.: P. Anstadt and Sons, 1895.

Brush, John C. *A Small Tract Entitled, A Candid and Impartial Exposition of the Various Opinions on the Subject of the Comparative Quality of the Wheat and Flour in the Northern and Southern Sections of the United States, with a View to Develop the True Cause of Difference.* Washington, D.C.: Printed by Jacob Gideon Jr., 1820.

Buckingham, James Silk. *The Slaves States of America.* 2 vols. London: Fisher, Son and Company, 1842.

Bullitt, Thomas W. *My Life at Oxmoor: Life on a Farm in Kentucky before the War.* Louisville: John P. Morton, 1911.

Bullock, William. *Virginia Impartially Examined and Left to Publick View.* London: John Hammond, 1649.

Burge, Dolly Sumner Lunt. *A Woman's Wartime Journal.* New York: Century, 1918.

Burke, Emily P. *Reminiscences of Georgia.* Oberlin, Ohio: James M. Fitch, 1850.

Burr, Virginia Ingraham, ed. *The Secret Eye: The Journal of Ella Gertrude Clanton Thomas, 1848–1889.* Chapel Hill: University of North Carolina Press, 1990.

Burwell, Letitia M. *A Girl's Life in Virginia before the War.* New York: Frederick A. Stokes, 1895.

Cable, George Washington, ed. "A Woman's Diary of the Siege of Vicksburg." *Century Illustrated Monthly Magazine* 30 (1885): 767–75.

Calvert, Rosalie Stier. *Mistress of Riversdale: The Plantation Letters of Rosalie Stier Calvert, 1795–1821.* Edited and translated by Margaret Law Callcott. Baltimore: Johns Hopkins University Press, 1991.

Carver, G. W. *How to Grow the Peanut and 105 Ways of Preparing It for Human Consumption.* Bulletin no. 31, March 1916. Experiment Station, Tuskegee Normal and Industrial Institute, Tuskegee, Alabama.

Catesby, Mark. "Mark Catesby's Natural History, 1731–47." In *The Colonial South Carolina Scene: Contemporary Views 1697–1774,* edited by H. Roy Merrins, 87–109. Columbia: University of South Carolina Press, 1997.

Chamberlayne, Churchill Gibson, ed. *Vestry Book of Blisland Parish, New Kent and James City Counties, Virginia.* Richmond: Library Board, 1935.

Chavarría-Cháirez, Becky. "Bertha M. Chavarría." In *From My Mother's Hands: Remembrances and Recipes from Texas Women,* edited by Susie Kelly Flatau, 65–72. Plano: Republic of Texas Press, 2000.

Cimarolli, Mary. *The Bootlegger's Other Daughter.* College Station: Texas A&M University Press, 2003.

City Directory of Macon, Georgia, 1897. Atlanta: Maloney Directory Co., 1897.

Claiborne, John F. H. "A Trip through the Piney Woods." *Publications of the Mississippi Historical Society* 9 (1906): 487–538.

Clay-Clopton, Virginia. *A Belle of the Fifties: Memoirs of Mrs. Clay, of Alabama, Covering Social and Political Life in Washington and the South, 1853–66.* New York: Doubleday, Page, 1905.

Connor, Jeannette M., trans. and ed. *Colonial Records of Spanish Florida.* DeLand: Florida State Historical Society, 1925.

Conrad, Georgia Bryan. "Reminiscences of a Southern Woman." Pts. 1, 3, 4, and 5. *Southern Workman* 30, no. 2 (February 1901): 77–81; 30, no. 5 (May 1901): 252–58; 30, no. 6 (June 1901): 357–60; 30, no. 7 (July 1901): 407–11.

Cooke, John Conrade. *Cookery and Confection.* London: W. Simpkin and R. Marshall, 1824.

Cooper, Thomas, and David J. McCord, eds. *Statutes at Large of South Carolina.* 10 vols. Columbia: A. S. Johnston, 1836–41.

Coulter, E. Merton, and Albert Berry Saye. *A List of the Early Settlers of Georgia.* Baltimore: Genealogical Publishing Company, 1983.

Craig, Tom Moore, ed. *Upcountry South Carolina Goes to War: Letters of the Anderson, Brockman, and Moore Families, 1853–1865.* Columbia: University of South Carolina Press, 2009.

Crane, Caroline Bartlett. *A General Sanitary Survey of Nashville, Tenn.* Kalamazoo, Mich.: n.p., 1910.

Cresswell, Nicholas. *The Journal of Nicholas Cresswell, 1774–1777.* New York: Dial Press, 1924.

Cumming, Kate. *Kate: The Journal of a Confederate Nurse.* Edited by Richard Barksdale Harwell. Baton Rouge: Louisiana State University Press, 1998.

Dallas City Directory. Dallas: John F. Worley Directory Co., 1941.

Dallas City Directory. Dallas: John F. Worley Directory Co., 1955.

Dallas City Directory. Dallas: R. L. Polk Co., 1961.

Danckaerts, Jasper. *Journal of Jasper Danckaerts, 1679–1680.* Edited by Bartlett Burleigh James and J. Franklin Jameson. New York: Charles Scribner's Sons, 1913.

D'Artaguiette, Diron. "Journal of Diron D'Artaguiette, 1722–1723." In *Travels in the American Colonies,* edited by Newton D. Mereness, 15–92. New York: Macmillan, 1916.

Denton [Tex.] Business Review and Directory. Denton: Blaine and Forshey, 1890.

Dimond, E. Grey, and Herman Hattaway, eds. *Letters from Forest Place: A Plantation Family's Correspondence, 1846–1881.* Jackson: University Press of Mississippi, 1993.

Douglass, Frederick. *The Life and Times of Frederick Douglass, from 1817 to 1882.* London: Christian Age Office, 1882.

Drums and Shadows: Survival Studies among the Georgia Coastal Negroes. Athens: University of Georgia Press, 1940. Reprinted with new introduction, 1986.

Du Bois, W. E. B. *The Negro in Business.* Atlanta: Atlanta University, 1899.

Dumont de Montigny, Jean-François-Benjamin. *Memoir of Lieutenant Dumont, 1715–1747.* Edited by Carla Zecher and Gordon M. Sayers. Chapel Hill: University of North Carolina Press, 2012.

Durand, of Dauphiné. *A Huguenot Exile in Virginia, or Voyages of a Frenchman Exiled for His Religion.* New York: Press of the Pioneers, 1934.

Eddington, Jane. "Bride's Cake." *Atlanta Constitution,* June 16, 1912.

————. "Lady Baltimore Cake." *Atlanta Constitution,* July 28, 1912.

Edmondston, Catherine Ann Devereux. *"Journal of a Secesh Lady": The Diary of Catherine Ann Devereux Edmondston, 1860–1866.* Edited by Beth G. Crabtree and James W. Patton. Raleigh, N.C.: Division of Archives and History, Department of Cultural Resources, 1979.

Edwards, William James. *Twenty-Five Years in the Black Belt.* Boston: Cornhill Company, 1918.

Elizer, Eleazer. *A Directory for 1803: Containing the Names of All the House-keepers and Traders in the City of Charleston.* Charleston: W. P. Young, 1803.

Eppes, Susan Bradford. *Through Some Eventful Years.* Macon, Ga.: J. W. Burke Company, 1926.

Evans, Oliver. *The Young Mill-wright and Miller's Guide.* Philadelphia: Oliver Evans, 1795.

Feltman, William. *The Journal of William Feltman of the First Pennsylvania Regiment, 1781–82.* Philadelphia: Historical Society of Pennsylvania, 1853.

Felton, Rebecca Latimer. *Country Life in Georgia in the Days of My Youth.* Atlanta: Index Printing Company, 1919.

Fithian, Philip Vickers. *Philip Vickers Fithian Journals and Letters, 1767–1774.* Edited by John Rogers Williams. Princeton, N.J.: Princeton Historical Association, 1900.

Fontaneda, Hernando de Escalante. *Memoir of Hernando de Escalante Fontaneda respecting Florida, Written in Spain, about the Year 1575.* Translated by Buckingham Smith. Washington, D.C.: Privately printed, 1854.

Fries, Adelaide L. *Records of the Moravians in North Carolina.* Vol. 1, *1752–1771.* Raleigh: North Carolina Historical Commission, 1922.

García, Genaro, ed. "Relación de los trabajos que la gente de una nao llamadad nuestra Señora de la Merced padeció y algunas cosas que en auqella flota sucederion." In *Dos antiguas relaciones de la Florida.* 153–226. México: Tip. y lit. de J. Auilar vera y Comp. (S. en C.), 1902.

Glen, James. *Description of South Carolina.* London: R. and J. Dodsley, 1761.

Grandy, Moses. *Narrative of the Life of Moses Grandy, Late a Slave in the United States of America.* London: C. Gilpin, 1843.

Greenhow, Rose O'Neal. *My Imprisonment and the First Year of Abolition Rule at Washington.* London: R. Bentley, 1863.

Hague, Parthenia Antoinette. *A Blockaded Family: Life in Southern Alabama during the Civil War.* Boston: Houghton, Mifflin, 1888.

Hamor, Ralph. *A True Discourse on the Present Estate of Virginia.* London: John Beals, 1615.

Hariot, Thomas. *A Briefe and True Report of the New Found Land of Virginia.* London: n.p., 1588.

Harland, Marion [Mary Virginia Terhune]. *Marion Harland's Autobiography: The Story of a Long Life.* New York: Harper and Brothers, 1910.

Harrison, Eliza Cope, ed. *Best Companions: Letters of Eliza Middleton Fisher and Her Mother, Mary Hering Middleton, from Charleston, Philadelphia, and Newport, 1839–1846.* Columbia: University of South Carolina Press, 2001.

Harrison, William. *Elizabethan England.* Edited by Lothrop Withington. London: Walter Scott, [1889?].

Hazard, Ebenezer. "The Journal of Ebenezer Hazard in Virginia, 1777." Edited by Fred Shelley. *Virginia Magazine of History and Biography* 62, no. 4 (1954): 400–423.

Hening, William Waller, ed. *The Statutes at Large: Being a Collection of All the Laws of Virginia, from the First Session of the Legislature, in the Year 1619.* 13 vols. Richmond: Samuel Pleasants Jr., 1809–23.

Hess, Karen, ed. *Martha Washington's Booke of Cookery and Booke of Sweetmeats.* New York: Columbia University Press, 1996.

Hinke, William J., trans. "Report of the Journey of Francis Louis Michel from Berne, Switzerland, to Virginia, October 2, 1701–December 1, 1702." *Virginia Magazine of History and Biography* 24, no. 2 (April 1916): 113–41.

Holmes, Emma. *The Diary of Miss Emma Holmes, 1861–1866.* Edited by John F. Marszalek. Baton Rouge: Louisiana State University Press, 1979.

Hopley, Catherine Cooper. *Life in the South: From the Commencement of the War.* 2 vols. London: Chapman and Hall, 1863.

Hughes, Louis. *Thirty Years a Slave: From Bondage to Freedom.* Milwaukee: South Side Printing, 1897.

Hundley, Daniel R. *Social Relations in Our Southern States.* New York: Henry B. Price, 1860.

Hunt, Gaillard, ed. *The First Forty Years of Washington Society in the Family Letters of Mrs. Samuel Harrison Smith (Margaret Bayard).* New York: Charles Scribner's Sons, 1906.

Iberville, Pierre Le Moyne d'. *Iberville's Gulf Journals.* Translated and edited by Richebourg Gaillard McWilliams. Tuscaloosa: University of Alabama Press, 1981.

Instructions to "Wear-Ever" Salesmen. New Kensington, Pa.: Aluminum Cooking Utensil Co., 1912.

"An Interview with James Freeman, 1712." In *The Colonial South Carolina Scene: Contemporary Views, 1697–1774,* edited by H. Roy Merrins, 38–55. Columbia: University of South Carolina Press, 1997.

Jackson, John Andrew. *The Experience of a Slave in South Carolina.* London: Passmore and Alabaster, 1862.

Jacobs, Harriet. *Incidents in the Life of a Slave Girl, Written by Herself.* Boston: n.p., 1861.

Jefferson, Isaac. *Memoirs of a Monticello Slave—Dictated to Charles Campbell in the 1840s by Isaac, One of Thomas Jefferson's Slaves.* Charlottesville: University of Virginia Press, 1951.

Jones, Hugh. *The Present State of Virginia.* London: Printed for J. Clarke, 1724.

Kalm, Peter, Margit Oxholm (trans.), and Sherret S. Chase (ed). "Description of Maize: How It Is Planted and Cultivated in North America, and the Various Uses of This Grain (Beskrifning om Mays; Huru den planteras och skötes i Norra America, samt om denna sädes-artens mångfaldiga nytta)." *Economic Botany* 28 (April–June 1974): 105–17.

Kennedy, John Pendleton. *Memoirs of the Life of William Wirt: Attorney-General of the United States.* 2 vols. New York: G. P. Putman and Sons, 1872.

Kercheval, Samuel. *A History of the Valley of Virginia*. Winchester, Va.: Samuel H. Davis, 1833.

King, Anna Matilda. *Anna: The Letters of a St. Simons Island Plantation Mistress, 1817–1859*. Edited by Melanie Pavich-Lindsay. Athens: University of Georgia Press, 2002.

King, Wilma, ed. *A Northern Woman in the Plantation South: Letters of Tryphena Blanche Holder Fox, 1856–1876*. Columbia: University of South Carolina Press, 1993.

Kingsbury, Susan Myra, ed. *The Records of the Virginia Company of London*. 4 vols. Washington, D.C.: Government Printing Office, 1933.

Lapidus, Jennifer. *Southern Ground: Reclaiming Flavor through Stone-Milled Flour*. New York: Ten Speed Press, 2021.

"Last Days of the Southern Confederacy." *Southern Historical Society Papers* 19 (1891): 329–33.

Laudonnière, René. *Three Voyages*. Translated by Charles E. Bennett. Tuscaloosa: University of Alabama Press, 2001.

Lawson, John. *A New Voyage to Carolina: Containing the Exact Description and Natural History of That Country*. London, 1709.

Le Moyne de Morgues, Jacques, and Theodor de Bry. *Brevis narratio eorum quae in Florida Americae provincia Gallis acciderunt*. Frankfort: D. Wechel, 1591.

Le Page du Pratz, Antoine-Simon. *History of Louisiana: Or of the Western Parts of Virginia and Carolina*. London: T. Becket, 1774.

Logan, William. "William Logan's Journal of a Journey to Georgia, 1745." *Pennsylvania Magazine of History and Biography* 36, no. 1 (1912): 1–16.

———. "William Logan's Journal of a Journey to Georgia, 1745 (Continued)." *Pennsylvania Magazine of History and Biography* 36, no. 2 (1912): 162–86.

Loughborough, Mary Ann Webster. *My Cave Life in Vicksburg with Letters of Trial and Travel*. New York: D. Appleton, 1864.

Maduell, Charles, Jr., comp. and trans. *The Census Tables for the French Colony of Louisiana from 1699 through 1732*. Baltimore: Genealogical Publishing Company, 1972.

Martire d'Anghiera, Pietro. *De Orbe Novo: The Eight Decades of Peter Martyr D'Anghera*. Vol. 2. New York: G. P. Putnam's Sons, 1912.

McGuire, Judith Brockenbrough. *Diary of a Southern Refugee during the War*. New York: E. J. Hale, 1867.

Michaux, André. *Journal of André Michaux, 1793–1796*. Cleveland: A. H. Clark, 1904.

Miller, Helen Hill. *The Kitchen in War Production*. New York: Public Affairs Committee, 1943.

Moody, Anne. *Coming of Age in Mississippi: An Autobiography*. New York: Dell, 1968.

Moore, John Hammond, ed. *A Plantation Mistress on the Eve of the Civil War: The Diary of Keziah Goodwyn Hopkins Brevard, 1860–1861*. Columbia: University of South Carolina Press, 1993.

Myers, Robert Manson, ed. *The Children of Pride: Selected Letters of the Family of the Rev. Dr. Charles Colcock Jones from the Years 1804–1868*. New Haven: Yale University Press, 1972.

"Nathan O. Tisdale." *Belle's Letters: A Collection of Family Letters, Papers, and Photos of Arabella Maria "Belle" Tisdale Booksh[op] (1855-1934)*. http://belletisdale.blogspot.com/2016/07/. Accessed August 30, 2021.

Neill, Edward D. *Virginia Carolorum: The Colony under the Rule of Charles the First and Second, a.d. 1625–a.d. 1683*. Albany: Joel Munsell's Sons, 1886.

Northrup, Solomon. *Twelve Years a Slave: Narrative of Solomon Northrup, a Citizen of New-York, Kidnapped in Washington City in 1841, and Rescued in 1853*. Auburn: Derby and Miller, 1853.

Olmsted, Frederick Law. *The Cotton Kingdom*. Edited by Arthur M. Schlesinger Sr. New York: Modern Library College Editions, 1984.

———. *Journey in the Seaboard Slave States: With Remarks on Their Economy*. New York: Dix and Edwards, 1856.

Padgett, James A., ed. "Journal of Daniel Walker Lord, Kept While on a Southern Trip." *Georgia Historical Quarterly* 26, no. 2 (June 1942): 166–95.

Pearson, Elizabeth Ware, ed. *Letters from Port Royal: Written at the Time of the Civil War*. Boston: W. B. Clarke, 1906.

Pember, Phoebe Yates. *A Southern Woman's Story*. New York: G. W. Carleton, 1879.

Pénicaut, André. *Fleur de Lys and Calumet: Being the Pénicaut Narrative of French Adventure in Louisiana*. Translated and edited by Richebourg Gaillard McWilliams. Tuscaloosa: University of Alabama Press, 1988.

Percy, George. "Discourse." In *Captain John Smith: Writings with Other Narratives of Roanoke, Jamestown, and the First English Settlement*. Edited by James Horn, 921–34. New York: Penguin Putnam, 2007.

———. "Observations Gathered out of a Discourse of the Plantation of the Southerne Colonie in Virginia by the English, 1606. Written by the Honorable Gentleman, Master George Percy." In *Narratives of Early Virginia*. Edited by Lyon Gardiner Tyler, 1–24. New York: Charles Scribner's Sons, 1907.

———. "A Trewe Relacyon." In *Captain John Smith: Writings with Other Narratives of Roanoke, Jamestown, and the First English Settlement*. Edited by James Horn, 1093–114. New York: Penguin Putnam, 2007.

Perdue, Charles E., Jr., Thomas E. Barden, and Robert K. Phillips, eds. *Weevils in the Wheat: Interviews with Virginia Ex-Slaves*. Charlottesville: University Press of Virginia, 1992.

A Perfect Description of Virginia: Being a Full and True Relation of the Present State of the Plantation, Their Health, Peace, and Plenty. London: Printed for Richard Wodenoth, at the Star under Peters Church in Cornhill, 1649.

Pickens, William. *The Heir of Slaves: An Autobiography*. Boston: Pilgrim Press, 1911.

Pickett, La Salle Corbell. *Pickett and His Men*. Atlanta: Foote and Davies, 1899.

Pringle, Elizabeth Waties Allston. *A Woman Rice Planter*. New York: Macmillan, 1914.

Pryor, Sara Agnes Rice. *My Day: Reminiscences of a Long Life*. New York: Macmillan, 1909.

Quincy, Josiah. *Memoir of the Life of Josiah Quincy Jun. of Massachusetts*. Boston: Cummings, Hilliard, 1825.

Rangel, Rodrigo. "Account of the Northern Conquest and Discovery of Hernando de Soto." Translated by John E. Worth. In *The De Soto Chronicles: The Expedition of Hernando de Soto to North America in 1539–1543*, edited by Lawrence A. Clayton, Vernon James Knight Jr., and Edward C. Moore, 1:247–306. Tuscaloosa: University of Alabama Press, 1993.

Reed, Lida Lord. "A Woman's Experiences during the Siege of Vicksburg." *Century* 71 (April 1901): 922–28.

Rolfe, John. *A True Relation of the State of Virginia in 1616*. Printed from the original manuscript in the private library of Henry C. Taylor, Esq. New Haven: Printing-Office of the Yale University Press, 1951.

Romans, Bernard. *A Concise Natural History of East and West Florida*. New York: B. Romans, 1776.

Ross, FitzGerald. *A Visit to the Cities and Camps of the Confederate States.* Edinburgh: William Blackwood and Sons, 1865.

Rowland, Dunbar, and Albert Godfrey Sanders, comps., eds., and trans. *Mississippi Provincial Archives 1704–1743 French Dominion, Vol. III.* Jackson: Press of the Mississippi Department of Archives and History, 1932.

Sadler, Genevieve Grant. *Muzzled Oxen: Reaping Cotton and Sowing Hope in 1920s Arkansas.* Little Rock: Butler Center for Arkansas Studies, 2014.

Salls, Helen Harriet, ed. "Pamela Savage of Champlain, Healthseeker in Oxford." *North Carolina Historical Review* 29, no. 4 (October 1952): 540–68.

Saxon, Lyle, Edward Dreyer, and Robert Tallant, comps. *Gumbo Ya-Ya: A Collection of Louisiana Folk Tales.* Boston: Houghton Mifflin, 1945.

Schaw, Janet. *Journal of a Lady of Quality: Being the Narrative of a Journey from Scotland to the West Indies, North Carolina, and Portugal, in the Years 1774 to 1776.* Edited by Evangeline Walker Andrews. New Haven: Yale University Press, 1921.

Schoepf, Johann David. *Travels in the Confederation* [1783–1784]. Vol. 2. Translated and edited by Alfred J. Morrison. Philadelphia: William J. Campbell, 1911.

Scott, D. M. "Selma and Dallas County, Ala." *Confederate Veteran* 24 (1916): 214–22.

Skrabanek, Robert L. *We're Czechs.* College Station: Texas A&M University Press, 1988.

Smedes, Susan Dabney. *Memorials of a Southern Planter.* 2nd ed. Baltimore: Cushings and Bailey, 1887.

Smith, John. "The Description of Virginia and Proceedings of the Colonies." In *Narratives of Early Virginia,* edited by Lyon Gardiner Tyler, 73–204. New York: Charles Scribner's Sons, 1907.

———. *The Generall Historie of Virginia, New-England, and the Summer Isles.* London: Michael Sparkes, 1629.

———. *A Map of Virginia: With a Description of the Countrey.* Oxford: Joseph Barnes, 1612.

Smith, Lee. *Dimestore: A Writer's Life.* Chapel Hill: Algonquin Books of Chapel Hill, 2016.

Smith, William R., ed. *Reports of the Decisions of the Supreme Court of the State of Alabama.* 10 vols. Tuskaloosa [sic]: William R. Smith, 1877.

Smyth, John Ferdinand Dalziel. *A Tour in the United States of America.* 2 vols. London: G. Robinson, 1784.

Sparkes, John, Jr. "The Voyage Made by M. John Hawkins Esquire, 1565." In *Early English and French Voyages, Chiefly from Hakluyt,* edited by Henry S. Burrage, 111–32. New York: Charles Scribner's Sons, 1932.

Srygley, Fletcher Douglas. *Seventy Years in Dixie: Recollections, Sermons, and Sayings of T. W. Caskey and Others.* Nashville: Gospel Advocate, 1891.

Stith, William. *The History of the First Discovery and Settlement of Virginia.* Williamsburg: Printed by William Parks, 1747.

Stone, Kate. *Brokenburn: The Journal of Kate Stone, 1861–1868.* Edited by John Q. Anderson. Baton Rouge: Louisiana State University Press, 1955.

Strachey, William. *For the Colony in Virginea Britannia: Lawes Divine, Morall, and Martial.* London: Walter Burre, 1612. Facsimile reprint, Washington, D.C.: [n.p.], 1836.

———. *Historie of Travell into Virginia Britania.* London: Hakluyt Society, 1953.

Stuart, James. *Three Years in North America.* 2 vols. Edinburgh: R. Cadell, 1833.

Swint, Henry Lee, ed. *Dear Ones at Home: Letters from Contraband Camps.* Nashville: Vanderbilt University Press, 1966.

Tailfer, Patrick, Hugh Anderson, and David Douglas. *A True and Historical Narrative of the Colony of Georgia, in America*. Charlestown, S.C.: Printed by P. Timothy, 1741.

Talley, Thomas W. *Negro Folk Rhymes*. New York: Macmillan, 1922.

Thomas, Jane Henry. *Old Days in Nashville*. Nashville: Publishing House Methodist Episcopal Church, South, 1897.

Thomson's Mercantile and Professional Directory for 1851–52. Baltimore: William Thomson, 1851.

Towne, Laura Matilda. *Letters and Diary of Laura M. Towne: Written from the Sea Islands of South Carolina, 1862–1884*. Edited by Rupert Sargent Holland. Cambridge, Mass.: Riverside Press, 1912.

Transactions of the New-York State Agricultural Society. Vol. 7, 1847. Albany: C. Van Benthuysen, Public Printer, 1848.

Tyler, Ronnie C., and Lawrence R. Murphy, eds. *The Slave Narratives of Texas*. Austin: Encino Press, 1974.

Vaughan, George Lester. *The Cotton Renter's Son*. Wolfe City, Tex.: Henington, 1967.

Vega, Garcilaso de la. "La Florida." Translated by Charmion Shelby. In *The De Soto Chronicles: De Soto to North America in 1539–1543*, edited by Lawrence A. Clayton, Vernon James Knight Jr., and Edward C. Moore, 2:25–560. Tuscaloosa: University of Alabama Press, 1993.

Weld, Isaac. *Travels through the States of North America, and the Provinces of Upper and Lower Canada, during the years 1795, 1796, and 1797*. London: Printed for John Stockdale, 1799.

White, C. C., and Ada Morehead Holland. *No Quittin' Sense*. Austin: University of Texas Press, 1969.

Wiggins, Sarah Woolfolk, ed. *The Journal of Sarah Haynsworth Gayle, 1827–1835: A Substitute for Social Intercourse*. Tuscaloosa: University of Alabama Press, 2018.

Wilcox, Georgia Griffing. "An Interrupted Wedding." *Sunny South*, May 15, 1897.

Williams, Samuel Cole. *Early Travels in the Tennessee Country, 1540–1800*. Johnson City, Tenn.: Watauga Press, 1928.

Wilson, George. Diary. William & Mary Digital Archive. https://digitalarchive.wm.edu/handle/10288/16116. Accessed August 29, 2021.

PATENTS

"Frozen Pie Crust Dough and Method of Preparation Thereof." 1954. Google Patents. https://patents.google.com/patent/US2726156A/en. Accessed August 29, 2021.

"Improvement in Dough-Kneading Machines." 1877. Google Patents. https://patents.google.com/patent/US186717A/en. Accessed August 29, 2021.

"Method and Means of Packing Dough." 1931. Google Patents. https://patents.google.com/patent/US1811772A/en. Accessed August 29, 2021.

ORAL HISTORY INTERVIEWS

Baylor University Institute for Oral History

Almanza, Adelaida Torres. Interviewed by Rebecca Sharpless, March 8–July 7, 1995. https://digitalcollections-baylor.quartexcollections.com/Documents/Detail/oral-memoirs-of-adelaida-torres-almanza-transcript/1546323?item=1546501.

Bielamowicz, Richard "Pop." Interviewed by Mary Jim Allen, June 11, 2012.
    https://digitalcollections-baylor.quartexcollections.com/Documents/Detail
    /oral-memoirs-of-richard-pop-bielamowicz-transcript/1557264.

Caufield, Alice Owens. Interviewed by Rebecca Sharpless, January 26, 1993.
    https://digitalcollections-baylor.quartexcollections.com/Documents/Detail
    /oral-memoirs-of-alice-owens-caufield-transcript/1565553?item=1565806.

Degrate, Ora Lee. Interviewed by Jay M. Butler, July 30, 1993.
    https://digitalcollections-baylor.quartexcollections.com/Documents
    /Detail/oral-memoirs-of-ora-lee-degrate-transcript/1581638.

Dodd, Myrtle Irene Calvert. Interviewed by Rebecca Sharpless, August 14–September
    19, 1990. https://digitalcollections-baylor.quartexcollections.com/Documents
    /Detail/oral-memoirs-of-myrtle-irene-calvert-dodd-transcript/1583747?item=1583753.

Folley, Della Inez. Interviewed by Rebecca Sharpless, September 4, 1990.
    https://digitalcollections-baylor.quartexcollections.com/Documents/Detail
    /oral-memoirs-of-della-inez-folley-transcript/1594972.

Guderian, Pearl Elizabeth Wynn. Interviewed by Anne Radford Phillips, December 7,
    1991. https://digitalcollections-baylor.quartexcollections.com/Documents/Detail
    /oral-memoirs-of-pearl-elizabeth-wynn-guderian-transcript/1604436.

Hernandez, Manuel, and Eva Hernandez. Interviewed by Sandra Denise Harvey, Octo-
    ber 1, 1994. https://digitalcollections-baylor.quartexcollections.com/Documents
    /Detail/oral-memoirs-of-manuel-and-eva-hernandez-transcript/1615165.

Hurtado, Luz Sánchez. Interviewed by Rebecca Sharpless, July 27 and August 2, 1995.
    https://digitalcollections-baylor.quartexcollections.com/Documents/Detail
    /oral-memoirs-of-luz-sanchez-hurtado-transcript/1622868?item=1622874.

Joe, Arthur Fred. Interviewed by James M. SoRelle, June 20, 2009. https:
    //digitalcollections-baylor.quartexcollections.com/Documents/Detail
    /oral-memoirs-of-arthur-fred-joe-sr.-transcript/1628579.

Kuykendall, Leota Wagner. Interviewed by Anne Radford Phillips, February 20, 1992.
    https://digitalcollections-baylor.quartexcollections.com/Documents/Detail
    /oral-memoirs-of-leota-wagner-kuykendall-transcript/1635230.

Malone, Vera Estelle Allen. Interviewed by LaWanda Ball, December 5, 1975. https:
    //digitalcollections-baylor.quartexcollections.com/Documents/Detail
    /oral-memoirs-of-vera-malone-transcript/1645346?item=1645411.

Matthies, Howard Herbert, and Olefa Koerth Matthies. Interviewed by Thomas L.
    Charlton, Deborah J. Hoskins, Thad Sitton, and Dan K. Utley, December 20,
    1991–December 2, 1994. https://digitalcollections-baylor.quartexcollections.com
    /Documents/Detail/oral-memoirs-of-howard-herbert-matthies-and-olefa-koerth
    -matthies-transcript/1647939?item=1648233.

Moreno, Susan Valerio. Interviewed by Lois E. Myers, July 15, 2003.
    https://digitalcollections-baylor.quartexcollections.com/Documents
    /Detail/oral-memoirs-of-susan-valerio-moreno-transcript/1658896.

Orrick, Bailis William. Interviewed by Rufus B. Spain, July 11, 1975–July 23, 1976.
    https://digitalcollections-baylor.quartexcollections.com/Documents/Detail
    /oral-memoirs-of-bailis-william-orrick-transcript/1668796.

Robles, Irene Palacios. Interviewed by Elizabeth Palacios, August 25, 2007.
    https://digitalcollections-baylor.quartexcollections.com/Documents/Detail
    /oral-memoirs-of-irene-robles-transcript/1687700.
Snyder, Carey H. Interviewed by William L. Pitts, June–July 1985. https:
    //digitalcollections-baylor.quartexcollections.com/Documents/Detail
    /oral-memoirs-of-carey-h.-snyder-transcript/1698711?item=1698721.
Washington, Maggie Langham. Interviewed by Doni Van Ryswyk and Marla Luffer,
    March 1, 1988–March 13, 1989. https://digitalcollections-baylor.quartexcollections
    .com/Documents/Detail/oral-memoirs-of-maggie-langham-washington-transcript
    /1714380?item=1714503.
Weir, Bernice Porter Bostick. Interviewed by Rebecca Sharpless, July 9–August 6, 1990.
    https://digitalcollections-baylor.quartexcollections.com/Documents/Detail
    /oral-memoirs-of-bernice-porter-bostick-weir-transcript/1716431.
Wharton, Anna May Peyrot. Interviewed by Julie Freeman, October 18, 2008.
    https://digitalcollections-baylor.quartexcollections.com/Documents/Detail
    /oral-memoirs-of-anna-may-peyrot-wharton-transcript/1717222.

Born in Slavery: Slave Narratives from the Federal Writers' Project, 1936 to 1938

Cannon, Sylvia. Interviewed by Annie Ruth Davis, August 4, 1937. www.loc.gov
    /resource/mesn.141/?sp=192.
Evans, Millie. Interviewed by Pernella Anderson, c. 1936. www.loc.gov/resource
    /mesn.022/?sp=254.

Southern Foodways Alliance

Carter, Billy. Interviewed by Kate Medley, February 22, 2018. www.southernfoodways
    .org/wp-content/uploads/sgp-005-billy-carter-2–22–18-final.pdf.
Gill, Graison. Interviewed by Kate Medley, February 1, 2018. www.southernfoodways
    .org/wp-content/uploads/sgp-004-graison-gill-2–1-18.pdf.
Lapidus, Jennifer. Interviewed by Kate Medley, October 19, 2017. www
    .southernfoodways.org/wp-content/uploads/sgp-001-jennifer-lapidus-10–19–17.pdf.
Lindley, Caroline. Interviewed by Kate Medley, May 15, 2018. www.southernfoodways
    .org/wp-content/uploads/sgp-006-caroline-lindley-5–15–18.pdf.

Southern Oral History Program, University of North Carolina at Chapel Hill

Allen, Ethelene McCabe. Interviewed by Barbara C. Allen, May 21, 2006. https://dc.lib
    .unc.edu/cdm/compoundobject/collection/sohp/id/4012/rec/1.
Chiltoskey, Mary Ulmer, and Rebecca Grant. Interviewed by Warren Moore, April 10,
    1984. https://dc.lib.unc.edu/cdm/compoundobject/collection/sohp/id/13581/rec/2.
Davis, Fredda. Interviewed by Ruth Dasmann, September 26, 1984. https://dc.lib.unc
    .edu/cdm/compoundobject/collection/sohp/id/10577/rec/80.
Durr, Virginia Foster. Interviewed by J. Clifford Durr, Jacquelyn Dowd Hall, and Sue
    Thrasher, March 13–15, 1975. https://dc.lib.unc.edu/cdm/compoundobject
    /collection/sohp/id/11143/rec/360.

Faucette, Ethel Marshall. Interviewed by Allen Tullos, November 16, 1978. https://dc.lib
.unc.edu/cdm/compoundobject/collection/sohp/id/11585/rec/20.

Hicks, Ray. Interviewed by Warren Moore, November 26, 1984. https://dc.lib.unc.edu
/cdm/compoundobject/collection/sohp/id/13659/rec/1.

MacDougall, Margaret McDow. Interviewed by Mary Frederickson, April 1, 1977.
https://dc.lib.unc.edu/cdm/compoundobject/collection/sohp/id/11193/rec/1.

Moss, Ida E., Jimmy [James Harold] Moss, John Moss, Suzanne Moss, and Wanda Moss.
Interviewed by Warren Moore, October 14, 1984. https://dc.lib.unc.edu/cdm
/compoundobject/collection/sohp/id/14143/rec/1.

Moss, Wanda. Interviewed by Warren Moore, September 12, 1984. https://dc.lib.unc
.edu/cdm/compoundobject/collection/sohp/id/14300/rec/1.

Oates, Hal, and Hattie Oates. Interviewed by Warren Moore, August 3, 1982.
https://dc.lib.unc.edu/cdm/compoundobject/collection/sohp/id/15025/rec/1.

Oates, Susan. Interviewed by Warren Moore, August 2, 1982. https://dc.lib.unc.edu
/cdm/compoundobject/collection/sohp/id/13759/rec/1.

Olive, Billy Brown. Interviewed by Jennifer Marsico, January 27 and February 15, 1994.
https://dc.lib.unc.edu/cdm/compoundobject/collection/sohp/id/12458/rec/1.

Pash, Jackie. Interviewed by Katie Otis, August 7, 2001. https://dc.lib.unc.edu/cdm
/compoundobject/collection/sohp/id/14739/rec/1.

Ridgle, Lawrence. Interviewed by Alicia J. Rouverol, June 3, 1999. https://dc.lib.unc.edu
/cdm/compoundobject/collection/sohp/id/12853/rec/1.

Robinson, Willa V. Interviewed by Malinda Maynor Lowery, January 14, 2004.
https://dc.lib.unc.edu/cdm/compoundobject/collection/sohp/id/8041/rec/1.

Shell, Mary. Interviewed by Warren Moore, September 27, 1984. https://dc.lib.unc.edu
/cdm/compoundobject/collection/sohp/id/15386/rec/2.

Snipes, John Wesley. Interviewed by Brent D. Glass, November 20, 1976. https://dc.lib
.unc.edu/cdm/compoundobject/collection/sohp/id/11701/rec/1.

Truitt, Herman Newton. Interviewed by Allen Tullos, December 5, 1978, and January 19
and January 30, 1979. https://dc.lib.unc.edu/cdm/compoundobject/collection/sohp
/id/12370/rec/1.

COOKBOOKS

All Saints Episcopal Guild. *Inverness Cook Book.* Inverness, Miss.: All Saints Episcopal
Guild, 1963.

Andrews, Mrs. Lewis R. [Wilson Hope Nelson], and Mrs. J. Reaney [Frances H.] Kelly.
The Hammond-Harwood House Cook Book. Annapolis: Hammond-Harwood House
Association, 1963.

Angelou, Maya. *Hallelujah! The Welcome Table.* New York: Random House, 2004.

Arlington County School Federation, Arlington County, Virginia, comp. *Washington Lee
High School Cook Book.* Arlington County, Va.: Arlington County School Federation,
1927.

Augusta, Ga., Second Presbyterian Church. *Choice Recipes of Georgia Housekeepers by the
Ladies of the Second Presbyterian Church, Augusta, Ga.* New York: Trow's Printing and
Bookbinding, 1880.

Benedict, Jennie C. *A Choice Collection of Tested Receipts: With a Chapter of Preparation of Food for the Sick.* Louisville: John P. Morton, 1897.

Bowers, Lessie. *Plantation Recipes.* New York: Robert Speller and Sons, 1959.

Breckinridge, Robert J. *From Soup to Nuts: Recipes That Have Made Kentucky and Louisiana Foods and Liquids Famous.* Lexington: Cardinal Dairies, 1935.

Brown, Marion. *The Southern Cook Book.* Chapel Hill: University of North Carolina Press, 1951.

Bryan, Lettice. *The Kentucky Housewife.* Columbia: University of South Carolina Press, 1991. Originally published 1839 in Cincinnati: "Stereotyped by Shepard & Stearns."

Bryant, Annie Mae Wood, ed. *Athens Woman's Club Cook Book.* Athens, Ga.: Athens Woman's Club, 1922.

Bullock, Helen. *The Williamsburg Art of Cookery.* Williamsburg: Colonial Williamsburg, 1938.

Butler, Cleora. *Cleora's Kitchen: The Memoir of a Cook and Eight Decades of Great American Food.* Tulsa: Council Oak Books, 1985.

Calvary Church Circle Cook Book. Memphis: n.p., 1925.

Carson, Jane. *Colonial Virginia Cookery.* Williamsburg: Colonial Williamsburg Foundation, 1968.

Central Presbyterian Church, Atlanta, Ga. Ladies' Missionary Society. *The Southern Housekeeper: A Book of Tested Recipes.* Atlanta: Franklin Printing and Publishing, 1898.

Charleston Recipes. Charleston: The Studio, 1928.

Chase, Leah. *The Dooky Chase Cookbook.* Gretna, La.: Pelican, 1990.

Child, Lydia Maria. *The American Frugal Housewife.* 16th ed. Boston: Carter, Hendee, and Company, 1835.

Circle of Service, King's Daughters, Norfolk, Virginia, comp. *The King's Daughters Cook Book: A Selected Collection of Several Hundred Choice Recipes from Old Virginia.* Norfolk: Circle of Service, 1924.

City Federation of Women's Clubs, Temple, Texas. *Feastin' with the Federation.* Temple: City Federation of Women's Clubs, 1955.

Claiborne, Craig. *Craig Claiborne's Southern Cooking.* New York: Times Books, 1987.

Colquitt, Harriet Ross. *The Savannah Cook Book.* New York: Farrar and Rinehart, 1933.

Community League Cook Book, Big Stone Gap, Va. N.p.: n.p., 1925.

Confederate Receipt Book: A Compilation of Over One Hundred Receipts Adapted to the Times. Richmond: West and Johnston, 1863.

Cook's Tour of Shreveport: Recipes Collected and Tested by the Junior League of Shreveport, Inc. Shreveport: Junior League of Shreveport, 1964.

Corbitt, Helen. *Helen Corbitt's Cookbook.* New York: Houghton Mifflin, 1957.

Council, Mildred. *Mama Dip's Kitchen.* Chapel Hill: University of North Carolina Press, 1999.

Cringan, Mrs. John W. [Harriet Curtis]. *Instruction in Cooking.* Richmond: J. L. Hill Printing, 1895.

Dalton Cook Book. Revised and published by the Women's Auxiliary of the First Presbyterian Church, Dalton, Ga., 1923. 4th ed. Reprinted in *Dalton Cooking: Past, Present, Future.* Dalton, Ga.: Whitfield County Library Board, 1979.

Darden, Norma Jean, and Carole Darden. *Spoonbread and Strawberry Wine: Recipes and Reminiscences of a Family*. Garden City, N.Y.: Anchor, 1978.

Dennis, Annie E., and Daisy A. Wright. *Annie Dennis' Cookbook: A Compendium of Popular Household Recipes for the Busy Housewife*. Atlanta: American Publishing and Engraving, 1893.

Dragonwagon, Crescent. *The Cornbread Gospels*. New York: Workman, 2007.

Dull, Henrietta Stanley. *Southern Cooking*. Atlanta: Ruralist Press, 1928.

Dupree, Nathalie. *New Southern Cooking*. Athens: University of Georgia Press, 2004. Reprint of 1986 edition published by Alfred Knopf.

Elliott, Sarah A. *Mrs. Elliott's Housewife. Containing Practical Receipts in Cookery*. New York: Hurd and Houghton, 1870.

Ellis, Belinda. *Biscuits*. Chapel Hill: University of North Carolina Press, 2013.

Favorite Recipes from Belle Haven Kitchens. Compiled by the Welfare Section of the Belle Haven Women's Club. Belle Haven, Va.: Belle Haven Women's Clubs, 1959.

Favorite Recipes of Alabama Housewives. Warm Springs, Ga.: Favorite Cook Book Company, 1937.

Favorite Southern Recipes. Atlanta: Southern Ruralist, 1912.

Fisher, Abby. *What Mrs. Fisher Knows about Old Southern Cooking, Soups, Pickles, Preserves, Etc.* Reprint, Bedford, Mass.: Applewood Books, 1995. Originally published in 1881 by the Women's Co-operative Printing Office, San Francisco.

Flexner, Marion. *Dixie Dishes*. Boston: Hale, Cushman and Flint, 1941.

Foose, Martha Hall. *Screen Doors and Sweet Tea: Recipes and Tales from a Southern Cook*. New York: Clarkson Potter, 2008.

Fox, Minnie C., comp. *The Blue Grass Cook Book*. New York: Fox, Duffield and Company, 1904.

Gasparilla Cookbook. Tampa: Junior League of Tampa, 1961.

Gibson, Marietta Fauntleroy Hollyd. *Mrs. Charles H. Gibson's Maryland and Virginia Cook Book Containing Numerous Valuable Receipts for Aid in Housekeeping*. Baltimore: John Murphy, 1894.

Glover, E. T. [Elizabeth Whitner]. *The Warm Springs Receipt-Book*. Richmond: B. F. Johnson, 1897.

Gulf City Cook Book Compiled by the Ladies of the St. Francis Street Methodist Episcopal Church, South, Mobile, Alabama. Dayton, Ohio: United Brethren Publishing House, 1878.

Guy, Jerrelle. *Black Girl Baking: Wholesome Recipes Inspired by a Soulful Upbringing*. Salem, Mass.: Page Street Publishing, 2018.

Handy Housekeeping: A Manual for Housekeepers and Collection of Thoroughly Tested Recipes Contributed by the Ladies of the Church and Many of their Friends. Charlottesville, Virginia. [Charlottesville: Woman's Auxiliary Society of the New Baptist Church, c. 1890s?].

Harbury, Katherine E. *Colonial Virginia's Cooking Dynasty*. Columbia: University of South Carolina Press, 2004.

Harland, Marion [Mary Virginia Terhune]. *The Dinner Year Book*. New York: Charles Scribner's Sons, 1883.

Hayes, Emma Allen. *Kentucky Cook Book: Easy and Simple for Any Cook, by a Colored Woman*. St. Louis: J. H. Tomkins, 1912.

Hearn, Lafcadio. *La Cuisine Creole*. New Orleans: Hansell and Brother, 1885.

Hill, Annabella P. *Mrs. Hill's Southern Practical Cookery and Receipt Book*. New York: Carleton, 1872. Reprint, with historical introduction by Damon Fowler, Columbia: University of South Carolina Press, 1995.

Hill, Sallie F. *Progressive Farmer's Southern Cookbook*. Birmingham: Progressive Farmer, 1961.

Hooker, Richard J., ed. *A Colonial Plantation Cookbook: The Receipt Book of Harriott Pinckney Horry, 1770*. Columbia: University of South Carolina Press, 1984.

Hounihan, John. *Bakers' and Confectioners' Guide and Treasure*. Staunton, Va.: n.p., 1877.

Housekeeping in Alabama. Anniston, Ala.: G. H. Norwood, 1893.

Huggins, Mollie. *Tried and True: Tennessee Model Household Guide*. Nashville: Publishing House Methodist Episcopal Church, South, 1897.

Hunter, Ethel Farmer. *Secrets of Southern Cooking*. Chicago: Ziff-Davis, 1948. Reprint, New York: Tudor Publishing Company, 1956.

Jamison, Minnie L., ed. *Tea Kettle Talk Recipes*. Greensboro: Alumnae Association of North Carolina College for Women, 1924.

Junior League of New Orleans. *The Plantation Cookbook*. Garden City, N.Y.: Doubleday, 1972.

Knoxville Woman's Building Association. *Knoxville Cook Book*. Knoxville, Tenn.: Bean, Warters, and Co., 1901.

Kyle Baptist Church (Kyle, Tex.) Ladies Aid and Missionary Society. *The Kyle Baptist Church Cook Book: A Selection of Tried and True Recipes*. Austin: Morgan Printing Co., 1904.

Ladies Aid and Sewing Society of New Orleans. *Up-to-Date Cookbook*. Compiled under the auspices of the Ladies Aid and Sewing Society of New Orleans. Rev. ed. [New Orleans: n.p., 1900?]

Ladies of the Guild of St. James' Parish Church, Pewee Valley, Kentucky. *Favorite Foods of Famous Folk with Directions for the Preparation Thereof Given for the Most Part by the Famous Folk Themselves to the Ladies of the Guild of St. James' Parish Church*. Louisville: John M. Morton, 1900.

"A Lady of Charleston." *The Carolina Receipt Book, or, Housekeeper's Assistant in Cookery, Medicine, and Other Subjects, Connected with the Management of a Family*. Charleston: James S. Burges, 1832.

Lane, Emma Rylander. *Some Good Things to Eat*. Self-published, 1898. Reprint, Clayton, Ala.: Clayton Record, 1976.

Lawrenceburg's Treasury of Personal Recipes Compiled by the Woman's Club of Lawrenceburg, Kentucky. [Kansas City, Mo.: Bev-Ron, 1961].

Lewis, Edna. *The Taste of Country Cooking*. 1976. Reprint, New York: Alfred A. Knopf, 2006.

Lewis, Nelly Custis. *Nelly Custis Lewis's Housekeeping Book*. Edited by Patricia Brady Schmit. New Orleans: Historic New Orleans Collection, 1982.

Lineback, Emily-Sarah. *Preserving the Past: Salem Moravians' Receipts and Rituals*. Boonville, N.C.: Carolina Avenue Press, 2003.

Lone Star Cook Book. Published by the Ladies' [sic] of the Dallas Free Kindergarten and Training School, Dallas, Texas. Dallas: Samuel Jones, 1901.

Lundy, Ronni. *Shuck Beans, Stack Cakes, and Honest Fried Chicken: The Heart and Soul of Southern Country Kitchens*. New York: Atlantic Monthly Press, 1994.

———. *Victuals: An Appalachian Journey, with Recipes*. New York: Clarkson Potter, 2016.

Lustig, Lillie S., S. Claire Sondheim, and Sarah Rensel, comps. and eds. *The Southern Cook Book of Fine Old Recipes*. Reading, Pa.: Culinary Arts Press, 1935.

MacDonald, Patty Vineyard, ed. *The Best from Helen Corbitt's Kitchens*. Denton: University of North Texas Press, 2000.

Mackey, Elbert. *The Tea Cake Roundup*. West Conshohocken, Pa.: Infinity Publishing, 2009.

Markham, Gervase. *Countrey Contentments, or The English Huswife*. London: I. B. for R. Jackson, 1623.

McDermott, Nancie. *Southern Cakes: Sweet and Irresistible Recipes for Everyday Celebrations*. San Francisco: Chronicle Books, 2007.

———. *Southern Pies: A Gracious Plenty of Pie Recipes, from Lemon Chess to Chocolate Pecan*. San Francisco: Chronicle Books, 2010.

McKey, Nola. *From Tea Cakes to Tamales: Third-Generation Texas Recipes*. College Station: Texas A&M University Press, 2016.

McLennan County Medical Auxiliary. *Gingerbread and More*. Waco, Tex.: McLennan County Medical Auxiliary, 1977.

McPhail, Mrs. Clement Carrington [Jane Millicent Powell]. *F. F. V. Receipt Book*. Richmond: West, Johnston and Co., 1894.

Meade, Martha. *Recipes from the Old South*. New York: Bramhall House, 1961.

Mendes, Helen. *The African Heritage Cookbook*. New York: Macmillan, 1971.

Moncure, Blanche Elbert. *Emma Jane's Souvenir Cook Book*. Williamsburg: [Moncure?], 1937.

Moncure, Mrs. M. B. *The Art of Good Living*. Baltimore: William K. Boyle's Steam Press, 1870.

National Council of Negro Women. *Black Family Reunion Cookbook*. New York: Fireside Books, 1993.

Neal, Bill. *Bill Neal's Southern Cooking*. Chapel Hill: University of North Carolina Press, 1989.

———. *Biscuits, Spoonbread, and Sweet Potato Pie*. New York: Alfred A. Knopf, 1990.

Neal, Moreton. *Remembering Bill Neal: Favorite Recipes from a Life in Cooking*. Chapel Hill: University of North Carolina Press, 2004.

Paddleford, Clementine. *The Great American Cookbook: 500 Time-Tested Recipes*. New York: Rizzoli, 2011.

Page, Linda Garland, and Eliot Wigginton, eds. *The Foxfire Book of Appalachian Cookery*. Chapel Hill: University of North Carolina Press, 1984.

Parks, Stella. *Bravetart: Iconic American Desserts*. New York: W. W. Norton, 2017.

Parloa, Maria. *Miss Parloa's Kitchen Companion: A Guide for All Who Would Be Good Housekeepers*. Boston: Estes and Lauriat, 1887.

Pinckney, Eliza Lucas. *Recipe Book of Eliza Lucas Pinckney, 1756*. Charleston: Charleston Lithographing, 1936.

Pohick Cookery: Old Southern Recipes. [Woodbridge, Va.?: n.p., c. 1960].

Porter, Mrs. M. E. Mrs. Porter's New Southern Cookery Book and Companion for Frugal and
    Economical Housekeepers; Containing Carefully Prepared and Practically Tested Recipes for All
    Kinds of Plain and Fancy Cooking. Philadelphia: John E. Potter, 1871.
Pretlow, Mary Denson. The Calendar of Old Southern Recipes. [New York?]: Dodge, 1900.
Raffald, Elizabeth. The Experienced English Housekeeper. 10th ed. London: Printed for R.
    Baldwin, 1786.
Randolph, Mary. The Virginia House-wife. With historical notes and commentaries by
    Karen Hess. Columbia: University of South Carolina Press, 1984. Originally pub-
    lished Washington: Printed by Davis and Force, 1824.
Recipes Collected by the Junior League of Columbus, Georgia. Columbus: Junior League, 1957.
Recipes of the Deep South, Quota Club of Macon, Georgia. Macon: Quota Club, 1948.
Rhett, Blanche S., comp., and Lettie Gay, ed. 200 Years of Charleston Cooking. New York:
    Jonathan Cape and Harrison Smith, 1930. Reprint, Columbia: University of South
    Carolina Press, 1976.
Richard, Lena. New Orleans Cookbook. New Orleans: Rogers Printing, 1939.
River Road Recipes. Baton Rouge: Junior League of Baton Rouge, 1959.
Roxboro Baptist Church Cook Book. Compiled by Circle No. 1, Roxboro, North Carolina.
    Roxboro: Circle No. 1, 1950[?].
Russell, Malinda. A Domestic Cook Book: Containing a Careful Selection of Useful Receipts for the
    Kitchen by Malinda Russell, an Experienced Cook. Paw Paw, Mich.: n.p., 1866.
Rutledge, Sarah. The Carolina Housewife. Charleston: W. R. Babcock, 1847.
Sloan, David L. The Key West Key Lime Pie Cookbook. Key West: Phantom Press, 2013.
Smart-Grosvenor, Vertamae. Vibration Cooking, or The Travel Notes of a Geechee Girl. Garden
    City, N.Y.: Doubleday, 1970.
Smith, Mary Stuart Harrison. Virginia Cookery-Book. New York: Harper, 1885.
Stone, Birdie K., comp. The Roanoke Cook Book: Favorite Recipes by Some of Roanoke's Good
    Housekeepers. Roanoke: Woman's Civic Betterment Club, 1907.
Stoney, Mrs. Samuel G., comp. Carolina Rice Cook Book. Charleston: Carolina Rice Kitchen
    Association, 1901.
St. Paul's Guild, Waco, Texas. Household Manual and Practical Cook Book. Waco: Brooks and
    Wallace Steam Print, 1888.
Strobel, Pamela. Princess Pamela's Soul Food Cookbook: A Mouth-Watering Treasury of
    Afro-American Recipes. New York: Rizzoli, 2017. First published 1969 by New American
    Library (New York).
Sturges, Lena E. Our Best Recipes. Birmingham: Oxmoor House, 1970.
Talk About Good! Lafayette, La.: Junior League of Lafayette, 1967.
Tartan, Beth. North Carolina and Old Salem Cookery. Chapel Hill: University of North
    Carolina Press, 1992.
Timlin, Octa Lee. Sandwiches, Salads and Desserts. By Octa Lee Stephen Timlin. [Galveston,
    Tex.: Octa Lee Timlin, c. 1929].
Tyree, Marion Cabell, ed. Housekeeping in Old Virginia: Containing Contributions from Two
    Hundred and Fifty Ladies in Virginia and Her Sister States. New York: G. W. Carleton, 1877.
Uhler, Alice Hough. A Collection of Valuable Receipts. Contributed by the Ladies of St. Paul's
    Church and Their Friends. Compiled by Lycurgus Edward Uhler. Alexandria, Va.:
    Ramey's Printing Office and Book-bindery, 1900.

Van Duzor, Alline P. *Fascinating Foods from the Deep South*. New York: Gramercy, 1962.

Vaughn, Kate Brew. *Culinary Echoes from Dixie*. Cincinnati: McDonald Press, 1914.

Verstille, Mrs. E. J. *Mrs. E. J. Verstille's Southern Cookery: Comprising a Fine Collection of Cooking and Other Receipts Valuable to Mothers and House-keepers. By Mrs. E. J. Verstille of Louisiana*. New York: Owens and Agar, Booksellers and Stationers, 1867.

Victuals and Vitamins. Greensboro: Junior League of Greensboro, North Carolina. Originally published 1942; revised and reprinted, 1952; supplement, 1962.

Villas, James. *My Mother's Southern Kitchen: Recipes and Reminiscences*. New York: Macmillan, 1994.

Virginia Cook Book. Compiled by the Women of the Presbyterian Church of Leesburg, Virginia. Baltimore: Lord Baltimore Press, [c. 1900?].

Warren, Mary Elizabeth. *The Mississippi Cook Book of New Southern Recipes*. Yazoo City, Miss.: Yazoo City Herald Print, 1922.

Watts, Edith, and John Watts. *Jesse's Book of Creole and Deep South Recipes*. New York: Viking, 1954.

Wilcox, Estelle. *The New Dixie Cook-Book*. Atlanta: L. D. Clarkson, 1889.

Willis, Virginia. *Bon Appétit, Y'all: Recipes and Stories from Three Generations of Southern Cooking*. Berkeley: Ten Speed Press, 2008.

Wilson, Mrs. Henry Lumpkin [Mary Elizabeth]. *Tested Recipe Cook Book*. Atlanta: Foote and Davies, 1895.

Woman's Auxiliary, Second Baptist Church, Richmond, Virginia, comp. *Second Baptist Church Cook Book: A Useful Collection of Practical Tested and Approved Recipes*. Richmond: Woman's Auxiliary, Second Baptist Church, 1925.

Woman's Club of South Jacksonville, compiler. *Cook Book*. Jacksonville, Fla.: The Woman's Club, [c. 1940s].

Young Men's Christian Association, Petersburg, Va., Ladies' Auxiliary. *The Old Virginia Cook Book of 600 Tested and Proved Recipes*. [Petersburg: Fenn and Owen, 1894?].

YWCA Cook Book. Pine Bluff, Ark.: [YWCA], 1924.

GOVERNMENT PUBLICATIONS

Agriculture of the United States in 1860 Compiled from the Original Returns of the Eighth Census. Washington, D.C.: Government Printing Office, 1864.

Atwater, Wilbur O., and Charles D. Woods. *Dietary Studies with Reference to the Food of the Negro in Alabama in 1895 and 1896*. U.S. Department of Agriculture Bulletin No. 38. Washington, D.C.: Government Printing Office, 1897.

Ballinger, Roy A. *A History of Sugar Marketing*. U.S. Department of Agriculture Economic Research Service Agricultural Economic Report No. 197. Washington, D.C.: Government Printing Office, 1971.

———. *Sugar during World War II*. U.S. Department of Agriculture War Records Monographs No. 3 (June 1946).

Burk, Margaret. "Pounds and Percentages." In *Food: The Yearbook of Agriculture 1959*, 591–99. Washington, D.C.: Government Printing Office, 1959.

Dashiell, L. T. *General Laws of the State of Texas Passed at the Regular Session of the Thirtieth Legislature*. Austin: Von Boeckmann-Jones, Printers, 1907.

Dickins, Dorothy. *Food and Health*. Mississippi Agricultural Experiment Station Bulletin No. 255. Agricultural College, Miss., 1928.

———. *A Nutrition Investigation of Negro Tenants in the Yazoo Mississippi Delta*. Mississippi Agricultural Experiment Station Bulletin No. 254. Agricultural College, Miss., 1928.

———. *A Study of Food Habits of People in Two Contrasting Areas of Mississippi*. Mississippi Agricultural Experiment Station Bulletin No. 245. Agricultural College, Miss., 1927.

Dickins, Dorothy, L. D. Welch, and W. E. Christian. "Industrialization and a Market for Food in the Kosciusko Trade Area." *Mississippi Agricultural Experiment Bulletin* No. 534, August 1954, 5–27.

Du Bois, W. E. B. *The Negroes of Farmville, Virginia*. Bulletin of the Department of Labor, vol. 3. Washington, D.C.: Government Printing Office, 1898.

Frissell, H. B., and Isabel Bevier. *Dietary Studies of Negroes in Eastern Virginia in 1897 and 1898*. U.S. Department of Agriculture Bulletin No. 71. Washington, D.C.: Government Printing Office, 1899.

Guin, Marvin. *An Economic Study of Dairy Farming in Oktibbeha and Lowndes Counties, Mississippi, 1936–1937*. Mississippi Agricultural Experiment Station Bulletin No. 324. State College, Miss., 1938.

Milanich, Jerald T. "Life in a 9th Century Indian Household: A Weeden Island Fall–Winter Site on the Upper Apalachicola River, Florida." *Bureau of Historic Sites and Properties Bulletin* No. 4, 1–44. Tallahassee: Florida Department of State, 1974.

Otto, John Solomon, and Russell Lamar Lewis Jr. "A Formal and Functional Analysis of San Marcos Pottery from Site SA 16–23, St. Augustine, Florida." *Bureau of Historic Sites and Properties Bulletin* No. 4, 95–117. Tallahassee: Florida Department of State, 1974.

Stiebeling, Hazel K., and Esther F. Phipard. *Diets of Families of Employed Wage Earners and Clerical Workers in Cities*. Circular 507. Washington, D.C.: U.S. Department of Agriculture, January 1939.

Swanton, John Reed. *Indian Tribes of the Lower Mississippi Valley and Adjacent Coast of the Gulf of Mexico*. Bureau of American Ethnology Bulletin No. 43. Washington, D.C.: Government Printing Office, 1911.

U.S. Senate. *Report on the Condition of Woman and Child Wage-Earners in the United States. Volume 16. Family Budgets of Typical Cotton-Mill Workers*. Senate Document No. 645, 61st Cong., 2nd sess. Washington, D.C.: Government Printing Office, 1911.

Wait, Charles E. *Nutrition Investigations at the University of Tennessee in 1896 and 1897*. U.S. Department of Agriculture Office of Experiment Stations Bulletin No. 53. Washington, D.C.: Government Printing Office, 1898.

DISSERTATIONS AND THESES

Anderson, Erin. "Molded Magic: Advertising the 'Joys of Jell-O' to the Modern American Housewife, 1920–1945." MA thesis, University of Wyoming, 2014.

Brown, David Arthur. "An Enslaved Landscape: The Virginia Plantation at the End of the Seventeenth Century." PhD diss., College of William and Mary, 2014.

Burton, Helen Sophie. "Family and Economy in Frontier Louisiana: Colonial Natchitoches, 1714–1803." PhD diss., Texas Christian University, 2002.

Cooper, Abigail. "'Lord, Until I Reach My Home': Inside the Refugee Camps of the American Civil War." PhD diss., University of Pennsylvania, 2015.

Cumbaa, Stephen L. "Patterns of Resource Use and Cross-Cultural Dietary Change in the Spanish Colonial Period." PhD diss., University of Florida, 1975.

Cusick, James Gregory. "Ethnic Groups and Class in an Emerging Market Economy: Spaniards and Minorcans in Late Colonial St. Augustine." PhD diss., University of Florida, 1993.

Franklin, Maria. "Out of Site, Out of Mind: The Archaeology of an Enslaved Virginian Household, ca. 1740–1778." PhD diss., University of California, Berkeley, 1997.

Galan, Francis X. "Last Soldiers, First Pioneers: The Los Adaes Border Community on the Louisiana-Texas Frontier, 1721–1779." PhD diss., Southern Methodist University, 2006.

Hoffman, Kathleen S. "Development of a Cultural Identity in Colonial America: The Spanish-American Experience in La Florida." PhD diss., University of Florida, 1994.

Luck, Katherine Adrienne. "Finding Margaret Haughery: The Forgotten and Remembered Lives of New Orleans's 'Bread Woman' in the Nineteenth and Twentieth Centuries." MA thesis, University of New Orleans, 2014.

McCleary, Ann. "Shaping a New Role for the Rural Woman: Home Demonstration Work in Augusta County, Virginia, 1917–1940." PhD diss., Brown University, 1996.

McKee, Lawrence William. "Plantation Food Supply in Nineteenth-Century Tidewater Virginia." PhD diss., University of California, Berkeley, 1988.

McReynolds, James Michael. "Family Life in a Borderland Community: Nacogdoches, Texas, 1779–1861." PhD diss., Texas Tech University, 1978.

Miller, Henry M. "Colonization and Subsistence on the 17th-Century Chesapeake Frontier." PhD diss., Michigan State University, 1984.

Parker, Susan Richbourg. "The Second Century of Settlement in Spanish St. Augustine, 1670–1763." PhD diss., University of Florida, 1999.

Schlotterbeck, John T. "Plantation and Farm: Social and Economic Change in Orange and Greene Counties, Virginia, 1716 to 1860." PhD diss., Johns Hopkins University, 1980.

Singleton, Theresa A. "The Archaeology of Afro-American Slavery in Coastal Georgia: A Regional Perception of Slave Household and Community Patterns." PhD diss., University of Florida, 1980.

Spencer, Maryellen. "Food in Seventeenth-Century Tidewater Virginia: A Method for Studying Historical Cuisines." PhD diss., Virginia Polytechnic Institute and State University, 1982.

Upton, Dell. "Early Vernacular Architecture in Southeastern Virginia." PhD diss., Brown University, 1980.

Vaughan, William Ashley. "Natchez during the Civil War." PhD diss., University of Southern Mississippi, 2001.

Wheeler, Robert Anthony. "Lancaster County, Virginia, 1650–1750: The Evolution of a Southern Tidewater Community." PhD diss., Brown University, 1972.

Young, Amy L. "Risk and Material Conditions of African American Slaves at Locust Grove: An Archaeological Perspective." PhD diss., University of Tennessee, 1995.

Young, Ashley Rose. "Nourishing Networks: The Public Culture of Food in Nineteenth-Century America." PhD diss., Duke University, 2017.

SECONDARY SOURCES

Abbott, J. S. *The Composition and Food Value of Margarine*. Washington, D.C.: National Association of Margarine Manufacturers, 1940.

Abernethy, Thomas P. *The Formative Period in Alabama, 1815–1828*. Montgomery: Brown Printing, 1922.

Adams, William Hampton, and Steven D. Smith. "Historical Perspectives on Black Tenant Famer Material Culture: The Henry C. Long General Store Ledger at Waverly Plantation, Mississippi." In *The Archeology of Slavery and Plantation Life*, edited by Theresa A. Singleton, 309–34. Orlando: Academic Press, 1985.

Agee, James. *Cotton Tenants: Three Families*. Brooklyn: Melville House, 2013.

Aggarwal-Schifellite, Manisha. "The Long, Strange Career of the Mrs. America Pageant." *Jezebel*, January 5, 2016. https://pictorial.jezebel.com/the-long-strange-life-of-the-mrs-america-pageant-1750888725.

Aldrich, Mark. "The Rise and Decline of the Kerosene Kitchen: A Neglected Energy Transition in Rural America, 1870–1950." *Agricultural History* 94, no. 1 (Winter 2020): 24–60.

Alsen, Dana J. "The Alabama Food Frontier: Development of a Cuisine, 800 to the Present." http://alabamafoodways.org/. Accessed August 30, 2021.

Anderson, E. N. *Everyone Eats: Understanding Food and Culture*. New York: New York University Press, 2005.

Anderson, Lucy London. *North Carolina Women of the Confederacy*. Fayetteville, N.C.: Lucy London Anderson, 1926.

Anderson, Virginia DeJohn. *Creatures of Empire: How Domestic Animals Transformed Early America*. New York: Oxford University Press, 2004.

Arnade, Charles. *Florida on Trial, 1593–1602*. Coral Gables: University of Miami Press, 1959.

Ash, Stephen V. *Rebel Richmond: Life and Death in the Confederate Capital*. Chapel Hill: University of North Carolina Press, 2019.

Atherton, Lewis. *The Southern Country Store, 1800–1860*. Baton Rouge: Louisiana State University Press, 1949.

Ayers, Edward L. *The Promise of the New South: Life after Reconstruction*. New York: Oxford University Press, 1992.

Baine, Rodney M., and Louis De Vorsey Jr. "The Provenance and Historical Accuracy of 'A View of Savannah as It Stood the 29th of March, 1734.'" *Georgia Historical Quarterly* 73, no. 4 (Winter 1989): 784–813.

Baird, Byron. "Baird, Ninia Lilla [Ninnie]." In *Handbook of Texas Online*. Texas State Historical Association. www.tshaonline.org/handbook/online/articles/fbaeq.

Balter, Michael. "Corn: It's Not for Cocktails." *Science*, March 23, 2009. www.sciencemag.org/news/2009/03/corn-its-not-cocktails.

Behr, Edward. "Eula Mae Doré." In *Cornbread Nation 6: The Best of Southern Food Writing*, edited by Brett Anderson, 145–48. Athens: University of Georgia Press, 2012.

Bell, Michael Everette. "Regional Identity in the Antebellum South: How German Immigrants became 'Good' Charlestonians." *South Carolina Historical Magazine* 100, no. 1 (January 1999): 9–28.

Benét, Stephen Vincent. *Western Star.* New York: Farrar and Rinehart, 1943.

Bennett, Helen Christine. "Cleaning Up the American City: How Mrs. Caroline Bartlett Crane Does It." *American Magazine* 76 (September 1913): 45–48.

Bentley, Amy. *Eating for Victory: Food Rationing and the Politics of Domesticity.* Urbana: University of Illinois Press, 1998.

Beoku-Betts, Josephine. "'She Make Funny Flat Cake She Call Saraka': Gullah Women and Food Practices under Slavery." In *Working toward Freedom: Slave Society and Domestic Economy in the American South,* edited by Larry E. Hudson Jr., 211–31. Rochester: University of Rochester Press, 1994.

Berenstein, Nadia. "Making a Global Sensation: Vanilla Flavor, Synthetic Chemistry, and the Meanings of Purity." *History of Science* 54, no. 4 (December 2016): 399–424.

Berry, Thomas S. "The Rise of Flour Milling in Richmond." *Virginia Magazine of History and Biography* 78, no. 4 (October 1970): 387–408.

Bienvenu, Marcelle, Carl A. Brasseaux, and Ryan A. Brasseaux. *Stir the Pot: The History of Cajun Cuisine.* New York: Hippocrene Books, 2005.

Billings, Warren M. *Sir William Berkeley and the Forging of Colonial Virginia.* Baton Rouge: Louisiana State University Press, 2004.

Bishai, David, and Ritu Nalubola. "The History of Food Fortification in the United States: Its Relevance for Fortification Efforts in Developing Countries." *Economic Development and Cultural Change* 51, no. 1 (October 2002): 37–53.

Blackman, Ann. *Wild Rose: The True Story of a Civil War Spy.* New York: Random House, 2006.

Blair, William. *Virginia's Private War: Feeding Body and Soul in the Confederacy.* New York: Oxford University Press, 1998.

Blejwas, Emily. *The Story of Alabama in Fourteen Foods.* Tuscaloosa: University of Alabama Press, 2019.

Blount, Roy. "Raising Cane: Finding Answers in a Sweet Syrup." *Garden & Gun,* June/July 2013. https://gardenandgun.com/articles/end-of-the-line-raising-cane.

Bobrow-Strain, Aaron. "White Bread Bio-politics: Purity, Health, and the Triumph of Industrial Baking." *Cultural Geographies* 15, no. 1 (2008): 19–40.

Boddie, William W. "Cornbread." *Southern Living* 1, no. 1 (February 1966): 44.

Bogin, Ruth. "Petitioning and the New Moral Economy of Post-Revolutionary America." *William and Mary Quarterly* 45, no. 3 (July 1988): 391–425.

Bollet, Alfred Jay. "Politics and Pellagra: The Epidemic of Pellagra in the U.S. in the Early Twentieth Century." *Yale Journal of Biology and Medicine* 65 (May/June 1992): 211–21.

Bolton, Charles C. *Poor Whites of the Antebellum South: Tenants and Laborers in Central North Carolina and Northeast Mississippi.* Durham: Duke University Press, 1994.

Bomgardner, Melody M. "The Problem with Vanilla." *Scientific American,* September 14, 2016. www.scientificamerican.com/article/the-problem-with-vanilla/.

Bond, Courtney. "Texas Sheet Cake." *Texas Monthly,* February 2016. www.texasmonthly.com/food/texas-sheet-cake-recipe/.

Booke, Erin. "Did You Know? The German Chocolate Cake Is Not Actually German, It's Texan." *Dallas Morning News*, May 7, 2018.

Bragdon, Kathleen, Edward A. Chappell, and William Graham. "A Scant Urbanity: Jamestown in the 17th Century." In *The Archaeology of Seventeenth Century Virginia*, edited by Theodore R. Reinhart and Dennis J. Pogue, 223–49. Richmond: Archaeological Society of Virginia, 1993.

Bragg, Rick. "Back to the Bayou." In *Cornbread Nation 3: Foods of the Mountain South*, edited by Ronni Lundy, 247–51. Chapel Hill: University of North Carolina Press, 2005.

Brasseaux, Carl A. *The Founding of New Acadia: The Beginnings of Acadian Life in Louisiana, 1765–1803*. Baton Rouge: Louisiana State University Press, 1987.

"Breads Made with Cornmeal." *Southern Living* 4, no. 9 (October 1970): 70–71.

Breen, T. H., and Stephen Innes. *"Myne Owne Ground": Race and Freedom on Virginia's Eastern Shore, 1640–1676*. New York: Oxford University Press, 1980.

Brewer, Priscilla J. *From Fireplace to Cookstove: Technology and the Domestic Ideal in America*. Syracuse: Syracuse University Press, 2000.

Briggs, Rachel V. "The Hominy Foodway of the Historic Native Eastern Woodlands." *Native South* 8 (2015): 112–46.

Brooke, Steven. *The Majesty of St. Augustine*. Gretna, La.: Pelican, 2005.

Brown, Joyce Compton, and Les Brown. "The Discourse of Food as Cultural Translation and Empowering Voice in Appalachian Women during the Outmigration Process." *Journal of Appalachian Studies* 7, no. 2 (Fall 2001): 315–29.

Brown, Stephen. "The Florida History Project: Key Lime Pie." *Naples Illustrated*, September 15, 2014. www.naplesillustrated.com/florida-history-project-the-key-lime-pie/.

Burkette, Allison. "'Stamped Indian': Finding History and Culture in Terms for American 'Cornbread.'" *American Speech* 86, no. 3 (Fall 2011): 312–39.

Burton, H. Sophie, and F. Todd Smith. *Colonial Natchitoches: A Creole Community on the Louisiana-Texas Frontier*. College Station: Texas A&M University Press, 2008.

———. "Slavery in the Colonial Louisiana Backcountry: Natchitoches, 1714–1803." *Louisiana History* 52, no. 2 (Spring 2011): 133–88.

Bushnell, Amy Turner. *Situado and Sabana: Spain's Support System for the Presidio and Mission Provinces of Florida*. New York: American Museum of Natural History, 1994.

Butterick Publishing Company. *The Story of a Pantry Shelf*. New York: Butterick, 1925.

"Butter Two Biscuits While They're Hot." *Southern Living* 4, no. 4 (May 1970): 101.

Calhoun, Creighton Lee. *Old Southern Apples*. Blacksburg, Va.: McDonald and Woodward, 1995.

Campbell, Jodi. *At the First Table: Food and Social Identity in Early Modern Spain*. Lincoln: University of Nebraska Press, 2017.

"Capsule Summary of 156 Prince George Street." Maryland Historical Trust, June 11, 2004. https://mht.maryland.gov/secure/medusa/PDF/AnneArundel/AA-1200.pdf.

Carney, Judith. "African Rice in the Columbian Exchange." *Journal of African History* 42, no. 3 (2001): 377–99.

Carney, Judith, and Richard Nicholas Rosomoff. *In the Shadow of Slavery: Africa's Botanical Legacy in the Atlantic World*. Berkeley: University of California Press, 2011.

Carr, Lois Green, and Russell R. Menard. "Immigration and Opportunity: The Freedman in Early Colonial Maryland." In *The Chesapeake in the Seventeenth Century: Essays in*

Anglo-American Society and Politics, edited by Thad W. Tate and David L. Ammerman, 206–42. Chapel Hill: University of North Carolina Press, 1979.

Carr, Lois Green, Russell R. Menard, and Lorena Walsh. *Robert Cole's World: Agriculture and Society in Early Maryland*. Chapel Hill: University of North Carolina Press, 1991.

Carson, Cary. "Banqueting Houses and the 'Need of Society' among Slave-Owning Planters in the Chesapeake Colonies." *William and Mary Quarterly* 70, no. 4 (October 2013): 725–80.

Carson, Cary, Norman F. Barka, William M. Kelso, Garry W. Stone, and Dell Upton. "Impermanent Architecture in the Southern American Colonies." *Winterthur Portfolio* 16 (1981): 135–96.

Carson, Cary, Joanne Bowen, Willie Graham, Martha McCartney, and Lorena Walsh. "New World, Real World: Improvising English Culture in Seventeenth-Century Virginia." *Journal of Southern History* 74, no. 1 (February 2008): 31–88.

Cashin, Joan. *War Stuff: The Struggle for Human and Environmental Resources in the American Civil War*. New York: Cambridge University Press, 2018.

Castle, Sheri. "The History behind the Legendary Lady Baltimore Cake." *Southern Living*. www.southernliving.com/desserts/cakes/lady-baltimore-cake-history. Accessed August 30, 2021.

———. "Mrs. Hanes' Hand-Made Moravian Cookies Keeps a Beloved Baking Legacy Alive." *Southern Living*, November 16, 2020. www.southernliving.com/christmas/mrs-hanes-moravian-cookies/.

———. "Ocracoke Fig Preserves Cake with Buttermilk Glaze." *Our State*, January 27, 2014. www.ourstate.com/ocracoke-fig-preserves-cake/.

Cave, Alfred A. *Lethal Encounters: Englishmen and Indians in Colonial Virginia*. Santa Barbara: Praeger, 2011.

Chaplin, Joyce E. *An Anxious Pursuit: Agricultural Innovation and Modernity in the Lower South, 1730–1815*. Chapel Hill: University of North Carolina Press, 1993.

Chapman, Jefferson, and Andrea B. Shea. "The Archaeobotanical Record: Early Archaic Period to Contact in the Lower Little Tennessee River Valley." *Tennessee Anthropologist* 6, no. 1 (1981): 61–84.

Chappell, Edward A. "Accommodating Slavery in Bermuda." In *Archaeology of Southern Urban Landscapes*, edited by Amy L. Young, 67–98. Tuscaloosa: University of Alabama Press, 2000.

———. "Housing Slavery." In *The Chesapeake House: Architectural Investigation by Colonial Williamsburg*, edited by Cary Carson and Carl R. Lounsbury, 156–78. Chapel Hill: University of North Carolina Press, 2013.

Chesson, Michael B. "Harlots or Heroines? A New Look at the Richmond Bread Riot." *Virginia Magazine of History and Biography* 92, no. 2 (April 1984): 131–75.

Christman, Jennifer. "Golden Goodness—Classic, Comforting Arkansas Cornbread." *Arkansas Living*, October 31, 2020. http://arkansaslivingmagazine.com/article/golden-goodness-classic-comforting-arkansas-cornbread/.

Cierzniak, Libby. "Indianapolis Collected: Butterine, Anyone?" Historic Indianapolis, March 17, 2012. https://historicindianapolis.com/indianapolis-collected-butterine-anyone/.

Cimprich, John. *Slavery's End in Tennessee, 1861–1865.* Tuscaloosa: University of Alabama Press, 1985.

Civitello, Linda. *Baking Powder Wars: The Cutthroat Food Fight That Revolutionized Cooking.* Urbana: University of Illinois Press, 2017.

Clark, John Garretson. *The Grain Trade in the Old Northwest.* Urbana: University of Illinois Press, 1966.

———. *New Orleans, 1718–1812: An Economic History.* Baton Rouge: Louisiana State University Press, 1970.

Clark, Libby. "Mary McLeod Bethune (1875–1955) Founded Bethune-Cookman College with Sweet Potato Pies: The Black Family Reunion Cookbook Heritage of African American Cooking." *Los Angeles Sentinel,* February 28, 1991.

Clayton, W. Woodford. *History of Davidson County, Tennessee.* Philadelphia: J. W. Lewis, 1880.

Click, Patricia C. *Time Full of Trial: The Roanoke Island Freedmen's Colony, 1862–1867.* Chapel Hill: University of North Carolina Press, 2001.

Cobb, James C. *The Most Southern Place on Earth: The Mississippi Delta and the Roots of Regional Identity.* New York: Oxford University Press, 1992.

Cofield, Rod. "How the Hoe Cake (Most Likely) Got Its Name." *Food History News,* Summer 2008, 1, 6–7.

Cooley, Angela Jill. "Freedom's Farms: Activism and Sustenance in Rural Mississippi." In *Dethroning the Deceitful Pork Chop: Rethinking African American Foodways from Slavery to Obama,* edited by Jennifer Jensen Wallach, 199–214. Fayetteville: University of Arkansas Press, 2015.

Cooper, Christopher A., and H. Gibbs Knotts. *The Resilience of Southern Identity: Why the South Still Matters in the Minds of Its People.* Chapel Hill: University of North Carolina Press, 2017.

Côté, Richard N. *Mary's World: Love, War, and Family Ties in Nineteenth-Century Charleston.* Mount Pleasant, S.C.: Corinthian Books, 2000.

Covey, Herbert C., and Dwight Eisnach. *What the Slaves Ate: Recollections of African American Foods and Foodways from the Slave Narratives.* Santa Barbara: Greenwood Press, 2009.

Cowan, Ruth Schwartz. *More Work for Mother: The Ironies of Household Technology from the Open Hearth to the Microwave.* New York: Basic Books, 1983.

Crane, Eva. *The World History of Beekeeping and Honey Hunting.* New York: Routledge, 1999.

Crosby, Alfred Worcester. *The Columbian Exchange: Biological and Cultural Consequences of 1492.* Westport, Conn.: Greenwood, 1972.

Crump, Nancy Carter. *Hearthside Cooking: An Introduction to Virginia Plantation Cuisine Including Bills of Fare, Tools and Techniques, and Original Recipes with Adaptations for Modern Fireplaces and Kitchens.* McLean, Va.: EMC Publications, 1986.

Cuevas, John. *Cat Island: The History of a Gulf Coast Barrier Island.* Jefferson, N.C.: McFarland, 2014.

Curry, Dale. "Lavishly Layered." My New Orleans.com, September 1, 2009. www.myneworleans.com/lavishly-layered/.

Dabney, Joseph E. *Smokehouse Ham, Spoon Bread, and Scuppernong Wine: The Folklore and Art of Southern Appalachian Cooking.* Nashville: Cumberland House, 1998.

David, Elizabeth. *English Bread and Yeast Cookery*. London: Grub Street, 2012. First published 1977 by Allen Lane (London).

Davis, Allison, Burleigh B. Gardner, and Mary R. Gardner. *Deep South: A Social Anthropological Study of Caste and Class*. Chicago: University of Chicago Press, 1941.

Dawdy, Shannon Lee. "'A Wild Taste': Food and Colonialism in 18th-Century Louisiana." *Ethnohistory* 57 (Summer 2010): 389–413.

Deagan, Kathleen. *Spanish St. Augustine: The Archeology of a Colonial Creole Community*. New York: Academic Press, 1983.

Deagan, Kathleen A., and Darcie A. MacMahon. *Fort Mose: Colonial America's Black Fortress of Freedom*. Gainesville: University Press of Florida, 1995.

DesChamps, Margaret Burr. "Early Days in the Cumberland Country." *Tennessee Historical Quarterly* 6, no. 3 (September 1947): 195–229.

Dickins, Dorothy. "Food Patterns of White and Negro Families, 1936–1948." *Social Forces* 27, no. 4 (May 1949): 425–30.

Dill, Alonzo Thomas, Jr. "Eighteenth Century New Bern: A History of the Town and Craven County, 1700–1800. Part II: The Founding of New Bern." *North Carolina Historical Review* 22, no. 2 (April 1945): 152–75.

———. "Eighteenth Century New Bern: A History of the Town and Craven County, 1700–1800. Part III: Rebellion and Indian Warfare." *North Carolina Historical Review* 22, no. 3 (July 1945): 293–319.

———. "Eighteenth Century New Bern: A History of the Town and Craven County, 1700–1800. Part V: Political and Commercial Rise of New Bern." *North Carolina Historical Review* 23, no. 1 (January 1946): 47–78.

Diouf, Sylviane A. *Servants of Allah: African Muslims Enslaved in the Americas*. New York: New York University Press, 1998.

Dow, George Francis. *Slave Ships and Slaving*. Salem, Mass.: Marine Research Society, 1927.

Downey, Salley A. "Robert C. Smith, Chairman of Pie Company." *Philadelphia Inquirer*, November 15, 2010.

Du Bois, W. E. B., ed. *The Negro American Family*. Atlanta University Publication No. 13. Atlanta: Atlanta University Press, 1908.

Duncan, Richard R. *Beleaguered Winchester: A Virginia Community at War, 1861–1865*. Baton Rouge: Louisiana State University Press, 2007.

Earle, Rebecca. *The Body of the Conquistador: Food, Race and the Colonial Experience in Spanish America, 1492–1700*. Cambridge: Cambridge University Press, 2012.

Edge, John T. *The Potlikker Papers: A Food History of the Modern South*. New York: Penguin Press, 2017.

Egerton, John. *Southern Food: At Home, on the Road, in History*. New York: Alfred A. Knopf, 1987.

Elie, Lolis Eric. "The Origin Myth of New Orleans Cuisine." In *Cornbread Nation 6: The Best of Southern Food Writing*, edited by Brett Anderson, 214–25. Athens: University of Georgia Press, 2012.

Engelhardt, Elizabeth S. D. *A Mess of Greens: Southern Gender and Southern Food*. Athens: University of Georgia Press, 2011.

Epperson, Terrence W. "Constructing Difference: The Social and Spatial Order of the Chesapeake Plantation." In "I, Too, Am America": Archaeological Studies of African American Life, edited by Theresa A. Singleton, 159–72. Charlottesville: University Press of Virginia, 1999.

Escott, Paul. Many Excellent People: Power and Privilege in North Carolina, 1850–1900. Chapel Hill: University of North Carolina Press, 1985.

Etheridge, Elizabeth W. The Butterfly Caste: A Social History of Pellagra in the South. Westport, Conn.: Greenwood, 1972.

Ethridge, Robbie. Creek Country: The Creek Indians and Their World. Chapel Hill: University of North Carolina Press, 2004.

Evans, Elliot A. P. "The East Texas House." Journal of the Society of Architectural Historians 9 (December 1952): 1–8.

Fairbanks, Charles. "The Plantation Archaeology of the Southeastern Coast." Historical Archaeology 18, no. 1 (1984): 1–14.

Farrish, Christopher. "Theft, Food, Labor, and Culinary Insurrection in the Virginia Plantation Yard." In Dethroning the Deceitful Pork Chop: Rethinking African American Foodways from Slavery to Obama, edited by Jennifer Jensen Wallach, 151–63. Fayetteville: University of Arkansas Press, 2015.

Feibleman, Peter S. American Cooking: Creole and Acadian. New York: Time-Life Books, 1971.

Feldman, Claudia. "Houston Says Goodbye to Beloved 'Cake Lady.'" Houston Chronicle, July 26, 2015.

Ferguson, Leland. Uncommon Ground: Archaeology and Early African America, 1650–1800. Washington, D.C.: Smithsonian Books, 1992.

Ferris, Marcie Cohen. The Edible South: The Power of Food and the Making of an American Region. Chapel Hill: University of North Carolina Press, 2014.

———. Matzoh Ball Gumbo: Culinary Tales of the Jewish South. Chapel Hill: University of North Carolina Press, 2005.

Fields, Barbara J. Slavery and Freedom on the Middle Ground: Maryland during the Nineteenth Century. New Haven: Yale University Press, 1985.

Figoni, Paula. How Baking Works: Exploring the Fundamentals of Baking Science. 2nd ed. Hoboken: John Wiley and Sons, 2008.

Francis, J. Michael, and Kathleen M. Kole. Murder and Martyrdom in Spanish Florida: Don Juan and the Guale Uprising of 1597. New York: American Museum of Natural History, 2011.

Francis, J. Michael, Gary Mormino, and Rachel Sanderson. "Slavery Took Hold in Florida under the Spanish in the 'Forgotten Century' of 1492–1619." Tampa Bay Times, August 29, 2019.

Franklin, Jay. "Bedrock Mortar Hole Sites on the Upper Cumberland Plateau in Tennessee." http://faculty.etsu.edu/franklij/BRM_page.htm. Accessed August 14, 2016.

Franklin, Maria. "The Archaeological and Symbolic Dimensions of Soul Food: Race, Culture and Afro-Virginian Identity." In Race and the Archaeology of Identity, edited by Charles E. Orser Jr., 88–107. Salt Lake City: University of Utah Press, 2001.

Franklin, Sara B. "Introduction." In Edna Lewis: At the Table with an American Original, edited by Sara B. Franklin, 1–14. Chapel Hill: University of North Carolina Press, 2019.

Fraser, Walter J., Jr. *Savannah in the Old South*. Athens: University of Georgia Press, 2005.

"Fried Pies Like Grandma Made." *Southern Living* 5, no. 9 (September 1970): 61.

"Frozen Bakery Items Aid Dessert." *Dallas Morning News*, August 18, 1966.

Fuller, Dorian Q., and Lara Gonzalez Carretero. "The Archeology of Neolithic Cooking Traditions: Archaeobotanical Approaches to Baking, Boiling, and Fermenting." *Archaeology International* 21 (2018): 109–21.

Fussell, Betty. *The Story of Corn*. New York: Alfred A. Knopf, 1992.

Gabaccia, Donna, and Jane Aldrich. "Recipes in Context: Solving a Small Mystery in Charleston's Culinary History." *Food, Culture and Society* 15, no. 2 (June 2012): 197–221.

Gallay, Alan. *The Indian Slave Trade: The Rise of the English Empire in the American South, 1670–1717*. New Haven: Yale University Press, 2002.

Galloway, J. H. *The Sugar Cane Industry: An Historical Geography from Its Origins to 1914*. London: Cambridge University Press, 1989.

Gantz, Carroll. "Corning Pyrex Bakeware." Industrial Design History, April 14, 2010. www.industrialdesignhistory.com/node/137.

Gill, Harold B., Jr. "Wheat Culture in Early Virginia." *Agricultural History* 52 (1978): 380–93.

Giraud, Marcel. *A History of French Louisiana*. Vol. 5, *The Company of the Indies, 1723–1731*. Translated by Brian Pearce. Baton Rouge: Louisiana State University Press, 1991.

Glatthaar, Joseph T. "Confederate Soldiers in Virginia, 1861." In *Virginia at War, 1861*, edited by William C. Davis and James I. Robertson Jr., 45–63. Lexington: University Press of Kentucky, 2005.

Glover, Lorri. *Eliza Lucas Pinckney: An Independent Woman in the Age of Revolution*. New Haven: Yale University Press, 2020.

Goldberg, Elyssa. "Why America Fell in Love with Pyrex." *Bon Appetit*, June 24, 2015. www.bonappetit.com/entertaining-style/pop-culture/article/pyrex-centennial.

Gorvett, Zaria. "The Delicious Flavour with a Toxic Secret." *BBC Future*, June 20, 2017. www.bbc.com/future/story/20170620-the-delicious-flavour-with-a-toxic-secret.

Govan, Gilbert E., and James W. Livingood. "Chattanooga under Military Occupation, 1863–1865." *Journal of Southern History* 17, no. 1 (February 1951): 23–47.

Granade, James A., III. "The Twilight of Cotton Culture: Life on a Wilkes County Plantation, 1924–1929." *Georgia Historical Quarterly* 77, no. 2 (Summer 1993): 264–85.

Gray, James. *Business without Boundary: The Story of General Mills*. Minneapolis: University of Minnesota Press, 1954.

Gray, Lewis Cecil. *History of Agriculture in the Southern United States to 1860*. 2 vols. Washington, D.C.: Carnegie Institution of Washington, 1933. Reprint, Clifton, N.J.: Augustus M. Kelley, 1973.

Greenwald, Erin M. *Marc-Antoine Caillot and the Company of the Indies in Louisiana: Trade in the French Atlantic World*. Baton Rouge: Louisiana State University Press, 2016.

Gregory, H. F., George Avery, Aubra L. Lee, and Jay C. Blaine. "Presidio Los Adaes: Spanish, French, and Caddoan Interaction on the Northern Frontier." *Historical Archaeology* 38, no. 3 (2004): 65–77.

Gremillion, Kristen J. "Human Ecology at the Edge of History." In *Between Contacts and Colonies: Archaeological Perspectives on the Protohistoric South East*, edited by Cameron B. Wesson and Mark A. Rees, 12–31. Tuscaloosa: University of Alabama Press, 2002.

Grimsley, Mark. *The Hard Hand of War: Union Military Policy toward Southern Civilians, 1861–1865*. New York: Cambridge University Press, 1995.

Grivno, Max. *Gleanings of Freedom: Free and Slave Labor along the Mason-Dixon Line, 1790–1860*. Urbana: University of Illinois Press, 2011.

Hale, William T. *History of DeKalb County, Tennessee*. Nashville: Paul Hunter, 1915.

Hall, Gwendolyn Midlo. *Africans in Colonial Louisiana: The Development of Afro-Creole Culture in the Eighteenth Century*. Baton Rouge: Louisiana State University Press, 1992.

Hall, Matthew R. "'The Reliable Grocer': Consumerism in a New South Town, 1875–1900." *North Carolina Historical Review* 90, no. 3 (July 2013): 259–87.

Hall, Robert L. "Food Crops, Medicinal Plants, and the Atlantic Slave Trade." In *African American Foodways: Explorations of History and Culture*, edited by Anne L. Bower, 17–44. Urbana: University of Illinois Press, 2007.

Hall, Wade. *Conecuh People: Words of Life from the Alabama Black Belt*. Montgomery: New-South Books, 2004.

Hamilton, Peter J. *Colonial Mobile: A Historical Study, Largely from Original Sources, of the Alabama-Tombigbee Basin from the Discovery of Mobile Bay in 1519 until the Demolition of Fort Charlotte in 1821*. Boston: Houghton, Mifflin, 1898.

Hann, John H. "Apalachee Counterfeiters in St. Augustine, Translation and Notes." *Florida Historical Quarterly* 67, no. 1 (July 1988): 52–68.

———. *A History of the Timucua Indians and Mission*. Gainesville: University Press of Florida, 1996.

———. "The Use and Processing of Plants by Indians of Spanish Florida." *Southeastern Archeology* 5, no. 2 (1986): 91–102.

Harbster, Jennifer. "The Great Sheet Cake Mystery." April 26, 2013. *Library of Congress: Inside Adams: Science, Technology & Business* (blog). https://blogs.loc.gov/inside_adams/2013/04/the-great-sheet-cake-mystery.

Hardeman, Nicholas P. *Shucks, Shocks, and Hominy Blocks: Corn as a Way of Life in Pioneer America*. Baton Rouge: Louisiana State University Press, 1981.

Harris, Elizabeth H. "Moravian Settlers during the Royal Period (1729–1775)." Carolana.com, 2007. www.carolana.com/NC/Royal_Colony/nc_royal_colony_moravians.html.

Harvey, Ray. *Want in the Midst of Plenty: The Genesis of the Food Stamp Plan*. Washington, D.C.: American Council on Public Affairs, 1941.

Hatch, Charles E., Jr. *The First Seventeen Years: Virginia, 1607–1624*. Charlottesville: University of Virginia Press, 1957.

Hatch, Peter. "Thomas Jefferson and Gardening." In *Encyclopedia Virginia*. Virginia Humanities. www.encyclopediavirginia.org/Jefferson_Thomas_and_Gardening#its4. Accessed September 1, 2021.

Hatcher, Halene. "Dairying in the South." *Economic Geography* 20, no. 1 (December 1944): 54–64.

Hatley, Tom. *The Dividing Paths: Cherokees and South Carolinians through the Era of Revolution*. New York: Oxford University Press, 1995.

Hayes, Marjorie. "A Brief History of Temperance Hall." In *Temperance Hall Remembers Book II*. N.p.: Dogwood Press, 1990. www.ajlambert.com/history/hst_th.pdf.

Hecht, Irene W. D. "The Virginia Muster of 1624/5 as a Source for Demographic History." *William and Mary Quarterly* 30, no. 1 (1973): 65–92.

Hendricks, Christopher E. *The Backcountry Towns of Colonial Virginia*. Knoxville: University of Tennessee Press, 2006.

Herman, Bernard. *Town House: Architecture and Material Life in the Early American City, 1780–1830*. Chapel Hill: University of North Carolina Press, 2016.

Hess, Karen. *The Carolina Rice Kitchen: The African Connection*. Columbia: University of South Carolina Press, 1992.

———. "Historical Notes and Commentaries on *The Virginia House-wife* (1824)." In *The Virginia House-wife* facsimile, ix–xlv. Columbia: University of South Carolina Press, 1984.

Higginbotham, Jay. *Old Mobile: Fort Louis de la Louisiane, 1702–1711*. Tuscaloosa: University of Alabama Press, 1977; reprinted with a new introduction, 1991.

"Hints on Cooking." *American Agriculturalist* 25 (1866): 865.

"Historical Review of the Rise of Mechanical Refrigeration." *Ice and Refrigeration* 22 (January 1902): 13–14.

Hockensmith, Charles D. *The Millstone Industry: A Summary of Research on Quarries and Producers in the United States, Europe and Elsewhere*. Jefferson, N.C.: McFarland, 2009.

Hofstra, Warren R. *The Planting of New Virginia: Settlement and Landscape in the Shenandoah Valley*. Baltimore: Johns Hopkins University Press, 2004.

———. "Private Dwellings, Public Ways, and the Landscape of Early Rural Capitalism in Virginia's Shenandoah Valley." *Perspectives in Vernacular Architecture* 5 (1995): 211–24.

Hofstra, Warren R., and Clarence R. Geier. "Beyond the Great Blue Mountain: Historical Archaeology and 18th-Century Settlement in Virginia West of the Blue Ridge." In *The Archaeology of 18th-Century Virginia*, edited by Theodore R. Reinhart, 209–40. Richmond: Spectrum Press, 1996.

———. "Farm to Mill to Market: Historical Archeology of an Emerging Grain Economy in the Shenandoah Valley." In *After the Backcountry: Rural Life in the Great Valley of Virginia*, edited by Kenneth E. Koons and Warren R. Hofstra, 48–61. Knoxville: University of Tennessee Press, 2003.

Hoganson, Kristin L. *Consumer's Imperium: The Global Production of American Domesticity, 1865–1920*. Chapel Hill: University of North Carolina Press, 2007.

Holt, Albert C., and Drury Breazale. "The Economic and Social Beginnings of Tennessee (Continued)." *Tennessee Historical Magazine* 8, no. 1 (April 1924): 24–86.

Holt, Sharon Ann. *Making Freedom Pay: North Carolina Freedpeople Working for Themselves, 1865–1900*. Athens: University of Georgia Press, 2000.

Horn, James. *Adapting to a New World: English Society in the Seventeenth Century Chesapeake*. Chapel Hill: University of North Carolina Press, 1994.

Hougland, Margaret W. "Mills of Washington County." Washington County, Tenn., Genweb, September 2007. http://tngenweb.org/washington/records-data/mills-of-washington-county/.

Hurt, R. Douglas. *Agriculture and the Confederacy: Policy, Productivity, and Power in the Civil War South*. Chapel Hill: University of North Carolina Press, 2015.

———. *Indian Agriculture in America: Prehistory to the Present*. Lawrence: University Press of Kansas, 1987.

Huse, Andrew T. *From Saloons to Steak Houses: A History of Tampa*. Gainesville: University Press of Florida, 2020.

Hussey, Scott. "Freezes, Fights, and Fancy: The Formation of Agricultural Cooperatives in the Florida Citrus Industry." *Florida Historical Quarterly* 89, no. 1 (Summer 2010): 81–105.

Ingersoll, Thomas N. *Mammon and Manon in Early New Orleans: The First Slave Society in the Deep South, 1718–1819*. Knoxville: University of Tennessee Press, 1999.

Johnson, Guy B. "Double Meaning in the Popular Negro Blues." *Journal of Abnormal and Social Psychology* 22 (April 1927): 12–20.

Johnson, Whittington B. *Black Savannah, 1788–1864*. Fayetteville: University of Arkansas Press, 1999.

Jones, Charles Colcock. *The History of Georgia: Aboriginal and Colonial Epochs*. Boston: Houghton, Mifflin, 1883.

Jones, Lu Ann. "Gender, Race, and Itinerant Commerce in the Rural New South." In *Other Souths: Diversity and Difference in the U.S. South, Reconstruction to Present*, edited by Pippa Holloway, 67–88. Athens: University of Georgia Press, 2008.

———. *Mama Learned Us to Work: Farm Women in the New South*. Chapel Hill: University of North Carolina Press, 2002.

Jones, Lu Ann, and Sunae Park. "From Feed Bags to Fashion." *Textile History* 21, no. 1 (1993): 91–103.

Joyner, Charles. *Down by the Riverside: A South Carolina Slave Community*. Urbana: University of Illinois Press, 1984.

Juneau, Sandra Scalise. *Celebrating with St. Joseph Altars: The History, Recipes, and Symbols of a New Orleans Tradition*. Baton Rouge: Louisiana State University Press, 2021.

Jurney, David H., and Timothy K. Perttula. "Nineteenth-Century Alibamu-Koasati Pottery Assemblages and Culinary Traditions." *Southeastern Archaeology* 14, no. 1 (Summer 1995): 17–30.

Kaczor, Bill. "Salesman Spends Latest Career Rolling in the Dough." *Lakeland [Fla.] Ledger*, January 30, 2005.

Karp, David. "The Case of the Tasty but Poisonous Nut." *Los Angeles Times*, February 20, 2002.

Kawash, Samira. *Candy: A Century of Panic and Pleasure*. New York: Faber and Faber, 2013.

Kayal, Michele. "Reviving the Tea Cake of Juneteenth Parties Past." *National Geographic*, June 15, 2015. www.nationalgeographic.com/culture/article/reviving-the -tea-cake-of-juneteenth-parties-past.

Kennedy, Cynthia. *Braided Relations, Entwined Lives: The Women of Charleston's Urban Slave Society*. Bloomington: Indiana University Press, 2005.

Kessler, John. "Fun of Factory Visit Is Off the Pie Chart." *Atlanta Journal-Constitution*, March 21, 2017. www.ajc.com/entertainment/dining v/fun-factory-visit-off-the-piechart/40k4H1YJhTmJcATB8xlK7H/.

Kindy, David. "For 100 Years, KitchenAid Has Been the Stand-Up Brand of Kitchen Mixers." *Smithsonian Magazine*, August 7, 2019. www.smithsonianmag.com/smithsonian-institution/100-years-kitchenaid-has-been-stand-brand-stand-mixers-180972838/.

King, Wilma. *Stolen Childhood: Slave Youth in Nineteenth-Century America*. Bloomington: Indiana University Press, 1993.

Kirby, Jack Temple. *Poquosin: A Study of Rural Landscape and Society*. Chapel Hill: University of North Carolina Press, 1995.

Kleber, John E., ed. *Encyclopedia of Louisville*, s.v. "Lively Burgess Willoughby." Lexington: University Press of Kentucky, 2001.

Kniffen, Fred. "The Outdoor Oven in Louisiana." *Louisiana History: The Journal of the Louisiana Historical Association* 1, no. 1 (Winter 1960): 25–35.

Koeppel, Dan. *Banana: The Fate of the Fruit That Changed the World.* New York: Penguin Books, 2007.

Kohler, Tim A. "Corn, Indians, and Spaniards in North-Central Florida: A Technique for Measuring Evolutionary Changes in Corn." *Florida Anthropologist* 32, no. 1 (1979): 1–7.

Kohn, Clyde F. "Development of Dairy Farming in Mississippi." *Economic Geography* 19, no. 2 (April 1943): 188–95.

Kolb, Carolyn. "'Hand-Held' before It Was Fashionable: The Story of the Hubig's Pie." *New Orleans Magazine* 38, no. 2 (November 2003): 132–33.

Koons, Kenneth E. "'The Staple of Our Country': Wheat in the Rural Farm Economy of the Nineteenth Century Valley of Virginia." In *After the Backcountry: Rural Life in the Great Valley of Virginia*, edited by Kenneth E. Koons and Warren R. Hofstra, 3–15. Knoxville: University of Tennessee Press, 2003.

Kukla, Jon. "Order and Chaos in Early America: Political and Social Stability in Pre-Restoration Virginia." *American Historical Review* 90, no. 2 (1985): 275–98.

La Fleur, J. D. *Fusion Foodways of Africa's Gold Coast in the Atlantic Era.* Boston: Brill, 2012.

Landers, Jane. "Spanish Sanctuary: Fugitives in Florida, 1687–1790." *Florida Historical Quarterly* 62 (1984): 296–313.

Landrey, Wanda A. *Boardin' in the Thicket: Recipes and Reminiscences of Early Big Thicket Boarding Houses.* Denton: University of North Texas Press, 1998.

Langhorne, Elizabeth Coles, K. Edward Lay, and William D. Rieley, eds. *A Virginia Family and Its Plantation Houses.* Charlottesville: University of Virginia Press, 1987.

Larsen, Clark Spencer. "Bioarchaeology of Spanish Florida." In *Bioarchaeology of Spanish Florida: The Impact of Colonialism*, edited by Clark Spencer Larsen, 22–51. Gainesville: University Press of Florida, 2001.

Larsen, Clark Spencer, Dale L. Hutchinson, Margaret J. Schoeninger, and Lynette Norr. "Food and Stable Isotopes in La Florida: Diet and Nutrition before and after Contact." In *Bioarchaeology of Spanish Florida: The Impact of Colonialism*, edited by Clark Spencer Larsen, 52–81. Gainesville: University Press of Florida, 2001.

Latshaw, Beth A. "The Soul of the South: Race, Food, and Identity in the American South." In *The Larder: Food Studies Methods from the American South*, edited by John T. Edge, Elizabeth Engelhardt, and Ted Ownby, 32–56. Athens: University of Georgia Press, 2013.

Laudan, Rachel. *Cuisine and Empire: Cooking in World History.* Berkeley: University of California Press, 2013.

Le Conte, René. "The Germans in Louisiana in the Eighteenth Century." Translated and edited by Glenn R. Conrad. *Louisiana History* 8 (1967): 67–84.

Levine, Lawrence W. *Black Culture and Black Consciousness: Afro-American Folk Thought from Slavery to Freedom.* New York: Oxford University Press, 2007.

Lewis, Kenneth E. "The Metropolis and the Backcountry: The Making of a Colonial Landscape on the South Carolina Frontier." *Historical Archaeology* 33, no. 3 (1999): 3–13.

Lich, Glen, and Lera Tyler. "When the Creeks Run Dry: Water Milling in the German Hill Country." In Built in Texas, edited by Francis Abernethy, 237–45. 2nd ed. Denton: University of North Texas Press, 2000.

Lichtenstein, Alex. "'That Disposition to Theft, with Which They Have Been Branded': Moral Economy, Slave Management, and the Law." Journal of Social History 21, no. 3 (Spring 1988): 413–40.

Locker, Melissa. "How Hello Dolly Bars Got Their Funny and Magical Name." Southern Living. www.southernliving.com/desserts/hello-dolly-bar-history. Accessed September 1, 2012.

Lundy, Ronni. "Cooking Fresh: That Old-Time Cornbread." Edible Kentucky and Southern Indiana, October 1, 2016. https://ediblekentucky.ediblecommunities.com/recipes /old-time-cornbread.

Lyon, Eugene. "Richer Than We Thought: The Material Culture of Sixteenth-Century St. Augustine." El Escribano: The St. Augustine Journal of History 29 (1992): 1–117.

———. Santa Elena: A Brief History of the Colony, 1566–1587. Research Manuscript Series 193. Columbia: Institute of Archeology and Anthropology, University of South Carolina, 1984.

MacLeod, Jessie. "Doll." George Washington's Mount Vernon. www.mountvernon.org /library/digitalhistory/digital-encyclopedia/article/doll. Accessed September 1, 2021.

Magee, David. MoonPie: Biography of an Out-of-This-World Snack. Lookout Mountain, Tenn.: Jefferson Press, 2006.

Mann, Charles C. 1491: New Revelations of the Americas before Columbus. New York: Random House, 2005.

Manning, Chandra. Troubled Refuge: Struggling for Freedom in the Civil War. New York: Alfred A. Knopf, 2016.

Manring, M. M. Slave in a Box: The Strange Career of Aunt Jemima. Charlottesville: University Press of Virginia, 1998.

Manucy, Albert C. Sixteenth-Century St. Augustine: The People and Their Homes. Gainesville: University Press of Florida, 1997.

Marcoux, Paula. Cooking with Fire: From Roasting on a Spit to Baking in a Tannur, Rediscovered Techniques and Recipes That Capture the Flavors of Wood-Fired Cooking. North Adams, Mass.: Storey Publishing, 2014.

Margavio, Anthony V., and Jerome J. Salomone. Bread and Respect: The Italians of Louisiana. Gretna, La.: Pelican, 2002.

Marie, Armand. Pellagra. Columbia, S.C.: State Company, 1910.

Martin, Ann Smart. Buying into the World of Goods: Early Consumers in Backcountry Virginia. Baltimore: Johns Hopkins University Press, 2008.

Massey, Mary Elizabeth. Ersatz in the Confederacy: Shortages and Substitutes on the Southern Homefront. Columbia: University of South Carolina Press, 1952.

———. "The Free Market of New Orleans, 1861–1862." Louisiana History 3, no. 3 (Summer 1962): 202–20.

———. Refugee Life in the Confederacy. Baton Rouge: Louisiana State University Press, 1964.

Mazzocchi, Jay. "Krispy Kreme Doughnut Corporation." In Encyclopedia of North Carolina, edited by William S. Powell. Chapel Hill: University of North Carolina Press, 2006. www.ncpedia.org/krispy-kreme.

McCann, James C. *Maize and Grace: Africa's Encounter with a New World Crop.* Cambridge, Mass.: Harvard University Press, 2007.

McCartney, Martha W., ed. *A Study of the Africans and African Americans on Jamestown Island and at Green Spring, 1619–1803.* Williamsburg: National Park Service/Colonial Williamsburg Foundation, 2003.

McCleary, Ann. "'Seizing the Opportunity': Home Demonstration Curb Markets in Virginia." In *Work, Family, and Faith: Rural Southern Women in the Twentieth Century,* edited by Melissa Walker and Rebecca Sharpless, 97–134. Columbia: University of Missouri Press, 2006.

McCorkle, James L., Jr. "Los Adaes and the Borderlands Origins of East Texas." *East Texas Historical Journal* 22 (1984): 3–12.

McCurry, Stephanie. *Confederate Reckoning: Power and Politics in the Civil War.* Cambridge, Mass.: Harvard University Press, 2012.

McDonald, Bryan L. *Food Power: The Rise and Fall of the Postwar American Food System.* New York: Oxford University Press, 2006.

McDonald, Roderick A. *The Economy and Material Culture of Slaves: Goods and Chattels on the Sugar Plantations of Jamaica and Louisiana.* Baton Rouge: Louisiana State University Press, 1993.

McGee, Harold. *On Food and Cooking: The Science and Lore of the Kitchen.* Rev. ed. New York: Scribner, 2004.

McGehee, Margaret T. "Krispy Kreme." In *Foodways,* edited by John T. Edge, 190–92. Vol. 7 of *The New Encyclopedia of Southern Culture,* edited by Charles Reagan Wilson. Chapel Hill: University of North Carolina Press, 2007.

McGough, Nella Bailey. "We Cracked the Case of the Hummingbird Cake." *Southern Living.* www.southernliving.com/desserts/cakes/mrs-wiggins-hummingbird -cake-recipe. Accessed September 1, 2021.

McInnis, Maurie D. *The Politics of Taste in Antebellum Charleston.* Chapel Hill: University of North Carolina Press, 2005.

McWilliams, James. *The Pecan: A History of America's Native Nut.* Austin: University of Texas Press, 2013.

Mehrländer, Andrea. *The Germans of Charleston, Richmond, and New Orleans during the Civil War Period, 1850–1870: A Study and Research Compendium.* Berlin: Walter de Gruyter, 2011.

Messner, Timothy C. *Acorns and Bitter Roots: Starch Grain Research in the Prehistoric Eastern Woodlands.* Tuscaloosa: University of Alabama Press, 2011.

Milanich, Jerald T. *Florida Indians and the Invasion from Europe.* Gainesville: University Press of Florida, 1995.

———. "Franciscan Missions and Native Peoples." In *The Forgotten Centuries: Indians and Europeans in the American South, 1521–1704,* edited by Charles M. Hudson and Carmen Chaves Tesser, 276–303. Athens: University of Georgia Press, 1994.

———. *Laboring in the Fields of the Lord: Spanish Missions and Southeastern Indians.* Gainesville: University Press of Florida, 2006.

Milanich, Jerald T., and Charles Hudson. *Hernando de Soto and the Indians of Florida.* Gainesville: University Press of Florida, 1993.

Miller, Adrian. *The President's Kitchen Cabinet: The Story of the African Americans Who Have Fed Our First Families, from the Washingtons to the Obamas.* Chapel Hill: University of North Carolina Press, 2017.

Miller Surrey, Nancy M. *The Commerce of Louisiana during the French Régime, 1699–1763.* New York: Columbia University, 1916.

———. "The Development of Industries in Louisiana during the French Regime, 1673–1763." *Mississippi Valley Historical Review* 9 (1922): 227–35.

Mintz, Sidney W. *Sweetness and Power: The Place of Sugar in Modern History.* New York: Viking, 1985.

Mizell-Nelson, Michael. "French Bread." In *New Orleans Cuisine: Fourteen Signature Dishes and Their Histories,* edited by Susan Tucker, 38–53. Jackson: University Press of Mississippi, 2009.

Montgomery, Lizzie Wilson. *Sketches of Old Warrenton, North Carolina.* Raleigh, N.C.: Edwards and Broughton, 1924.

Morgan, Philip D. *Slave Counterpoint: Black Culture in the Eighteenth-Century Chesapeake and Lowcountry.* Chapel Hill: University of North Carolina Press, 1998.

Mormino, Gary Ross, and George E. Pozzetta. *The Immigrant World of Ybor City: Italians and Their Latin Neighbors in Tampa, 1885–1985.* Urbana: University of Illinois Press, 1987.

Morton, Paula E. *Tortillas: A Cultural History.* Albuquerque: University of New Mexico Press, 2014.

Moss, Buelon R. "Pete." "Dairy Industry in Alabama." In *The Encyclopedia of Alabama,* September 26, 2017. http://encyclopediaofalabama.org/article/h-1393.

Mrozowski, Stephen, Maria Franklin, and Leslie Hunt. "Archaeobotanical Analysis and Interpretations of Enslaved Virginian Plant Use at Rich Neck Plantation." *American Antiquity* 73, no. 4 (2008): 699–728.

Mullenweg, Matt. "The Houston Doberge Project." Matt Mullenweg Unlucky at Cards, June 19, 2019. http://ma.tt/2019/06/doberge-project/.

Mullins, Paul R. *Glazed America: A History of the Doughnut.* Gainesville: University Press of Florida, 2008.

———. *Race and Affluence: An Archaeology of African America and Consumer Culture.* New York: Kluwer Academic/Plenum Publishers, 1999.

Munro, John. "The Consumption of Spices and Their Costs in Late-Medieval and Early-Modern Europe: Luxuries or Necessities?" Home page of John Munro. Paper delivered 1983. www.economics.utoronto.ca/munro5/SPICES1.htm. Accessed August 30, 2021.

Nadasen, Premilla. *Household Workers Unite: The Untold Story of African American Women Who Built a Movement.* New York: Beacon Press, 2016.

Newcomb, W. W., Jr. *The Indians of Texas: From Prehistoric to Modern Times.* Austin: University of Texas Press, 1961.

Nicholls, Michael L. "Aspects of the African American Experience in Eighteenth-Century Williamsburg and Norfolk." Colonial Williamsburg Foundation Library Research Report Series 330. Williamsburg: Colonial Williamsburg Foundation, 1991.

Norton, J. Dean. "'An Abundance of Every Thing': Mount Vernon's Fruit and Vegetables Gardens." In *Dining with the Washingtons: Historic Recipes, Entertainment and Hospitality from Mount Vernon,* edited by Stephen A. McLeod, 79–94. Chapel Hill: Mount Vernon Ladies Association, 2011.

Nystrom, Justin. *Creole Italian: Sicilian Immigrants and the Making of New Orleans Food Culture.* Athens: University of Georgia Press, 2018.

Okihiro, Gary Y. *Pineapple Culture: A History of the Tropical and Temperate Zones.* Berkeley: University of California Press, 2009.

Olmert, Michael. *Kitchens, Smokehouses, and Privies: Outbuildings and the Architecture of Daily Life in the Eighteenth-Century Mid-Atlantic.* Ithaca: Cornell University Press, 2009.

Opie, Frederick Douglass. *Hog and Hominy: Soul Food from Africa to America.* New York: Columbia University Press, 2008.

Orso, Ethelyn. *The St. Joseph Altar Traditions of South Louisiana.* Lafayette: Center for Louisiana Studies, University of Southwestern Louisiana, 1990.

Otto, John S. *Cannon's Point Plantation, 1794–1860: Living Conditions and Status Patterns in the Old South.* Orlando: Academic Press, 1984.

Ownby, Ted. *American Dreams in Mississippi: Consumers, Poverty, and Culture, 1830–1998.* Chapel Hill: University of North Carolina Press, 1999.

Pack, M. M. "Got Milk? On the Trail of Pastel de Tres Leches." *Austin Chronicle,* February 13, 2004.

Paddleford, Clementine. "Batting for Butter: Modern Margarine Is an Able Substitution." *Atlanta Constitution,* January 31, 1943.

Page, Frederick G. "Baking Powder and Self-Rising Flour in Nineteenth-Century Britain: The Carbon Dioxide Aerations of Henry Jones and Alfred Bird." *Bulletin for the History of Chemistry* 38, no 2 (2013): 140–54.

Pando, Trilla. *Stirring Up Memories All the Times: Recollections and Recipes from Southwest Georgia.* Bainbridge, Ga.: Post Printing, 2006.

Parent, Anthony S. *Foul Means: The Formation of a Slave Society in Virginia, 1660–1740.* Chapel Hill: University of North Carolina Press, 2003.

Parker, Joseph B. "Making Do on the Macon Ridge: The Eating Patterns of Southern Farm Families during World War II." Paper presented at "Eating for Victory: American Foodways and World War II," Boulder, Colo., October 8–9, 1993. https://biglittlemeals .files.wordpress.com/2018/09/making-do-on-the-macon-ridge-1.pdf.

Patterson, Hadassah. "Kernels of Truth about Corn." *The Bitter Southerner,* November 17, 2020. https://bittersoutherner.com/feature/2020/features /2020/kernels-of-truth-about-corn.

Pearce, George F. *Pensacola during the Civil War: A Thorn in the Side of the Confederacy.* Gainesville: University Press of Florida, 2000.

Peckenpaugh, Douglas J. "Más Cubano." *Snack Food and Wholesale Bakery* 104, no. 5 (May 2015): 10–13.

Perdue, Theda. *Cherokee Women: Gender and Culture Change, 1700–1835.* Lincoln: University of Nebraska Press, 1998.

Perry, Mary Allen. "The South's Most Storied Cakes." *Southern Living.* www.southernliving .com/food/holidays-occasions/classic-southern-layer-cake-recipes. Accessed August 29, 2021.

Perttula, Timothy K. "Caddo Agriculture on the Western Frontier of the Eastern Woodlands." *Plains Anthropologist* 53, no. 205 (February 2008): 79–105.

———. "Caddoan Area Archaeology since 1990." *Journal of Archaeological Research* 4, no. 4 (December 1996): 295–348.

———. "Material Culture of the Koasati Indians of Texas." *Historical Archaeology* 28, no. 1 (1994): 65–77.

Peterson, Arthur G. "Flour and Grist Milling in Virginia: A Brief History." *Virginia Magazine of History and Biography* 43, no. 2 (1935): 97–108.

Plater, David D. "Building the North Wales Mill of William Allason." *Virginia Magazine of History and Biography* 85, no. 1 (1977): 45–50.

Poppendieck, Janet. *Breadlines Knee-Deep in Wheat: Food Assistance in the Great Depression.* Berkeley: University of California Press, 2014. First published 1986 by Rutgers University Press.

Postlethwayt, Malachy. *The Universal Dictionary of Trade and Commerce, with Large Additions and Improvements.* 4th ed. Vol. 1. London: Printed for W. Strahan, 1774.

Potorti, Mary. "'What We Eat Is Politics': SNCC, Hunger, and Voting Rights in Mississippi." In *The Seedtime, the Work, and the Harvest: New Perspectives on the Black Freedom Struggle in America*, ed. Jeffrey L. Littlejohn, Reginald K. Ellis, and Peter B. Levy, 115–53. Gainesville: University Press of Florida, 2018.

Purvis, Kathleen. "The Mystery of the Hummingbird Cake." *Southern Living.* www .southernliving.com/desserts/cakes/hummingbird-cake-history. Accessed September 1, 2021.

Ramsay, David. *Ramsay's History of South Carolina, from Its First Settlement in 1670 to the Year 1808.* Newberry, S.C.: W. J. Duffie, 1858.

Ransome, David R. "'Shipt for Virginia': The Beginnings in 1619–1622 of the Great Migration to the Chesapeake." *Virginia Magazine of History and Biography* 103, no. 4 (October 1995): 443–58.

———. "Wives for Virginia, 1621." *William and Mary Quarterly* 48, no. 1 (1991): 3–18.

Raskin, Hanna. "Beckroge's Was Icing on Cake for City's German Bakery Tradition." *Charleston Post and Courier*, May 16, 2018.

———. "Bullwinkel's Whipped Cream Cake." *Charleston Post and Courier*, December 2, 2014.

Rees, Jonathan. *Refrigeration Nation: A History of Ice, Appliances, and Enterprise in America.* Baltimore: Johns Hopkins University Press, 2013.

Revels, Tracy J. *Grander in Her Daughters: Florida's Women during the Civil War.* Columbia: University of South Carolina Press, 2004.

Reynolds, Cynthia Furlong. *"JIFFY": A Family Tradition: Mixing Business and Old-Fashioned Values.* Chelsea, Mich.: Chelsea Milling Company, 2008.

Reynolds, John. *Windmills and Watermills.* New York: Praeger, 1970.

"Rhea's Mill Ledger." Community and Conflict: The Impact of the Civil War in the Ozarks. www.ozarkscivilwar.org/archives/3535. Accessed September 1, 2021.

"Richard Barton Haxall." *Northwestern Miller*, January 20, 1882, 35.

Richter, Julie. "Christiana Campbell ca. 1723–1792." In *Encyclopedia Virginia.* https://encyclopediavirginia.org/entries/campbell-christiana-ca-1723-1792/. Accessed September 1, 2021.

Riley, Elihu Samuel. *"The Ancient City": A History of Annapolis, in Maryland, 1649–1887.* Annapolis: Record Printing Office, 1887.

Rivers, Larry. "'Dignity and Importance': Slavery in Jefferson County, Florida, 1827–1860." *Florida Historical Quarterly* 61 (April 1983): 404–30.

Roark, Carol. "Cooking for a Living: Lucille Bishop Smith." In *Grace and Gumption: The Cookbook*, edited by Katie Sherrod, 233–62. Fort Worth: Texas Christian University Press, 2010.

———. "Cracking the Glass Ceiling: Entrepreneurs and Professionals." In *Grace and Gumption: Stories of Fort Worth Women*, edited by Katie Sherrod, 229–56. Fort Worth: Texas Christian University Press, 2007.

Robert, Joseph C. "Lee the Farmer." *Journal of Southern History* 3, no. 4 (November 1937): 422–40.

Rockman, Seth. *Scraping By: Wage Labor, Slavery, and Survival in Early National Baltimore.* Baltimore: Johns Hopkins University Press, 2009.

Rodrigue, John C. *Reconstruction in the Cane Fields: From Slavery to Free Labor in Louisiana Sugar Parishes, 1862–1880.* Baton Rouge: Louisiana State University Press, 2001.

Roe, Daphne. *A Plague of Corn: The Social History of Pellagra.* Ithaca: Cornell University Press, 1973.

"Rolls You Buy, Then Bake." *Popular Science* 157, no. 3 (September 1950): 118–19.

Rood, Daniel. "Bogs of Death: Slavery, the Brazilian Flour Trade, and the Mystery of the Vanishing Millpond in Antebellum Virginia." *Journal of American History* 101, no. 1 (June 2014): 19–43.

"Rosegill." In *Historic Buildings in Middlesex County, Virginia, 1650–1875*, by Louise E. Gray, Evelyn Q. Ryland, Bettie J. Simmons, Richard A. Genders, and Walter C. C. Johnson. N.p.: n.p., 1978. www.rosegill.com/Library/HistoricBuildings/History.html.

Ruhl, Donna L. "Archaeobotanical Data from La Florida." In *Foraging and Farming in the Eastern Woodlands*, edited by C. Margaret Scarry, 255–83. Gainesville: University Press of Florida, 1993.

———. "Spanish Mission Paleoethnobotany and Culture Change: A Survey of the Archaeobotanical Data and Some Speculations on Aboriginal and Spanish Agrarian Interactions in La Florida." In *Columbian Consequences.* Vol. 2, *Archeology and History of the Spanish Borderlands East*, edited by David Hurst Thomas, 555–80. Washington, D.C.: Smithsonian Institution Press, 1990.

Rushing, Erin. "Stovetop Waffle Iron Patented." *Smithsonian Libraries and Archives Unbound* (blog), August 24, 2010. https://blog.library.si.edu/blog/2010/08/24/waffle-iron-patented/#.Xxh-WJ5KiUk.

Rutman, Darrett B., and Anita H. Rutman. *A Place in Time: Middlesex County, Virginia, 1650–1750.* New York: W. W. Norton, 1984.

Samford, Patricia. *Subfloor Pits and the Archaeology of Slavery in Colonial Virginia.* Tuscaloosa: University of Alabama Press, 2007.

Sassaman, Kenneth E. *Early Pottery in the Southeast: Tradition and Innovation in Cooking Technology.* Tuscaloosa: University of Alabama Press, 1993.

———. "The Multicultural Genesis of Stallings Culture." In *Archaeology in South Carolina: Exploring the Hidden Heritage of the Palmetto State*, edited by Adam King, 14–33. Columbia: University of South Carolina Press, 2016.

Saunt, Claudio. *Black, White, and Indian: Race and the Unmaking of an American Family.* New York: Oxford University Press, 2005.

Scarry, C. Margaret. "Variability in Late Prehistoric Corn from the Lower Southeast." In *Corn and Culture in the Prehistoric New World*, edited by Sissel Johannessen and Christine A. Hastorf, 347–68. Boulder: Westview Press, 1994.

Scarry, C. Margaret, and Elizabeth J. Reitz. "Herbs, Fish, Scum, and Vermin: Subsistence Strategies in Sixteenth-Century Spanish Florida." In *Columbian Consequences.*

Vol. 2, *Archeology and History of the Spanish Borderlands East*, edited by David Hurst Thomas, 343–54. Washington, D.C.: Smithsonian Institution Press, 1990.

Scarry, John F. "Resistance and Accommodation in Apalachee Province." In *The Archaeology of Traditions: Agency and History before and after Columbus*, edited by Timothy R. Pauketat, 34–58. Gainesville: University Press of Florida, 2001.

Scroggs, William O. "An Assize of Bread at Mobile, Alabama." *Quarterly Journal of Economics* 21, no. 2 (February 1907): 330–32.

Severson, Kim. "Festiveness, Stacked Up Southern Style." *New York Times*, December 15, 2009.

Shapiro, Laura. *Something from the Oven: Reinventing Dinner in 1950s America.* New York: Viking Penguin, 2004.

Sharpless, Rebecca. *Cooking in Other Women's Kitchens: Domestic Workers in the South, 1865–1960.* Chapel Hill: University of North Carolina Press, 2010.

———. *Fertile Ground, Narrow Choices: Women on Texas Cotton Farms, 1900–1940.* Chapel Hill: University of North Carolina Press, 1999.

———. "'She Ought to Have Taken Those Cakes': Southern Women and Rural Food Supplies." *Southern Cultures* 18, no. 2 (2012): 45–58.

Sharrer, G. Terry. "The Merchant-Millers: Baltimore's Flour Milling Industry, 1750–1860." *Agricultural History* 57 (1982): 138–50.

Shephard, Steven J. "The Spanish Criollo Majority in Colonial St. Augustine." In *Spanish St. Augustine: The Archeology of a Colonial Creole Community*, edited by Kathleen Deagan, 65–98. New York: Academic Press, 1983.

Shields, David S. *The Culinarians: Lives and Careers from the First Age of American Fine Dining.* Chicago: University of Chicago Press, 2017.

———. *Southern Provisions: The Creation and Revival of a Cuisine.* Chicago: University of Chicago Press, 2015.

Shurtleff, William, and Akiko Aoyagi. "History of Soy Oil Shortening." Soy Info Center. www.soyinfocenter.com/HSS/shortening2.php. Accessed September 1, 2021.

Sims, Elizabeth. "Layers of Love: The Legend of Apple Stack Cake." Edible Asheville. www.edibleasheville.com/apple-stack-cake/. Accessed September 1, 2021.

Singleton, Theresa. "The Slave Tag: An Artifact of Urban Slavery." *South Carolina Antiquities* 16, nos. 1–2 (1984): 41–65.

Sitterson, J. Carlyle. *Sugar Country: The Cane Sugar Industry in the South, 1753–1950.* Lexington: University of Kentucky Press, 1953.

"Sixteenth Annual Convention of the Texas Association." *Bakers Review* 33, no. 1 (April 1916): 76–77.

Smith, Andrew F. *Starving the South: How the North Won the Civil War.* New York: St. Martin's Press, 2011.

Smith, Bruce D. "Eastern North America as an Independent Center of Plant Domestication." *Proceedings of the National Academy of Science* 103, no. 33 (August 2006): 12223–28.

Smith, Nelson F. *History of Pickens County, Alabama.* Carrollton, Ala., 1856. Spartanburg, S.C.: Reprint Co., 1980.

Smith, Timothy B. *Mississippi in the Civil War: The Home Front.* Jackson: University Press of Mississippi, 2010.

Smith, Warren B. *White Servitude in Colonial South Carolina.* Columbia: University of South Carolina Press, 1961.

Snyder, Terri L. "Berkeley, Frances Culpeper Stephens (1634–ca. 1695)." In *Encyclopedia Virginia*. Virginia Humanities, 2021. www.encyclopediavirginia.org /Berkeley_Frances_Culpeper_Stephens_b_ap_1634-ca_1695.

Spruill, Julia Cherry. "Virginia and Carolina Homes before the Revolution." *North Carolina Historical Review* 12, no. 4 (October 1935): 320–40.

Stanonis, Anthony J., and Rachel Wallace. "Tasting New Orleans: How the Mardi Gras King Cake Came to Represent the Crescent City." *Southern Cultures* 24, no. 4 (Winter 2018): 6–23.

Steen, Herman. *Flour Milling in America*. Minneapolis: T. S. Denison, 1963.

Steiner, Bernard C. *Beginnings of Maryland, 1631–1639*. Baltimore: Johns Hopkins Press, 1903.

Stephenson, Mary A. "Mills in Eighteenth Century Virginia with Special Study of Mills Near Williamsburg." Colonial Williamsburg Foundation Library Research Report Series 0116. Williamsburg: Colonial Williamsburg Foundation, 1999.

Sterling, Justine. "A Brief, Delightful History of the Bundt Pan." Food and Wine, May 23, 2017. www.foodandwine.com/news/brief-delightful-history-bundt-pan.

Stevens, J. Sanderson. "A Story of Plants, Fire, and People: The Paleoecology and Subsistence of the Late Archaic and Early Woodland in Virginia." In *Late Archaic and Early Woodland Research in Virginia: A Synthesis*, edited by Theodor R. Reinhart and Mary Ellen N. Hodges, 185–211. Richmond: Archeological Society of Virginia Special Publication 23, 1991.

Stewart, Kayla. "The Fine Legacy of Lucille's." *Gravy* 78 (Winter 2021): 44–58.

Stone, Garry Wheeler. "St. John's: Archaeological Questions and Answers." *Maryland Historical Magazine* 69, no. 2 (Summer 1974): 146–68.

Storck, John, and Walter Dorwin Teague. *Flour for Man's Bread: A History of Milling*. Minneapolis: University of Minnesota Press, 1952.

Stringer, Tommy W. "Collin Street Bakery, Corsicana." *Handbook of Texas Online*. Texas State Historical Association. www.tshaonline.org/handbook/online/articles/dico1. Accessed September 1, 2021.

Strom, Claire. "Problems Confronting the Dairy Industry in the American South, 1900–1930." Unpublished paper presented at the European Rural History Organisation, Girona, Spain, 2015. In author's possession.

Sturges, Lena. "The South Takes to Cakes." *Southern Living* 1, no. 2 (March 1966): 42–43.

Sturtz, Linda L. *Within Her Power: Propertied Women in Colonial Virginia*. New York: Routledge, 2002.

Sumler-Edmond, Janice. *The Secret Trust of Aspasia Cruvellier Mirault: The Life and Trials of a Free Woman of Color in Antebellum Georgia*. Fayetteville: University of Arkansas Press, 2008.

"Sweet History: Dorchester and the Chocolate Factory." The Bostonian Society, 2005. https://earlybirdpower.com/wp-content/uploads/2014/04/SWEET_HISTORY _2005.pdf.

Takagi, Midori. *Rearing Wolves to Our Own Destruction: Slavery in Richmond, Virginia, 1782–1865*. Charlottesville: University of Virginia Press, 2000.

Taylor, Amy Murrell. *Embattled Freedom: Journeys through the Civil War's Slave Refugee Camps*. Chapel Hill: University of North Carolina Press, 2018.

Texas Almanac for 1872. Galveston: Richardson, 1872.

Thomas, Gertrude I. *Foods of Our Forefathers*. Philadelphia: F. A. Davis Company, 1941.

Thomas, Larissa. "The Gender Division of Labor in Mississippian Households: Its Role in Shaping Production for Exchange." In *Archaeological Studies of Gender in the Southeastern United States*, edited by Jane M. Eastman and Christopher Bernard Rodning, 27–56. Gainesville: University Press of Florida, 2001.

Thomas, Mary Martha. *Riveting and Rationing in Dixie: Alabama Women and the Second World War*. Tuscaloosa: University of Alabama Press, 1987.

Thompson, Bette. "All Around the Town." *Amarillo Globe-Times*, October 10, 1960.

Thompson, Mary V. "Martha Washington's Cookbooks." In *Dining with the Washingtons: Historic Recipes, Entertainment and Hospitality from Mount Vernon*, edited by Stephen A. McLeod, 31. Chapel Hill: Mount Vernon Ladies Association, 2011.

———. "'Served Up in Excellent Order': Everyday Dining at Mount Vernon." In *Dining with the Washingtons: Historic Recipes, Entertainment and Hospitality from Mount Vernon*, edited by Stephen A. McLeod, 37–56. Chapel Hill: Mount Vernon Ladies Association, 2011.

Tomblin, Barbara Brooks. *Bluejackets and Contrabands: African Americans and the Union Navy*. Lexington: University Press of Kentucky, 2009.

Tuten, James H. *Lowcountry Time and Tide: The Fall of the South Carolina Rice Kingdom*. Columbia: University of South Carolina Press, 1991.

Upton, Dell. "White and Black Landscapes in Eighteenth-Century Virginia." In *Cabin, Quarter, Plantation: Architecture and Landscapes of North American Slavery*, edited by Clifton Ellis and Rebecca Ginsburg, 121–40. New Haven: Yale University Press, 2010.

Usner, Daniel H., Jr. "Food Marketing and Interethnic Exchange in the 18th-Century Lower Mississippi Valley." *Food and Foodways* 1 (1986): 279–310.

———. "The Frontier Exchange Economy of the Lower Mississippi Valley in the Eighteenth Century." *William and Mary Quarterly* 44, no. 2 (1987): 165–92.

———. *Indians, Settlers, and Slaves in a Frontier Exchange Economy: The Lower Mississippi Valley before 1783*. Chapel Hill: University of North Carolina Press, 1992.

Veit, Helen Zoe. "Eating Cotton: Cottonseed, Crisco, and Consumer Ignorance." *Journal of the Gilded Age and Progressive Era* 18, no. 4 (October 2019): 397–421.

Velden, Dana. "Yes or Noyaux: Using Stone Fruit Kernels in the Kitchen." *Kitchn*, July 15, 2013. www.thekitchn.com/yes-or-noyaux-using-stone-fruit-kernels-in-the-kitchen-192153.

Vidal, Cécile. "Antoine Bienvenu, Illinois Planter and Mississippi Trader: The Structure of Exchange between Lower and Upper Louisiana." In *French Colonial Louisiana and the Atlantic World*, edited by Bradley G. Bond, 111–33. Baton Rouge: Louisiana State University Press, 2005.

Vlach, John Michael. *Back of the Big House: The Architecture of Plantation Slavery*. Chapel Hill: University of North Carolina Press, 1993.

———. "'Snug Li'l House with Flue and Oven': Nineteenth-Century Reforms in Plantation Slave Housing." *Perspectives in Vernacular Architecture* 5 (1995): 118–29.

Vogt, Paul L. *The Sugar Refining Industry in the United States: Its Development and Present Condition*. Philadelphia: University of Pennsylvania, 1908.

Walker, Melissa, ed. *Country Women Cope with Hard Times: A Collection of Oral Histories*. Columbia: University of South Carolina Press, 2004.

Wallach, Jennifer Jensen. *Every Nation Has Its Dish: Black Bodies and Black Food in Twentieth-Century America.* Chapel Hill: University of North Carolina Press, 2019.

———. *How America Eats: A Social History of U.S. Food and Culture.* Lanham, Md.: Rowman and Littlefield, 2013.

Walls, Lauren, and Scot Keith. "Cooking Connects Them: Earth Ovens as Persistent Places during the Woodland Period." In *Baking, Bourbon, and Black Drink: Foodways Archaeology in the American Southeast,* edited by Tanya Peres and Aaron Deter-Wolf, 119–39. Tuscaloosa: University of Alabama Press, 2018.

Walsh, Lorena S. *From Calabar to Carter's Grove: The History of a Virginia Slave Community.* Charlottesville: University Press of Virginia, 1997.

———. "The Wider Context." In *A Study of the Africans and African Americans on Jamestown Island and at Green Spring, 1619–1803,* edited by Martha W. McCartney, 15–25. Williamsburg: National Park Service/Colonial Williamsburg Foundation, 2003.

Warman, Arturo. *Corn and Capitalism: How a Botanical Bastard Grew to Global Dominance.* Translated by Nancy L. Westrate. Chapel Hill: University of North Carolina Press, 2003. First published in Mexico in 1988.

Washburn, Beatrice. "French Market of New Orleans Inspiration for Colorful Cookery." *New York Herald,* May 10, 1925.

Watson, Alan D. "Public Poor Relief in Colonial North Carolina." *North Carolina Historical Review* 54, no. 4 (October 1977): 347–66.

Watson, Harry L. "'The Common Rights of Mankind': Subsistence, Shad, and Commerce in the Early Republican South." *Journal of American History* 83, no. 1 (June 1996): 13–43.

Wattigny, Catherine. "Food for Thought: Eula Mae Doré—a Life Served with Love—and Good Food." *Daily Iberian* (New Iberia, La.), September 16, 2018.

Weatherwax, Paul. *Indian Corn in Old America.* New York: Macmillan, 1954.

Weigl, Andrea. "Alongside Shrimp and Bluefish: Ocracoke Fig Cake." *Southern Cultures* 21, no. 1 (Spring 2018): 135–36.

Weiner, Marli. *Mistresses and Slaves: Plantation Women in South Carolina, 1830–80.* Urbana: University of Illinois Press, 1998.

Werlin, Otto. "Tales of a Traveler." *Bakers Review* 33, no. 1 (April 1916): 93–96.

Westervelt, James. *American Pure Food and Drug Laws.* Kansas City, Mo.: Vernon Law Book Co., 1912.

Wightman, Orrin Sage, and Margaret Davis Cate. *Early Days of Coastal Georgia.* St. Simons Island, Ga.: Fort Frederica Association, 1955.

William, Hayden. "Quick-Bake Roll Pioneers' Suit over Funds Is Settled." *Tampa Tribune,* January 21, 1951.

Wilstach, Paul. *Mount Vernon: Washington's Home and the Nation's Shrine.* Garden City, N.J.: Doubleday, Page, 1916.

Winters, Donald L. *Tennessee Farming, Tennessee Farmers: Antebellum Agriculture in the Upper South.* Knoxville: University of Tennessee Press, 1994.

Wolfe, Brendan. "Angela (fl. 1619-1625)." In *Encyclopedia Virginia.* https://encyclopediavirginia.org/entries/angela-fl-1619-1625/. Accessed September 2, 2021.

———. "Peirce, William (d. btw. 1645 and 1647)." In *Encyclopedia Virginia.* Virginia Humanities. www.encyclopediavirginia.org/Peirce_William_d_btw_1645_and_1647. Accessed September 2, 2021.

Wood, Betty. *Women's Work, Men's Work: The Informal Slave Economies of Lowcountry Georgia.* Athens: University of Georgia Press, 1995.

———. *Slavery in Colonial Georgia, 1730-1775.* Athens: University of Georgia Press, 2007.

Wood, Minter. "Life in New Orleans in the Spanish Period." *Louisiana Historical Quarterly* 22, no. 3 (July 1939). 641–709.

Wood, Peter. *Black Majority: Negroes in Colonial South Carolina from 1670 through the Stono Rebellion.* New York: W. W. Norton, 1974.

Woods, Patricia D. "The French and the Natchez Indians in Louisiana: 1700–1731." *Louisiana History* 19 (1978): 413–35.

Worth, John E. "Spanish Missions and the Persistence of Chiefly Power." In *The Transformation of the Southeastern Indians, 1540–1760,* edited by Robbie Ethridge and Charles Hudson, 39–64. Jackson: University Press of Mississippi, 2002.

Wright, Muriel H. "American Indian Corn Dishes." *Chronicles of Oklahoma* 36, no. 2 (1958): 155–66.

Yarbrough, Steve. "Grandma's Table." In *Cornbread Nation 3: Foods of the Mountain South,* edited by Ronni Lundy, 92–99. Chapel Hill: University of North Carolina Press, 2005.

"Yeast Breads Rise to the Occasion." *Southern Living* 4, no. 5 (June 1970): 69.

Yentsch, Anne. *A Chesapeake Family and Their Slaves: A Study in Historical Archeology.* New York: Cambridge University Press, 1994.

———. "Excavating the South's African American Food History." In *African American Foodways: Explorations of History and Culture,* edited by Anne L. Bower, 59–98. Urbana: University of Illinois Press, 2007.

York, Patricia S. "Classic Cola Sheet Cake." *Southern Living.* www.southernliving.com /food/soda-cake-recipes. Accessed September 2, 2021.

Yost, Genevieve. "Ludwell-Paradise House Historical Report, Block 18 Building 7 Lot 45." Colonial Williamsburg Foundation Library Research Report Series 1407. Williamsburg: Colonial Williamsburg Foundation, 1940.

WEB PAGES AND WEBSITES

"About Us." Edwards Desserts. www.edwardsdesserts.com/our-story.htm/. Accessed August 30, 2021.

"About Us." Lucky Leaf. www.luckyleaf.com/about/. Accessed September 1, 2021.

"About Us." Mary B's Biscuits. https://marybsbiscuits.com/about/. Accessed August 30, 2021.

"About Us." Sauer Brands. https://sauerbrands.com/pages/about/. Accessed September 1, 2021.

Alliance of Native Seedkeepers. www.allianceofnativeseedkeepers.com/. Accessed August 30, 2021.

Aijana W. "Publix Bakery Beginnings." *The Publix Checkout* (blog), December 26, 2016. https://blog.publix.com/publix/publix-bakery-beginnings/.

"Armour's Vegetole." Justia Trademarks. https://trademarks.justia.com/700/23/armour -s-vegetole-70023291.html/. Accessed August 30, 2021.

Barton Springs Mill. https://bartonspringsmill.com/. Accessed August 30, 2021.

"Beignet History and Recipe." What's Cooking America. https://whatscookingamerica .net/History/BeignetsHistory.htm/. Accessed August 30, 2021.

"Butchers, Caterers, Bakeries, and Groceries." Atlanta Jewish Life. www.atljewishlife. com/Visiting/Kosher-Food/butchers-caterers-bakeries-and-groceries/. Accessed August 30, 2021.

"Candied Cherries." Cooks Info, December 5, 2019. www.cooksinfo.com /candied-cherries/.

The Cast Iron Collector. www.Castironcollector.com. Accessed August 30, 2021.

Chocolate for Basil (blog). www.chocolateforbasil.com/. Accessed August 20, 2021.

"Citrus Industry History." Florida Citrus Mutual. http://flcitrusmutual.com/citrus-101 /citrushistory.aspx/. Accessed June 3, 2019.

"Don't Call Me Angel Biscuits." Anson Mills. https://ansonmills.com/recipes/434 /. Accessed August 30, 2021.

"Enjoying the Sweet Life: Mr. James Onobun's Rise to the American Dream." Majority. www.majority.com/en/community/article/enjoying-the-sweet-life/. Accessed August 30, 2021.

EuroIndo Mideast Market. http://euroindomideastmarket.com/menu/. Accessed August 30, 2021.

Family Baking Bakery and Café. www.familybakingchamblee.com/. Accessed August 30, 2021.

"Find Members." Bread Bakers Guild of America. www.bbga.org/find_members /. Accessed August 30, 2021.

"The First Africans." Jamestowne Rediscovery. https://historicjamestowne.org/history /the-first-africans/. Accessed August 30, 2021.

"Forbidding Fruit: How America Got Turned On to the Date." *The Salt*, June 10, 2014. National Public Radio. www.npr.org/sections/thesalt/2014/06/10/320346869 /forbidding-fruit-how-america-got-turned-on-to-the-date/.

"Fox's Steam Bakery." *Waves Magazine of Galveston*. https://wavesgalveston.com /patrick-lemire/f/fox%E2%80%99s-steam-bakery-%7C-est-1837/. Accessed June 22, 2019.

"From Metal Working to Food Production." Jamestowne Rediscovery. http://historicjamestowne.org/archaeology/map-of-discoveries/blacksmith -shopbakery/. Accessed August 31, 2021.

"From the Sweet Past to the Delicious Present." Karo Syrup. www.karosyrup.com /our-history/. Accessed August 30, 2021.

"George Washington's Gristmill." George Washington's Mount Vernon. www .mountvernon.org/the-estate-gardens/gristmill/. Accessed August 31, 2021.

"Georgia Gilmore." Equality Archive. https://equalityarchive.com/history/georgia -gilmore/. Accessed August 31, 2021.

"Governor's House." Texas Beyond History, Los Adaes. www.texasbeyondhistory.net /adaes/images/f-gov-house.html/. Accessed August 31, 2021.

Hansen, M. V. "How a Threshing Machine Works." February 9, 2011. www .farmcollector.com/equipment/how-a-threshing-machine-works/.

Helen [no surname given]. "Early Rotary Egg Beaters." Home Things Past, February 19, 2012. www.homethingspast.com/antique-egg-beaters/.

Hémard, Ned. "Madame Langlois, Fact or Fiction?" New Orleans Nostalgia: Remembering New Orleans History, Culture and Traditions. www.neworleansbar .org/uploads/files/Madame%20Langlois,%20Fact%20or%20Fiction.pdf/. Accessed September 1, 2021.

"Heyward-Washington House." Visit-Historic-Charleston.com. www.visit-historic -charleston.com/heyward-washington-house.html#gallery[pageGallery]/5 /. Accessed September 1, 2021.

"Historic Charleston Foundation." https://charleston.pastperfectonline.com /archive/949436A1-AFD8-49ED-8108-202957225655/. Accessed June 19, 2019.

"History." Franklin Baker. www.franklinbaker.com/our-company/history/. Accessed September 1, 2021.

"The History." King Biscuit Time. https://king-biscuit-time.myshopify.com/pages /about-us/. Accessed September 1, 2021.

"History." King Biscuit Blues Festival. https://kingbiscuitfestival.com/history/. Accessed September 1, 2021.

"History." National Cornbread Festival. http://nationalcornbread.com/about/history /. Accessed September 1, 2021.

"History." Sunbeam Products. www.sunbeam.com/history.html/. Accessed September 9, 2019.

"History and Founders." Southern Foodways Alliance. www.southernfoodways.org /about-us/history-founders/. Accessed September 1, 2021.

"History of Fleischmann's Yeast." Fleischmann's Yeast Company. www.breadworld .com/history.aspx/. Accessed March 17, 2019.

"History of Gelatin, Gelatine, and JELL-O." https://whatscookingamerica.net/History /Jell-o-history.htm/. Accessed September 1, 2021.

"Huguenot Torte History and Recipe." http://whatscookingamerica.net/History/Cakes /HuguenotTorte.htm/. Accessed September 1, 2021.

"Introduction." Mount Clare Museum House. www.mountclare.org/history/intro _mountclare.html. Accessed September 1, 2021.

"Jamestown Rediscovery, Dig Updates, 2012." Historic Jamestowne. https:// historicjamestowne.org/archaeology/dig-updates/2012-2/. Accessed September 1, 2021.

"Jamestown 1624–25 Building Records." Virtual Jamestown. www.virtualjamestown.org /Muster/buildings24.html/. Accessed September 1, 2021.

"Jamestown 1624/5 Food Records." Virtual Jamestown. www.virtualjamestown.org /Muster/food24.html/. Accessed September 1, 2021.

John, Visitor Services [no surname given]. "A Learning Experience." Stratford Hall Blog: New Projects and Innovative Ideas (blog), June 14, 2012. http://stratfordhallprojects. blogspot.com/2012/06/learning-experience.html/.

Jolly Jolly Bakery. www.jollyjollybakery.co/. Accessed September 1, 2021.

"Meet Ms. Dean." Dean's Cake House. http://deanscakehouse.com/meet-ms-dean /. Accessed September 1, 2021.

Memorial Page for Christian Anton Borchert (January 17, 1804–October 4, 1870). Find a Grave, database and images. www.findagrave.com/memorial/116796671 /christian-anton-borchert. Accessed September 3, 2021.

Memorial Page for Lucile P. Plowden Harvey (June 23, 1901–February 1987). Find a Grave, database and images. www.findagrave.com/memorial/60125515/lucile-p -harvey. Accessed September 3, 2021.

"The Mill." Farm and Sparrow. www.farmandsparrow.com/the-mill/. Accessed September 1, 2021.

"A North Carolina Flour Mill since 1755." Lindley Mills, Inc. www.lindleymills.com /about-lindley-mills/history.html/. Accessed September 1, 2021.

Old Mill of Guilford. http://Oldmillofguilford.com/. Accessed September 1, 2021.

"Our Definitive List." Southern Kitchen, March 21, 2018. www.southernkitchen.com/articles/eat/ our-definitive-list-of-the-best-biscuits-from-fast-food-chains-in-the-south/.

"Our Heritage." Sara Lee Desserts. https://saraleedesserts.com/about/. Accessed September 1, 2021.

"Our History." Hobart Corporation. www.hobartcorp.com/about-us/history/. Accessed September 1, 2021.

"Our Story." Adams Extract Company. www.adamsextract.com/history.asp/. Accessed September 1, 2021.

"Our Story." Leidenheimer Baking Company. https://leidenheimer.com/pages /our-story/. Accessed September 1, 2021.

"Our Story." Ximenz-Fatio House Museum. ximenezfatiohouse.org/our-story/. Accessed September 1, 2021.

"Pa Mac" [Gary McWilliams]. "How'd They Used to Build a Fireplace and Chimney without Bricks and Mortar?" Farm Hand's Companion. www.farmhandscompanion. com/how_did_they_used_to_do_that_files/688a0bad3b352f0655e27545078e545a-7 .html/. Accessed September 1, 2021.

"Powdered Sugar Pillows: The History of the Beignet." *Joe Gambino's Bakery, Bakery Blog*, November 6, 2019. https://gambinos.com/new-orleans-food/powdered-sugar -pillows-history-beignet/.

Preservation Society of Charleston. www.preservationsociety.org/program _currentdetail.asp?icID=64/. Accessed August 21, 2015.

Proof Bakery. https://theproofbakery.com/. Accessed September 3, 2021.

Ross, Paige, and Joanna Rothkopf. "Best Bagel Shops in America." *Epicurious*. www .epicurious.com/archive/diningtravel/restaurants/bagels/. Accessed September 1, 2021.

Sammy's Bakery. www.sammybakery.com. Accessed April 26, 2021.

"Shipley Do-Nut Flour and Supply Company." Shipley Do-nuts. www.myshipleydonuts. com/about-us/shipley-history/. Accessed September 1, 2021.

Slave Voyages. www.slavevoyages.org/assessment/estimates/. Accessed September 1, 2021.

"Society for the Preservation of Old Mills." Society for the Preservation of Old Mills. www.spoom.org. Accessed September 1, 2021.

Sweet Potato Comfort Pie. www.sweetpotatocomfortpie.org/. Accessed September 2, 2021.

Tea Cake Project. www.teacakeproject.com/. Accessed September 2, 2021.

"The VIP Biscuit Bash." King Biscuit Blues Festival website, https://kingbiscuitfestival
.com/events/biscuit-bash/. Accessed August 30, 2021.

"What You Need to Know about Corn." Anson Mills. https://ansonmills.com/grain
_notes/13/. Accessed September 2, 2021.

"Who We Are: A Family Bakery." Little Debbie McKee Foods. www.littledebbie.com
/6.4/who-we-are/. Accessed September 2, 2021.

"Who We Are: Glenn Roberts. Anson Mills." https://ansonmills.com/biographies
/. Accessed September 2, 2021.

Index

Page numbers in italics refer to illustrations.